Happy

G000255775

Bumping

About

Brittany

with Charles Davis

DISCOVERY WALKING GUIDES LTD

Bumping About Brittany

First published - August 2008

Copyright © 2008

Published by
Discovery Walking Guides Ltd
10 Tennyson Close
Northampton NN5 7HJ
England

Photographs
Photographs in this book were taken by the author,
Charles Davis, and Jeanette Tallegas.

ISBN 9781904946441

Text and photographs* © Charles Davis 2008

Contents

Foreword: Brittany Blank

In a word association game like Blankety-Blank, most people from the British Isles would probably complete the phrase 'Brittany ------ ' with the word 'ferries', understandably given that the company carries over two million passengers a year, the vast majority of them English speakers. In fact, when you think about it, there really isn't any other option. If the key word was 'French ------', there'd be no end of alternatives: 'farce', 'poodle', 'letter', 'pack', 'revolution', 'resistance', 'food', 'wine', 'cheese', 'restaurant', 'muck', possibly even 'bastards' if you were mixing in euro-sceptic circles . . . Even the substantive 'France -----' would only cause a moment's hesitation before inspiring 'profonde', 'Telecom', 'Soir', 'riots', 'retreats', 'protests', 'cheats' and the much relished 'loses'. But when it comes to Brittany, the only thing that really suggests itself is 'Ferries', and few people without an avowed passion for all things Celtic would be able to tell you much about the region even without the grammatical constraints of the game.

Moreover, if you asked those who came up with 'Brittany Ferries' to elaborate a little and tell you something about the history of the company, the conversation would probably be fairly short. Given it's English name, many people are surprised to hear that Brittany Ferries is a French company, and they're downright astonished when you tell them that it was originally set up to shift cabbages, cauliflowers and artichokes rather than holidaymakers. Yet when Alexis Gourvennec and the Roscoff Chamber of Commerce founded Brittany Ferries in 1972, their principal motive was to promote the local agricultural co-operatives. They weren't actively averse to making money from the tourist trade, but the main purpose was exporting produce rather than importing people.

This gap between what we 'know' about Brittany and the idiosyncratic reality of the place is revealing, for Brittany is a region of unsung charms and unexpected histories. And it's the unsung charms and unexpected histories that we explore in this book. Bumping about, we discover the eccentricities of Brittany and the foibles of its people. We delve into a Brittany that lies just a little way off the beaten track, and if it's on the beaten track, we approach it from a sufficiently eccentric angle to see it in a new light. Each chapter describes a recreatable outing or, in the case of geographically movable feasts like the Tro Breiz pilgrimage and wheedling your dinner out of a rock pool, an outing designed to trigger a comparable exploration wherever you happen to find yourself. And in each case, we look at an aspect of Breton character or Breton history or Breton landscape or Breton life that might otherwise be missed by casual visitors.

And why Bumping About? Well, it's the happenstance of travel we want to celebrate here, the chance encounters and oddities that crop up when we're wandering around, not quite aimlessly, but ready to enjoy whatever we find, even if it wasn't precisely what we were looking for in the first place. If you want to know where the theme parks are, you'll probably be disappointed. But if you want to know what the Bretons think of France and vice-versa, if you want to know how to climb an imaginary mountain, if you want to know why the slippers look a little peculiar, if you want to know what city invented International Non-Diet Day, how to be rude to a Parisian, where to search for little green men, which shellfish should go on the sex offenders register, why the pope provoked a scandal, who brews the best beer, where the President buys his cider, how to find the way to hell and back, the approved technique for nicking a garden gnome, and the correct word for suggesting something is a lot of old cobblers, then this might be the book for you.

Acknowledgements

This book would not have been possible without the generous advice and suggestions of people who know Brittany far better than I do, above all Jeannette for family stories and family life, Yves-Marie for intoxicated talk and inebriating ideas, Xavier for home-made music and a very eccentric tour, and Michel and Jacqueline for fishing lore and more. Any errors of fact or interpretation are entirely down to my own invincible nitwittedness. My thanks to David Brawn for the original concept of 'Bumping'.

1. Becoming Plouc
and the Unpredictable Art of Bumping About

ACCESS - **Erquy** is in Côtes d'Armor northeast of St. Brieuc. Access via the D786 from St. Brieuc through Pleneuf-Val-Andre, from St. Malo through Matignon, and from Dinan (via the D794) through Plancoët.

Land of Granite

One small village of indomitable Gauls. It shouldn't be that difficult to locate, but when you start Bumping About Brittany, you realize that distinguishing fact from fiction is not so easy in a topsy-turvy world where things are not always what they seem. In Brittany, nobody bats an eye at the notion of a landlocked island, yet the Bretons will argue fiercely over whether an islet accessible on foot at low tide is really a distinct land mass. In Brittany, many otherwise sane people maintain the delirious fiction that the peninsula is partitioned by a range of mountains that is, to all intents and purposes, invisible to the naked eye. In Brittany, ancient monuments are sacrosanct, yet the most famous medieval city was built after the Second World War. In Brittany, saints sailed in granite boats, rocks sing and stones rock, and the Anglo-Saxon image of a typical Frenchman evolved in a form unrecognized by most typical Frenchmen. And even when you turn to a reliably fictional character like Asterix The Gaul, the real and the surreal are never far apart.

Look at the sketch map on the opening page of an Asterix album and you'll see that his native province of Armorica covers the area we know as Brittany. Consult the 1:25,000 scale maps of France and you'll find that Asterix's village is located on the site of modern Erquy. Look more closely and a remarkable correspondence emerges between Uderzo's sketch map and the actual beaches, quarries and islands near Erquy. Above all, there's a cluster of rocks that lie to the left of the magnifying glass in the sketch map that match almost perfectly La Pointe des Trois Pierres to the northwest of Erquy.

Asterix's illustrator, Uderzo, admits he was inspired by the area around St. Brieuc, where he was a refugee during the war, but denies consciously modelling his village on Erquy. The writer, Goscinny, wanted his Gauls beside the sea so they could travel more easily and, since the only stretch of sea Uderzo knew was in Brittany, Brittany it was. But it was only a sketch map and the bit under the magnifying glass could have been anywhere between St. Malo and Roscoff. When, after decades of success and some thirty albums, he was taken up in a helicopter to see the Trois

Pierres, he was flabbergasted by how closely they matched the rocks on his own map.

And yet, latching onto the cartoonist's disclaimers, some respectable historians have pretended Asterix and his 'village of madmen' weren't in Brittany at all, but in Normandy. The Normans are like that, though. As we'll see later on, they have always had a penchant for getting their hands on other people's monuments. And if you know your Asterix, you'll recall that the Normans are infamous for being pathologically fearless, drowning their food in cream, and not giving a straight answer - "Maybe no, maybe yes", is their refrain. Can't be trusted, you see. Certainly not for something so important as the whereabouts of the world's most famous Frenchman. Asterix comes from Brittany and don't listen to anybody who tells you otherwise. And that is why we are on the road to Erquy. If we're going to bump about Brittany, it's as well to know who we're liable to bump into, and since a lot of the jokes in the Asterix albums are about national stereotypes, it seems fitting that we should visit his village in search of the stereotypical Breton.

Leaving the dual carriageway of the *voie expres* to the east of St. Brieuc, we find ourselves amid a patchwork of pleasant country lanes crowded with clusters of weekend cyclists. The rolling, lightly wooded landscape to the south gradually gives way to larger more open fields laced with tracks as we approach the head of the peninsula, where the coastal car parks are crowded with camper vans. As yet there's no sign that we are nearing Asterix's village, no brown plaques or tourist luring hoardings, but doubtless that's some cunning Celtic plan to baffle the Romans. The Bretons like to think themselves adept at baffling outsiders.

Nations rarely have an entirely unique or coherent picture of what they are and the Bretons' image of themselves is as varied as any people's, but one often repeated anecdote is revealing. It's not a story restricted to Brittany, being rather more in the nature of a modern myth, surfacing wherever the countryside has had to confront the predatory intrusions of the urban world, but it reflects at least one aspect of the Breton character. A Parisian tourist is tooling along a country lane in the depths of Brittany when he sees a shabby old bloke sat by the roadside with a shabby old dog and a gold bowl full of water. The bowl's tarnished, but clearly valuable and it's equally obvious the old boy has no idea how valuable given that he uses it for his dog. Barely able to believe his good fortune, the Parisian pulls over and approaches this rustic pair. Unwilling to give the game away, he ignores the bowl and admires the dog instead, asking if it might be for sale. The old boy admits it might and names a price that's dear for the dog but a bargain for the bowl. Deal done, money paid, the Parisian slaps his head and says, "But I forgot, I haven't got any accessories for a dog! Can I take the bowl, too? Then, at least, I can give it some water". And the old boy bows his head regretfully and says: "Ah, *non, monsieur*. I'm afraid that will not be possible. I can get any number of dogs like that. I've sold three today already. But a bowl like this is irreplaceable". That's how the Bretons like to see themselves, apparently simple people but shrewd enough to put one over on sophisticated outsiders seeking to take advantage. Which could serve as a definition of Asterix, too. It's not, however, a view shared by the rest of France.

Look at the map again. Dotted about Brittany are places like Plouec, Plouescat, Plouezoch, Plougasnou, Plougastel, Plougras, Plouguerneau . . . there are 180 towns and villages beginning with 'plou', a prefix that has given French the word *plouc* and, by derivation, *Ploukistan* for Brittany. And what is a *plouc* apart from a resident of Brittany? There's the rub. Since this has become a derogatory, slang word, many French dictionaries (which are considerably more conservative than their English counterparts: sniggering adolescents would have a thin time of it leafing through looking for dirty words) simply ignore it altogether. But it translates as something like 'bumpkin', 'clodhopper', or 'peasant' with a dash of 'pleb' thrown in for good measure, the Latin word for 'people' being its etymological source, from the days when being plebian was a matter of administration rather than denigration.

You see where we're heading here? Someone may occasionally claim *ploucdom* as a badge of honour, in the same spirit that American political parties proudly identify themselves with donkeys and elephants, but despite the sale of nigh on 300 million Asterix albums, your average Breton doesn't get a great press in the rest of France. By comparison, Britain's Celtic fringe gets off rather lightly with Taffy, Jock and Paddy. The English may have done some dreadful things, but the larceny, parsimony and stupidity evoked in the jokes are not implicit in the nicknames. If the rest of France were to baptize the Bretons with an Asterix style name, it would probably be Dimwitix or Hayseedix or something like that.

It's a stereotype that has varied through history, but always with a common theme. For the Romantics, the Breton was Quixotix - archaic, passionate, fierce, devout, brave and imaginative to the point of folly; for Royalists he was Fidelitix - rustic, simple, loyal, virtuous, and in harmony with the 'natural' laws of feudalism; and for Republicans he was Fanatix, a sort of noble but woefully backward savage. Later incarnations included Nannyix, the loyal but comical Breton servant, and Miserabilix, the poor peasants and poor fishermen who lived in such alluring poverty and suffered so much their wretchedness was positively picturesque. Alcohol has played it's part, too, but we'll be looking at that in detail later on. In the meantime, a catalogue of the major themes in the Breton stereotype should read something like this: old fashioned, chauvinistic, drunk, pious, mistrustful, taciturn, prudent to the point of reticence, but capable of impetuous violence, and above all as hard, intractable and enduring as the granite of which the region is made.

And Asterix? How does he match up to this image? Well, he's shrewd, loyal, cunning, stubborn, resourceful, fearless, a battler, and he's always ready for an adventure. Likes his magic potion, too. There are plenty of echoes of the stereotype there. But most revealing in historical terms is the fact that he does all the dirty jobs nobody else wants to do.

Someone has to venture into the big, dangerous city, it's Asterix who volunteers; someone has to build a palace in an impossibly short time, Asterix does the work; something missing, something stolen, something distant and difficult to get, Asterix does the finding, fetching and getting. Doing the dirty, difficult jobs for other people is something the Bretons would understand. For centuries, they were the foot-soldiers, mercenaries, sailors and gendarmes press-ganged into fighting other people's wars, exploring other people's empires, and policing other people's streets. And before Europe started pilfering hands and brains from beyond the continent, the Bretons were the pool of cheap labour on which France called when a lot of earth needed shifting or blood needed shedding or Madame acquired a dozen infants with a regrettable tendency to soil their undergarments. To this day, the Breton *bonne* (maid, nanny, or wet nurse depending upon the imperatives of the moment) is a recognizable cliché of popular French culture, despite the fact that she has long been replaced by migrants from points south and the overseas dependencies. I'm not suggesting Asterix ever worked as a wet nurse, but as the doer of other people's dirty work, he has a distinctly Breton history.

The first impression of Erquy is not good, the heart of the village being hemmed in by large pink granite houses, second homes for holiday makers and the bourgeoisie of St. Brieuc. The houses are not overtly ugly in themselves, but most are shuttered out of season, lending them an air of redundancy, and there's something about the architecture, a mismatch between the chunky design and the pale pink stone, that is at once cumbersome and inconsequential, like a cartoon hippo in a tutu.

In the Tourist Information Office, I tell the girl I'm looking for Asterix's village, fully expecting her to start edging toward the door, smiling fixedly and groping for the panic button. Instead she unhesitatingly takes out a local map and indicates the Pointe des Trois Pierres. I'm on the right track. We're repeatedly told that Asterix lives in 'a village of madmen'. This has got to be the place.

The centre of the village is more attractive than the outskirts and, this being a Saturday, is crowded with market stalls overflowing with a tempting range of charcuterie, cheeses, vegetables and an array of products qualified by the modifier *artisanal,* a word that doesn't have a precise English translation but suggests phrases like home-made, arts & craft, and cottage industry. There are stalls selling honey, others are laden with cider and mead, one stand is flushed with fresh new strawberries, and an entire alley is dedicated to sailing clothes and loose woven, loose fitting, smock-like garments. And there's a rotisserie advertizing roast pork with a cartoon of a grinning pig that seems inexplicably pleased by the prospect of being grilled. It's not exactly a wild boar, but close enough for someone looking for Asterix's village. The two high street chemists, however, are a disappointment. No long white beards or Celtic goblets, but in each a quartet of professional looking women dispensing the dull packets of pills to which the French are so addicted, the nation being far and away the biggest consumers of pharmaceuticals in Europe and the third largest drugs market in the world.

On the terrace of the main bar in the Place de l'Eglise other magic potions are being dispensed. It's only 10am, but already three burly men in shorts revealing bulging cyclists' legs are knocking back glassfuls of strong Trappist beer. Scanning the crowd though, there comes the realization that the people thronging the market are not strikingly Asterix-like. True, there are a scattering of gallic moustaches and there is one, ageing and rather etiolated Obelix type. But that's all. The Obelix is the key, though.

The Asterix books are full of puns and Obelix is called Obelix because an obelisk is both a large lump of tailored rock and the dagger symbol used for a secondary footnote that comes after an asterisk. The symbol was also used in old manuscripts to mark passages that scholars believed had been corrupted over the centuries, texts in which one copyist's error had been compounded by another. It is, in one sense then, a signifier of the ravages of time, and the Obelix-like figure in Erquy is nothing if not a signifier of the ravages of time. He has the hair, most of it, he has the moustache, minus a bit of bushiness, he has the nose, albeit blued by rather too many purplish blood vessels, he has the braces and high-waisted trousers, maybe he has the personality for all I know, but the muscles are gone, the belly is slack, his posture is none too clever, and I rather doubt he could lift an oversized pumice stone, let alone a menhir. He's wilting rather than weight-lifting, more Simpson than Samson, more Golem than Goliath, and even the weediest centurion in the empire could probably tweak his moustaches with impunity. In fact, he looks bloody knackered and I wonder whether it wouldn't be a kindness to offer him a roast pork sandwich and a sip of magic potion.

A closer look at the market places reveals that the vast majority of the shoppers are united not by any very obviously Gaul-like qualities, but by maturity. Average age must be about sixty, though most are in considerably better nick than Obelix. The camper vans in the coastal car-parks on the approach roads were already flagging up the phenomenon, for these motorized homes are now so popular among pensioners, they have become a synonym for retirement, to such a degree that the French education minister announced an extension to teachers' retirement age by saying "the camper van will have to stay parked in the drive for another couple of years".

Inundated by Dormobiles, many popular resorts have had to restrict their circulation, banning them from village centres after dark, and curtailing access to well known beauty spots and beachfront car-parks . . .

in theory, at least. There's an adage contrasting English and French attitudes to authority that claims the French respect all politicians and despise all laws while the English despise all politicians and respect all laws. It's a cliché, but like all clichés, it's marked by truth, and the regulations about overnight parking are widely ignored. Blue horizons are what these Dormobile Pilgrims are looking for and blue horizons are a bit limited when twenty vans are crammed onto a patch of concrete round the back of the water treatment plant, so people park where they like.

The summer invasion of itinerant retirees is matched in Brittany by a parallel year-round sedentary phenomenon. Many villages have doubled in size in the last ten years as the baby-boomers reach retirement age and come home after careers elsewhere. Join a queue in mid-winter and the chances are every head will be grey. This greybearding of Brittany has revitalized many communities, but it has also made younger residents with young families worry that a disproportionate number of senior citizens means local authorities will be more inclined to serve the interests of age than nonage. It doesn't seem to work like that, though. When our local school was threatened with closure, it was the grandparents rather than the parents who were out in the street protesting. And in Erquy, the reason I notice there are so many retired people is that the bookstall in front of the bar is lined with greybeards, all assiduously leafing through picture books for children. These are not illiterate or infantile people. But the summer holidays start soon and in a couple of weeks the grandchildren will be arriving.

You'd have thought that with so many well-heeled pensioners in the vicinity, presumably with time on their hands and in need of diversion, Erquy would be packed with gift shops peddling Asterix statuettes, Getafix goblets, and other vital accoutrements for cluttering up the mantelpiece. But stroll around the streets of Erquy and you'll see that Asterix is conspicuous by his absence. The Tourist Office may have resigned themselves to humouring the odd passing lunatic, but otherwise the link is wholly unexploited. There are no themed bars, no Asterix menus, no souvenir menhirs, no Gallic baseball caps or bottles of Official Magic Potion - the marketing potential has completely passed them by.

It's quite refreshing, really. Here's a place given a golden opportunity to put itself on the map and all they do is say, "Yeh, right, there's three stones up there". Otherwise it is what it is, a small quarrying and fishing village grown beyond its original raison d'être into a community of holiday homes. If you want Parc Asterix, go to Paris. You won't find it in Erquy. As for authentic Gallo-roman ruins, Erquy has a patch of scrubland called the Camp de Cesar, the hump of a Gallic earthwork, the *fossé Catuelan*, and that's about it. The real attraction, what draws all those greybeards (who have not on the whole constructed for themselves a well-paid early retirement by being fools), the reason why the old *bourg* is surrounded by weekend retreats, is the extraordinary coast that lies immediately to the north. The beaches between Cap d'Erquy and the Pointe du Champ du Port are utterly lovely, each a broad expanse of white

Plage de Lourtuais

sand bracketed by azure blue seas and verdant dunes. Elsewhere, on a less privileged coastline, any one of them would inspire the development of a discrete resort, but here there's at least three kilometres of beach without a building in sight.

Spend any time in France and you'll notice that the lack of marketing nous is characteristic of the country. I'm not saying it's a nation of consumer virgins. They can stuff unwanted glossy paper through your letter-box with the best of them and there's the same gluttony for gadgetry you get anywhere in the western world. But there's a certain innocence about it, too, even naiveté. There is, for instance, a stunning artlessness to French TV commercials, many of which are still at a nine-out-of-ten-housewives-prefer level. In an age when every three year old is expected to have a highly developed understanding of marketing techniques, the French ineptitude at selling itself (an ineptitude that becomes positively pathological in Brittany) is endearing. Or perhaps they just don't care. Certainly, no one in Erquy is interested in flogging you a Gag-This-Bard T-shirt, or a pair of Gaul-Grip sandals, or a druid-shaped soap on a rope. As for Asterix himself, there's no sign of him whatsoever.

At first, the absence of the plucky Gaul is a bit disappointing, but as we stroll along the footpath behind the beaches to the North, it occurs to me that it really doesn't matter, because a large part of the pleasure of bumping about is bumping into the unexpected. We came to Erquy looking for the prototype of a stereotype. Instead, we've found the archetype of a Breton coastal town, and within it the lineaments of what Brittany is all about. Like Erquy, Brittany inspires elaborate and elaborately successful fantasies, but rarely tries to profit from the fruits of imagination by turning them into a tangible product; it is a holiday destination that is the very antithesis of pushy, a place that draws in a discerning public who have seen enough of life to know that the simple pleasures of an ancient culture and a wild coast are infinitely superior to the flashy charms of brasher, better known resorts; and it is a place that takes quiet pride in defying expectation.

A village of madmen? Perhaps we'll bump into some of them later. In the meantime, a visit to Erquy is as good a way as any of getting a first impression of Brittany. And if you spot Obelix, for God's sake, give him a sandwich. He needs feeding up.

2. Coasting

ACCESS - **Primel-Tregastel** is in the *commune* of Plougasnou in Finistère north of Morlaix. Access via the N12, D64 and D76 from Lanmeur or along the coast road (D76/D46a) from Morlaix. Park in front of the 'Residence de la Baie' and the Dormobile car-park. The walk starts along the **'Rue des Freres Poupon'**.

Look at a regional map of Brittany and you'll see that the peninsula is defined by a thin red ribbon, a dotted line that roughly corresponds with the contours of the coast. It may be marked as the GR34 or the *sentier cotier* or the *sentier douanier*, but whatever it's called it is one of the great customs paths of Europe and, wherever you go on the Breton

Belles de la Plage

coast, you can be certain there's at least one stunning walk within easy striking distance.

It's one of the few things that seem to make any sense to the Bretons when I try to explain why so many English people come here to buy second homes, or up sticks altogether and settle in some isolated, windswept, rain lashed farmhouse that's been on the market for decades, during which time prudent locals refused to go anywhere near the place with their cheque books, just in case they were overcome by a *coup de foudre* and ended up buying the blessed thing, landing themselves with a leaky roof and a lot of dodgy plumbing.

"Why are they coming here?" exclaim disbelieving Bretons.

I should point out that their incredulity is not a symptom of excessive modesty. The Bretons are as proud as any people of their land, maybe more than most. But they don't nurture many illusions. Or at least they do, but not the sort that suppose anyone born elsewhere is disadvantaged in life unless they remedy the situation by moving to Brittany. And they certainly don't look to England and see a windswept, rain lashed island, and think, "Yes, they'll be coming over here shortly to benefit from our uncommonly balmy climate". So why are the English coming here?

I try to explain. I point out that you practically have to own a Building Society before you can buy a house in England and that, while the tales of forty room *châteaux* in rural France being sold for the price of a prefab bungalow in the suburbs of Bournemouth, are nowadays mostly that, just tales, you still need a fairly large footstool if you're to get on the housing ladder in Britain, whereas in Brittany you can generally jump several rungs without breaking sweat. The sweat comes afterwards when you get stuck into the plumbing.

"Yes, but what about the weather?" they insist.

I'm a bit stumped when it comes to this. Truckloads of northerners decamping to the *costas* of Spain may create some peculiar juxtapositions of culture and climate, but you can understand the motive. One too many a wet Sunday afternoon sat in front of the telly wondering whether there'll be leaves on the track tomorrow morning and heading south seems eminently sensible. But Brittany's not really south enough to make a difference and it faces a large ocean that frequently calls in the removal clouds with a view to relocating to the mainland.

"Countryside's very nice," I suggest. "Lot less crowded than in England."

"Yes, but what about the weather?"

"Home from home?"

"Yes, but why here?" The Bretons are nothing if not tenacious.

"Communications are good. Roscoff and St. Malo are just down the road if the continentals do something disturbingly continental like have one of their wars".

I may then mention, in case they're harbouring any illusions on this point, that the immigrants aren't coming to embrace Breton culture. The English love the idea of France (can't stand the French but love France), but for the most part only have a very hazy notion of how that idea is translated into reality, and certainly wouldn't think to make any radical distinction between the Breton bit and the rest of it.

The startling revelation that other people are not acutely aware of the uniqueness of the Breton way of life generally induces such dismay, I take pity, and suggest that perhaps the reason so many English people come here is the coast path, a notion that normally elicits a huge sigh of relief.

"Ah, oui! Le sentier cotier."

Smiles break out, a tender, possibly faintly moist look enters the eye, arms are waved expressively, lips are smacked, fingertips held together to honour the ineffable essence of this inexpressible truth, and if we're really lucky, the two might come together for a bit of kissing of fingers.

"Moooauh!"

"Moooauh!"

Pointe de Grouin - Ille et Vilaine

Every Breton understands that the Breton coastal path is a wonderful phenomenon, the like of which is not to be encountered elsewhere. That *must* be why the English are coming here. Of course, in truth its like *is* to be encountered elsewhere and I don't suppose many people settle in Brittany because there's a nice bit of path running along the edge, but the *sentier cotier* is sufficiently fine that, if they did, I would not regard the move as being wholly whimsical. For if you are a dedicated walker or sea bather or simply like to get out and stare at the waves, you'll soon notice a difference between the two sides of the channel.

"*Moooauh!*"

Le Crapeau - Finistère

There are places on the South Coast of England, where access is so restricted by upmarket housing estates that the beach has effectively been privatized, and there are plenty more where coastal walks have, until recently, only remained open thanks to the public spirited generosity of private landowners. Not so in Brittany. Naturally, you do get the odd uptight, twisty-lipped, sniffy-faced fence maker who resists. But that's all it is, resistance, with all the weaker-party implications of the word. In France, when it comes to coastal walking, the boot has long been on the other foot. And very nice, too. Even in those areas where the development of holiday homes has achieved a density comparable to that in England, the path is still there, the coast is still open to the public. The only exceptions to this rule are those strategic locations where the state has seen fit to park a nuclear submarine base or *gendarmerie maritime*. Otherwise, the coast belongs to everybody.

It wasn't always like that, not quite, though there's been some form of state imposed access ever since 1681, when Jean-Baptiste Colbert, Louis XIV's Minister of Finance, established a right of way across private land for those charged with coastal surveillance. A little over a century later, France had 35,000 customs officers, which suggests just how many people must have been busying themselves with contraband, resulting in the *sentier douaniers* being established in 1791. The customs officers didn't patrol every corner of the coast, just those places liable to be a good landing or embarkation point for smugglers (engagingly known as *coureurs de lunes* or moon-runners), but after 300,000,000 years of wind and water, Brittany has an awful lot of secluded bays and creeks and beaches just begging for someone to slip by with a barrel of brandy, so there were stretches of path in most areas and the basic infrastructure was already in place when walking was transformed from an arduous necessity into a pleasurable pastime.

The GR34, which generally follows but occasionally diverges from the coastal path, was conceived in the 1960s. As late as 1968, there wasn't a single waymarked walk in Brittany. Now there's some 3000 kilometres of signposted paths, the coastal stretches protected by the popular *Loi Littoral*, which prohibits new building within 100-metres of the coast and stipulates that private landowners leave a three-metre right-of-way between their property boundary and the high-water mark. The three-metre rule maybe a bit irksome if you happen to own a house within spitting distance of a crumbling cliff, and you still do get the occasional legal battle between the local authorities and a landowner who claims the public land is that heap of rubble on the rocks down there *et ici c'est à moi!,* but it guarantees an extraordinary resource for everyone else.

Just how extraordinary is suggested by a glance at the names given to distinct sections of the coast, for like so many things in Brittany, the seaboard is not seen as a homogenous unit but as a multifarious thing, each region possessing its own special character and inviting its own intensely local loyalties. And yet, evocative though they may be, those names are not exclusive claims to the properties they embody. Pink granite is to be found beyond the coast that bears its name, the seas are emerald everywhere, not just between St. Malo and St. Brieuc, while legends and megaliths, the names given to two other coastal regions, are virtually ubiquitous in Brittany. As for Côte Sauvage, well, nobody suffered any illusions on that score - there are no less than five of them!

What is most interesting about the coastal path as a cultural phenomenon though, is the fact that it owes its existence to the voluntary efforts of local people and organizations like the FFRP (the French rambling association) and the Breton based *Amis des Chemins de Ronde.* Local authorities will do some work on the paths, but as soon as things get a bit hairy, which they often do, it's the volunteers that are out with their Strimmers and adzes. They don't always get it right (some paths were originally placed too close to fragile cliff-tops, while neat railway-sleeper stairways may look very nice, but can actually exacerbate erosion), but they work with an admirable passion for the public good.

I'm allergic to anything that smacks of chauvinism (a French word, by the by, from Nicolas Chauvin, a veteran of the Napoleonic wars), but I can't help admiring the French engagement with nation. Walking on the coastal path at Le Guildo near St. Malo, we met a man who spent his free time reconstructing 'something' (he didn't know what it was, but thought it might be a pigeon coop) beside a medieval castle. It wasn't of any architectural merit, it wasn't featured in guidebooks, it wasn't something people visited, and he knew absolutely nothing about what he was doing, but it was part of the fabric of his nation and he was damned if he was going to stand by and see it fall apart. In the same spirit that no self-respecting French executive would ever dream of buying a foreign made car, ordinary people get out and about and work to hold their country together, quite literally when they're shoring up the fabric of a coastal path that defines the shape of the land.

That said, not everyone who walks the coastal path does so in a spirit of benign amateurism. Not long ago, a walker fell over and sued the FFRP for negligence, in essence seeking to profit from the work of volunteers. It was a very worrying precedent. Successive French governments have been at great pains to resist the Americanization of their culture, pretending with fabulous condescension that there's no such thing as globalization and that they can carry on just as they always have, while introducing some wonderfully dim laws stipulating how much of what language you're allowed to hear on radio and at the cinema. But if people start to believe they can sue their way out of responsibility, *l'exception Française* is in trouble. Happily, in this case, the litigant was walking on a stretch of path that was off the waymarked trail. She didn't have a leg to stand on.

The *sentier cotier* defines the shape of the land, but it is a shape that is constantly shifting, which makes this an even more satisfying frontier. When I say frontier, I'm not talking about a rigid line and a rule book, but about a more fluid border between two worlds, the aspect of which changes throughout the day. At high tide, its course can seem like an act of daring brinkmanship, delicately negotiating a narrow line along the edge of the terrestrial world, beyond which all is wind and water and turmoil. But with tides of such startling amplitude (especially in the north, where some islands multiply their size a hundredfold at low water), there are times when the more exhausting stretches of path, dipping up and down an endless string of rises, can seem positively perverse given that only a few metres away you have an expanse of hard packed flat sand where walking would be considerably easier. The tides change the character of coastal walking. Add the shifting patterns of light and skies from which a cloud can drop quicker than a bride's nighty, and you begin to understand why this is such a satisfying path. Repeat the same walk day after day and you will always see it in a new light, a new humour, because what's around you is changing all the time. And if you do get bored, just keep on walking. The GR34 is a

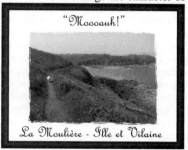

"*Moooauh!*"

La Moulière - Ille et Vilaine

part of the E9, an LDP that follows the coast from the Baltic to Gibraltar.

I doubt such a drastic recourse will be necessary, though. Whether you're exploring one of the tempestuous western headlands, or strolling through the dunes at Goulven, or tapping on the 'singing' stones at St. Jacut to hear them ring, or tiptoeing along the giddying cliffs of Cap Frehel, or labouring uphill and down dale on the remorseless roller coaster of Beg an Fry, the Breton coastal path is a source of constant pleasure. *"Moooauh!"*

But enough of this continental lip-smacking. Where precisely are we bumping about? Well, when it comes to the coastal path, everywhere and anywhere is good, but in order to illustrate the way in which the history of Brittany is etched into the landscape itself, I've selected a short walk round the Pointe de Primel in the *commune* of Plougasnou, which lies to the northeast of Morlaix.

Plougasnou is a typically sprawling Breton *bourg* in that the comparatively small town centre is the administrative hub for a starburst of satellite hamlets and over thirty kilometres of coast, including the immense beach and headland at Primel-Tregastel. We set off from the Plage de Tregastel car-park between the harbour and the Residence de la Baie, formerly the Hôtel Poupon. Built in 1892 in response to the new fashion for taking a seaside break and served until the 1930s by a narrow gauge railway link with the mainline station at Morlaix, the Hôtel Poupon was one of twenty-four in the Plougasnou district and there were also twenty-two *colonies des vacances*, kids holiday centres run by local authorities, corporations, and co-operative societies. That was then, though, and this is now. Despite having more money and more leisure time, few French families can afford a month in a hotel anymore, and cash-strapped local authorities are divesting themselves of 'superfluous' expenses like subsidized holidays for kids, as a result of which only five hotels and two *colonies* remain in Plougasnou.

Strolling along the Rue des Freres Poupon, we pass a tiny cottage tucked into a bulbous rock. The cottage is another memento of times gone by, being all that remains of the Ferme des Rochers, the farm that was once the only domestic development on this headland. The name is fitting because Brittany is built on and out of granite, and a little further along we come to the large shrubbery filled bowl of the Men Gleuz quarry. Similar excavations can be seen all along the coast, many so small they were clearly only exploited for building a single farmhouse, and there are places along the shore where tide-line quarries form what look like tiny mooring bays. The path then burrows between hedgerows, passing a patch of the synthetic stone that is almost as integral to the coast as granite, the concrete base of a gun emplacement which was part of the German Atlantic Wall fortifications during the Second World War. Toward the end of our walk, at the western end of the Plage de Primel-Tregastel, we will see another remnant of the Atlantic Wall, a blockhouse that has been converted into a private holiday home.

These blockhouses are a feature of the coastline and are visited in much the same spirit as one would a striking natural phenomenon. Most are open to both the elements and the public, exposed to the wear and tear of wind and water, detritus and graffiti, but they are not simply a scar on the landscape, indeed they are now protected for their historical significance. Take shelter in a blockhouse on a wet winter's day when the coast is deserted and you can still get a frisson of the grim history they represent. Just imagine what it must have felt like to be some luckless German conscript, sat in a grey concrete box under a grey sky, peering at a grey horizon, waiting for the allies to invade, knowing all the while that there was a large population of fishermen and farming folk at your back, people well equipped with gutting knives, gaff hooks, pitchforks and scythes, people who'd really rather you weren't there and would readily see to it that you weren't if no very severe consequences were forthcoming. Look, too, at the field of fire across the featureless expanse of the bare sands, and imagine what it would have taken to jump from a landing craft, wade through the water, and set yourself up as a moving target. Even after the war, these blockhouses had a sad history, several children being killed by booby traps or forgotten grenades, but nowadays, as memories of the fighting fade, a curious kind of alchemy is taking place and the crumbling fortifications are almost an additional attraction. For obvious reasons, they're always located in commanding positions and are so well incorporated into the landscape, they are like superior bird hides. Stumbling across one of the better preserved burrows is an event accompanied by a thrill of discovery for children of all ages.

Before crossing the small rise onto the *pointe* itself, it's worth looking back across the bay toward the fishing port of Le Diben, where the local authorities want to construct a marina. You can imagine how pleased the fishermen are about the prospect of sharing their port with a lot of amateur yachtsmen and many of them are hoping the plan will go the way of another recent project for developing the port. A couple of years back, it was decided that a division of the *gendarmerie maritime* should be stationed at Le Diben. The project was approved, housing was built for eight *gendarmes* and their families, and it was only when the keys were being passed out and everyone was about to move in that someone noticed the harbour was too shallow for the draught of the police launch!

Following the path over the rise, we enter the Salle Verte, a green 'room' formed by a ring of rocks enclosing a shallow grassy arena. The Romans had relatively little impact on this area of Brittany, but the Salle Verte was the site of one of two Roman lookout posts on the *pointe*, and is still known by some as the *Kastell ar Sal,* or Chateau de la Salle. When the Roman empire started to

The 'Green Room'

implode in the third century, pirates began raiding these coasts with rather more success than a reading of Goscinny and Uderzo might suggest, and Primel soon became one of their strongholds. Between 878 and 882, the Viking chieftain Hastings had a base on the Pointe de Primel, which was subsequently taken over and reinforced by his successor, Rollo. Known as The Walker because he was so big no horse could carry him, Rollo caused such havoc the French gave him Normandy, reasoning that, if the Norsemen had their own country to play with, they'd be less inclined to go gallivanting about Paris sacking and burning the sackables and burnables. But you can't keep a good Viking down and it was a squabble over the Norman inheritance that eventually lead to the Hundred Years War, in which Anglo-Norman nobles did a sort of inverted UKIP number, desperately trying to get back into a Europe from which they'd been ejected. And it was during the Hundred Years War that the burghers of Morlaix, fed up with the English raids that took place with monotonous regularity, erected their own watchtower in the *Kastell ar Sal*, the foundations of which can be seen in the partially interred stones at the heart of the *salle*.

Scrambling over the band of rock behind the Kastell or contouring round via the main path, we leap forward several centuries to the First World War, during which German POWs worked the local quarries. The large walled cave tucked into the big rock immediately north of the *salle* was used to store the quarry's dynamite and as a munitions dump during the next war. Our path then traverses the grassy flatlands at the heart of the headland, known as the *Poull ar Yeot* or Bight of Grass. Apart from the turf, the main growth is of ferns, a plant so prevalent in Brittany there's even a town named Fougères. Furze and moss are plentiful, too, and there's a scattering of what the Bretons call *louzou*, a word that can mean either weeds or medicinal herbs, suggesting the nearby farm of Ty Louzou was once the home either of a very poor husbandman or a notable herbalist. On the Pointe de Primel, the *louzou* fit both definitions, for among the vegetation are bugle, a traditional salve for wounds, and belladonna, which doesn't salve anything very much apart from a death wish.

The topographical terminology takes a turn toward the surreal as we approach the coastguard hut on the back of Kerniou, a modest band of rock and scrub local historians are pleased to describe as the headland's "*grand massif central*" and the "*chaîne transversale*". Cast your mind back to the Breton stereotypes and you will recall that Quixotix is imaginative to the point of folly. Nothing exemplifies this better than the Breton take on mountains. How anyone could dub this little rise a "*grand massif central*" or a "*chaîne transversale*" is beyond me. It would make an impressive garden rockery and bits of it might not look amiss on the back of a dinosaur, but it's about as *grand* and *massif* as a pigeon's brain. Local 'mountaineers' are undeterred though and several of the rocks have waymarked ascents, while one or two are even topped with climbers' cleats. Hyperbolae notwithstanding, there's a great view from the coastguard hut, which was built in the aftermath of 1806 when Napoleon prohibited trade with England because he feared a Nation of Shopkeepers would come barging in and muck up his carefully laid fiscal plans, a sentiment shared by many French politicians to this day.

To the northeast, we can see the fin like rocks of the Plateau de la Mêloine, rimed with a ruff of white foam from the breaking waves, whereby hangs another tale. It's said that the Pointe de Primel was once the domain of a siren, Morgan, who spent her time spinning wool on a jenny stretching from the Cairn de Barnénez in Plouezoc'h to the dolmen of Guimaëc, a passage consequently dubbed the Spinner's Bed or *Gwele an Inkinerez*. Apart from spinning wool, Morgan also enjoyed more outward bound activities, like luring sailors onto the rocky shoreline and whooping it up when the ships sank and everyone drowned. And, as is only right and proper for a legendary figure, she also had a great treasure which was guarded by a *korrigan*.

A korrigan is (I use the present tense as they are still said to pop up near dolmens on All Souls Night hoping to kidnap whoever comes to hand) a sort of short fairy with a bad attitude, *korr* meaning dwarf, while *ig* and *an* are diminutives, making it a double short dwarf, I suppose. They are said to have lovely hair, flashing red eyes, and be able to change shape and move very very fast; they hate piety, have a talent for making men fall in love with them and a tendency to damage those that do; they sing and dance a lot and are very keen on combing their hair: in other words, ideal candidates for the Big Brother house.

You know how it goes with these things, though. There you are, an unassuming hobgoblin or comely siren or some minor animist deity, minding your own business and whiling away the days worrying the natives, when along comes some Christian saint who reckons pagan sprites are a diabolic blot on the landscape that need cleaning up with a bit of the old white spirit. In this instance it was the sixth century anchorite and co-founder of Plougasnou, Primel (Prim Aël - The Agile Angel), who rolled in from Wales (along with Ireland, the traditional recruiting ground for Breton saints) to establish a hermitage on the *pointe*. It hardly needs stating in the modern world, but indigenes don't take kindly to immigrants piling in and telling them how to live, and Morgan got shirty with Primel, for which she received a most saintly duffing up. Realizing Celtic saints were made of sterner stuff than the usual run of wailing sailors, Morgan beat a speedy retreat to the Rochers des Méloines, which she haunts to this day, the surf actually being the suds of the linen she is forever washing.

In her haste to get away, Morgan's korrigan and gold got left behind. Magnanimous in victory, Primel allowed that both might remain on his Pointe, on condition that the treasure be buried and the korrigan only come out once a year to get a breath of fresh air. The korrigan's annual outing takes place during mass on Palm Sunday. If you haven't already spotted the opportunity, you've got none of that rapacious entrepreneurial spirit the French regard as being typically English. Once a year, Morgan's treasure is unprotected! It is even said that come Monday morning, there are signs that some optimist has skipped visiting the supermarket in order to scrape about in search of treasure.

Ghostly soap suds are not the only symptom of haunting on the Pointe de Primel. Another story reports that during the first French revolution, the priest in Plougasnou continued to serve throughout the Terror until one night, having received his honorarium for a service, he was chased away by a bunch of *sans-culotte* before he could say mass and was forced to flee to England. Full of remorse for his failure to fulfill his sacerdotal duties, he languished in England (all Frenchmen languish when in exile, especially in England) until the Concordat of 1801 secured the future of the Catholic church in revolutionary France and he was able to embark for Brittany. But a great storm blew up as they approached the coast, the boat sank, all hands were lost, and the priest never performed the expiatory ceremony. Tormented by guilt, his ghost is said to haunt the *pointe*, coastguards reporting weird shrieks in the night and eerie lights glimmering in the dark. Listen to the wind when a good storm's blowing up, watch the glowworms in early summer, and you maybe persuaded yourself.

On the far side of the *"grand massif central/chaîne transversale"*, we descend past a shallow depression (invisible in Summer when it's overgrown with ferns) reinforced by a rough stone wall. It is the work of Vauban, the great seventeenth century military architect who fortified some 300 cities and constructed from scratch nearly forty new forts. In his leisure hours, he was an accomplished essayist and something of a visionary, proposing for instance a single European currency and correctly predicting that by the year 2000 the population of Canada would be 30 million. He also had the temerity to tell the king that the common people were overtaxed and overworked and underfed, and that the government should introduce a graduated income tax, which the nobility and the king himself would pay, too. The military marvel of the age, Vauban's forts have achieved an even more sublime status in modern times, for the man had as good an eye for a picturesque line as he did for a strategic location, and the places he chose for their military attributes are precisely the sort of places we choose nowadays for their aesthetic merits. Of itself, the Pointe de Primel gun emplacement isn't particularly impressive, you probably wouldn't even notice it if you weren't looking for it, but it did the job, participating in the defeat of an English squadron attempting to land 7000 soldiers on the 11th September 1793. Sit here for a while and you'll appreciate why it was effective, overlooking as it does the harbour entrance and being shielded from behind by treacherous rocks and easily defensible positions. And when it comes to appreciating nature, this is a great place to be in a storm, when swollen seas come rolling in to smash against the fangs of rock at the harbour's mouth.

Our next stop is a less alluring spot for contemplating wild water and should be avoided by anyone without a head for heights. I'm not having a *grand-massif-central-chaîne-transversale* moment here, but Le Gouffre (chasm, abyss, whirlpool, vortex) is a precipitous little drop and no place to be when the seas are running high. A narrow channel between the main headland and the rocks at its tip, Le Gouffre really does become a kind of vortex when the conditions are ripe, and the footbridge that spanned the gap in the first two decades of the twentieth century was aptly named Le Pont du Diable.

Nowadays Le Grand Rocher or Penn ar Hastell (lit. Castle Head) is only accessible at low tide, and even then some hands on scrambling is involved. The scramble isn't exactly alpine, but a fall would hurt and it's not recommended if you're unsure of the tide's movements or after a spell of heavy rain when there's a risk of rockslides from the crumbling turf along the tide-line. If you do want to get to the top . . . er . . . be it on your own head. The easiest way is to descend onto the rocks twenty-five metres to the east of Le Gouffre then scramble up the right hand side of Le Grand Rocher, where a narrow but natural path zigzags onto the top.

The history of this diminutive lump of rock is surprisingly rich. It was the site of the second of the Roman lookout posts mentioned earlier and probably served a similar function as far back as Mesolithic times.

However, it only really gained notoriety when it was fortified in the sixteenth century, during that most dismal of dismal conflicts, the French Wars of Religion between factions of Catholic and Protestant fundamentalists and pragmatists, aided, abetted, and provoked by the English and the Spanish. Basically a dispute about who ate the wafer and who wore the crown, the French Wars of Religion did the job most wars do best, bringing scum to the surface and making ordinary people miserable. The local narrative is confused, I've read at least four versions of what happened in Plougasnou, but in one respect all accounts agree - it was a story of turncoats, fanatics, and bandits, often as not all rolled up in one handy package.

In 1593, the Duc de Mercoeur, governor of Brittany, member of the Catholic League, and self-appointed Protector of the Roman Catholic Church, put Francois de Goëzbriand in charge of the Pointe de Primel. To call Goëzbriand fickle would be like saying Caligula was a little bit smutty. He had started out as a royalist, supporting the claim to the throne of the protestant Henry of Navarre, but after being imprisoned by the *ligueurs* and obliged to pay a ransom for his liberty, he joined the league himself, aiming to recuperate his lost fortune by robbing 'royalists', to wit anyone who had any money. What ensues is a bit like that eighties spoof TV serial, Soap, each episode of which began with a plot résumé and the refrain: "Confused? You will be".

Goëzbriand got Primel after being kicked out of his previous fiefdom by another sometimes-yes-sometimes-no *ligueur* and all round ruffian, Guy Eder La Fontenelle, who was convicted a few years later of lèse-majesté and conspiracy, broken on the wheel and executed. When Henry wrong-footed both the Protestants and the Catholic *ligueurs* by converting to Rome and pocketing the French crown, Goëzbriand promptly changed sides again, somewhat atypically as it happens, the Bretons generally displaying an uncanny knack for staying on the wrong side. As a result, he held onto the fort at Primel and continued much as before, except now he called his victims *ligueurs* rather than royalists, the definition once again being premised more upon the size of their purse than the shape of their convictions. Insofar as such turbulent times allowed, Henry was one of history's Good Guys, and he soon realized that the only thing Goëzbriand deserved was his P45. But by then, Goëzbriand had acquired a taste for the business of brigandage, and retreated to his castle on Le Grand Rocher, chained off access to the only landing stage, armed three boats, and turned pirate.

Set a thief to catch a thief or, in this instance, get a bloodthirsty brigand to dislodge a bloodthirsty brigand. The *pointe* was beset by Goëzbriand's old sparring partner, La Fontenelle, who had previously been busy doing much the same as Goëzbriand from his Île Tristan stronghold at Douarnenez, and the unsavory pair conspired in a bout of blood-letting that would make Smithfield look anaemic. Eventually, with the help of a Spanish expeditionary force and a band of Irish adventurers, Goëzbriand was captured, the Spaniards took the castle and La Fontenelle took everything else, setting up a new bastion for the Catholic League, and carrying on much as his predecessor had done. But being a man of such predatory ambition he might have been designed as an exemplar of the wonderful French phrase "*il racle le tapis avec ses dents*" (he scrapes the carpet with his teeth), La Fontenelle wasn't content with 'everything else', he wanted the castle, too. Turning against his erstwhile allies, he attempted to storm Le Grand Rocher, failed and, in a fit of pique worthy of a Hollywood villain, stabbed his lieutenant to death. When, at length, the Spaniards vacated the castle, allegedly because they were homesick, Boiséon de Coëtnizan, the governor of Morlaix, nipped in quick and partially destroyed it. End of story, right? Wrong.

In 1616 a new bunch of renegade *ligueurs*, Les Routiers (no relation to the fine tradition of roadside restaurants), took over the ruined fortress and began putting themselves about a bit, until they in turn were shifted, once again by Boiséon (you can imagine what he thought about Plougasnou: one set of bandits can be put down to bad luck, two is beginning to look like a habit, three is becoming pathological). This time the governor was taking no chances and the fortifications were completely razed. Nowadays, all that remains on Le Grand Rocher are the windbreak-like foundations of a tower and the only bloodletting is done by fishermen, who come here in search of Coley, Mullet, and the occasional John Dory and Bass.

Taking the path to the southeast away from Le Gouffre, we pass the Menhir Marsouin, so called because it was re-erected by the marines, who are nicknamed The Porpoises or *Marsouins*. Despite the maritime associations, it seems a curious choice of name. These are big strapping lads we're talking about here, lads with a costly education in acts of extreme prejudice, yet they're identified with a mammal that spends ninety per cent of its time playing games and making love. Given its strategic location, Brittany has long been a naval base and one may still occasionally see marines marching along the coastal path on a training exercise, machine guns strapped to their backs. Directly behind the menhir, on the path nearer the main outcrop of rock, two upright stones mark the entrance to twin tumuli from the Bronze Age. When the tumuli were explored by archeologists, they found sarcophagi, granite tools, a skeleton, a bronze bracelet and an earthenware vase dating back to 1800BC, all of which are

Tumuli entrance

now lodged at the Musée de Morlaix. We then pass a fallen menhir and, amid the last rise of rocks on the right, a prehistoric cave-dwelling, before traversing the site of a final memorial to all those years of bloodletting.

With such a mêlée of militants clubbing one another about the head and sheathing their swords in one another's vital organs, there were a lot of bodies piling up in sixteenth century Primel, so a cemetery was established in the northeasterly dune. It has long since been eroded by the waves, but fragments of bone are still said to appear in the shingle on the Grève Beleg. *Grève* literally means beach or shore, but is used locally to specify a pebble beach, while *Beleg* comes from the chapel that used to stand beside the cemetery, the Chapelle Beleg or Priest's Chapel being named in memory of the unfortunate ecclesiastic said to haunt the *pointe*. Though photos exist of it, the chapel has now gone the way of the bones, washed out to sea by the unremitting assault of the waves, all that remains being two sections of the wall.

To end our walk, we follow the path skirting the campsite, which is located on the site of the 'Chambre aux Boeufs' where livestock for the fortress used to be corralled. I'm none too sure what the modern day camper is supposed to make of this association, but if visitors would rather be linked with rebels than cattle, they need only look to the Roc'h ar Banniel just beyond the campsite, which was where the rebel *ligueurs* raised their banner. The coastal path then drops down onto the fine sandy expanse of the Plage de Primel-Tregastel, where a swim provides a refreshing conclusion to our outing.

The walk described here is short, yet it touches on three thousand years of history. A similar trajectory can be followed on virtually any stretch of the coastal path as we stroll back in time, bumping into a very Breton mix of fact and fancy, of tall tales and improbable history, encountering pirates and shipwreckers, saints and sirens, smugglers and coastguards, bandits and buried treasure, big stones and imaginary

Indisputably "Moooauh!"

The Emerald Coast - Ille et Vilaine

mountains, sinister washerwomen and marauding Englishmen . . . . We'll be bumping into all of them in more detail later on. As for the coastal path itself, one word says it all: *"Moooauh!"*

3. Fest Noz:
La Mutine - 6 / Les Gavottes - 0

ACCESS - **Plouezoc'h** is in Finistère north of Morlaix on the D76. Temporary panels will indicate the field in which Celtytud is being held and guide you through the provisional one-way system.

I don't know the statistics, but I wouldn't be surprised to hear that Brittany is the festival capital of France. Admittedly, nowadays pretty well any town in Europe where the mayor's got a minimum of gumption can find some pretext for a festival, but visit Brittany in the Summer and you'll find the blessed things everywhere: festivals of the sea, festivals of the earth, festivals of seaweed, festivals of chestnuts, festivals of *crêpes*, festivals of *galettes*, festivals of cider, festivals of harps, harvest festivals, horse-racing festivals, bagpipe festivals, parish festivals, festi-this-and-that-and-the-other . . . it's as if the entire region is festering. You could stumble from one to the other the whole summer long and never leave the circuit except perhaps for the odd non-festival breakfast now and again.

In particular, there are dozens of music festivals, the most famous of which are Les Vieilles Charrues at Carhaix, the Festival du Bout de Monde on the Presqu'île de Crozon, and the Festival Interceltique at Lorient. Vieilles Charrues has become France's biggest rock festival, featuring eighty odd concerts in front of a quarter of a million spectators, but when it began in 1992 it was little more than an irreverent jest made by a group of students cocking a snook at official celebrations in Brest. The Festival du Bout de Monde, meanwhile, wittily takes its location at the 'End of the World' to celebrate World Music, and tries to maintain a human scale by restricting attendance to a 'modest' 50,000 over the three days. As for the Festival Interceltique, well, that's a legend all to itself. Curiously, most of the tales I've heard about it seem to relate to the antics of the Irish contingent. There was, for instance, the year a Brittany Ferries boat had to spend three hours sailing round in circles because *festivaliers* en route from Ireland had suffered a little access of joy and chucked a lot of deck chairs over the back of the boat. Only problem was, nobody knew whether there'd been anyone in the chairs when they went overboard! The same year, a man of my acquaintance was strolling through the streets of Lorient when he was assaulted from behind, receiving a roundhouse punch on the jaw, after which he was spun about to be confronted by a profusely apologetic Irishman, who insisted he hadn't actually meant to hit Yves but had mistaken him for 'a friend'.

But if you want a really authentic Breton experience, rather than bumping about one of these big events, you've got to go to a *fest noz*. Apparently. I say 'apparently' because I don't actually know anything about this. A 'night party' as opposed to the day party of a *fest deiz*, the *fest noz* is a celebration of traditional Breton music and dance. And that is all I know.

Otherwise, I am perfectly ignorant on the topic.

The *fest noz* we're attending is at Plouezoc'h in Finistere. It's called Celtytud and is organized by the local dance circle. Wherever you go in Brittany, you'll see signs advertizing *fest noz,* ranging from an old pallet daubed with a spot of leftover paint and propped beside a country lane to professionally printed banners strung across major thoroughfares, and I would guess the events vary accordingly. Plouezoc'h has the banners. Not that we were swayed by the advertizing. We chose Celtytud partly because it's on our doorstep, but mostly because the headlining group was recommended by an internationally renowned fiddler, a professional singer of sea shanties, a philosopher stone mason, and a psychoanalyst, a roster of references that could hardly be bettered. Add the bank manager and the chemist, and you'd have a good part of life's necessities covered.

We cross the field that serves as a car-park, hand over our tickets, get our hands stamped and stroll into the makeshift compound where the *fest noz* is being staged. The bank manager and the chemist are already there. And the girl from the supermarket checkout. A kind of laager has been laid out for the occasion. On one side, the stage folds out from an eighteen wheeler with a flap in its side. Opposite the stage is a three-sided marquee. Sealing either end of the laager are large tents, one housing the bar, the other serving crêpes, cider and coffee. The ground in the middle and in the marquee is covered with a temporary wooden floorboard. This, apparently, is important. The programme proudly proclaims that Celtytud takes place "*sur parquet, en plein air et sous chapiteau*". The *chapiteau* or big top is perhaps pushing it a bit for the marquee, but given that rain is rarely far away in Brittany, some shelter is essential and it is big enough to house a fair few people if needs must. As for the *plein air*, there's always plenty of that in Brittany, sometimes a little too much, and *fest noz* generally take place outdoors so that as many people as possible can attend. The *parquet* I'm not sure about yet. But it's obviously significant.

Actually, I'm not being strictly honest about my unblemished ignorance. I have spent an afternoon on the internet checking out the background. I know, for instance, that there are dances called *gavottes* and *jabadaos* and *danses ficelles* and *an dros* and *hanter dros* and *plinns*. I know there was a great revival of Breton folk music in the second half of the twentieth century, climaxing with the international acclaim for the multi-instrumentalist Alan Stivell. And I know that if you're to bump about Brittany with any authority, you've got to go to a *fest noz* sooner or later. But I don't know what any of this means. I don't know my *an* from my *hanter*, and I'm a bit hazy about my *binious* and my *bombardes*. The one's a bagpipe, the other a shawm or oboe, but I have an unfortunate tendency to get them muddled up with *bigorneaux*. *Bigorneaux* are winkles and, even in Brittany, where they make some strange sounds with some strange instruments, winkles are not susceptible to being blown into for the purposes of popular entertainment. So, like Donald Rumsfeld, there are things I know I know and things I know I don't know, but I've got a nasty feeling there might be a lot of things I don't know I don't know.

The first band, the Breizh Brothers, are already on stage when we arrive. *Breizh* (also spelled Breiz or occasionally Vreiz), meaning Brittany, is regularly used as a prefix to give commonplace words a local flavour, most strikingly perhaps in Breizh-Cola, but naming a Breton band the Breizh Brothers is particularly neat. As it happens, they don't bear a very great resemblance to Jake and Elwood Blues, and the rhythm section's not nearly as tight as Booker T's old sidemen, but they are wearing the regulation white shirts and black trousers.

The band includes accordion, percussion, electric violin, *bombarde*, whistles, electric bass, and semi-acoustic guitar, five of which are in the line-up thanks to Alan Stivell. The electrification of *fest noz* came before his time, but he was the man that revived neglected instruments and integrated new ones into the traditional dance tunes. That may not sound like a very great achievement, but anyone who has ever heard a *bombarde* will be able to tell you it's not the most accommodating of instruments.

Look in the dictionary and among the definitions for 'bombard' you will see 'an early cannon', 'an old form of bassoon', 'a large liquor jug' and 'a black-jack'. The instrument was in fact named after the cannon, which isn't hugely encouraging, and if it's played badly, a large jug of liquor might prove a pretty essential piece of equipment because the sound it makes can feel like a blow round the back of the head. It is, in short, one of those instruments like the banjo or the bagpipe that can be slotted into Mark Twain's definition of a gentleman as a man 'who owns a banjo/bagpipe/*bombarde* (take your pick), but doesn't play it'.

I once heard a Breton *bombarde* player jamming with a German guitarist in a Pyrenean bar. The German was playing Blowing In The Wind. Given the look on the Breton's face, I reckon he'd have been happier blowing in the wind than in a *bombarde*. You can say what you like about Bob Dylan, but his compositions are not a natural vehicle for the *bombarde*. The Breton was paralyzed for about fifteen seconds, his face creased with concentration, but after a few tentative blue notes, he did it. He played Blowing In The Wind on the *bombarde*. And it was good, too.

The problem, if problem it is, is that the *bombarde* doesn't fit into the prevailing western tradition. Like the *biniou* (the bagpipe, not the winkle), it's not a tempered instrument, which effectively means that to get the same harmonics out of two different *bombardes*, they'd have to be made from the same tree. Bach may have had a well-tempered clavier, but the Bretons have got a bad-tempered *bombarde* that doesn't mix easily.

I'm none too sure what to make of this. It's an unknowable known or perhaps a known unknowable. It could be a recipe for anarchy or a pretext for unbridled individualism. Or one might suppose it a means of promoting local loyalties since, on the surface at least, the implication is that

Blowing in
the winkle

no two Breton musicians can play together unless they've got access to the same tree. And yet they do. And well, too. Despite the fact that they play an instrument that shares its etymology with a bomb. Nor is a peculiar tonality the only eccentric aspect of Breton music. Governed by the rhythmic patterns of set dance steps, it also resists classical musical notation.

Bags and coats lie untended inside the marquee, which is otherwise empty. No one seems concerned that anything might be stolen and just about everyone is out on the *plein air parquet*. And I mean everyone. From the age of four to somewhere in the region of eighty-four, the floor is full of Bretons having a good time. Leastwise, I suppose they're having a good time. Nobody's forcing them out there. There's no frantic Nashville caller barking orders. But nobody seems to be smiling very much. They're all remarkably solemn, dancing in circles, perhaps fifty people in each, holding hands and decorously rotating clockwise, elbows jigging back and forth. It's all in the elbows as far as I can see. The feet move, but only enough to keep the circle turning. It looks pretty silly, actually. A bit Mr. Beanish. Especially the guy wearing brown velveteen *saroual* and the man with the hair I'd swear was a wig if it wasn't cut so artlessly.

That's easy, I think, adding as an afterthought, You won't catch me doing that.

Everybody's dancing except half a dozen blokes standing under the *chapiteau* nursing their beers. They're standing there, casual like, trying to give the impression they could be dancing if they wanted to, because it's easy that, anybody could do it, but they're not dancing right now because they don't want to, that's all. It's got nothing to do with being frightened of standing on someone's toes or spinning off to the left when everyone else is spinning off to the right, or doing something else that will make them look like right bloody wallies. I go and stand beside them.

It might be easy, but watching the slow spinning of four or five adjacent circles has a slightly hypnotic effect, drawing one into a world of alternative perception, like trying to decipher an animated computer *trompe l'oeil*. And it's also strangely touching, the steady repetitive movement, maybe five generations conjoined in a single circle, affinity unbroken by time or age or the troubling compulsions of self-assertion and divisive ambition. A phrase comes to mind, one I would have despised in my dissolute youth: this is good clean fun. Taking care not to get caught in one of the circles, I make my way to the bar.

Now this is a known known: La Mutine, one of the best beers in Brittany. A dozen beakers are lined up on the bar, brimful and just yearning to be drunk. Two euros a shot, which isn't bad in a country where a decent pint in a pub can set you back a fiver. The dances maybe a bit decorous, the dancers may not be smiling very much, but the beer is good and cheap, and I am further cheered by the sight of a druid arriving at the *fest noz*, all long white hair and long white beard and long white clothes. They're not quite flowing robes he's wearing, but about as near to flowing robes as a collarless shirt and baggy trousers can get. I take his presence to be yet further testimony to the quality of the headlining act. I must keep an eye on this man. Meet him and I'll be in touch with an authentic bit of Breton history. The real thing.

Back in the marquee during a break between numbers, I overhear the admiring observation that everyone 'knows' the dances. What's to know? You stand in a circle, hold hands, and jig your elbows. It's easy. Ring-a-ring-of-roses. I could do that. Except then the dancers confuse me by pairing off for a *bal a deux*. Nothing much else changes, though. They still dance side by side, the movement is still mostly in the elbows, and everyone still looks pretty solemn.

Music is a reflection of character and the Bretons are a bit like the Irish without the gaiety. Reels and jigs are now part of the repertoire, but the definitive line of Breton chanson is "*Ach, c'est triste, c'est pas rigolo*", "Oh, it's sad, it's not funny". *Gwerz*, they call it, unaccompanied folk songs all about doom and gloom and death and unrequited love: Breizh Blues. Done well, by a performer of the calibre of Denez Prigent for instance, it can be extraordinarily powerful, a haunting lament sending shivers down your spine. Done badly, it will also send shivers down your spine, but for different altogether more lamentable reasons.

Life in Brittany hasn't always been a barrel of laughs, not in a country where most people were either dirt poor farmers scraping a living from smallholdings or sailors and fishermen who faced drowning as an everyday work hazard. But the Irish had it just as hard, if not harder, and still came up with the *craik*. In Brittany, the only *craik* was the one in the ceiling when it was raining, which it always was. There is a lurking sense of stoicism in the face of impending disaster about the Bretons, a resignation that I'm told was encouraged by the church. The assumption was that one had to be miserable on earth to merit your reward in the afterlife. But the misery ought not to be expressed too forcefully as it wasn't quite moral to display either happiness or sadness. Which may well be why pleasure is taken tight-lipped. To make matters worse, the church proscribed dances that were *kof-a-kof*, that is tummy-to-tummy, for the obvious reason that jigging about *kof-a-kof* was altogether too much fun in a world of carefully balanced woes, which is why so many dances are danced side by side.

For the next number, the patterns become more complex, one circle turning within another, lending the dance a faintly heliocentric symbolism, an interpretation confirmed by the fact that the druid's out on the dance floor now. Must be a bit of sun-worshipping in there somewhere. I really must meet this man. He can give me deep insights into the Celtic mysteries and open my mind to new and marvellous worlds. Deep insights notwithstanding, the immediate effect of watching circles turning within circles is to compound the hallucinatory quality of the experience. It maybe simple, but by the time it's all over, I feel quite dizzy and have to stagger off to the bar to get another Mutine.

Returning two euros the lighter, I secrete myself behind the small group of non-dancing guys. We're not exactly wallflowers, but there's certainly something a bit mossy about us. I take a sip of Mutine, two, three, four, then realize that something strange is happening with this 'easy' dancing. People are dancing in pairs again, side-by-side, but they're turning more, and occasionally two pairs will face each other, daring a bit of the old *kof-a-kof*, albeit *à quatre* and at a distance. Then suddenly the squares break and the couples hold one another, real *kof-a-kof*, nothing dissembled, and are whirling round very fast. It's such a shock the first time it happens, I nearly drop my Mutine. Then they stop just as abruptly. Side-by-side again. Bit of decorous jigging. Then a foursome. Then whirling again. I look for a pattern. It's clear everyone is doing the same thing at the same time, so they must know what to do and when to do it, and I have to admit, it ain't looking all that easy, but I can't for the life of me work out the musical cues. At first it seems to be a sprightly *bombarde* solo, but then the same solo repeats itself when the dancers are side-by-side or in squares, so that's not the signal to embark on a meeting and greeting of tummies. As time goes on, I begin to wonder whether they're not counting steps. There seems to be no other explanation for the sudden shifts, which aren't in the least ragged, but take place with the same unfathomable precision that a flight of birds will suddenly change course without breaking formation. By the time the Breizh Brothers finish their set, I'm thoroughly disoriented. I need another Mutine.

The next act is an accordion-vocal duo, Patrick Lefebvre and Marie-Claire Lavanant. From what I can gather after pestering the people around me, this duo is closer in spirit to the original *fest noz* which, before it was revitalized and amplification was introduced by Loeiz Ropars in the 1950s, generally consisted of two people, each sat on a cider barrel, and making as much noise as they possibly could, hence the popularity of the accordion and the *bombarde*, which are nothing if not loud.

No instrument is more French than the accordion, right? Get the old stripy T-shirt on, a rakishly angled beret, a bit of fishnet stocking, and Bob's your *tantie, je ne regrette rien*. Well, actually, no. Invented in Germany in the 1820s, the instrument was only really popularized in France at the end of the nineteenth century. We may think of it as typically French, but Robespierre, Balzac, or Victor Hugo certainly wouldn't. When, however, it was introduced into Brittany, it was an instant success. First, you could make a helluva racket with an accordion, which was handy when you were sat on a cider barrel with two hundred people stamping their clogs on a wooden floor; second, it was cheap; third, it was

Making as much noise as they possibly could.

a lot easier to play than a bagpipe or a violin or a winkle; and fourth, the *boite du diable,* as it was also known, was associated with lascivious big city dances like waltzes and mazurkas, and whatever the church had to say on the matter, a certain sensuality was vital at these shindigs. One social function of the *fest noz* was to let young people meet and, er, size one another up. You couldn't be sizing one another up if you were standing side-by-side bending your elbows. You needed a bit of *kof-a-kof* and you got more *kof-a-kof* for your *livre* with an accordion than you did with a fiddle, as a result of which the latter instrument virtually disappeared from the Breton repertoire until Alan Stivell reintroduced it three-quarters of a century later.

Marie-Claire's voice is a bit scratchy at first, but it soon warms up and, between them, she and Patrick fill the dance floor for some decidedly *kof-a-kof* stuff, which I'm informed is a 'Scottish'. Nobody explains how the Scots got to be such specialists in *kof-a-kof*, but there you go. In the meantime, somebody, not me, has spilled beer on the *parquet*. That may not seem very remarkable of itself. Some of the dancehalls I've been in down the years, most of the beer appeared to be kept on the floor, along with the dog ends and the drunks. What is remarkable though is that the culprits are on their knees, wiping it up with their bare hands and sweeping it through a gap in the planks. I can't for the life of me imagine why. It doesn't seem very likely anybody would slip over, especially given that they're all holding onto each other. Surely one cup of spilled beer couldn't bring down fifty people? And if someone did momentarily slip, the momentum of the circle would keep them turning. But then I catch sight of Marie-Claire. Maybe she's the explanation. House proud, I surmise. I can't say for sure whether she's seen the spilled beer, but she stands on stage looking like a stern housewife from some fifties Hollywood confection, hand firmly fixed on hip as if expressing displeasure at the woeful incompetence of her menfolk. It may be the stance all Breton *chanteuse* adopt, but faced with this particular known unknown, I feel faintly discomfited and fetch myself another Mutine.

Marie-Claire and Patrick work in the *kan han diskan* tradition, originally a strictly vocal call and response style, in which two singers, the *kaner* and the *diskaner* played off one another, repeating and modifying phrases with an hypnotic effect to match the whirling circles of the dances. At different stages both the clarinet, or 'cauliflower stick' as the Bretons call it, and the accordion have been popular instruments for accompanying a solo vocalist, since each could mimic the phrasing of the human voice and provide the *diskan*. Songs can tackle any subject, but must match the metre of the dance they're meant to accompany, as a result of which nonsense phrases are used to fill out a line where necessary. The most common of these Breizh-scat phrases, *tra-la-la-la-leh-no*, has become so integral to the music, songs can even start with it, rather than just tacking it onto the end of a line for the purposes of scansion.

By the end of the set, I have to admit that there's more to Breton dancing than I'd supposed. I'd thought it was just sort of jiggy-jiggy-jig, hoppety-hop, push-the-elbows-out and shuffle-round-the-circle, then repeat. But the more I look, the more I realize there's something else going on here. First, there were the mysterious breaks in dance patterns with no apparent musical cue. Now there's a bit of heel kicking coming in and knees are being raised. And there's more crossing of legs than could be explained by a simultaneous urge on the part of two hundred people to have a pee. And several dancers are spinning around, for all the world like kids making themselves dizzy. Above all, everything is being done with faultless synchronicity. I expect the druid could enlighten me about the intricacies of the dance. He'd know about things like this. Deep Breton stuff, you see. But I can't locate him at the moment. He must be off doing mysterious druidical things in a mysterious Breton way.

Instead, I get myself another Mutine and go to talk to our neighbour, himself a fine musician and a man with an encyclopedic knowledge of traditional music, which he is very ready to share. Very ready. You wouldn't want to get him talking about the history of the chanter and the drone in the Breton bagpipe, not if you had any very pressing appointments in the next couple of months. But he is an absolute mine of information, better still, a volcano - you don't have to dig it out of him, he gives forth of his own accord. Tentatively, I ask what was happening with those bewildering shifts between lateral pairs, quadrilles, and twirling couples.

"We dance like that," he says, "because of you English."

Oh, no, I think, here we go, the English have done it again.

To be honest, amid the torrent of information that ensues, I don't quite catch everything and only have the haziest notion why the English are to blame for the way the Bretons dance. In my defence, I should say that I am a bit befuddled by all those spinning circles. And I really want to talk to the authentic Breton druid, get the inside druidical gen, you understand, but I've just seen him emerging from the *pissoir* buttoning up his trousers, which rather takes the shine off the anticipated deep Breton stuff and inside druidical gen. And I have drunk five Mutines. Not to mention the best part of a bottle of wine at dinner. But as far as I can work out, the key to the changing patterns of the dance is, as I had surmised, counting. If you are to carry off a Breton dance with a becoming grace, you need to know your eight-times table. Eight steps, shift, sixteen steps, shift, thirty-two steps, shift. Little wonder no one is smiling. Get a few Mutines inside me and I'd be hard pressed to remember the coefficient, let alone apply it to my feet.

And the English are to blame, I believe, because all that breaking apart and coming together again has its origins in English country dancing, and is found specifically in northern Finistere and Côtes d'Armor, the two *departements* facing England. How it got here, is another known unknown. Insofar as I'd understood the narrative of the Anglo-Breton take on the Entente Cordiale, the English came to Brittany to plunder and pillage and rape. They didn't go wafting about giving dancing classes for the general betterment of Breton folk culture. But somehow they left their mark.

It's time for Skolvan. This is not a beer-truck. It's the violinist-shantyman-philosopher-mason-psychoanalyst recommended band. But it's a good enough pretext to head for the bar and get another Mutine. Weaving back to the marquee . . . sorry, walking sedately back to the marquee, I check out the line-up. Again, Stivell's influence is manifest: the percussionist is very minimalist and state of the art, playing a sort of bodiless bongo and flamenco-style box-stool, and there's an alto-saxophonist, all cheek and frizzy hair, but he plays like an angel. Perhaps angels always have big cheeks and frizzy hair, but Bernard le Dreau looks like he just came in from the farm, and yet he's making some extraordinary jazz-inflected sounds that are a perfect counterpoint to the *bombarde*, tempered or no. That was perhaps Stivell's most significant contribution to the revival of Breton music, blending it with other styles including jazz, blues, mainstream rock, roots music from various traditions, and latterly even incorporating elements of hip-hop.

One of the first dances is a *jabadao*, which is distinguished from those that went before primarily by the fact that it involves a lot of stamping. And this is why the parquet is so important. Apart from its percussive qualities, it is said to be a measure of how well you dance, for in the past it was judged that the 'best' circle of dancers were those that cracked the floorboards with their clogs. When I ask where all this stamping comes from, I'm told (by somebody who's looking a bit blurred for some reason) that the origin of many of these dances was the communal stamping down of dirt for the foundations of a new house or to make a threshing circle. If you experience a Breton storm, which you probably will, you'll appreciate that you'd want firm foundations for building a house. Standing in a circle and stamping hard is a vital part of communal living.

Later, I believe (there may have been another Mutine in there somewhere; I was trying to find the druid and thought he might be at the bar, though it's possible he was off in the *pissoir* again), the circles are leaching into one another again, except this time an internal ring is facing out and an external ring is facing in, so it's a sort of communal *kof-a-kof*. More than that though, the circles seem to be winding through one another like waves, or a human representation of a Venn diagram, subsets within subsets within subsets, shifting all the while to accommodate different configurations and different truths.

Ah! There he is. The druid. He's dancing again. He definitely looks enlightened.

And the man with a wig that's not a wig, he's back on the dance floor, too.

I can do this. This is easy.

Then the man with the wig that's not a wig does something complicated with his feet and I'm lost again. The atmosphere has warmed up. There's still not much smiling. True, the druid's smiling, a smile of gentle understanding and deep wisdom. He does it by instinct, I expect. Doesn't need to recite his times-table. The rhythm resides deep in his genuine Breton soul along with other arcane yet illuminating lore. Everyone else though is still too busy concentrating on the counting to be smiling. Nonetheless, several foreheads gleam with sweat and a few Yee-haas! are echoing round the dance floor. They're not exactly rebel-yells but they are undeniably symptoms of excited pleasure.

Looking over the dancers' heads, I realize not every circle is doing the same thing. Some dance slow, some dance fast, and yet they all seem to be in time to the music. One string of dancers is skipping sideways incredibly quickly, snaking their way between circles in a sort of Breizh-conga, snapping back and forth like a whip, curling against themselves, nearly colliding, never quite, all moving as one and at remarkable velocity.

And then I get an insight. This is the glory of Breton dance. They're all there together, all types, all walks of life, all ages, all holding hands, and they're all doing the same dance, but each group is doing it in its own way. And it's the group that counts. You've got to keep in time with your group, else you're lost and so is everyone else. You can keep your jitterbug and your break and your mashed potato. This is not a place for displays of individual athleticism. Nobody stands back to admire the best dancers. It is a collaborative act, an affirmation of community. Complicity is required, but otherwise, there's room for everyone. So long as the circle is unbroken, every dance can be done with whatever degree of facility you may have. I repeat, there's room for everyone: fast or slow, young or old, fat or thin, bewigged or not; there's even room for an ungainly Englishman.

The floorboards are rocking beneath my feet, propelling me from the marquee onto the dance floor. The bar's on the other side and I need another Mutine. I squeeze between the spinning cogs of a Breton community, a bit like Charlie Chaplin in Modern Times, swallowed up by something larger than myself, but not defeated. I get to the bar. It's crowded, but I edge forward till I'm within ordering distance. And I find myself standing by the druid. He's just one step away to my left. This is it! The real thing. I'm at my first *fest noz*. I've got a gutful of Mutine. I've understood the nature of Breton dance. I'm groping toward the convivial heart of Breton identity. And I'm standing next to a druid. And I sidle up to him. And I smile shyly and duck my head in deference to the mystic truths embodied by this man. And I lean forward to introduce myself, ready to extract the deep Breton stuff and inside druidical gen. And he turns to speak to his wife. And he's English.

4. Round Brittany:
'Them Next Door' in the Next Country

ACCESS - See www.tro-breiz.com or trobreizh.free.fr for details of which stretch of the route is scheduled for any given year. The itinerary links the cathedrals of **St. Malo, Dol-de-Bretagne, Vannes, Quimper, St. Pol de Leon, Treguier** and **St. Brieuc**. Between Dol and Vannes the itinerary passes through Meillac, Bécherel, St. Méen, Mauron, Josselin, and Plumelec. Between Vannes and Quimper: St. Anne, Hennebont, Pont Scorff, Quimperlé, and Rosporden. Between Quimper and St. Pol: Briec, Pleyben, Brassparts, Commana, and Pleyber-Christ. Between St. Pol and Treguier: Morlaix, Lanmeur, Plestin, and Lannion. Between Treguier and St. Brieuc: Pontrieux, Paimpol, Plouha and Etables-sur-Mer. Between St. Brieuc and St. Malo: Lamballe, Jugon, and Plancoët. Between St. Malo and Dol: Cancale and Vivier-sur-Mer. The devil's garage is at **Ploumanac'h** in Côtes d'Armor beside the **'Maison du Littoral'** behind the **Men Ruz** lighthouse, which is accessible from the car-park at 48° 49'.405 / -3° 28.115.

Pilgrim's Progress

Seven is a vital number in Celtic mythology and nowhere more so than in Brittany. Dotted about the region are the seven sleeping saints, the seven witches, the seven sisters, the seven isles, the seven stones representing seven loaves of bread a baker refused to give Saint Hervé, and there is a monument to seven thousand seven hundred and seventy seven martyrs. There are also tales of seven bishops embarking with seven hundred and seventy men, of seven hundred and seven score and seven saints meeting at a convention, multiplied elsewhere to seven thousand, seven hundred, seven score and seven. And, perhaps not unsurprisingly, the monument to the seven thousand seven hundred and seventy seven martyrs at Lanrivoaré is a place of pilgrimage if you think you're going mad. Contemplate all those sevens long enough and you probably will be. But perhaps the most significant seven if you're bumping about Brittany are the seven bishoprics of the nation's seven founding saints.

Nowadays the region is divided by *departements* like the rest of France . . . oops! Shouldn't say that, really. Got to watch your language when you're talking about Brittany and France. The Bretons don't always take kindly to phrases like Brittany and 'the rest of France'. 'Brittany and France' is better, as it implies an equality of status, but on the whole the Bretons are like a well upholstered woman who can't quite bring herself to dismiss the witless propaganda that promotes an anorexic ideal of beauty: each would really rather you ignored altogether the existence of the big bit stuck onto their hind end. It has no bearing on their true identity and is, in any case, an unsightly and entirely superfluous excrescence that any well bred and polite person would decline to mention in public. So, let's try that again.

Nowadays, Brittany is divided into five *departements*: Ille et Vilaine, Côtes d'Armor, Finistère, Morbihan and Loire-Atlantique. And they are all a matter of the most perfect indifference to your actual Breton. Nobody would dream of identifying themselves by their *departement*. Such things are merely a legal fiction manufactured for the convenience of the big bit stuck onto the hind end. You maybe a Breton, but you're not a Loire-Atlantiquean or an Ille-et-Vilainian, and not just because pronouncing it would involve a degree of oscular gymnastics that could lead to the swallowing of one's own head. Take the most virulent, rabidly disbelieving, materialistic atheist you can find in Brittany and ask him where he's from, and the chances are he'll name his village followed by his diocese, or in some cases a region within the diocese. Forget about Finistère and Côtes d'Armor . . . well, don't forget about them, you'll get lost if you don't bear in mind that these places have a juridical validity reflected on maps and signposts. But to bump about Brittany in Breton mode, the bishoprics are the important thing.

This is because localism is important in Fra . . . sorry, Brittany. Some Canadian friends were touring the region a few years ago and were looking for a campsite. This is not exactly a daunting challenge. Virtually every village, both in Brittany and the big bit stuck onto the hind end, has it's own campsite, but accustomed to distant vistas, great plains, mountain fastness and so forth, the Canadians couldn't see the wood for the trees, and eventually stopped and asked an old boy if he knew where the nearest campsite was. After grimacing a bit and scratching his head, the old boy announced gloomily: "I know *all* the countries round here and there's not a campsite in any of them". The Canadians were flabbergasted. France, Belgium, Luxembourg, Germany, Switzerland, Italy, Spain couldn't rustle up a single campsite between them?! What was the world coming to? Europe was pretty quick off the mark when it came to cobbling together a couple of world wars that a lot of Canadian backwoodsmen had to come and sort out, but when said Canadians wanted to pitch a tent, it was suddenly a major logistical challenge. Of course, when the old boy said 'countries' he was talking about discrete regions within the more immediate area, it was just a question of usage. But the anecdote does suggest a notion of borders that is, to say the least, a little different from the norm. Place is important.

Due to the vagaries of administrative expedience, there are actually nine dioceses in Brittany, corresponding to the areas around St. Malo, St. Brieuc, Vannes, Nantes and Rennes, and the regions of the Trégor, Léon and Cornouaille, though Rennes and Nantes are rather peripheral to the Breton identity - something else you shouldn't say in front

The Dioceses of Brittany

a Breton, as they can get quite vociferous about Nantes being Breton. But definitions of what's Breton and what's French aside, why seven bishoprics and seven saints?

The most attractive explanation is the most improbable, so we'll go with that. The story goes that an Irish queen took to dabbling in genetics, or what passed for genetics back in the dark ages, and after much pondering and staring into the middle distance, declared that any woman giving birth to twins must indubitably have slept with two different men. All hell was going to break loose therefore when the queen herself gave birth to septuplets (I mean, she may well have been a queen, but that's just plain greedy), so to avoid a scandal she gave the seven boys to her servant with instructions that they be drowned. But the servant knew the fairy tales, knew too that servants who did the dirty work did not get a glowing press, and duly approached the king. King took pity on the babes, took them in, raised them as bishops and packed them off to Brittany.

Now I freely confess, there are a number of holes in this story. First, just what sort of a king is it that can either not notice his wife has a bun full of wannabe bishops, or fail thereafter to cotton onto the fact that said bun has shrunk from a seven bishop bun to a bit of belly entirely innocent of ecclesiastic ambition? And what about this queen? Can you picture her face when the king comes in with seven bundles of swaddling cloth capped with seven mini-mitres? "Look what I found my dear, the Episcopalettes". And what about the genetics? "Who's been sleeping in *my* bed?" demands the Big King Bear. "Well, there's him and him and him and him and him and him, and er . . . oh, and him, too". That was practically the whole court. Forget about the sword-dipping escapades of Lancelot. The entire Round Table had been queuing up to take a turn. This is *kof-a-kof* on an heroic scale. You'd need a bucket of linctus to soothe a *kof* like that. And yet, despite or possibly because of the farcical overtones, it's still the best story around.

One way to explore Brittany is to follow the route of the Tro Breizh, the round Brittany pilgrimage that links the seven cathedrals of (clockwise) St. Malo, Dol-de-Bretagne, Vannes, Quimper, St. Pol de Leon, Treguier and St. Brieuc. It is, as we shall see, one of the very few things that do link the different dioceses, for each has its distinct identity, indeed the bishopric of Cornouailles round Quimper boasts several, identities that are defined as much by bad-mouthing their neighbours as asserting their own individual qualities.

In medieval times, the 600 kilometre Tro Breizh was the Breton equivalent of the Hadj, a relatively simple way of guaranteeing your place in paradise, presumably on the assumption that there was no point cluttering up your life with good deeds if you could just go for a long walk instead. Not that the pilgrimage was without its hardships and risks. For one thing, they didn't have Vibram in those days and they could have done with something solid under their feet as there was a wayside plant said to grow in the Monts d'Arrée that did not take kindly to being trodden on. Step on it and the hapless pilgrim would lose his way and end up wandering into the Yeun Elez marsh, wherein lay the gates of hell. The gates of hell notwithstanding, apparently some ten thousand Bretons took the risk every year, ten thousand out of a total population of six hundred thousand.

The turmoil during the Wars of Religion somewhat curbed this enthusiasm and the pilgrimage had died a death by the nineteenth century, but it was revived in the 1990s, and is now an annual event attracting thousands of modern day pilgrims for a five to six day hike along one portion of the trail, progressing between Quimper and Saint Pol de Leon (120km), Saint Pol and Treguier (127km), Treguier and Saint Brieuc (57km), Saint Brieuc and Saint Malo (91km), Saint Malo and Dol (24km), Dol and Vannes (140km), and finally back to Quimper (116km), with communal sleeping quarters in sports halls along the way and a range of ancillary services that would not disgrace the Tour de le Big Bit Stuck Onto the Hind End. Now I am not, of course, suggesting we try to squeeze a 600-kilometre itinerary into a single day, but I do recommend joining the pilgrimage as spectator or participant if you happen to be in Brittany when it's taking place, which is generally in the last week of July and the first week of August. To locate which stretch is slated for any given year, see www.tro-breiz.com or trobreizh.free.fr.

The old route is largely asphalted now and even the adapted itinerary includes long stretches on tarmac, but it's still a worthwhile walk, attracting as it does an extraordinary mix of dedicated ramblers, devout Christians, desperate dieters, and Breton nationalists. You'll see plenty of Breton flags, the nine stripes representing the nine bishoprics, the five black stripes standing for the  Gallo or French speaking areas of Dol, Nantes, Rennes, Saint Malo and Saint Brieuc, and the four white stripes for the Breton speaking Trégor, Léon, Cornouaille and Vannes. The division is notable, for what's really interesting about the pilgrimage is the them-next-door-in-the-next-country factor, since it traverses all the 'countries' in Brittany.

It has been said, with some justification, that the Bretons aren't racist because they exhaust their racist instincts among themselves. Putting aside for a moment the fact that Nantes and St. Malo weren't behindhand when it came to piling up filthy lucre through the slave trade, this seems largely true. There are other explanations, such as the instinctive kinship of people subjected to stereotyping and exploitation (the first overseas

migrants who came to do the dirty work in the Big Bit Stuck Onto The Hind End were called *Bretons Noirs*); but there's a pleasing logic to the notion of a culture in which racism is kept in the family. As we'll see shortly, according to the popular prejudices that come from without, it wasn't the only thing that was kept in the family.

Anyway, let's not beat about the bush here: the people of Vannes are dumb, the Cornouailles lively, the Léonards light-fingered, and the Trégorois treacherous: *"Sot comme un Vannetais, vif comme un Cornouaillais, voleur comme un Léonais, traître comme un Trégorais."* The dictum is quoted in *Fils de Ploucs* (Editions Ouest-France 2005) by Jean Rohou, who goes on to point out that it is a saying from Cornouailles, which you may have guessed already given that they get the only positive attribute. He also mentions that the Trégorois call the Cornouaillais *er C'herne*, i.e. Donkeys.

Of all the clichés, the key one is that of the Léonards, for in some ways that is the identity against which the others are defined. The Léonards are, in character if not religion, the Calvinists of Brittany. The work ethic is strong, wealth and salvation are won by the sweat of one's brow, order is preeminent in the world as in religion, and the Leonard would have no difficulty identifying with that 1960s sketch with John Cleese and the Two Ronnies which, after going down the grades, ends with Ronnie Corbett saying, "I know my place". Almost the exact phrase was current in the Leon, *pep hini en e renk,* each to his place, a conviction that was extended to pleasure. Booze, for instance, was shameful and not to be brought into the house, so bottles were stashed in the fields, and music and dancing (don't even mention *kof-a-kof*) were deemed so inappropriate among a god-fearing people they were actually banned during the nineteenth century.

This melancholy creed did not go down well with other Bretons. To the south the Cornouaillais were spontaneous, impulsive, insouciant, free thinkers, perhaps a little pretentious, but happily dancing and singing their way to damnation. And to the east, the Trégorois were scarcely less jolly, priding themselves on being impious, vivacious jokers, the very antithesis of the hardworking Léonards. They might be untrustworthy, they might be lazy, but they knew how to live, regarded themselves as *philosophes*, and delighted in mocking their austere neighbours. They knew what the Léonards were like: men who married religion with a love of money, men who had one hand on their missal, the other in their neighbour's pocket.

Perhaps the perfect affront the Trégorois offered the Léonards is to be found behind the Men Ruz lighthouse at Ploumanac'h. A little to the west of the house near the end of the headland is a most singular garage. Asked if there were any particular stipulations concerning the garage's style, the builders were given a free hand, so they built a pastiche chapel and decorated it with a mini bell tower housing a devil flanked by a couple of griffins. This impious jest would have been enough to elicit catalepsy amid the people of Léon, who were nothing if not clerical, boasting more priests per square foot than anywhere else in Brittany. More people, too, and therein lay their revenge. Despite the strictures against *kof-a-kof*, the Léonards were more numerous than the Trégorois and always short of land. Many farms on the Trégorois side of the Baie de Morlaix were left to languish in a pitiable state, because their carefree owners pretended it was poor land and there was no point trying to farm it when one might be better employed fishing and drinking and swanning about having a good time. Then the Léonards came over, bought up the Trégorois farms, fertilized the land with the old sweat of the brow, and prospered.

The notion that a people can be readily defined in this manner is, of course, total nonsense, but as nonsense goes it's rather good fun, and even if the clichés only ever embodied a tenuous truth, they shaped the way Bretons from different regions reacted to one another. Indeed, they still do. Woe betide anyone from north Finistère who is the slightest bit careful with his money. You can be sure everyone will be muttering behind his back: "Of course, he's a Léonard".

It was not merely a question of where you were born, though, for there were also more nebulous divisions of class allegiance, between the landlocked peasants and the seafaring coastal dwellers, between the rural and the urban, the Breton speaking west and the Gallo speaking east, the 'truly' Breton and the fragments of the Big Bit Stuck Onto The Hind End that had infiltrated themselves onto Breton territory, like the military and administrative centre of Rennes and the naval port of Brest. But perhaps the most striking differences were in folk dress.

Erwan Vallerie, in his droll essay, *Ils Sont Fous Ces Bretons* (Coop Breizh 2003), suggests the mania for distinguishing oneself from others was fomented by the Jacobin misconstruction of egalitarianism as uniformity. The Bretons have always been of a contrary disposition, being royalist when everyone else was republican, republican when everyone else was royalist, on the right when everyone else was on the left, on the left when everyone else was on the right, so no sooner than they got a whiff of communalism, they were busy asserting their individuality. The revolutionaries may have wanted a cohesive nation in which everyone was French and looked the part, but the Bretons didn't want to look like anyone else at all, certainly not one another, and there ensued a century of desperate differentiation, in which every region, every country, every village, every hamlet, sought to distinguish itself from it's neighbours by adding an extra ribbon to the traditional costume, or lengthening or flattening the hat, or working a different and more elaborate coif. The search for difference continued until World War One, when the non-Francophone Breton soldiers were hurriedly put in the front line, and a generation of Breton women were condemned to a uniform black dress. But even today, when some pageant involves dressing up in traditional

Glad to be different

costume, you will hear people saying, "Ah, no, that's not a proper coif from round here, that's a Bigouden coif", or "Oh, dear me, no. The lacework on that shawl, that's not right, my granny wouldn't have been seen dead in one of them". They don't quite say it's from 'another country', but the sentiment is implicit.

So what, apart from a pilgrimage, unites these disparate peoples that spend their time bad mouthing one another and dressing up the difference? You'd have thought they had nothing in common but borders and even those are argued over. First and most simplistically, there is an externally imposed unity. I know people who grew up in the Breton countryside in the fifties and sixties never imagining they were anything other than French, until they went to Paris and were told they were Breton, often as not by second generation expatriate Bretons whose great dream was to return to the homeland. But that's not enough to make a nation.

There is something else, though, something nearly all Bretons have in common, one thing that unites Léonards, Trégorois, Cornouaillais, *moi-je-suis-moi-je-ne-suis-pas-celle-ci-ou-celui-là*, impious and pious, gay and austere, all and sundry. No matter how lively local rivalries, no matter that my coif is bigger than yours, that you stitch your tassels this way and I stitch my tassels that way, no matter that this man sails, that man tills, this man tinkers with telecommunications, and that man sits around all day waiting for his supplementary benefit cheque, there is one subject that elicits a universal and comprehensive response in Brittany: Paris . . . or more particularly, the Parisians.

Parisien, tête de chien! Parigot, tête de veau!

Go anywhere in Brittany and you'll get an entrée with that phrase. Quite how the Parisians contrived to get heads that are at once dog-like and resemble a calf, I couldn't say, but whatever shaped head they've got, the Bretons don't like them. There are several reasons for this antipathy. There are ancient enmities stemming from the centralizing impetus of both pre and post revolutionary France, there are the inevitable resentments of a people long subjected to an annual influx of boisterous and alien holiday-makers, but if you push a Breton on the subject, the chances are he'll say it is an inevitable reaction to the nature of your average Parisian.

One aspect of this is the metropolitan know-it-all disdain suggested earlier in the tale about the golden dog bowl. We used to have an Old English Sheepdog called Bati that we'd picked up in an Andalusian refuge. Walking the dog one day, we bumped into a holidaying Parisian who instantly dissolved into baby talk, bending down, tapping his knees and cooing terms of endearment - toward the dog, that is, he didn't seem much interested in us.

"*Oooh, mon fou-fou, woooh, wooooh, moooauh! C'est le chien de mes rêves. Viens ici, viens ici, mon petit, mon petit choux, viens voir papa, viens ici.*"

Despite being called a little cabbage, Bati firmly ignored the invitation to come and see daddy. You can understand it really. I'm sure I wouldn't take kindly to some middle aged bloke bending down, calling me his little cabbage and inviting me to come and see daddy. I've read about people like that in the papers.

We watched awhile as the Parisian drooled all over the tarmac, then told him that Bati didn't 'speak' French. He 'spoke' English and Spanish. The Parisian snorted and snapped his fingers derisively.

"*Pouf! Des clopinettes. Tout le monde sait que c'est l'intonation qui compte. Viens ici, mon petit, viens, viens, viens, viens voir papa*".

Bati remained imperturbable.

"*Essayez en anglais*".

The Parisian, dropped his shoulders, glanced heavenward and sighed exaggeratedly at our woeful ignorance, but to humour us said, "Come!", and the dog went to him directly. Rarely is the comeuppance so immediate, but it is precisely this sort of know-better-than-you-you-dim-hick attitude that sets the Bretons against the Parisians. But there is more - and this is where it all gets rather delicate.

Parisien, tête de chien! Parigot, tête de veau! They are not pretty sentiments, I grant you, but neither is the contumely to which Bretons have been subjected by the big bit stuck onto the hind end. First of all, there was the immediate and inevitable riposte of the calf heads: *tête de Breton, tête de cochon*! But that's just name calling. Before the name calling began there was outright calumny.

When we were bumping about Erquy looking for Asterix, there was something about the Breton image that I omitted to mention. I ducked out of it because it's not the sort of thing you like to discuss in polite company and I'm still none too sure how to say this without shocking the children. Let's put it this way. Suppose you were frustrated to find yourself enamoured of an attractive young woman (and this is only supposition, so don't take it personally), an attractive young woman who tells you with the utmost sympathy and kindness, that she thinks you're really very nice and she really really likes being with you and she's really very fond of you and she thinks you're a really nice man but she doesn't really feel about you 'like that' and really she loves you 'like a brother' - you could always suggest moving to Brittany. That's the other bit of the Breton image in France: flat head, jug ears, low brow, limited cranium, and inbred. Degenerate, in a word. It's not quite the Appalachian hillbillies in John Boorman's Deliverance, but it's a near thing.

Truth be told, I did actually once meet a Breton who appeared to satisfy all these criteria, but he was attached (surgically insofar as I could work out) to the end of a bottle of Ricard and propped (with, to all appearances, equal permanence) on a stool in a fly-blown bar in West Africa behind an old slaving station, so he doesn't really count. Spend too long in a place with such unhappy memories and you too would end up with a flat head etc.

You may suppose this prejudice about inbred degeneracy utterly passé, a ridiculous attitude from a less enlightened epoch than our own, in which case you would suppose wrong. Not long ago, we were in a campsite near St. Brieuc and standing in the middle of the campsite was a Parigot who had clearly had a bad experience with a Breton. He'd cornered a local woman and was telling her at great length, great length, that he didn't care what you said, but the Bretons were all degenerate, all degenerate, that he had a chum who was a psychologist, a psychologist mind, a man who knew about these things, and he'd confirmed it, it was a well known fact, proven statistically, that is with numbers, that they were all, all of them, all degenerate, there was no denying it, he didn't mind saying so, either, he was from Paris, him, yes, and he knew, it was a truth, indisputable, beyond doubt and irrefutable, degenerate, every one of them, degenerate, I tell you, degenerate. He went on and on and on. It was none too clear what had been done to him that was so outrageously degenerate, but he clearly liked the sound of the word and seemed to have a few genetic deficiencies himself, or at least had failed to cultivate those bits of the brain that dish out discretion, respect and courtesy. Eventually, after about fifteen minutes of this echoing round the campsite, Jeannette, a former maths teacher, fluent in four languages, and my partner since 1989 (so clearly an all round clever bod), could take no more. She strolled up to the man, wished him good-day on the part of a degenerate, and mildly wondered what he was doing so far from home amid so many degenerates when he might easily get himself packed up and go elsewhere. Parigots - *nul points*; Dégénéres - *dix points*! The man took one look at her, clearly astonished that anyone so manifestly degenerate was capable of coherent speech let alone irony, and fled.

Parisien, tête de chien! Parigot, tête de veau!

Practice that phrase, walk the Tro Breizh, mimic the local rivalries, and you'll be well on your way to becoming deg . . . Breton yourself.

5. Bedding In:
Of Castles, Flowers and Four-Posters

ACCESS - The **Chateau de Kerjean** is in northern Finistère just west of **Plouzevéde** between Landivisiau, Plouescat and Lesneven. Access via the D30 (south and north) and D788 (west and east).

Rampart chapel at Kerjean

Though less famous than the Châteaux de la Loire or the Cathar strongholds of the south, the castles of Brittany feature some of the finest military architecture in France. Long fought over by the French and English and resisting each with equal vigour, the Bretons were bound to feel the need to hide behind a bit of stone, and there are some 4000 fortified châteaux and manor houses scattered about the peninsula. Constructed in the course of the Middle Ages and during the early Renaissance, they constitute a heritage so rich it attracted T.E. Lawrence, who came to Brittany in search of medieval buildings and ruins, though whether his studies stood him in good stead when he was giving stick to the Ottomans is a moot point. In honour of this tradition (the building of forts, that is, not giving stick to Ottomans), we're bumping about the Château de Kerjean today.

There are four categories of castle in Brittany. Best known are the coastal defences like Fort de la Latte at Cap Fréhel, the Château du Taureau in the bay of Morlaix, and the citadels of Port Louis and Belle-Île in the south. Then there are the castles with grand literary associations, like the Château de Comburg, the childhood home of Chateaubriand and dubbed *le berceau de romantisme* or 'the cradle of romanticism'. Perhaps the least celebrated but in some ways most coherent category encompasses the castles of the Breton marches, built to keep the big-bit-stuck-on-the-hind-end unstuck and forming a defensive line between Fougères, Vitré, Châteaubriant, Ancennis, Nantes and Clisson. By far the most widespread though are the homes of what local historians like to call *'les grandes familles'* - a label that begs the question, just what was so *grande* about these *grandes familles*?

Doubtless, like all families in the middle ages, they were as extensive as possible, breeding as a hedge against high child mortality rates, but I suspect the *grande* here is intended more in a forelock tugging way than as a merely numerical description. For the most part, the names of these *grandes familles* are not the sort you'll find in history books, but as with their saints, the Bretons are great ones for inventing aristocrats no one else has heard of, and often as not the seat of a *grande famille* in Brittany is clearly just a big farmhouse belonging to people with a bit more land than everyone else.

The manor, fortified or otherwise, may be very fine, but the scions probably wouldn't have got very far clumping about Versailles in their clogs. In the case of Kerjean though, the *grande famille* was a cut above your local rich bloke, and the Barbier were determined to prove it by building a château that would function as the template for renaissance architecture in Brittany. That's why we're here, that and because we've got to get some flowers.

Brittany's castles come in all shapes and sizes and many degrees of degradation, ranging from ruins like the Château de Guildo at St. Jacut, a place in a state of such perfect decline it makes you want to sit down, whip out your quill and pen a few romantic verses, through to immaculately restored and readily habitable residential châteaux like Roche Jagu near Treguier; and there is a corresponding range of financing and management. Some, like the Château de la Hunaudaye near Lamballe, are left to nature and a little light tourism (sometimes not so light depending on how heavy-handed the animators are), while other better preserved stately homes pull out all the stops to make themselves as vital to the modern tourist economy as they once were to the local agricultural economy. Kerjean tends toward the pull-out-all-the-stops school. I'm not saying you can expect to see merry minstrels gamboling about the lawns amid giggling wenches wearing pointy hats with a bit of chiffon floating about the crown, not all the time, at least. But the place does endeavour to pay its way, staging a variety of events such as treasure hunts for kids, workshops, exhibitions and concerts. Some of these are regular fixtures recurring throughout the year, others one-off happenings, while others are annual events. In the last category are the *Journées des Plantes de Collection*, held every Autumn in the enceinte and courtyard of the castle. Hence the flowers. We're going to the château to buy a plant. I guess it's a step up from the Garden Centre.

Château de Kerjean is significant not only because it's an attractive building in its own right, but because it had such a strong influence on the civil and religious architecture of the region, especially on the *enclos paroissiaux,* or churchyards, the tour of which has become one of Brittany's best known cultural attractions. To be honest, once you've craned your neck to admire one grinning gargoyle, photographed a couple of calvaries, and played spot-the-saint in the panelling, you'll probably have had your fill of *enclos*, and even your most refined culture vulture will get a slightly glazed look about the eye if they tackle the whole tour, but they are undoubtedly a marvel of vernacular architecture and no trip to Brittany would be complete without visiting at least one.

The attractions of Kerjean itself are manifest as soon as we turn into the car-park, which is located in an alley alongside the main drive. It's a very impressive pile of stones, large enough to be imposing, small enough to be habitable, and possessed of an alluring symmetry. Even the dovecot is well proportioned and looks like it could comfortably house a small family. That said, I'm not wholly persuaded an admission fee is justified in the present circumstances. This is, after all, a shop. It's not a flower show in the sense of this-is-my-garden-pretty-good-huh? It's a flower show in the sense that a lot of professional nurseries have paid their whack to have a stall within the walls in the hope that Joe Public are going to buy a plant or two. Can you imagine paying to go into Tesco or IKEA? I might pay to get out of one, I'd probably pay quite a lot if I'd been in there for more than about three minutes, but paying to get *into* a shop? This does however help explain a puzzling sign one can see on the doors of some French shops: *'Entrée Libre'*. I've always been peculiarly outraged by this. Of course it's bloody 'free entry', you're a shop, aren't you? I'm not very keen on coming in there and giving you my money in the first place. If I've got to give you my money in order to come in there and give you my money, you can forget about it, chum! There's probably something vital I've missed here. I never did understand the finer points of shopping. So I hand over the admittedly modest entrance charge for our party, and carry on as if I do this sort of thing everyday and it's all perfectly normal.

The enceinte is certainly a very eye-catching shop, each nursery decorating its pitch below the walls with considerable grace and artistry. The Autumn show at the Château de Kerjean is famous among plant lovers. They tell me the plants are highly unusual, very healthy, and most reasonably

"*Give us yer money!*"

priced. They tell me. Plant lovers do. Personally, all I know about horticulture is that it sounds like a euphemism for pornocracy. I have no memory for plant names and can never recall which wildflower is which from one walk to the next. I do like a bit of green stuff, not just on my dinner plate, but out in the woods and up in the mountains. And I'm full of admiration for the colours flowers make. But ask me what they're called and I'm flummoxed.

Even when the plants are helpfully labeled, I'm a bit taxonomically challenged. I see one display of Asters, the given names of which suggest nothing so much as an upper crust family tree, featuring as they do the *Hon Vicary Gibbs*, *Edwin Beckett*, and their incontinent tea lady *Rosie Weie*. Below them is the rather more literary Achilleas family, the louche *Carla Hussey*, her respectively romantic and revolutionary sisters *Heidi* and *Rosa Luxembourg*, and their fading dowager aunt *Old Brocade*. Elsewhere, we have the faintly painful sounding *Cornus Norman's Hadden*, kin to the more acute *Cornus Weise Foutain*, while the stall of Anne Plouhinec really pushes the boat out, promoting things called *Mystery*, *Freak of Nature*, *Bolero*, and *Gay Baby*. Really, I'm not cut out for this sort of stuff. The pictures conjured are not pictures of flowers.

We shuffle along, me doing my damnedest not to look too dazed by so many evocative names attached to a bit of green stuff, until we come to the pitch belonging to Cathy Bernabe's *Pepiniere Fleur et Senteurs*, and I'm really brought up short. There's this little shrubby thing and it's got a big sign on it saying *Mulberry Jam*. Sorry, Cathy, old girl, you're not getting that one past me. I've picked mulberries in Spain. They come off trees then spread up your fingers and along your arms until your T-shirt looks like a spectacularly unsuccessful tie-and-dye experiment. And -here's the clincher- jam doesn't grow on trees! Or, if it does, I want to know why I've spent the last few months boiling pans full of summer fruits and painstakingly sealing the product with paraffin wax. But a closer look suggests I'm out of my depth again. Another sign says *Hot Lips*, another *Sierra San Antonio*. And it dawns on me that they are more in the nature of descriptions than proper names. The plants are all *salvia* something or others, Hot Jam and Mulberry Lips simply attempts to sex things up. It's time for me to turn aside from flowers before I get myself in a real jam.

If Kerjean was the template for renaissance architecture in the region, it's also a perfect exemplar of how all this fine art was paid for. Remember, this was a poor country, yet kilometre for kilometre Brittany boasts an extraordinary number of manorial buildings and delicately wrought churches. Check their history and you'll find most were built on the proceeds of linen and hemp, which were so vital to the Breton economy between 1650 and 1830 that there now exists a tourist *Route du Lin*, following the flax growing, processing and trading routes, above all in Côtes d'Armor near Saint-Thélo and Quintin, where there are museums and an annual festival celebrating the weaving tradition. The precision of those dates may seem surprising, but they can be justified. While fighting the English in Brittany in the mid-seventeenth century, the Spanish realized Breton linen was the perfect material for clothing their colonists in South America, so giving birth to a trade that grew and grew for the next hundred years. The first blow came in 1779, when a change in Spanish fiscal policy made imported linen more expensive. Then the turmoil of the French Revolution gave English industrialists a chance to flood the South American market with cheap cotton, after which the newly independent South American republics gradually cut their trading links with the enfeebled and non-industrialized Breton linen manufactories. Widespread misery ensued and the 1830s saw the first mass migrations from Brittany.

Nowadays, linen production is largely an *artisanal* sideline sustained by the heritage industry. However, flax is used in baking, particularly in the loaf known as a *bannette coeur du lin*, since it's rich in Omega 3 acids, which are good for the cardiovascular system. Nonetheless, there are still some septuagenarian farmers who remember the tail end of the Breton linen trade and can tell you what a very earthy business it was. Ordinarily, flax was sown on the 1st of April and harvested 100 days later, but there was also a more precise method for timing planting than the inflexible dictates of the calendar. To judge whether the soil was ripe for sowing, you had to drop your cacks and place your bare buttocks on the field. If the soil was warm, the seed could be sown. If not, not. I'm not sure how this sort of thing would go down on an episode of Groundworks nowadays, but I expect there's people would pay good money to see some of the celebrity gardeners give it a go.

Defeated by the flowers, I slope off to inspect the rest of the castle, crossing the central courtyard where a hopscotch grid rather hopefully suggests a passage from earth to heaven, *TERRE* and *CIEL* being written at either end of the grid. The mottos of the various families that owned the castle are displayed in a cloister on the far side of the courtyard. Taken at face value, they suggest an aristocracy rapidly resigning itself to extinction, or at least giving up any great hope of hopping to heaven. The mottos begin with a complacent 'It would be meet', then decline through diminishing hauteur from 'If God pleases', to 'Have good heart', to 'It is time, it will be time', before ending with a slightly ambiguous *'Je me contente'*, which according to my book can indicate resignation, complacence or self-indulgence. Whichever way you look at it, they're all dead now and several of them are lined up amid the mortuary statuary below the chapel. The chapel itself is rather lovely, with a superb wooden frieze and a vaulted wooden ceiling. Slightly disconcertingly, there's an ashtray on the altar, suggesting a Dave Allen sketch in which the officiating priest likes to have a fag with his communion wine.

Thinking outside the box

Of the permanent fixtures inside the château, the most striking are the *lits clos*, the Breton take on a four poster bed except that in the Breton climate nobody was going to trust to a bit of flimsy curtain to keep the elements out, preferring instead to immure themselves in a wooden box with a secure sliding door. Nowadays, you're most likely to see a *lit clos* (*gwele kloz* in Breton) converted into a bookshelf or sideboard, but time was when these box-beds were the principal piece of furniture in a farmhouse, often including several levels and serving as bed, wardrobe, linen closet, and trunk all at the same time.

Look at the examples on display at Kerjean and you maybe forgiven for thinking Brittany was once populated by a bunch of Hobbits. Of course, people were shorter in the past, but not quite that short. In fact, the traditional Breton diet was such a punishing affair it would make your stereotypical deep-frying Scot look like a model of fastidious Californian, calorie-counting, cranberry-quaffing, Omega-3 food faddism. Prior to the invention of Rennies, most Bretons slept propped upright on a heap of pillows in a vain attempt to keep the digestive juices in their place. Moreover, they slept not on a mattress but between feather quilts, so the *lit clos* was more like a nest than a bed.

Some people have fond memories of these nests, recalling a cozy and intimate retreat. Others talk of a stifling claustrophobia. Either way, intimacy was one of the key functions of the *lit clos*. Legend claims such beds were necessary to protect adults against prowling wolves and guard infants against greedy, indiscriminate pigs and, wait for it, *poules rapaces* (yup, that's it, 'rapacious hens') that would as soon peck at a baby's ear as a husk of corn. Doubtless fraught parents did occasionally shut toddlers in the *lit clos* while they were out in the fields, and I know for a fact that babies slept strung from a hammock above their parents' heads, but the chief purpose of a *lit clos,* apart from keeping out the cold, was privacy. In a culture where entire families slept in a single room and in which *kof-a-kof* was frowned upon, a *lit clos* was an essential piece of equipment.

The box-bed was such a potent emblem of Brittany, it was taken for the title of a collection of verse legends about the region, *Contes du Lit-Clos* (Tales from the Box Bed), by Theodore Botrel. Now vilified as a poetaster romanticizing a Brittany he never knew and that never really existed, Botrel was hugely popular in the Francophone world at the end of the nineteenth century, strutting his stuff decked out in the *bargou-braz* or traditional Breton costume with which he's identified to this day. He was in large measure responsible for promulgating the Miserabilix image of Brittany, which is perhaps why he's despised by many contemporary commentators otherwise inclined to acclaim anything remotely Breton. He has even been dismissed as a 'Breton de Montmartre': in a nation of *Parigots* and 'another country', the insults don't get much worse than that.

Check out the man's lyrics on the internet and you may begin to sympathize. Try to imagine if you can a cross between "Two Little Boys Had Two Little Toys" and Max Bygraves' "I'm a Pink Toothbrush, You're a Blue Toothbrush" rewritten by Leonard Cohen and being sung by Morrissey the day after his granny died, and you'll be halfway there. Add the sort of sentiment aimed at by one of those posters picturing a winsome street urchin with a tear in the corner of his eye and you'll almost have it.

'La Mouchoir Rouge de Cholet', for instance, is narrated by a soldier dreaming of giving three red hankies to his distant love. But war intervenes and he ends up with only the one red hanky, and that one's red because it's soaked with the blood he cheerfully sheds so he can die for his king. In 'L'Horloge de Grand-Mère', a long case clock is compared to a coffin and, by a curious process of metempsychosis, gets granny's heart ding-donging away inside it. "*Dong! Dong! elle sonnait ainsi*" / 'Dong! Dong! it rang like that.' Well, yes. "*Et Grand Maman, dans son lit-clos, agonisa . . .*" / 'And grandma gasped her last in her box bed.' Spend too much time reading Botrel and you get quite gaspy yourself. 'Marie ta Fille' is happier, but includes the baffling and vaguely asinine refrain "*Youp, youp, youp*". As for 'Le Petit Gregoire', well! Petit Gregoire is a peasant boy so small he's deemed unfit for joining the hunt or serving the King he worships. Come the revolution, he joins the royalist *chouans*, but for awhile he's even beneath the bullets. Eventually, he gets it between the eyes and heads heavenward, only to be told by St. Peter that he's too small for heaven! He finally gets into paradise through the intervention of Jesus. And Botrel turned these things out by the hundred!

I don't want to sound too cynical here. I'm a sucker for sentimentality. Charles Trenet singing *Quand notre coeur fait boum* made me feel nostalgic the very first time I heard it. And the moment Edith Piaf begins warbling away on the radio, I have to reach for my hankie. I'm sure Botrel's songs were all very moving at the time. But, frankly, nowadays this sort of stuff moves me to tears of an entirely different stripe.

By the time I've finished peering into the dark heart of the Botrelian *lit clos*, those of our party who came in search of flowers have found the plants they want and are ready to buy. At which point, we get another of those wonderful moments that exemplify the cut and thrust of French commercial instincts. Grandma can agonize all she likes, Marie can *youp-youp-youp* till the cows come home, you can wave your *mouchoir rouge de Cholet* till you're blue in the face, get as plaintive as you wish about the fate of Petit Gregoire, go *Dong! Dong! Dong!* for all eternity, but it's one o'clock and all the stall holders have buggered off to lunch. Perhaps that's why we had to pay to get in. Nobody actually expected to sell anything. *Vive les commercants Gaulois*! Give 'em a choice between a good lunch and selling a couple of potted plants and they'll go for the lunch everytime.

Even once the *pépiniéristes* have been tracked down to the dining hall, persuading someone to sully their hands with money mid-meal proves quite a challenge. When the would-be purchaser pokes her head round the refectory door and suggests it might be nice if someone in the vending line left the table and came outside to supervise this uncommon commercial transaction, there is a sharp intake of breath on all sides followed by some strong comments about the sanctity of lunch. One man wordlessly gestures at his plate, as if to indicate he is involved in a delicate manoeuvre, like defusing a mine, and a distraction at this critical moment could well prove fatal. Another is so shocked, he is momentarily paralyzed, fork frozen midair, and only recovers the power of animation when a lump of lamb slips off his fork and disappears under the table. Finally, a rather shame-faced, shifty looking figure, possibly a Leonard, condescends to sacrifice himself on the altar of Mammon, though whether he has anything to do with the owners of the plants is anybody's guess. The handing over of moneys is sufficiently noteworthy for a slightly deranged looking individual to ask if he can take our picture for the local paper. We make our excuses and leave. As we drive past the entrance, several people scurry out of the flower show pushing barrow-loads of plants. Whether they paid anyone for them, I wouldn't know. But I'm fairly sure the stallholders haven't finished their couscous yet.

6. Perfidious Albion

ACCESS - Boats to the Château du Taureau depart from the western and eastern sides of the Baie de Morlaix from **Carantec** (D58) and **Le Diben** (D76/D46a). For timetables and bookings, see www.chateaudutaureau.com or call 02-98-62-29-73.

One might be forgiven for supposing the tradition of sending coach parties of kids back and forth across the Channel to promote the *entente cordiale* with a little light shop-lifting, the purchase and ignition of an unfeasibly large quantity of *petards*, and spewing copious quantities of green chartreuse onto the feet of unsuspecting passers-by, a relatively recent phenomenon. Doubtless this is one of those worthy projects encouraged by the Erasmus foundation with a view to advancing intra-communal relations and fostering an understanding that well-heeled adolescents are capable of

The fountains ran red.

abominable behaviour, wherever they may have been sired, and no matter how expensively educated.

As it happens, this exchange should be viewed rather more in the light of an historical enthusiasm, for the Napoleonic and Hundred Years Wars are only the highpoints of a long and happy Anglo-French tradition of gleefully abusing one another, and the Bretons, who are in many things barely French at all, have not been behindhand in participating. Indeed, their participation goes way back to the thirteenth century, for it was to Breton mercenaries that the Plantagenets turned when the barons were kicking up strong back home and laying the foundations of parliamentary government.

In fact, if there's one thing that unites the Bretons more than their loathing for the Parigots, one thing that might even make them grudgingly admit a distant affinity with the Big Bit Stuck On The Hind End, it's their dislike of the English . . . the English, mind. If you do happen to be channel hopping and carrying a British passport, never call yourself English. British is better, but ideally you should dig back in the family tree and identify some Scottish, Welsh, Irish or Cornish roots. There's no better shoe-in for a Brittany holiday. The English are just too tricky to be trusted.

It is a well known fact in France that the English can be relied on for one thing and one thing alone, to wit to do the dirty on the French. Why else did we arbitrarily and without warning sink the French fleet at Mers-el-Kebir in 1940, including 1300 sailors, most of them Breton? Why else was Perfidious Albion busily exporting all those mad cows if not to undermine the hard work of the French education system by rendering Gallic youth gaga? Why are we 'in' Europe at all if not to wreck their welfare system with our vicious Anglo-Saxon mercantilism? And when the MSC Napoli ran aground in Lyme Bay in January 2007, the French were quick to point out that, while the English were busy salvaging BMW motorbikes off Branscombe Beach, and dishing out consolation prizes of exhaust pipes, beauty cream, and steering wheels, the Bretons got a lot of mini-packs of Turkish biscuits full of tar washed up on their shore. It was a typically devious contrivance on the part of a people who willfully refuse to eat Breton artichokes, not because they don't like artichokes (*everyone* likes artichokes), but because they know exporting artichokes would nicely complement the winter trade in cauliflowers and cabbages. Can't be having that. That would be tantamount to fraternizing with the enemy.

These prejudices go far, very far, so very far in fact that people are perfectly capable of revising history to fit with the well know 'facts' about English perfidy. There was, for instance, the glorious story touted a few years back about a French minister visiting a holocaust memorial where there was a map of Europe indicating the number of Jews deported to concentration camps during the war. There was, however, one puzzling anomaly. Why, he asked, was Britain not featured on the map? It was pointed out to him that Britain had not actually been overrun by the Nazis and hadn't actually arranged to have its own indigenous fascist regime. Well, yes, yes, there was that, he admitted. But what did they do with their Jews? They *must* have sent them somewhere!

As for the former French prime-minister, Edith Cresson, and her notorious assertion that all Englishmen were homosexuals, well, my dear . .

Perhaps most entertaining, though, is the commemoration of ancient animosities in commonplace idioms. *Filer à l'anglaise* means to do a runner; when a woman has her period, she is said to *avoir les anglais* - which must cause no end of complications during Rotary Club exchange visits; and most famously, a French letter is *une capote anglaise*. There is, by the by, some sense of fair play here though, for whilst the French may 'spin an English' when they're short of money, 'have the English' when they're menstruating, and wear 'an English overcoat' for reasons not strictly related to keeping warm, they do have the good grace to *faire une carte de France* when they have a wet dream.

You maybe beginning to get a little worried here. You maybe thinking, I don't want to go there, not with all them Anglophobic French people littering up the place. But it should be stressed, it is highly unlikely that you'll actually encounter any in-yer-face Anglophobic sentiment in Brittany. This is more in the nature of inverted Anglophilia, a little like the jubilant and fundamentally affectionate Francophobia of the redtops in Britain. It's a question of these being the people we love to hate . . . or, perhaps: these are the people we love, to hate.

In Brittany, the idiomatic tradition of linking the English linguistically with discharge and flight has been complemented by another charming turn of phrase. Whenever the Bretons finish a bottle of wine, they say, "That's another one the English won't have". Leastways, I presume it's a tradition. Perhaps it's just something they say when I'm around. Maybe they're not saying, *Ça c'est une autre que les Anglais n'auront pas* at all. Maybe they're saying, *Ça c'est une autre que l'Anglais n'aura pas.* Generally too late, though.

And wherefore this uncharitable sentiment? Well, it's fairly obvious, isn't it? The English are a very thirsty people. And if there's one thing we've always admired about the French, it's their wine. True, there's little viniculture in Brittany. But they've got cellars, haven't they? And we've got boats!

Bump about pretty much anywhere in Brittany and, sooner or later, you'll come across some evidence of English perfidy. There's the story of the duel on the Place du Marché at Dinan in 1359 between Bertrand du Guesclin and Thomas of Canterbury, after the latter had kidnapped his opponent's younger brother despite having signed a truce. This was a typically

Eiffel viaduct in Morlaix

underhanded English thing to do, though it's worth noting that Bretons don't always let partiality cloud their judgment. One nationalist historian describes Bertrand as being short, dark and hairy, with disproportionately long arms, big fists, a flat nose, and greenish, globulous eyes; and as if that wasn't enough, he says Bertrand was a cantankerous, vicious illiterate who liked nothing so much as a good scrap. It makes you wonder. With heroes like that, who needs the English?

Well, the Bretons apparently because elsewhere they still talk about the sack of Roscoff in 1375, the massed duel of the Combate des Trente at Ploërmel in the same century, the Bataille des Cardinaux in 1759, in which the French flagship was scuttled and the fleet was blockaded in Port de la Roche Bernard for two years . . . the list goes on, but rather than merely cataloguing all the dastardly things we've done to the Bretons, I propose bumping about the scene of one particular piece of treachery, the raid on Morlaix in Finistére in 1522. I choose this instance not because we English were unusually perfidious, but because the event is commemorated in both stone and song, and because following its traces makes for a particularly pleasing day out.

Tucked into a narrow valley formed by the confluence of two rivers and straddled by a couple of spectacular viaducts, Morlaix is an attractive market town, the appeal of which is only marginally marred by the fact that it's entirely unsuited to modern living, and has been badly scarred by the *mairie*'s decision to concrete over a stretch of the river and turn it into a car-park. Nowadays, it has a faintly decayed air, for it hasn't the space to burgeon into a modern metropolis, is not sufficiently well preserved to draw in huge numbers of tourists, nor accessible enough to make its port a viable marina for yachtsmen; but in its day, Morlaix was the hub of regional commerce, a centre for trading paper, leather, skins, livestock, honey, bacon, wheat, wine and above all linen, and the birthplace of several celebrated corsairs. You can guess what the English liked about that list . . . and what we didn't like. We were all for the wine, probably not averse to a bit of bacon, either, but we didn't like those corsairs one little bit.

In 1522, learning that most of the townspeople and their defensive garrison had decamped to Guingamp for the annual fair, Admiral Howard, in his devious English way (or maybe a devious Welsh way given that he was Henry VIII's admiral), landed a thousand devious Englishmen, who set about doing what the devious English always do when we go to the continent: drinking all the drink, womanizing all the women we can get our hands on (few enough in view of the drink, but there you go), and smashing up everything else. Though just how devious we were about all this depends on which account you read.

Some sources say we did a bit of burning and looting en route before investing the town itself, which probably wouldn't have done a lot for the surprise element of the surprise attack; others say we snuck up through the woods (pretty devious, I grant you) then bundled in at night to do our dastardly deeds; others that we disguised ourselves as merchants (plausible enough being English), slipped in unnoticed, then did a Trojan Horse job, popping out at night and getting down to the dastardlies; a fourth source claims there was a fifth columnist within the city walls who treacherously opened the gates to us.

Anyway, no matter how we got in there, get in there we did, and once in, did the dastardlies with right good gusto, burning the eminently burnable half-timbered buildings in the narrow streets, pillaging the churches, robbing the rich merchants' houses, drinking the wine, and having our way with the women, some of them at least. I say some of them because the story is told of one resourceful but anonymous chambermaid who hid herself in the cellar and opened a trap door at the bottom of the steps which gave directly onto the subterranean waters of the Jarlot. Inflamed with liquor and lechery, the raiders tumbled down the stairs and, one by one, dropped through the trap-door like a trail of Keystone Cops. So much for being devious.

As it happened, the men that raided Morlaix in 1522 were rather more hapless than devious. I'm not saying they were very nice people or anything. But you'd have thought any self-respecting pirate would know that, once you've done your dastardlies, you high-tail it out of there. Not this bunch of stumblebums. They waddled out of Morlaix, bloated with booze and burdened with booty, only to find the ships that were meant to meet them hadn't been able to sail upriver because a bunch of Breton peasants had felled a load of tall trees and blocked the river's course - now *that's* what I call devious. And rather than cottoning onto the fact that something was going badly wrong, this band of topers thought it would be a really cunning plan if they had a bit of a sleep in the Bois de Styvel. Alerted to the disaster that had befallen their city, the local militia hastened back from Guingamp and surprised the comatose tourists. In fact, they must have downright astonished them, because the English were slaughtered in such numbers that the waters of a nearby spring ran red, and ever since the spring has been known as the Fontaine des Anglais. Ooh, that's mean!

What most of the French accounts don't tell you is that the English raiders were from Bristol, and the reason they were so bloody irate and unwilling to do the gentlemanly thing by the local girls was that the local corsair, Jean de Coatanlem, had being doing exactly the same sort of things along the English coast, in particular in Bristol, for the preceding few months. It's worth noting here that Morlaix's city motto is "S'ils te mordent, Mords-les!" - *If they bite you, bite them back*. You see what I mean about unruly school trips to Dieppe and Brighton being nothing new? The English and French have always gone round to each other's place in order to behave badly and probably always will. If they'd just get on with it and stick that in the European Constitution, everyone would vote for it straight away and everything would be hunky-dory. Business as usual.

Article One: thou shalt cross the Channel and thou shalt set about thy neighbours and their persons with right good will, and thou shalt steal their goods and do unto them as they would do unto you and will doubtless do in short measure. Tick this box now.

If you care to see the site of this dreadful event (I'm talking about the massacre of the English here, not the European Constitution), set off from the Quai de Treguier between Morlaix town hall and the railway viaduct, and follow the right bank of the river along the Plougasnou road. The Fontaine des Anglais lies on the right of the road, below the residential neighbourhood of Coat Serhô, and between the GAN insurance office and Le Tempo bar. To see a more substantial monument, we then fork left on the Plouezoc'h road (either by car or the Plougasnou-Morlaix bus which leaves from just after the railway viaduct). Our next destination is the Château du Taureau.

Understandable, really. The Morlaisiens didn't have so many fountains they could afford to be tainting them with English blood every few months, and it was said that it took the town ten years to recover from the 1522 raid, so something had to be done to stop Perfidious Albion sailing upriver whenever we took a fancy to do so, and the best way to do this was to make sure we never got past the mouth of the bay in the first place. The Château du Taureau is a sea fort that can be reached from Carantec on the western shore of the bay and Le Diben in Plougasnou. Either will do (see www.chateaudutaureau.com for seasonal variations in timetables), but the latter offers more water for your money, and the approach road takes us past the pretty little fishing port of Dourduff-en-Mer, wherein lies yet more testimony to our indefatigable perfidy.

One of the few people who makes a point of the fact that the 1522 raid was actually a sort of prototype exchange scheme, is Fanch Le Marrec. Fanch, one of Brittany's foremost shanty singers, only has to sniff an Englishman in the house and he'll launch into a heartfelt and wholly well-meaning version of the ballad of *Marivonig an Dourduff,* generally dedicated to "nos bons voisins d'Outre-Manche" or some similar, not necessarily so polite circumlocution.

It is an affecting tale of a virtuous young maid from Dourduff who . . . well, you can probably guess what happens to her, can't you? Yup, the English. Up they sail and away they sail with Marivonig on board, blubbing her little heart out, for she knows that once the English get their hands on you, you're done for. "Aaar! Never fear, my pretty," says 'the Big Englishman', or words to that effect, "your life's in no danger. Aaar! You'll not lose your life, but as for your honour, well I can't answer for that. Aaar!" But Marivonig's having nothing English done to her; the priests have told her all about the English and their *kof-a-kof* ways, and she throws herself overboard, preferring to drown rather than have some grubby *outre-manche* matelote pawing at her privates. Whereupon, a great fish rises out of the waters and carries the unconscious Marivonig back home to Dourduff, rousing her father from his grief with a shout, demanding he open the door because his daughter has not lost her honour. Yeh. Well, this is Brittany. Anything can happen.

***

The day we embark for the Château du Taureau, the weather is foul with a lowering sky crowding the black waves and sheets of Breton *crachin* scudding across the bay. You'd better get used to the idea of *crachin* because it's Brittany weather par excellence. Literally 'spitting', you'd think it ought to be entirely familiar to someone from the British Isles. But our British spitting isn't at all like Breton spitting. Ours is a devious, untrustworthy sort of rain, spitting here and there, the odd drop, maybe large, maybe small, never quite declaring itself, not really rain, but tricky enough to have you rushing out to take the washing in to no purpose, and occasionally catching you a good gob in the eye to make you blink - in a word, English. Breton spit on the other hand is like another element altogether, not quite water, not quite air, but a fine vapor, as if there's some great god of the sea out in the Atlantic pressing his finger on the button of an enormous aerosol. It's actually quite pleasant to walk in, and is said to be very good for the skin, but it's not necessarily the sort of thing to encourage you out on the seas - not when you're a solitary Englishman among a boatload of Bretons visiting a fort their ancestors were obliged to build because your ancestors kept coming over and doing dastardly things to their ancestors' wives and daughters. Chin up, though.

On board, I take a good place at the front of the boat. The day maybe a study in gray, but I'm going to show these Frenchies what an Englishman is made of. Devious? Perfidious? Not a bit of it. We're foursquare, straightforward, open, honest, and not afraid to be exposed to the elements. Everyone else crowds into the perspex cabin of the boat.

Even if you don't take one of the boats, it's hard to miss the Château du Taureau when you take a turn round the Baie de Morlaix, as every picnic spot along the coast has been fixed up with sighting points indicating the thing and explaining, in helpful multilingual signs, the degree of grief it brought to English privateers.

Built in the 1540s by the burghers of Morlaix, the château takes its name from the island on which it was built, *toro*, so called because it was said to have the form of a bull, though later amateur etymologists claimed the name came from the wind tearing through the casements like the bellowing of a bull. It must have been a terrible disappointment to the English to see this strategic defense being raised, but had they only known, insult was being heaped on injury because the fort and its garrison were to be maintained on the proceeds of a tax on all the wine that passed through the port of Morlaix. The wine! Wine we might have been nicking and knocking back like there was no tomorrow - which there wouldn't have been if you had a kip in the Bois de Styvel. The very stuff of our debauchery was to be the means of us no longer getting our hands on it. The price of perfidy is steep, indeed.

As it happens, Morlaix wasn't entirely free from English goings-on, albeit by proxy. In 1611, the commander of the fort, Jacques Deleau, had a distinctly Marivonig moment during a visit to town with his daughter to hear a sermon from a famous Capuchin friar. They were leaving the church after dark when a gang of Irish sailors abducted his daughter and took off with her with a view to doing unto her some dastardly English things - our influence has always been extensive. They were, however, caught before anything English came to pass. The captain's throat was slit open, a personal attention on the part of Deleau, and the crew were bound hand and foot and tossed overboard. There is no report of the big fish being involved in this encounter.

Back in Le Diben, I'm having my own Marivonig moment, though it does not actually involve me diving overboard. More a case of the overboard diving onboard. I'm still sat in the prow of the boat, the good place, looking stoical and English and doubtless a little devious, too. The moment we leave the harbour, a bloody great wave breaks over the port bow and soaks my left hand side. This may explain why the Bretons all scurried off under the perspex. I detect a distant tittering behind me, but I don't react. Never mind. I can do this. Dignity's the thing. As I say, show these Frenchies what an Englishman's made of.

In the seventeenth century, mounting rivalry between England, Spain, Holland and France raised the strategic stakes along the Breton coast, and Louis XIV decided it would be really rather nice if the burghers of Morlaix gave him their castle. In 1689, the great military architect, Vauban, whom we've already encountered on the Pointe de Primel, set about rebuilding the municipal fort, though the work was not finished for another fifty odd years. Constrained by space and practicalities, Vauban stuck to the same basic design, maintaining the principal artillery tower, La Tour Française, and extending the fortifications across the remainder of the island. The main battery of cannon were arranged in a fan on La Tour Française so they could control the navigable western channel, while short range guns were placed lower down to hole ships at the waterline.

I do vaguely wonder about Vauban's military prowess here. The French are very fond of Vauban and there's a much quoted saying: *"Ville assiégée par Vauban, ville prise; ville défendu par Vauban, ville imprenable"*; but in 1793 the Château du Taureau was nearly taken by the English. You'd have thought he'd have remembered how devious we were. It was the 16th of March when a frigate and two vessels of the line engaged the fort from the main channel. And while they were busy blasting away, a launch carrying a platoon of marines made it's way round to the far side of the fort, where they didn't have any guns! They're behind you! As it happened, a French corsair intervened and the English were driven off, but for a man of alleged military genius it's a bit of major oversight.

Major oversights and exposed fronts are something of an issue back on the tourist launch, too. I'm still up-front, jaw set, braving the slings and arrows. But I reckon there's an agenda going on here, the revenge of Marivonig and all those dishonoured *Morlaisiennes*. We've cleared the harbour and the dangerous rocks flanking its entrance, and the pilot swings the boat round to the west, and another bloody great wave breaks, over the starboard bow this time, soaking my right hand side. There's a distinct giggling behind me. More water for your money, like I said. Perhaps dignity isn't all it's cracked up to be. All right, I admit it, I've had enough. I'm done with dignity. There's a narrow dry patch running down my middle and I don't want that soaked, too. I stagger back to the shelter of the perspex canopy. There are no seats left, so I sit on the fibreglass bin housing the life belts. My fellow passengers are smiling at me. I ignore them. I'm above this.

Apart from a few skirmishes, the Vauban fort was never actually engaged in any major military clashes, but its isolation meant it was an ideal prison, and, in 1745, it became a gaol for errant Breton nobles, who were locked up because they'd broken the law, displeased the king, or their families thought they were barmy. Best known among the last category was Quentin Tapin de Cuillé, dubbed *l'ecrivain fourbe et menteur* - the sly, lying writer. Whatever his literary merits, Quentin's dad reckoned his son was a profligate libertine and Tapin minor was duly shut up in 1757. When his father died, the family were in no hurry to have Quentin back doing sly and mendacious things with the family fortune (perhaps he had English blood in him?), and he stayed in the château for another twenty years, writing the endless defamatory letters that earned him his nickname, often as not in solitary confinement on bread and water, for the garrison considered him mad, bad and dangerous to know.

Doubtless they had their reasons, but look at a list of the charges on which people were locked up, and you might begin to wonder. Among the more common pretexts for imprisoning the scions of the Breton nobility were debauchery, fickleness, a desire to marry beneath one's station, licentiousness, drunkenness, imbecility, madness, prodigality, impertinence, disrespecting your parents, a fondness for peccadilloes, a penchant for knavish tricks, and diverging from the true path of religion. There were a few representative thieves, rapists and murderers bunged in there, too, but for the most part criminality appears to have come from progressing through the commonplace stages of youth.

The alleged madness of those interned on the island was not always of a frivolous nature, though. In 1764, the magnificently named Louis René Caradeuc de la Chalotais (I could have gone far with a name like that) was imprisoned for protesting against the unjust fiscal impositions of the French monarchy on Brittany. He only spent 35 days on the island, but they were 35 days that earned him a place in the pantheon of Breton heroes, that and a withering dismissal from the Duc d'Aiguillon, the governor of Brittany, who said La Chalotais was nothing more than "an overheated brain".

The Château du Taureau was used as a prison during the French Revolution, when it housed various nobles, priests, Girondins and Montagnards, but the most famous of its prisoners did not take up residence until 1871, when the communard agitator and tireless revolutionary, Louis Auguste Blanqui, did a six month spell guarded by 25 men and a warship. This was a man who was imprisoned more often than most people go to the dentist, spending some 37 years behind bars, but he seems to have found his time in the Château du Taureau particularly galling, complaining, with typically Parigot contrariness, that the roar of the waves kept him awake at night.

To while away the time, he wrote *L'Eternité par les Astres*, Eternity Through The Stars, a scientific and political study with a cosmological angle, which may sound a bit fanciful but isn't bad for a man who spent 90% of the day in a room called 'la salle de discipline', a damp windowless cell rimed with saltpetre. In the book, he writes: *"Ce que j'écris en ce moment dans un cachot du fort du Taureau, je l'ai écrit et je l'écrirai pour l'éternité."* That which I write at this moment in a cell of the Château du Taureau, I have written and I will write for eternity. I don't think he meant it was going to be a very long book, but one that would please posterity. Of course, if he'd been English his work would have taken a far more practical turn, something along the lines of *101 ways to sneak up on an unsuspecting Frenchman and give him a hell of a nasty surprise*.

Blanqui was the last prisoner at the château, which was decommissioned in 1881. The English proved somewhat less than perfidious in 1914, when we blockaded the Channel (the *English* Channel, not La Manche, hah!), spoiling German plans to land an army in the Baie de Morlaix and open a second front in Brittany, but we don't want to dwell on that, lest it undermine a much loved, time-honoured animosity. At the end of World War One, some aggrieved French nationalists reckoned it would be a nice idea to lock the Kaiser up in the Château and see how he liked the sound of the waves, but it never came to pass. The fort was briefly bought back into service by the Germans during the Second World War, but otherwise has enjoyed a generally peaceful decline into old age, being used as a holiday home cum literary salon during the 1930s, and as a sailing school in the 1960s, before being abandoned in 1980 for lack of funds to maintain the infrastructure. It was only restored in the new millennium and was opened to the general public in 2006.

This particular bit of the general public is sitting on the fibreglass bin housing the life belts. It's immediately in front of the door, the open door, the one through which the third wave sends a spattering of spray just dense enough to do for my dry patch. This occasions great, unfeigned and undissembled merriment among the Frenchies, and I begin to feel a sneaking regard for those lads from Bristol. They may not have been too hot on the post-pillage strategy, but they certainly had a way with them.

There's a grating sound. At first, I think we've run aground and a moment's wild delight fills my heart since I'm still sat on the lifebelts and anyone who wants one has to get past me first, but then I realize it's the voice of the girl who is our guide for the day, a rather raucous sounding girl whose delivery is in no way improved by the boat's sound system. She claims there's a Breton-speaking association on board, though I have my doubts because when she passes the microphone to the alleged president of this alleged Breton-speaking association and he addresses them in Breton, of the fifty odd other people on board there are only two who appear to understand what he's saying, and one of them promptly falls asleep. There is some hesitation as we approach the fort's jetty, which is understandable, since the waters are choppy and even the main channel in the Baie de Morlaix is notoriously difficult to negotiate. Dozens of ships have foundered here, scores of people lost their lives, and when the château was still a working fort and had no jetty, the supply boat seems to have been wrecked almost as often as it landed. Considering how treacherous these waters are, the 1522 raid was a remarkable feat of seamanship. The channel was not marked, nor mapped until the job was done in 1776 by local corsair, Charles Cornic. So for Howard to land a thousand strong force and sail to a point at which the river was narrow enough to be bridged by a tree trunk, then get away again without losing all his ships, suggests seamanship of the first order. There again, I guess the French would say only someone from perfidious Albion could be so devious as to negotiate these waters without local know-how to help them.

Eventually, the skipper decides which approach offers the safest landing and the boat is moored against the quay. It's still bouncing about a lot, though, and a couple of the crew are required to help everybody disembark, and even then one man slips and falls on the decking. I didn't push him. Honest.

Inside, we all huddle together, the guide waving people forward and, well, bellowing at them, really, like a bull, telling them to come close because she won't bite. I'm none too sure myself. She looks like she might very well bite. She's aggressively gregarious and I wouldn't fancy the chances of any unfortunate Bristolian privateer who made the mistake of dragging her off in his boat. She wouldn't be needing any big fish. In fact, she reminds me of a gag told by a friend from Quebec. The Quebecois have got a bit of a chip on their shoulder about the supercilious disdain the French display for their colonial cousins, and are not behindhand when it comes to a story disparaging the mother country.

There's these three animals -a polar bear, a monkey, and a crocodile- and they're discussing their holiday plans.

"Well," says the bear, "I've got long, thick fur, and my wife's got long, thick fur, and all my children have got long, thick fur, so we're going to the Arctic for our holidays."

Says the monkey: "I've got long arms and a prehensile tail, and my wife's got long arms and a prehensile tail, and all my children have got long arms and a prehensile tail, so we're going to the jungle".

"I've got a big gob (*grande gueule*)", beams the crocodile, "and my wife's got a big gob, and all our children have got big gobs . . . we're going to France."

This girl's got a *grande gueule* and I don't want to hear any more of it, so I slope off on my own as she launches into her spiel about the castle. It's my first wise move of the day and, if you detect anything in the nature of a *grande gueule* when you visit the Château du Taureau, I recommend you do likewise. Let the guide chunter on, she's not going to tell you anything that isn't detailed in the explanatory panels, and if you're quick about it, you can see the fort for yourself before the crowds start muddling the vista. It's an impressive place (not just because it was designed to keep people like you and me out) and is best seen when its lines are at their cleanest before other people start clicking their cameras and cluttering up the perspective.

What's most striking about the place is how prison like it is, even though it wasn't designed as such. The deep central well is lined with walkways giving onto cell-like rooms, and all you'd need would be a bit of key-clanking and door slamming and lock turning, and you'd reckon yourself in the opening sequence of an episode of Porridge.

As I stand there, imagining what it must have been like to be here as a prisoner rather than a tourist, I do indeed hear some strange, slightly sinister sounds. They're not really metallic, but there's a groaning and gurgling and growling going on, the sort of slurred burbling you might hear in a rough Breton bar at about two in the morning. I eventually track the noise down to a trunk in a corner of an otherwise bare room. Next door, someone else seems to be inside a barrel, drinking and belching and sighing. They are sound effects, designed to conjure the life of the fort in former times. Not hugely successful, either. The grim grey stone and the incessant susurrus of the waves are more than enough to make the imagination fly. But it's better than having a lot of shabby wax models draped about the place depicting Quentin Tapin de Cuillé being sly and mendacious, or Blanqui reaching for the stars and coming up with a bushel load of politics. The first room, the one that sounds like a rough Breton bar at about two in the morning, turns out to be the officers' mess.

Visiting the château when the weather is bad is actually quite a good idea, as it gives a real idea of what it must have been like for those stranded here. Seeing each empty room on your own, you can well imagine somebody going stir crazy here. The cells are a mere fourteen square metres and, though they'd go for a fortune nowadays if they were turned into holiday let studios, they must have been grim when all you had was a table, a chair, a bed, and a fitful little fire, and were banged up all day long watching the saltpetre form on the walls. The restoration, however, is immaculate and, according to the official pamphlets, has all been done using traditional techniques dating back to the eighteenth century: I presume that doesn't include the noises-off in the barrels and trunks; you wanted noises-off in a barrel back then, you stuck a bloke in there.

Perhaps the most spectacular part of the château and something you should definitely visit before everyone else, is the roof. The view is superb and, when you tire of the great expanse of sea and the ring of ragged rocks protruding from the waves, there's a series of information panels and a couple of entertaining signs. There is, for instance, engagingly for a former prison, a panel explaining the 'Plan de Evacuation'. Another indicates where the latrines used to be. Apparently, they were dismantled in the nineteenth century, though it doesn't explain where residents were meant to relieve themselves after that. What's nice, though, is that at first glance the sign looks like an invitation to piss against the wall.

The prison was garrisoned by Les Invalides, though judging by their depredations on the local population, these old soldiers were anything but invalid. In fact, many of them carried on as if they were English, mistreating the local peasants, stealing what they wanted, and, in one evocative but faintly obscure phrase, *"faisant l'amour les poings fermés"* - *making love with their fists balled*. One evening in 1800 a couple of inebriated soldiers rolled up at the house of a certain Bellec in the village of Plouezoc'h, where they were billeted for the night. Asked if they needed to eat before turning in, they wanted to know what was on offer. The same as me and my family eat, said Bellec, but the soldiers weren't having any of that. They said they'd eat what they wanted to eat, and it was his job to go out and get it if he didn't have it. Things got a bit rambunctious then. The Bellec family's stock of crêpes got scattered about the floor, the sideboard was smashed, Bellec *père* had his jacket torn apart, and Bellec *mère* and Bellec *fille* received some rather unappetizing proposals. Roused by the hubbub, the neighbours came to the family's aide and the soldiers were ejected, whereupon a great and violent banging on the door began. Fearing the door would break under such a pounding, Bellec opened it, revealing one soldier carrying a five pound rock, which rock was promptly dropped on the head of one Louis Guéguen ... well, you get the picture. We're not a million miles from a brawl in an Asterix book here. Makes you wonder why they got so vexed about the English.

As the stipulated time for visiting the château draws to a close, the *crachin* gives way to rain, real rain. The skies open up and it starts tipping down. The thing is, having sloped off early and visited the fort before everyone else, I've finished before them, too. And I'm in a position to get on the boat a bit quick, installing myself under the perspex, out of the rain, well away from any wave beckoning apertures.

I'm English, me. Devious.

Maybe they've got a point about Perfidious Albion.

Maybe they do need us, after all.

7. Huellogorrhoea: Forest of Stories

ACCESS - **Huelgoat** is in the centre of Finistère, northwest of Carhaix. Access via the D784 and D14. The walk starts from the municipal car-park behind the town hall (signposted 'Mairie' throughout the village) via a walled alley (signposted 'Ancien Mine') descending to the leat canal.

We're bumping about Huelgoat, the forest at the heart of Finistère that was discovered by sightseers and anglers in the nineteenth century, and which has remained popular ever since with ramblers, romantics, daytrippers and myth-makers. Myth-makers, above all. There's scarcely a stone, stream or tree that doesn't have some tale attached to its genesis. Stand still too long and one will probably spring up around you.

Push-me-Pull-you: the Roche Tremblante

Despite its popularity, the village remains a pretty place with a pleasant central square, and none of the trippery trimmings that can spoil celebrated beauty spots. We begin at the Armorique, a typical Breton country bar, with its token alcoholic propped in the corner, a pile of laundry and an ironing board beside the counter (booze is a very domestic business in Brittany), and an old boy who pops in with his poodle at 10.30 every morning for his *petit coup de rouge*. A couple of chimney sweeps turn up, too, but since the fireplace is in use, they have a coffee then disappear into the back garden and don't return, a vanishing act that seems slightly sinister in light of the stories we are about to encounter. Otherwise, the atmosphere is very amenable, everyone seems to know everyone else, and after an agreeable half hour cultivating a mutual admiration society with the old boy's poodle, we head for the woods.

There are dozens of waymarked walking itineraries around Huelgoat and we set off on the 'Circuit de Ancien Mine', following a broad leat canal from an eighteenth century reservoir created to feed the silver-lead mines to the southeast of the village. Once used to crush and wash the ore, the canal now serves a small hydro-electric plant and, rather more rewardingly, the bumping about of people like us. It's a lovely stroll, the clear rusty water dappled with light and mottled by the shifting shadows of shrubs and trees, the patterning of

which occasionally shades to black beneath a more densely woven awning of leaves. Dark baby trout, carp and perch dart about the bed of the canal, dragon flies flicker from bank to bank, while pondskaters and waterboatmen scamper and scull across the surface of the stream. The woods grow deeper and denser, so dark even the dragonflies seem to be black, and

The Leat Canal

we pass the first of the huge mossy boulders for which the forest is famed.

There's a thousand hectares of woodland round Huelgoat, the remnant of a forest that once covered the entire Breton hinterland from here to Paimpont, which came to be associated with the Broceliande of Arthurian romance. The name comes from the Breton for high (*huel*) wood (*goat*) and shares its etymology with the word for the interior, Argoat, or land beside the forest, as opposed to the land beside the sea of Armor. Aside from being exploited for forage and smelting, the most extensive wood based industry was clog making. The traditional Breton *sabot* took many forms, including a stilt variety for wading through farmyard mud, but has nowadays settled into a leather and wood affair resembling the clogs that were fashionable in the sixties, except with a closed heel. These are still widely worn and, if you happen to be shopping for a pair of slippers and are puzzled by a rather close-cut thin sole, you're probably looking at a slipper designed to be worn inside clogs, which are left at the door on entering a house. Clumpy but practical, the clog and slipper combination is not the most elegant concept in footwear, but it's ideal for visiting neighbours on a wet winter's evening.

Strolling alongside the leat, we pass increasingly massive boulders, scattered about the woods like the discarded building blocks of a disgruntled giant, which is what they are according to one legend. Geologists claim these stones are the detritus of a subterranean borborygmus, liquid rock bubbling out of the ground and solidifying, after which erosion abraded the more friable granite, leaving behind large boulders of the denser rock. Locals know better, though. Huelgoat is the Forest of Stories and nobody's going to let mere science get in the way of a good anecdote. Indigestion was involved, but it had little to do with the underworld, not at least until Christian theologians set about demonizing the pagan gods of the Celts. These stones were a gift from Gargantua.

One may be forgiven for wondering what the satirical writings of a sixteenth century friar from Touraine could possibly have to do with a Breton legend, but Rabelais' giant was inspired by Gargan, a manifestation of a long tradition of Celtic giants personifying fertility and primordial chaos. Subsequently 'tamed', insofar as such things can be tamed, Gargan became a symbol of resistance against foreign aggressors, notably the Romans and later on, of course, the English. Sound familiar? Big pagan bloke decked out in Celtic paraphernalia beating up invaders? Once again, there are echoes of the Asterix books here and Obelix tossing the legionnaires about.

Gargantua's mum and dad, Gargamelle and Grandgousier, were the sort of couple that give social services nightmares. Gluttons and drunks, they gorged themselves on tripe and red wine, then danced, sang and quarreled so frenetically that when Gargantua came to term, he popped out of his Mum's left ear mid-binge and promptly demanded his own barrel of booze. Left to his own devices, the infant Gargantua ate, drank and slept, and rolled in ordure as the whim took him, eventually branching out to travel the land, tossing rocks about, kicking up hills and cliffs, defecating mountains, pissing rivers (I'm not talking figuratively here, but generatively) and reforming the landscape as the whim took him, the scars of his travels round France bearing his name and/or a linked legend to this day. Mont St. Michel, for instance, was associated with the Gargan-Gargantua cult before the monks got their hands on it, the Rocher de Tombelaine is said to be the burial place of Gargantua's parents, and there are numerous Monts Gargans in the big-bit-stuck-on-the-hind-end, notably at Rouen and Limoges.

Come the day Gargantua (or, depending on who's telling the story,

A giant's tantrum?

either Hok Bras or Le Gaor, as in the Welsh Red Giant, Rhudda Gawr) fetched up in Huelgoat, the boy was feeling a bit peckish and wanted to know what the locals were going to feed him. Huelgoat was a poor place and all they could spare was porridge or *bouillie*. This was not smiley faced Quaker Oats porridge, but a solid slab of boiled buckwheat, which can still be bought in Breton supermarkets. It's not a particularly appetizing looking lump of fodder and, though considered a delicacy among many Bretons (scoop a hole in the middle and spoon a dob of butter in to establish your Breton credentials), it fair put the wind up Gargantua. Couple of days later, our flatulent friend got a better meal further down the road, decided he'd been insulted by the Huelgoatians, gathered a load of boulders and lobbed them back in the general direction of his parsimonious hosts, hence all these dirty great rocks littering up the forest.

There is, however, another story explaining the presence of these stones and, in view of the lamentable state of neighbourly relations within Brittany, the alternative does have an authentically Breton ring to it. The villages of Berrien and Plouyé lie six kilometres to the north and south of Huelgoat and loathe one another's guts, leastwise so the story goes and it's perfectly feasible because the communities are close enough to be in entirely different countries. Mists of time stuff this, but within the Christian era since the villages' respective clerics, who cared more for local pride than catholicity, encouraged their parishioners to line up and chuck rocks at one another with a view to crushing their rivals' homes. Only being mere mortals, or at least Bretons, rather than burly great giants, none of the villagers could throw their rocks far enough and all the stones landed midway, to wit around Huelgoat.

When the leat reaches a small generating plant, we leave the Circuit de Ancien Mine and cut down to the site of the mine itself to join the Circuit de Arquellen. The mine is nothing much to look at, just an open cast scar on the landscape, but it has also left its toponymical mark since the river *Fao* (Breton for beech) on which it was sited is now known as the Rivière d'Argent. Needless to say, several more stories are attached to this river, the first of which describes how the deposit was discovered.

Young man wandering along the riverbank at the dead of night . . . Yes, I know, daft, isn't it, what with witches and demons and fairies and so forth knocking about the night scene. But legends are a bit like Hollywood scenarios. If the bimbo with low morals has got to get in the shower with that knife slashing music building up in the background, she'll do it, no matter how many Norman Bates' are lurking in the corridor; and if a young man's got to be out on a riverbank at the dead of night, he'll do it, no matter how many banshees are banging about the treetops and swinging from the branches. When you live in a forest of stories, life has its own ineluctable illogic.

So, young man wandering along the riverbank at the dead of night when he chances upon a weird and creepy al fresco washhouse where weird and creepy al fresco washerwomen are beating their linen against the boulders. Now he's a fly one this lad, he knows these are the Washerwomen of the Night, seeing as how it's night and they're out washing (what *was* the boy doing there?), condemned to launder their winding sheets at the mercy of the elements until relieved by a Christian saviour. Evidently, our hero wasn't it, because he fears his time has come when one old crone asks him to help wring her winding sheet, adding that if he does so, he'll be rich all his days. Well, our hero knows that if you're called upon to wring a winding sheet with a Washerwomen of the Night, it's essential to twist the sheet in the same direction she does, information nobody ever bothered telling me. Possibly Washerwomen of the Night were a bit thin on the ground in the south London suburb where I grew up, but it's the sort of handy tip you'd like to know. Anyway, Washerwoman of the Night sees she's dealing with a bright boy, so she fills his pockets with silver and precious stones. He returns to Huelgoat, shows his haul to the lads down the bar, and the Huelgoat Silver Rush begins.

However, not every encounter between local youth and riparian ladies of the night had such a happy outcome. Further up the river, we pass the Mare aux Fées, or Fairies' Pool. Young fairy spent too much time chatting up the boys and got bunged in the pool as a punishment, there to lurk about the depths coiffing her blonde locks with a gold comb. It's said that if you look into the pool by moonlight, she'll gull you in and you'll drown. Meanwhile, her colleagues roam the village in the guise of hideous witches, about which I will make no comment, save to observe that this smacks of the sort of story put about by villagers next door in another country. Further upstream we reach Le Gouffre, a sample of that very Breton phenomenon the *chaos*.

We'll see the most famous chaos later when we return to the village of Huelgoat, but it's worth noting that there are others dotted about Brittany, particularly in Côtes d'Armor, where there's the Chaos de Gouët near St. Brieuc and, further south toward Rostrenen, those of Toul Goulic and Corong. A chaos in the Breton sense is a concentration of the stones Gargantua had such a gay time tossing about, a kind of cataract of boulders crowded into and generally submerging a watercourse, and surrounded by forest so dense and tangled it aspires to a tropical fecundity. Associated with all manner of pagan deities and fertility rites, these places were demonized by Christian missionaries, giving rise to their present names - chaos, *gouffre* (abyss or chasm), *pierres du diable*, and so forth.

Another legend we'll be looking at later concerns the Celtic Atlantis, the Ville d'Ys, swallowed up by the waves as punishment for the anti-social antics of the daughter of the royal household, Dahut. Not the sort of girl you'd want to bump into down the disco on a Friday night (not for long, at least), Dahut lead a dissolute life, picking a new lover from among the local beaux every night. So far so good. More power to her elbow. As Chuck Berry was told by his father, a Baptist minister, "There's nothing wrong with sex, son. Not a thing wrong with sex! Nothing wrong with sex! Nothing wrong with sex! It's just the way you handle it, you see". Sadly, Dahut had a heavy hand. It's that 'new lover every night' gives the game away. Once Dahut had had her way, her lover's way was had, and the unfortunate chap would be strangled or boiled alive, his body whisked away along a subterranean passage by L'Homme Noir (a ghoulish creature of the night rather than an early incarnation of Johnny Cash's Man In Black) to be dumped in Le Gouffre. Ever since, the water chute at Le Gouffre is said to run red with the blood of her victims, whose ghostly lamentations can be heard in the torrent at night, in which case one must recite '*Doue da bardono d'an Anaon'*, 'God pardon their trespasses'.

Enter the avenging Saint Guénolé (also spelled Gwennole), a man one would do well not to antagonize, given that not only he but both parents and no less than three siblings were canonized - you can imagine what a bundle of laughs a get-together round the Guénolé household must have been. Anyway, enter Guénolé and it's bye-bye Ys and *bonjour* eternity. Dahut was transformed into a siren and swiftly took the Man In Black's subterranean passage to Huelgoat and Le Gouffre, where she now whiles away her days singing to conceal the cries of her victims. She spends here evenings above Le Gouffre in the Kastell Ar Guibel or Chateau du Gouffre, where it is said one can also see at midnight a beautiful Woman In White waiting for some dashing knight to rescue her from captivity, only drawback being she has a hideous serpent wound about her neck. Whoever overcomes their horror and rescues the distressed damsel will receive a gift equivalent to all of Brittany.

The Kastell Ar Guibel is reached by a steep but brief climb along a narrow stepped path. Though its defensive advantages are immediately obvious, there is little to see apart from a few pit-like earthworks and a modern stele, raised to commemorate a more verifiable if no less morbid literary event that took place on this site.

Born in Brest toward the end of the nineteenth century, Victor Segalen was a bit like a Breton Robert Louis Stevenson. The two writers' books and the genres they worked in are very different, but there's the same brief life, the same intensity of living and creativity, the same ill health, the same questing love of travel and adventure, and a shared passion for the South Seas. Poet, novelist, doctor, explorer, archeologist and anthropologist, Segalen travelled throughout Polynesia and China, reaching Tahiti three months after the death of Gauguin, whose last sketchbooks he was lucky enough to consult. For Segalen, travel was more than an elaboration of sightseeing, a mere ticking off of exotic sights and sensations, but a means of exploring oneself, and in fifteen restless years between the completion of his studies and his death at the age of 42, he built up a voluminous and varied body of literary works, between times bearing witness to the destruction of Maori culture, fighting in the First World War, and practicing medicine, including a spell battling the Spanish Influenza Epidemic of 1918-19. As he himself observed, it was a life lived with irreparable and exhausting intensity, as if in pursuit of its end, and death is an abiding image in his work, appearing in his most famous book, the prose poems *Stèles*:

Je suis sans désir de retour, sans regrets, sans hâte
　　　　　et sans haleine. Je n'étouffe pas. Je ne gémis
　　　　　point. Je règne avec douceur et mon palais
　　　　　noir est plaisant.

Certes la mort est plaisante et noble et douce. La
　　　　　mort est fort habitable. J'habite dans la mort
　　　　　et m'y complais.

He met his own accommodating death on the 21st of May 1919 while walking in Huelgoat. Quite how is a mystery. Normally, his demise is ascribed to exhaustion, the man was simply worn out by living, but suicide is occasionally mooted, too. His body was found at the Kastell Ar Guibel, a copy of Hamlet lying open at his side.

A couple of years later and some two thousand miles to the west, another writer was born who would incarnate a similar itinerant romanticism. Jack Kerouac was not a Breton writer, but there is a Breton connection, since *Ker* is the Breton equivalent of the French *chez*. It can be translated as town or village, but most often is a prefix for 'the house of' and everywhere you go in Brittany you will see signs for *ker* something or other. That somebody with Breton origins should become one of America's most celebrated writers is not necessarily all that surprising. I make no claims for the imperial scope of the Breton literary genius, but migration is almost as much a theme of Breton history as it is of Irish history. Entire villages would up sticks and set off for a new life in the New World, leaving their mark from Nova Scotia, where the Cap Breton area is home to one of the liveliest folk music scenes in the Celtic diaspora, to New York where there is to this day a dynamic Breton speaking community, the offspring of migrants who emigrated before French became the *lingua franca* in Brittany. No surprise then that someone with a Breton name should have achieved fame in the States. In this instance, the name reached the New World through the emigration in 1721 of Urbain François le Bihan de Kervoach, son of the public notary in Huelgoat.

After visiting the Kastell Ar Guibel, we retrace our steps to Le Gouffre, and follow the D769a back toward the village to pick up the Sentier du Clair Ruisseau, which soon passes Le Mare aux Sangliers, or Wild Boar's Pool. Strangely enough, the Fairies' pool was far deeper, which doesn't seem right somehow. You'd have thought a big brawny pig would want to splash about a bit more than Tinkerbell. Why the pool is named after the *sangliers* is unclear, some sources claiming it's because the heads of wild boar can be made out in the shape of the rocks, others because this is where the boar came to drink. Either way, there are wild boars hereabouts, and inevitably there is a story attached to them.

God and St. Peter descend to Huelgoat disguised as a labourer and a lumberjack with a pregnant pig . . . I'm not making this up, somebody did, but it wasn't me. Meeting an old woman, a poor baker, they give her the pig on condition that she keep half the piglets for them, saying they'll be back in a week to pick up their part of the litter. Pig gives birth to eight piglets, old woman decides these shabby woodsmen aren't to know how many piglets were born and resolves to tell them there were only four, that way she'll be six pigs the richer, not counting the sow, so she duly hides four piglets in the bread oven. God and St. Peter come back and ask how many piglets were born. Four, she says. What about those ones over there in the oven, says God, didn't you count them? Ooh . . . er . . . Woman begs forgiveness, St. Peter opens the oven, and the missing piglets tumble out covered in soot and ash and dash off into the forest - hence the dusky skin of their offspring. I confess, Just So it ain't, but it's my intention to report every story associated with this wood, so you'll have to live with 'so so' as well as 'Just So'.

The Boars' Pool is potentially a nice place for a break, particularly on a warm summer's day. I say 'potentially' because it depends on the company you keep. What I am about to describe, may come as a shock. Everyone in England, indeed pretty much everyone everywhere, knows foreigners and foreign places are inherently inferior. The French, for instance, will return from a trip abroad, sigh with relief, and say, "*On est bien chez nous*", i.e. we're better off at home. But in England, though we know foreigners are inferior, we have a nasty suspicion they possess some secret insight into the Art of Living that we don't quite comprehend. Take the French. Take 'em and keep 'em is the instinct of most English people. Lovely country, but all those French people! And yet we still have a sneaking regard for their sense of style. It's *haute couture*, we talk about, not 'lofty needlework'. And when we consider the continent, it is with the uneasy feeling that they're rather more elegant than us and have rather more refined tastes. *Haute couture, haute cuisine* . . . inferior they maybe, but they're still more *haute* than me and you. Well, let me tell you, vulgarity knows no national boundaries. You can have all your *haute couture* you want, but there is in France a *basse couture*, too, *très basse*, and it goes with the *basse culture,* and it's manifesting itself in the Mare aux Sangliers.

Half a dozen people are paddling and splashing about the pool. They're wearing an assortment of sagging pink shell suits and ill-fitting T-shirts with the pictorial equivalent of FCUK plastered across the chest on plastic logos. They've got curves and bulges in places where curves and bulges really ought not to be. There's more than a hint of builders' crack and a fair bit of barmaid's bosom. Mops of bottle blonde hair flop about beds of undyed roots. And everybody is shrieking and shouting and snorting and snickering and swigging Kronenbourg and dropping their fag butts in the water. Yves Montand it is not. I don't doubt that they are fine and upstanding people, raising their children with loving kindness, caring for aged relatives, taking pleasure of a life that is not necessarily a long quiet river. But the sight of the pleasure taking is not an edifying spectacle. My companions, a couple of friends over from England for the weekend, are looking on with faintly fixed grins, as if fearful lest one of these lumpen *fées* is about to bounce out of the pool bellowing *Voulez vous couchez avec moi*. The only member of our party who regards the scene with unmixed happiness is Alud, a large and unfeasibly friendly Pyrenean Mountain Dog whose motto is "take love where you find it", and she finds it everywhere, no matter how unwillingly bestowed. She has a technique for bullying people into petting her, herding them into a corner then standing in front of them, looking big, until they stroke her. Confronted with this animated crowd, she can't help but see it in terms of stroking potential, and she's off splashing about the pool with her newfound friends. But to her dismay, indeed downright incomprehension, these are not dog-loving people, and all they do is use her as a shield to avoid being splashed by one another. After recovering one bedraggled and very bewildered dog, we continue our wanderings.

Next objective is the Camp d'Artus, a hill fort dating back to the first century BC and latterly associated with Arthurian legend. The man's said to have buried a fabulous treasure hereabouts, guarded by will-o'-the-wisps, which seems a pretty sorry sort of protection compared to the standard *korrigan* and strapping great demons. No winding sheets to be wrung out, either. Just a bit of marsh gas to puff aside and the treasure could be ours. But the afternoon is getting warm and none of us are much tempted to chance our arm digging up the earthworks, so we head for the Sentier des Amoureux and the main concentration of Huelgoat's sights at the Chaos du Moulin.

If you don't fancy the steep climb to the Camp d'Artus, there is an alternative Arthurian route back to Huelgoat. Crossing the footbridge at the Boars' Pool and heading back downstream, we come to the Grotte d'Artus, a sort of natural dolmen rather than a cave and hardly regal in its dimensions, but big enough for the Breton imagination to conjure a tale of Arthur sleeping in one of its nooks, waiting till he's summoned from his slumbers to save the country from some unspecified danger that can doubtless be laid at the door of the English. If you take this option, simply follow the track past the cave back to the D769a then take the Allée Violette alongside the river to the Chaos.

Either way, via the *camp* or via the *grotte*, a word to the wise: if you can visit the main sites in winter rather than summer, or during the week rather than at the weekend, or early in the morning rather than in the afternoon, and preferably all three, DO SO! Huelgoat is a lovely place and, despite the Boars' Pool, most of what we've seen so far will be a serene experience at any time of the year, week, or day. But the Chaos du Moulin is very well known and very close to the village and very easy to get to and therefore very easily inundated with visitors.

Later excursions will prove that visiting the Chaos du Moulin can be a delightful experience, but on our first trip, we have a very nasty shock. Elsewhere in the woods, the prevailing mood was one of peace and quiet, of chuckling streams and close-stitched canopies of leaves, good clichés like that. You might laugh at the legends, but you can still understand why such tales were told in the first place. The atmosphere is right for myths and fantastic stories. Come the Chaos, that air of timelessness has all but disappeared, and we're plunged into another sort of chaos, one that is all too common in our day and age, a chaos of sightseers dragging unwilling infants round sights seen by so many eyes so many times before, one half suspects the marvel and mystery that made them worth seeing in the first place has evaporated.

There's a man busking beside the path, tootling on a penny whistle, but nobody can hear him because another busker further up the Chaos is doing something unspeakable to a bagpipe. A bickering couple look like they might come to blows shortly. Dazed tourists shuffle past the buskers, guiltily glancing the other way. There's a Chihuahua having a crap on a small child's shoe, while the small child looks on with fascinated horror, uncertain whether to bawl, stick the boot in, or just stand about awhile to see how things develop. People are everywhere! Alud is delighted and before you can say 'kiss-me-quick', she's herding a family of potential admirers into a corner, gently groining the grandfather just in case he gets up to any funny business. Enough!

Flash forward a few months for a moment to a Friday morning in February, when we return to Huelgoat on a fact-checking trip. The atmosphere has changed entirely. There are no bagpipes, no excreting Chihuahuas, no children contemplating the unsavory pile accumulating on their feet, no tourists apart from ourselves, no people whatsoever as it happens, just us and the chaos. And what a chaos it is, a great cascade of glistening rocks rimed with moss, boulders improbably perched on one another in precarious and splendidly imaginative positions, as if engaged in some peculiarly ingenious gymnastics, an orgy of rock that is so very spectacular you want to rush out and grab somebody by the arm and say, "Here, come, come and look at this, look what we've found!". We resist the temptation, though. You probably will, too, if you manage to visit when the place is empty.

The most famous attraction in the chaos is the *Roche Tremblante*, a seven-metre long, three-metre high boulder weighing 137 tons, and so balanced by nature that it is said a ten year old child can make it rock by pushing on a precise point with their back, or even a finger. Whether this is true or not, I couldn't say. In the summer, it's generally surrounded by a lot of puzzled tourists pointing at likely pressure points and vainly trying to shift the thing. Mum has a go, then dad has a go, then son has a go, then granddad has a go, but the stone doesn't even shimmer, let alone tremble - possibly because another mum, dad, son and granddad are pushing on the other side at the same time.

Lower down in the heart of the chaos lies the *Ménage de la Vierge*, which translates as something like The Virgin's Chattels. These erosion scars in the rocks are variously said to resemble the bed, cauldron, spoon, crib, dish, butter churn, and umbrella of the Virgin Mary - 'variously' because different people see different things. I confess, all I see is a few vague shapes in the rock, so very vague I'm still not sure I found the right place. Nonetheless, the sight, if sight it was, leaves me full of admiration for the imagination that can conjure so much from the simple forms of a few damp rocks. This is typically Breton, though. A modest cave becomes the resting place of the greatest Celtic king, a peck of water is turned into the snare of a predatory fairy, and an erosion scar is translated into a souvenir of divinity . . .

Mind you, maybe it's not just imagination. After all, Kerouac came from here and he wasn't averse to experimenting with mind altering substances. And there's a sign indicating 'mushrooms' further up the path. The guide books say it's a 200-ton stone shaped like a mushroom, but I'm reserving judgment on that. That may just be a blind. A predilection for psychotropic fungi would explain much about the Breton character.

Climbing back toward Huelgoat village, we pass the raked amphitheatre of the open air *Théâtre du Verdure* and, down to our right, the most spectacular of the sights and the one that really merits an early morning visit, the *Grotte du Diable*. At first, the narrow ladder dropping into a hole between the rocks appears to be descending to a simple viewing platform. In fact, this is just the first of several steps into the underworld, for thereafter we walk underneath enormous boulders into the heart of the chaos itself.

Like many places in Brittany, the *Grotte du Diable* is reputed to be the entrance to hell, and it must be said that, given the Breton penchant for the bottle, the present legend does at least sound bona fide. The thing is, this particular gateway is not a one-way route like that bewildering side trail encountered by Tro Breiz pilgrims in the Yeun Elez bog. It is said that beyond the Huelgoat gate lie ninety-nine *auberges,* each and every one of them a purveyor of strong liquor. Would be revenants need only reach the last auberge without getting drunk and they can come back. This may explain why Bretons are so fond of drinking - they're practicing. If, however, you do this infernal pub crawl and succumb to the strong liquor, the devil nabs you, pours toad and snake blood inside you, then whisks you off to hell. I've had a few nights like that myself.

Another more prosaic but possibly more factual tale recounts how a revolutionary partisan was being pursued by *chouans* (royalist peasants) and took refuge in the *Grotte du Diable*. It was dark and damp and cold, so he lit a fire, and in so doing, gave his hiding place away. Cornered by the *chouans*, he took up his pitchfork and pulled on his cap, which happened to be decorated with a couple of red feathers, and went out to defend himself. The *chouans* took one look at this spectral, horned figure looming out of the flames with a fork in his hand, and promptly took to their heels, hollering "The devil! It's the devil!" Anyone for a mushroom? And yet, once inside the *grotte*, you can understand their fear. Surrounded by rock and deafened by roaring water, one is humbled to a degree ordinarily only prompted by the most daunting mountains. To be perfectly honest, I wouldn't be too happy myself if I happened to be here on a quiet night and somebody suddenly appeared with a fire behind him and horns on his head and a fork in his hand.

Thirsty work all this, so where should we go for refreshment after the chaos? Where better in a forest of stories than a *café-librairie*. There are nineteen *café-librairies* in Brittany, hybrid bar-bookshops, and one of the finest and most civilized is just round the corner. Indeed, we passed it a little earlier, so if the trails and tales prick your appetite en route, all you need do is turn right at the signposted turning just before the Boars' Pool, and stroll uphill to the hamlet of Restidiou Braz and the welcome refuge of *L'Autre Rive*. Otherwise, to extricate yourself from the chaos (touristic and granitic), take the lakeside road round to the D769a, hang a left, then left again just after the Sentier du Clair Ruisseau, and follow the road up to the hamlet.

L'Autre Rive is a lovely place, a home from home, except that somebody else is pouring the drinks and providing the food. Furnished with large tables, armchairs, benches from *lits clos*, and decorated with discriminating good taste that's just the right side of a Homes & Gardens double-page spread, it's a bit like being in somebody's living room. Admittedly, someone of a powerfully gregarious disposition, but it's all very domestic, and they don't even have to fetch out the ironing board to create the illusion. The background music is so good you wouldn't mind it being a bit more in the foreground, internet access is available in an unobtrusive niche round the corner, books line the walls, there's a chess set, a table full of books of local interest, and a kids' corner with kid-sized table and chairs, picture books, drawing paper and past visitors' pictures strung from the window. Refreshment consists of soups, salads, and a selection of savoury and sweet cakes, and an impressive array of local beers from the Brasserie An Alarc'h. Their standard *bière blonde*, Tantad, is an excellent cloudy beer with only one serious drawback - it needs to stand in the glass for a minute or two before its full range of flavours emerge. But it doesn't matter. Time is most decidedly not of the essence here. Just sit back and enjoy. The only risk is that L'Autre Rive is so very agreeable, you may find it hard to tear yourself away. I sense a new legend evolving here. Ah, him. Yes, well, he went to The Other Bank and was never seen again. They do say that if you go down to the woods at closing time ...

8. Facing the Void

ACCESS - The Monts d'Arrée are in the centre of Finistère between Pleyben and Morlaix. Main access is via the D785 (north-south) and D11/D784 (northwest/southeast). The itinerary begins at the **Col de Trévezel** at the intersection of the D784 & D785 then traces a clockwise circuit via the D784, D36, D14, and D785. The **Col de Trédudon** is on the D36 slip-road linking the D785 and D764 immediately south of **Plounéour-Ménez**.

Precious time is slipping away

We're in the Monts d'Arrée. They're really most remarkable. They're not here. It's the first thing you notice when you reach the Breton mountains: no mountains. As far as the eye can see, not a single blessed mountain. The unmountainness of the vista is impeccable. Yet woe betide anyone who comments on the fact. This is a sensitive subject in Brittany, a sort of don't-mention-the-war, emperor's-new-clothes job, and Missing Mountain posters or jokes about bandaging the Invisible Man are not welcome.

It's strange really. For all their myth-making, the Bretons are not an entirely credulous people. Fairly credulous, yes, but not entirely. How could they be when their word for god, *an doue*, sounds remarkably close to French *andouille* (chitterlings) and its diminutive *andouillette* (tripe sausage)? It would not, after all, do much for your sense of faith if you found yourself chanting "Our Chitterling who art in heaven" or lauding Tripe Sausage, who is presumably the son of Chitterling. So they can't be entirely credulous. And yet, they all believe in their mountains with a fervor that is tantamount to infatuation. I choose my words carefully. They believe *in* them. You may believe in the Tooth Fairy. I might believe in Father Christmas. The Bretons believe in the Breton mountains.

Drive across Finistère from north to south with a Breton and, sooner or later, your companion will feel compelled to nudge you out of your inexplicable negligence in not mentioning the phenomenon yourself, by saying something like, "And these are our mountains. Pretty neat, huh?"

Neat's not the word. They're so tidy, they've been filed away in a drawer somewhere.

"What mountains?" you may ask, glancing nervously at your travelling companion, trying to recall if there is any history of mental instability in the family, at which point you'll get a faintly hurt look from the far side of the car.

"Those ones, back there," he'll say, going onto to expound the mildly delirious fantasy that in times past these 'mountains' were a major obstacle to communication between the north and the south, like the Pyrenees and the Alps. In this case though, the obstacle was rather more vital since, instead of serving a trifling function like merely keeping France and Spain apart, or separating Italy from the rest of Europe, the Monts d'Arrée prevented the Leonards getting at the Cornouailles, and vice versa. Breton history wouldn't have been the same without them. "Good Breton mountains, they are," he might add, smugly.

"What, you mean that little hummocky thing? Bit like a sleeping policeman? With knobs on it?"

Only after a minute or two will you realize this conversation is in deadly earnest and that your hoots of delighted derision aren't going down at all well. Your companion may sink into wounded silence at this stage, or mutter defensively about them being "very old mountains". Too right they are, chum. They're so old they no longer possess any discernible relation to mountain reality. THEY DON'T EXIST!

I had this and comparable conversations on numerous occasions over the course of several deeply puzzling years until the day I realized the slightly high heath we kept driving across was it, that was the 'mountain'.

In the end, one of the more breathtaking and possibly most admirable qualities of the Bretons, is their capacity for confronting want. Faced with a total lack of something in themselves or their culture or their land, they just go ahead and make it up, creating by naming, and then enjoy the fantasy quite as much as if it really existed. All you need do is identify a patch of land as 'the mountains' and ensure that enough people do the same thing, and Presto! You got mountains. They haven't installed any ski stations in them yet, but I'm sure it's only a matter of time.

They're not shy about the science, either. Even otherwise serious and reliable publications will solemnly explain that the Monts d'Arrée are among the oldest 'mountains' in France along with the Massif Central and the Ardennes, dating back some 200 to 300 (being Brittany, there's room for disagreement, probably depending on which bishopric you adhere to) million years to the Primary Era and the Hercynian orogenic fold, since which they have . . . um . . . 'eroded' - a lot. It's at this point that the conversation becomes a bit post-modern, in the sense that you realize the word 'mountain' does not represent some verifiable objective reality on which everyone can agree, but is actually a fancy foreign intellectual concept that can be applied to anything the speaker chooses, and that said concept will henceforth enjoy a correlative denotative validity within the subjective perceptual framework of the denotee's internal conceptual analytical matrix of the signifier and the signified. Or some tosh like that.

I suppose this all rather begs the question of when is a mountain not a mountain. I'd always understood a mountain was a sticky up bit that topped 600 metres. Admittedly, that's not exactly a technical definition and is of itself pretty arbitrary, but at least it's a measurable reality everyone can agree on - it is a mountain or it isn't a mountain, end of story. The Monts d'Arrée don't even reach 400 metres, and most of that is climbed on the agricultural plain approaching the 'mountains', which of themselves might at best make for a nice little fell. Generally, they bear a closer resemblance to Hay Tor on Dartmoor than anything really mountain-like; not entirely incidentally, perhaps, since the Monts d'Arrée come from the Devonian period in geological terms. Really, you could dump them down in Devon and nobody would notice, always supposing they weren't standing in the middle of the dumping site, leaving a little person shaped outline in the landscape. Scattered outcrops of rock protruding from upland moor, that's all it is. The only difference is that Hay Tor is higher.

Perhaps, though, what we're really talking about here is not something peculiar to Brittany, but a fundamental difference between France and Britain. The French are always talking about, usually bemoaning, occasionally praising, British pragmatism, and it has to be said that as a stereotype it does have some application. In Britain, our philosophers come up with free market economics, statistical analyses, predictions of catastrophic population growth, justifications for an autocratic state, and the common-sense assertion that we have to make compromises in choosing one good over another; in France they invented revolutionary idealism, the dissolution of the individual within the state, collective dissent as an assertion of identity, anthropological structuralism, linguistic post-structuralism, post-structuralist philosophical deconstructionism, and existentialism, for the most part each incompatible with the other. It's little wonder they're a bit shaky when it comes to defining what a mountain may or may not be. Us Brits get out a ruler. The French think it through a while, conclude that one man's mountain maybe another man's inselberg, always supposing, that is, that the man exists in the first place, so it doesn't really matter one way or another what you call it because every individual's image of what a mountain may be is bound to be different; they then decide where they would like to have a mountain, et *Voila! Une Montagne!* Northeast of Paris, for instance, in one of France's flatter regions, there lies the 'Parc National de la Montagne de Reims'.

In case you have any doubts about this idiosyncratic definition of mountains, I refer you to the entry in the encyclopedic, five-volume *Larousse du XXeme Siecle*, published in the first decades of the last century. The entry for *montagne* begins conservatively enough, saying it's an "*Elévation du sol, naturelle et très considerable*", but the moment they get into details, they start tergiversating, hiding behind vague phrases like "*des parties élevées de la surface du globe par rapport au niveau de la mer*". Evidently, the compilers were acutely aware they were straying into dangerous territory, that my *considerable, natural elevation of the ground* might well be your *high surface in relation to the sea*. Brittany's highest point above sea level is in the Monts d'Arrée; ergo, they are mountains.

Still with me? Still with your disgruntled Breton travelling companion? What's he saying? I wouldn't mind betting it's something along the lines of: "*En tout cas. Peut-être elles sont petites, mais elles sont nos montagnes à nous et on les aimes bien*".

Key phrases if you really want to wind up a Breton mountain

enthusiast are:

- Sorry, I must have blinked.

- Oh, yes. I thought I felt the car go bump.

- Hang on a moment, I'll get my glasses.

- What, that tufty bit?

- I beg your pardon, where did you say? (this accompanied by squinting into the distance and using your right hand to shield your eyes from the glare)

And, best of all, as this implies you noticed something, but are putting it firmly in its place: Nice hills.

So what are we doing up here if these 'mountains' are so risible. Well, the thing is, they are nice hills, very nice hills. And being in Brittany they provide us with a pleasing ambiguity. I'm not talking about their non-existence as mountains. In fact, I'd better stop banging on about that if I want anyone here to acknowledge my existence in the future. Question the reality of the Breton mountains too often and you'll end up enduring your own existential dilemma. No, the interesting ambiguity about the Monts d'Arrée is that they are the locus of what has long been identified as a Breton cult of death, yet are a remarkably stimulating and life-enhancing experience both for casual visitors and long-term residents. This being a topsy-turvy world, we'll begin with the death.

Approaching the Monts d'Arrée from the north, they are immediately identifiable, not because there's a dirty great *elévation du sol* looming ahead of us and winking through the permafrost, but because the chain (no, don't laugh) is pricked by an immense telecommunications mast that serves as a waypost for most of the approach roads. This antenna has been famous ever since it was blown up by the Front de Libération de la Bretagne in 1974 as a protest against the lack of Breton language broadcasting, which was a bit rich given that their own name was in French, but so it goes. Breton nationalism isn't exactly the most virulent of the various brands that have made headlines in the modern world, indeed nowadays it bears much the same relationship to other nationalisms as the Breton mountains do to other mountains: it is, by and large, a strictly cultural phenomenon verging on the fictional. Nonetheless, it did have its day, and its night, too, some of it quite murky, for there are still tales told of impressionable young men becoming embroiled in the clandestine cause then, one way or another, not being 'let go' when they became disillusioned and wanted to leave. When the Trévezel antenna was blown up, Brittany went without television for over a month. Nine months later there was a sharp rise in the birthrate.

Keep your eyes peeled as you approach the antenna, not because there might be a lot of iffy-looking men in stripy T-shirts and balaclavas scurrying about beside the road trying to appear inconspicuous, but because this is your cue to admire the 'mountains' (no, stop it!). As we cross either of the principal access points from the north, the Col du Trédudon or the Col du Trévezel . . . oh, yes, I didn't mention that, they've got cols, too. You can't put anything past these Bretons. They know that a range of mountains (Please! Simmer down in the back rows there) is defined as much by its depressions as its summits, so they've duly gone round identifying their cols, just in case some snooty English pragmatist starts poking about with his ruler. As we cross the principal access points from the north, the Col du Trédudon or the Col du Trévezel, a splendid view opens out incorporating all the main sights of the Monts d'Arrée: Ménez Mikel, Ménez Kador, the Yeun Elez marsh, the Brennilis nuclear reactor .. huh? Now this is where the ominous stuff begins.

When the idea for this book was first mooted, it was suggested that it might be interesting to do a chapter on a community living beside a nuclear reactor. Until very recently, nuclear power was the ultimate taboo in Britain, and anyone wanting to promote it was treated as if they'd expressed a partiality for eating small children. France meanwhile has been happily scattering nuclear reactors about the place for the past forty years and nobody seems to mind. Drive cross country and you're almost bound to see a shapely cooling tower belching clouds of white steam into the air, and just beside it there'll be a prosperous little town, often as not made prosperous by the presence of the reactor. Surely this would make an interesting outing, contrasting mores on either side of the channel? Well, no. Not in Brittany, at least. The Bretons aren't like the big-bit-stuck-on-the-hind-end and they haven't got any nuclear reactors and they don't bloody want any.

Several decades ago, conservative Breton peasants living near Locquirec on the Finistère-Côte d'Armor frontier, were outraged to discover that a bunch of hairy hippies were using the remote coast around Beg an Fry to lounge about in the sun, naked as a cold cabinet of plucked *poulets*. I mean really outraged. They were revolted. It was disgusting. They went back time and again to make sure their eyes weren't deceiving them, but there was no mistaking it. "Look at her, look at that big one down there, that's horrible, that is, did you see the way she crossed her legs? Here, give us those binoculars, will you. I can't believe I'm seeing this. I'm going to have to come back tomorrow to make sure . . . that'll be five francs for use of the stool, please, M. Le Curé." As you can imagine, relations between peasants and nudists were none too cordial, and the atmosphere was about as conducive to a coming together as a field full of rotting cauliflower.

Then some bright spark in the big-bit-stuck-on-the-hind-end suggested Beg an Fry, occupied as it was by nothing more than a pack of inbred Breton peasants and a handful of filthy hippies, was an ideal location for a nuclear reactor. Instantly, common cause was found. Nudists and peasants united to protest against the project, arm in arm, shoulder to shoulder, bare breast to grubby working vest, chanting and waving banners about proclaiming, "*Non aux neutrons! Oui aux nichons!*" - *No to neutrons! Yes to nipples!* The nipples won and this famous beauty spot remains much the same as it was in the sixties, only with a few more swimming costumes and a few less cloth caps.

I say the Bretons haven't got any nuclear reactors, but they do have some rather large, secretive, and faintly sinister submarines lurking about in the Rade de Brest, and they've got Brennilis. Descending from the col toward Brennilis, we pass through a bleak, barren landscape largely devoid of tree cover. The austerity of the terrain is not the result of some hitherto hushed up nuclear disaster, but is the natural scenery of the Monts d'Arrée. Story goes that when Christ was born, the Breton woods were ordered to hop off to Bethlehem to offer obeisance. With the exception of the pine, heather and gorse, the trees and shrubs of the Monts d'Arrée declined to get their feet wet, and were duly cursed, condemned to dry up and disappear. If that sounds a bit far fetched for you, the alternative explanation ascribes the flora to the high acidity of the soil, and the impact of the constant wind and rain that comes chuntering in from the ocean.

From the village of Brennilis, a broad lane descends to the lake and the former heavy-water reactor, which was active from 1967 to 1985, and is now being dismantled, though the site won't be reclaimed for another twenty years. It's always a bit galling for lovers of wilderness sites (anyone who has walked in the Lake District will know what I'm talking about) when military bases and potentially hazardous power plants are located in remote beauty spots, but the logic is simple enough. If it's unpopular and security is an issue, stick it somewhere that doesn't have many people. There are less than forty inhabitants per square kilometre in the Monts d'Arrée and, in the absence of an unholy alliance of reactionary peasants and radical nudists, it was the perfect place to have a nuclear power station.

I presume the authorities know what they're doing here and the decommissioned reactor is safe, though apparently, a few years ago, heavy rainfall raised the water-table to a level above safety norms for a nuclear installation. I've also read that, though the reactor was up and running by the mid sixties, it didn't reach full capacity till the seventies because it kept 'breaking down'. Doesn't exactly inspire confidence, does it? Somehow, the deserted building looks more menacing than the bigger, functioning reactors found elsewhere. There's something almost clean about all that fluffy white steam, but this scruffy superannuated lump of concrete with its mucky white trunk and dirty black domed cap, looks like nothing so much as a giant toadstool from which some satanic gardener has been trimming the gills. It puts me in mind of an altogether less stable and less salubrious installation than the big modern power stations, the sort of thing that would seem more at home in one of the more obscure central Asian republics, the sort of thing that might well be leaking.

Before I get the French government and EDF slapping gagging orders on me and issuing libel writs, I hasten to add that I'm sure the place isn't leaking. I don't even know if there's anything in there that can leak. I've visited the site several times and I haven't started glowing in the dark or anything like that. It's just that it's a bit of a blot on the landscape. Nothing like those evocative little hydroelectric generating plants that were built in remote Spanish valleys during the forties and fifties, and which are now crumbling into romantic ruins. True, you wouldn't really want a nuclear reactor crumbling into romantic ruins, but neither do you want it sat on the shore of an otherwise lovely lake, located in such a way that anyone doing the walk round the Yeun Elez marsh has to end or begin their itinerary with four kilometres of tarmac.

Still, it didn't take atomic boffins to lend this depression at the heart of the Monts d'Arrée a morbid aspect. Nature and the fanciful Breton imagination had long since seen to that. I mentioned earlier in Chapter 4 that Tro Breizh pilgrims were terrified by this place. Walking along the mist shrouded crests surrounding the marsh, they were ever alert to the risks of a plant called *l'herbe d'oubli* that made wayfarers lose track of the path and stray into the heart of Yeun Elez to disappear through the Youdic gateway to hell. *L'herbe d'oubli* has subsequently been identified with the springy matted undergrowth of the heath and it is said that, without the benefit of waymarks or a clear trail, the clotted yielding vegetation can easily beguile you down the gentle slopes of the 'mountains' into the peat bog. A cold, damp marsh may seem an odd place to situate hell, but the Bretons have always known that things are relative and need to be adapted to the locale. Living in a wintry, windswept land, they didn't find the burning hell developed by desert dwelling Christians such a terrible prospect, so their theologians invented the *ifern yen*, or cold hell, in which one froze as much as one burned, hence its location in the dismal, dank quagmire of Yeun Elez.

According to most sources, there's no risk of encountering Youdic nowadays, since it lay at the centre of what was to become the Lac St. Michel, a manmade reservoir dating back to 1935. You'd have thought it a pretty popular idea, sealing up the gates to hell with a lot of water, but not everybody in Brittany was pleased by the innovation. The thing is, the Bretons have always been mightily conscious of death and have consequently elaborated many rituals aimed at averting the more disagreeable aspects of the after-life. These rituals and the concomitant superstitions were so prevalent that the Breton folklorist, Anatole le Braz, published a book in 1893 entirely dedicated to the subject, *La Légende de la Mort chez les Bretons armoricains*, in which he went so far as to state that "*toute la conscience de ce peuple est orientée ves les choses de la mort*". That maybe a bit strong, there was *kof-a-kof* after all, not to mention the stimulating rivalries with them-next-door-in-the-next-country, but it's true that the Bretons aren't exactly what you'd call a bright and breezy people. They know it's going to end badly. Worse though, they have customarily supposed it wouldn't just end badly, but would go on badly thereafter, hence their misgivings about the lake.

In the past, Bretons were possessed of a powerful antipathy toward the unquiet dead. Fair enough. Nobody's keen on the idea of some zombie stumbling through the living room. But the Bretons had a solution for the problem. If a revenant soul, known locally as *anaon*, was troubling the living, the priest would exorcize the spirit, transforming it into a black dog, which was then returned to hell by the simple expedient of bundling it up in the priest's stole and dumping it in Youdic. Happily, at least for the local black dog population, the lake put paid to that particular custom.

Sticking with the other-worldly theme, our tour of the Monts d'Arrée continues via two chapels, the first in the hamlet of St. Herbot to the southeast of Brennilis. The word chapel suggests something subordinate, but the peculiarity of St. Herbot is that it is, in part, modelled on a cathedral, the tower, which dwarfs the rest of the building, being inspired by the Minster at Quimper. The original building was destroyed during the wars of succession and the current edifice was financed by indulgences the pope granted in 1389 to all those who made the pilgrimage and added their mite to the reconstruction programme, which took 100 years to complete.

Nothing exceptionally doomy about that one might suppose, save that this was the place where our old friend Gaor/Gargantua is said to have met his end. Herbot the hermit, AKA *Elghez* ('long-chin' due to his big beard), was doing his hermitic stuff one day when Gaor, driven to distraction by the cleric's incessant prayers, got up to his usual tricks and began bunging rocks about with a view to reducing Long-Chin to Flat-Head. All was going well for the giant until a particularly large rock toppled back on him, tipping him over and impaling him on the chapel's steeple.

The present tower appears to have been restored quite recently and not entirely happily, either, the clean, white, precisely pointed stone proving an ill match for the weathered facade of the nave. Nonetheless, it's still worth visiting, in part for the interior with its fine retable, but also for some of the structural and decorative details outside, like the vaulted ceiling of the porch housing statues of the disciples, and the charming smiling dog perched on the outside corner of the western gable.

Nowadays, St. Herbot is best known as the patron saint of cattle and as a guarantor of good dairy products, a reputation won by virtue of the fact that he landed in Brittany in the sixth century with two white bulls of phenomenal strength. When he died, the bulls were left to the local peasants on condition that they were brought back to his tomb every night. Needless to say, somebody forgot and the bulls disappeared, but their successors can still be seen at the annual *pardon* (the Friday preceding Trinity Sunday), when livestock are paraded round the chapel three times, and supplicants leave oxtails, butter and milk on the altar.

Our next point of call is Lannedern, which lies to the west on the D14. Like nearly every village in the Monts d'Arrée, Lannedern seems to have got stuck in time. It's not that they cultivate a consciously archaic image. These are not places that cultivate images. But isolation, poverty and the much vaunted rigors of 'the mountain climate' mean the communities of the Monts d'Arrée have long been marginalized and have still not quite caught up with the turn of the millennium, remaining very much as they were forty or fifty years ago. This is La Bretagne Profonde.

Lannedern is named after Edern, who is sometimes said to have been a monk, but is also linked with the Arthurian cycle and features as Lord of the Underworld in Celtic mythology. The latter seems more fitting because, like most of the older parishes in the Monts d'Arrée, Lannedern is closely associated with the Breton cult of death. Visit the church and you will see on the ossuary a couple of skull and crossbones images, and to the left of the nearside window of the main building, a gleeful looking grim reaper. Despite being obsessed by death, both pagan Celts and christianized Bretons have not generally feared mortality as such,

regarding it at once as a natural, simple fact, and the point of transition into a better life; but they were none too keen on being told that their personal transition was nigh. Death was all right. It was his messenger that appalled them.

The *ankou* is the Breton version of the grim reaper, appearing in traditional form

Ossuary carving Lannedern

(skeleton, cloak, scythe), or as a very tall, extremely thin man wearing a broad felt hat. I confess, I was slightly alarmed when I read about this second manifestation. I'm very tall and, though not quite so skinny as I once was, might be described as extremely thin; and I've been known to wear broad felt hats. Being English, I'm already labouring against the odds in Brittany. If the neighbours identify me with the *ankou*, my social life will be at an end. *Ank* is a miserable root word in Breton, *anken* meaning sorrow, *ankoun* oblivion, so you can understand why the Bretons were disinclined to grapple with such a dismally named embodiment of the grim reaper. Despite the gleeful image at Lannedern, the *ankou* was all grim, with no positive overtones of harvesting your reward.

Unlike the *anaon*, who, according to Anatole le Braz, could be appeased with a plate of *crêpes,* scared away with a loud cough, or stuffed inside a dog if they weren't, a meeting with the *ankou* was invariably fatal, and anyone who heard the creaking wheels of his cart, the *karrig* or *karriguel an Ankou*, knew that their time was near. Other signs were the scent of a burning candle, a cock crowing at midnight, or the ringing of a handbell. Depending upon where you lived (remember, the Bretons do like to distinguish themselves from one another) the *ankou* was personified either by the last or first parishioner to die in any given year. Come the designated month, everyone was waiting, watching one another nervously, because one's own well-being over the next 365 days might well depend upon the age of the year's *ankou*. If the first to die was someone young, the *ankou* would spend his time in office claiming the old; if the *ankou* was old, it was the youngsters who were in trouble. And if the *ankou* was a famously nice man, everyone breathed a sigh of relief, persuaded that he, at least, would not be indulging in too many nasty tricks.

Images of the Ankou are often accompanied by cheery little messages. At Brasparts, a stone inscription proclaims, "*Je vous tue tous*" - *I kill you all*; at La Martyre we are told, "*La mort, le jugement, l'enfer froid: quand l'homme y pense, il doit trembler*" - *Death, judgment, cold hell: when man ponders these things, he must quake*; and at La Roche Maurice we are offered a helpful reminder, "*Souviens-toi, homme, que tu es poussière*" - *Remember, man, you are dust*. They certainly knew how to win friends and influence people. Yet men did forget and they didn't always quake . . . and I mean men.

In many Breton communities, religion was considered women's business and, while their wives and daughters attended mass, the men would congregate at the local café (if you're in need of a bar in Brittany, the first place to look is in front of the church) for a *petit coup de rouge* and a game of cards. The male population only attended church on high days, like Christmas, Easter, and All Saints. As a result, the *Toussaint* homily became something of an institution, for it was then that the priest had to counter all the hands of cards and *petits coups de rouge* that were the order of Sunday the rest of the year round, preaching his most vivid hell-and-damnation sermon in an attempt to terrify the men into sobriety. Odd logic, really. Bad news is bad news, whatever way you look at it, and when an experience proves disagreeable, you don't go hurrying back to get more of the same. Certainly, anecdotal evidence suggests the principal effect of the hellfire sermonizing was to drive the men to drink. The kids, meanwhile, were scared witless, and more than one mother was woken in the middle of the night by an anxious child concerned that they had committed a mortal sin.

To complete our tour of the Monts d'Arrée's morbid side, we must enter the Yeun Elez marsh itself. North of Brasparts on the D785 you will find the *Ferme des Artisans*, the region's co-operative craft shop (well worth a visit), and beyond that, in the lee of Ménez Mikel, a track leading to the Ty Blaise *Centre de Formation Chasse-Nature*. If you take the 'Landes et Tourbieres' path to the north from the Ty Blaise car-park, then turn left just before the line of pine separating the pasture from the marsh, you will find Eured Ven, a megalithic alignment of twenty small menhirs that is also known as La Noce de Pierres or The Wedding of Stones.

As megalithic monuments go, Eured Ven is a bit shoddy and looks like it was put together by some Sunday afternoon DIY enthusiast with more zest than talent, but it was enough for the Bretons to embroider a tale about its genesis. Legend claims a wedding party was dancing on this spot when the priest of Brasparts happened to come along, en route to delivering extreme unction to a dying parishioner. Deep in their cups and possessed by the demon of dance, the irreverent celebrants refused to let the priest pass, forcing him to scramble through the brush and across the heath to reach the dying man. As punishment, when the last dance was done, the wedding party were promptly turned to stone.

Seems a bit mean really because in many ways weddings brought out the best in the Bretons. There was, for instance, a charming custom ensuring an equitable redistribution of the wedding banquet among the wider community. Few people could afford to wine and dine the entire village, so one member of each household was invited - on the understanding that the one member would surreptitiously pocket enough food to give the rest of the family a sample of the feast, too. Guests would turn up, regardless of the weather, wearing large coats with capacious interior pockets, or, if they didn't have a poacher's coat, would bring a loosely furled umbrella, the folds of which would become tighter and tighter as the meal progressed and the family's portion was stuffed inside the brolly. Heaven forbid they were caught in a shower on the way home.

Our next objective lies directly to the north of Eured Ven and can be reached either by carrying on along the waymarked 'Landes et Tourbieres' itinerary or by a narrow embankment path traversing the rise behind Eured Ven before dropping down to join the 'Landes et Tourbieres' boardwalk. When I was planning this outing, all the sources I consulted were most emphatic about the fact that the Yeun Elez gates of hell had been submerged by the reservoir. Only as I was browsing over the map, did I notice there's still a Youdig (the -ic and -ig suffixes are interchangeable in Breton) that is not underwater and, according to IGN, is located just to the west of the lake. This was too tempting. To be honest, I don't place a huge amount of faith in the IGN maps, certainly not for locating the supernatural, despite the fact that I personally find some of their mapping a bit paranormal; but really, I ask you, in how many other countries could you hope to have hell marked on a map? Every estate agent on the planet will claim to offer you a patch of paradise, but poor old hell rarely gets a look in, and when it does, it's attached to some perfectly blameless valley in one of the warmer catholic countries. But this is the real thing. We're not talking metaphors here. These are the gates to hell itself and they're marked on the map.

Anyone familiar with the fens or moorland will have a pretty good idea of what to expect in the Yeun Elez peat bog: basically something big and flat and wet and wild. It's not the sort of place in which to go wandering on a whim and there's a large, moss-blotched sign advising us to stick to the boardwalk and signposted paths. We are accompanied by a white dog and a black dog. Compared to the black dog, the white dog does not possess any strikingly superior literacy skills, yet she wisely follows the boardwalk. The black dog, meanwhile, keeps bounding off into the bog, as if all he wants of life is the opportunity to become a Breton scapedog. There are places here where a dog might well get stuck, maybe even disappear. If we're to discover Youdig today, I've got a nasty feeling I know who's going to find it first.

If you don't get soaked by one of the storms that regularly sweep in from the Atlantic, when it really is a cold hell, Yeun Elez is an extraordinary place. Perfectly flat (these are the Breton mountains, after all), it stretches out on all sides, like some matted, living, growing thing - which it is, of course. The fact that the ground is composed of compacted combustible vegetation means that this wetland can actually be a fire hazard during a long spell of hot weather. Locals still recall the summer of

1977 when the drought and heat dried out the peat. A group of farmers were clearing the upland heath one day when the blade of a power tool hit a rock, sent out a spark, and set fire to the peat. The farmers just had time to get themselves and their tractor out before the hillside was engulfed in flames. The ensuing fire spread across the bog and burnt for three months, kicking up such clouds of ash that every surface was black to the touch and washing hung out on the line was grizzled by the time it was dry.

Today, though, there's a heavy shower barreling in off Ménez Kador and I suspect we could spend the entire morning tossing lighted dog-ends into the scrub with impunity. On the subject of dog-ends, our increasingly bedraggled black dog eventually concludes the white dog has made the politic decision, and even deigns to trot at heel as we scamper back to the car, pursued by what appears to be a large dollop of the Atlantic. Whether he or we found Youdig before the rain drove us back, I couldn't really say. As far as I can work out, it's about four hundred metres south of the Reservoir de St. Michel's westerly tip. To be honest, though, apart from the fact that you could then boast you'd been to hell and back, it doesn't make much difference. Youdig literally means 'small porridge'. It's not the most evocative name for the gates of hell, nor even a very accurate description of the bog, but it does suggest something mushy that lacks firm features and is much the same wherever you dip into it, and that *is* a fair depiction of the terrain. Like the Breton mountains themselves, Youdig could be anywhere you wanted it to be, since there's no easy way to distinguish one patch of porridge from another. Picking a precise spot for hell is strictly for the birds - and the black dogs.

It should be said here that, despite their elaborate obsession with the business of passing on, the Bretons knew how to defeat death, too, in their own manner. There's a delightful story told of a man who was so terribly keen on mourning he prided himself on being the first to present his condolences after a bereavement, until the day he was in such a hurry to console a grieving widow, he rushed off to the dead man's house, only for the 'deceased' to open the door. Now that's what I call defeating death. Presumably the apprentice cadaver in question had opted for the Huelgoat Grotte du Diable entrance to the underworld rather than the Youdic way in, and had visited the ninety-nine auberges without getting drunk. As for the precipitate mourner, he was never quite the same again.

It's a hungry business death and, if you haven't brought a well-stocked umbrella with you, you may be getting a bit peckish by now, in which case you should continue along the D785 to the more northerly of its two junctions with the D42, where you will find what is, for my money, the best restaurant in Brittany.

There are plenty of 'fine' restaurants dotted about Brittany, the sort that feature in conventional guide books, several of them boasting Michelin stars, but an awful lot of these establishments suffer from the inverted commas bracketing that 'fine'. They are too 'fine', places with all the life and gusto refined out of them, temples to Good Taste in which the atmosphere is heavy with piety, suffused with a soft glow from muted pink curtains, pale yellow lampshades, and overly deferential waiters; places of softly murmured apparently mortal conversations and couples trying not to catch one another's eye across the dazzling desert of the snowy white table linen; places with far too many forks and not enough food; shrines to nouvelle cuisine in which I always end up feeling as if I've been stuffed and stuck in a glass case on display in a museum. Not stuffed with food, either; just stuffed. There's a stifling sense of propriety about such 'restaurants', a smothering blanket of politesse that leaves the diner with a pervasive fear of overturning the wine glass with its nine-foot long stem (spilling the quarter inch of wine that is allowed to sully the bottom of the glass' gigantic glistening balloon), or that someone, probably oneself, is going to embarrass your oh-so-seemly hosts by doing something unforgivably vital like break wind.

I can still recall the bitter disappointment of sitting in a highly recommended restaurant in Roscoff, disconsolately pushing four Brussels sprout leaves about my vast and vastly vacant plate. They weren't my leftovers. That was what I'd been presented with, direct from the kitchen. Talk about facing the void. Four of them! I counted them several times just to make sure; checked under the plate, inspected the underside of each leaf. Leaves, mind you! I even briefly scanned the ceiling in case it was Autumn. I like Brussels sprouts, too. For a moment, I thought perhaps the waiter had scoffed my sprouts en route to the table, but judging by his pallor, he hadn't eaten anything for about four and a half years. After a while, I began to wonder whether there wasn't perhaps a commis chef in the kitchen whose sole responsibility was selecting and carving the evening's sprout. Or perhaps each diner had their very own sprout, one sprout all to themselves, and the heart of the sprout was discarded after the four greenest leaves on the outside had been peeled away and placed at strategic intervals about the big white plate. Maybe there's a small mountain of disrobed sprouts developing somewhere in Roscoff even as I write. If ever called upon for a definition of disbelief, I shall try to evoke my feelings in that restaurant. The memory smarts to this day.

What the purpose of such places is, apart from flattering snobbery, feeding people who don't need to eat, and sending your credit card debt spiraling off into the stratosphere, I don't know, but I'm pretty sure their function in life has precious little to do with food. La Croix Cassée, on the other hand, is something different. La Bretagne Profonde doesn't get any deeper than this, not unless you successfully locate Youdic.

At first glance, it just looks like a rundown roadside bar, and one that maybe closed at that, an impression confirmed by a door that requires a good firm hand if you're to get the thing open. Even once inside, the word 'restaurant' is not one that leaps to mind, not unless there's something bubbling in the pot. The business has been in the same family for over a century, the decor doesn't appear to have changed for about fifty years, and the ashtrays look like they're emptied every decade or so. Even the electricity supply is so antediluvian they can't have the oven on and run the coffee machine at the same time. But if there is something bubbling in the pot, I guarantee you'll start salivating like one of Pavlov's dogs - a big black one having its last meal before the priest wraps it in his stole. Give thanks for the chichi mausoleums in the richer resorts on the coast! If it wasn't for them keeping the 'fine' palates away from the unfashionable interior, the sign of the broken cross might not be such a symbol of rude life and good eating.

I say *if* there's something bubbling in the pot because the restaurant works on a reservation basis only. You don't just turn up and look at the menu. There is no menu. You phone several days in advance (0298-996-295 in French, I'm afraid), say how many you are, and ask what they're prepared to make for you - and don't quibble: if they suggest it, it's worth eating. As it happens, we were lucky the day we discovered the place. We'd only popped in for a coffee, but a dozen hunters had ordered a *kig-ar-farz* for their post-hunt repast - 'repast' is the sort of word that comes to mind here, with its overtones of 'good, solid fayre' as described in an eighteenth century novel peopled by gluttonous squires and bibulous clergymen. One whiff of what was cooking was enough. We sat down and refused to move till a table for two was set in the living room between the TV, the dog's bed and the kitchen corner.

Kig-ar-farz is one of the great traditional dishes of Brittany and nowhere prepares it better than La Croix Cassée, though you need to be part of a large party or muscle in on somebody else's large party, since it takes nearly five hours to cook and is not the sort of dish you rustle up for a handful of people. A variant on the better known *pot au feu*, *kig-ar-farz* is a broth of beef, ham, belly pork, smoked sausage, *andouillette*, carrots, cabbage, potatoes and, the Breton touch, *farz* (literally 'stuffing') boiled in a bag in the stock. The nearest thing to *farz* in Britain is Yorkshire pudding, only in Brittany the batter mix is boiled rather than baked, and comes in two varieties, a pale *farz* made from wheat flour, and a darker one based on buckwheat. And as if all that isn't enough, there's a shallot and butter sauce that should cast such shame on your average *Chef des Feuilles de Choux de Bruxelles,* he'd do the decent thing and curl up and wither away.

If further testimony to the quality of the food at La Croix Cassée is required, I can tell you that regular customers come from as far away as Australia, have been known to make the six hundred kilometre trip from Paris expressly to eat the *kig-ar-farz*, and include Jacques Chirac, a man, whatever else you may think of him, not known for being careless about what he puts in his mouth.

***

A trip to the Monts d'Arrée inevitably involves us in the darker end of bumping, conjuring things that go bump in the night and threaten to bump you off. Despite La Croix Cassée, you may have been wondering where, amid all these *ankous*, petrified dancers, black dogs and gates to hell, the life-enhancing stuff comes in. Well, it is in the 'mountain' itself.

I may laugh at the alleged Breton mountains, but any mountain, even one manifestly mountain-like let alone one concocted entirely by the eye of the beholder, exists as much in the imagination of people as it does as a physical agglomeration of rock, earth and vegetation, and as I've indicated, the Bretons are nothing if not imaginative. They believe in their mountains and, like any dearly held belief, their faith is its own reward, one that I wouldn't mind converting to myself.

So, to crack the mystery of the Breton mountains, I'm going to do a Mallory. I don't mean disappear, but scale the highest summit "because it's there" - perhaps. And in the tradition of plucky British explorers battling against the odds in a hostile climate, I've borrowed a couple of native porters to do all the hard work for me. I'm taking Samson (age 4&¼) and Segal (age 2&¾) into the Breton mountains. Breton born and bred, they've got to start seeing mountains sooner or later, and it suits me (plucky British explorer, age 45&¾) that it's sooner.

"Ah, you're taking them to discover their *patrimoine*," says their grandmother.

No, I'm not, I think. I'm taking them to carry the beer. That's what plucky British explorers do with native porters. But I suspect this might not go down too well. Bretons can get exceedingly misty-eyed about their *patrimoine*, but it is as nothing to grandmothers and grandsons burdened with plucky British explorers' beer. Instead, I make a noise intended to convey sentiments of derision: "Their *patrimoine*! It's entirely imaginary."

"The *patrimoine imaginaire*", I am told, "is the best sort."

This maybe true. Wikipedia seems to agree because it describes the Monts d'Arrée as being on the border of the illusory, a place where legends write themselves in the landscape and are embodied in the stones, a place that is, in short, *le royaume de l'imaginaire*.

We park at the Col du Trédudon lay-by. It's a bright breezy October day, the sun is high in the sky, there's a nip in the wind, and the moor . . . sorry, the mountain is patched with puddles and splashes of marshy ground after the recent rains. The light is exquisite, picking out the rude encaustic of distant dry stone walls, and dressing the rough heath with a magical luminosity. The mountains may be surreal, but in this light their flora is hyper-real. To the north lies a windfarm and, behind it, the blue expanse of the big sky above the Baie de Morlaix. To the south, we can see the grey smudge of Lac St. Michel, flanked by the Brennilis nuclear reactor and the smooth curve of Ménez Mikel, the latter pricked by the distinctive nipple of its diminutive chapel. When the wind blows, this is a genuinely wild place and, I have to admit, it certainly has a mountain feel to it; just doesn't have any mountains around to justify the sensation.

Where we set off from was a matter of some dispute, not between Samson (age 4&¼) and Segal (age 2&¾), they'll go anywhere, but among the sources I consulted to find out which is Brittany's highest peak. You may find it strange that this should be a matter of doubt, but life's like that in Brittany. Major debates engender modest heat, but if you want some really lively argy-bargy, you need to dispute something that is of very little significance and makes no difference either way. The culminating point of Brittany is perfect. It's a matter of a few modest centimetres on some very modest rocks on some very modest uplands, but get the Bretons onto the subject and a molehill can soon become a mountain.

Traditionally, Roc'h Trévezel (383 metres) a kilometre or so to the west was thought to be the highest point, and you can understand why as it's the craggiest and most distinctive *roc'h* around here. I specify *roc'h* because Bretons don't do things by halves. Not content with inventing a bunch of non-existent mountains, they went on to distinguish between them. The rough outcrops to the north and east of the Yeun Elez basin that have historically vied with one another for the title of Brittany's highest peak, are *roc'hs*, quartzite peaks that have been exposed by water erosion wearing away the surrounding layer of schist. You see what I mean about the Bretons not being shy of science? Give them a pebble and they'll promptly produce half a dozen technical terms to describe it, and will probably see a new world in it, too. More widespread but no less venerated are the *ménez*, like Ménez Mikel and Ménez Kador to the west of Yeun Elez, Ménez Hom near Chateaulin in Finistère, and Ménez Bre near Guingamp in Côte d'Armor. Less rocky than the *roc'h* and more downlike, the *ménez* are granite or sandstone uplands that have been shaped into smooth rounded hills by erosion. You've got to admire the Bretons. Once they apply themselves, they do a really thorough job. They leave no stone unturned, not when they're looking for a mountain.

For the most part, it is the *roc'h* that have been identified as Brittany's highest points, though some partisans have put forward Ménez Mikel (more widely known as Mont Saint-Michel de Brasparts - though Disgusted of Saint Rivoal will inform you it actually falls within their parish, not that of those thieving sods next door in the next country), claiming the chapel's cross is an integral part of the 'mountain', thus pushing its height up to 391 metres! Following that logic, we should be scaling the Trévezel telecommunications antenna, but pluck has its limits and my own stock is severely restricted when it comes to climbing vertiginous antenna. Roc'h Trévezel itself is still often cited as the highest summit by publications that really ought to know better, though as I say there is some excuse for this. It is the craggiest of the crags and, if you were to go for my earlier definition of a mountain as a 'sticky up bit', Roc'h Trévezel certainly looks more sticky up than any of the other sticky up bits of Brittany. The other long-standing candidate and official holder of the title for the last few decades is Tuschenn or Tosenn ar Gador, which appears on the map as Ménez Kador (384 metres). But glance at the IGN 1:25,000 map for the region - well, no, don't glance, you actually need to look quite closely .... Look closely at the IGN map and you'll see that between Roc'h Trévezel and Roc'h Trédudon (385 metres) there's an unnamed summit of 387 metres. I'm sorry if this sounds petty, but in the Monts d'Arrée every metre counts and, if we want to really assimilate the Breton experience, we have to get stuck into the nitty-gritty of Breton identity, so we've got to be picky about identifying The 'Mountain' among 'mountains'. The 387-metre summit is called Roc'h Ruz or Red Rock. It's not actually red, but as I suggested earlier, words can mean anything you want them to mean when we're talking about the Breton mountains.

So, that's pretty straight forward, isn't it? Well, not really, no. This is Brittany after all. I double-checked all this on the internet and the latest word on the matter is as follows. In the course of a recent survey conducted by the Service des Impôts de Morlaix ... yes, that's right, the tax office. Don't ask why, I really wouldn't know, and I suspect I'd prefer not to. In the course of a recent survey conducted by the Service des Impôts de Morlaix, it was determined that Roc'h Ruz *is* the highest at 385.01 metres (not 387 metres as marked on the map), followed by Ménez Kador at 384.91 metres, then Roc'h Trévezel at 384.89 metres, and Ménez Mikel at 381.96 metres. Got it? I thought I had. Then I looked at another website quoting the same survey in which they confirmed that Roc'h Ruz is indeed the highest at 385.01 metres, and number two is Ménez Kador at 384.91 metres, and number three Roc'h Trévezel's 384.89 metres, but number four is Roc'h Trédudon at 383.29 metres, and Ménez Mikel is nowhere in sight. Well, at least we can all agree that Roc'h Ruz is number one. Ernest Géréc, the mayor of Plounéour-Ménez, the *commune* within which it falls, even cites a source from 1836 that already identified the Roc'h Ruz crag. That must be it, then. Maybe.

Then I made the mistake of triple-checking and I discovered the latest measurements were based on a GPS survey. GPS, though spot on for mapping the horizontal plane, is a bit dicky when it comes to the vertical. To make matters worse, Roc'h Trédudon and Roc'h Ruz, though four hundred metres apart, are often assimilated into a single *roc'h*, so it's none too clear who has been measuring what. And all these measurements are IGN approved, yet IGN tolerate a margin of error of up to ten centimetres, so any of the top three candidates could be the highest point! And as if that wasn't enough, the actual culminating point of the Massif Armoricain, of which the Monts d'Arrée are a part, isn't in Brittany at all, but is Mont des Avalois in Mayenne. To cap it all, when I started talking about Roc'h Ruz, I discovered that nine out of ten Bretons had never heard of it. They all 'knew' about their mountains, 'knew' that the mountains were real mountains, not imaginary ones, 'knew' (invariably wrongly and invariably in violent disagreement with one another) which was the highest, but hardly anybody had heard of Roc´h Ruz. Takes some doing, doesn't it? They make up a bunch of mountains because that's what national pride requires then they completely overlook the little bit of rock that is actually the highest! True, it's quite easy to overlook a Breton mountain, but even so.

On the ground though, the niceties of determining altitude are brushed aside. Segal (age 2&¾) is already striding out of the car-park, leaving me, the plucky British explorer (age 45&¾) to hurry after him, hopelessly stabbing at the buttons of my own GPS receiver in a vain attempt to record this extra-ordinary expedition. Segal (age 2&¾) falls over twice within the first ten metres and decides it might be politic to hold my hand. Sherpa Tenzing he's not, but he's game, and barely blubs at all when he inadvertently sits in a puddle, soaking his blue corduroys.

Meanwhile, Samson (age 4&¼) is supplementing the necessary expenditure of energy by leaping across the ruts in the track we're following. "*C'est rigolo*," he says. *It's funny!* This boy's got some way to go if he's to become a truly Botrelian Breton. He needs schooling in the "*Ach! C'est triste, ce n'est pas rigolo*" approach to the Breton way of life. That said, there's one aspect of being Breton he's mastered already. There's a half-metre rise as we leave the parking area, which he promptly dubs *une montagne*. "*La montagne est très, très haute, c'est sympa*", he observes.

Très haute it may be, but so far as I can see, we're following a perfectly flat track across a perfectly flat moor that, with every step, puts me increasingly in mind of Dartmoor and Hay Tor. There is another difference, though, apart from the fact that Hay Tor is higher. There are no coach parties here. Perhaps they got confused by the conflicting claims for Brittany's highest point. Maybe there are bus drivers dotted about Brittany, men of insufficiently vivid imaginations, scratching their heads and apologizing to exasperated sightseers, "Well, I *thought* it was here". Whatever the reason though, we have the place to ourselves. Segal (age 2&¾) takes advantage of this uncommon privilege and sits in another puddle.

"It's here that we're going," says Samson (age 4&¼) pointing, correctly as it happens, west toward the Trévezel antenna. He's still jumping across the ruts, but a hundred metres later, he decides the walk is too long, adding for good measure that there's a *mechant serpent*, a wicked snake, hiding in the heath. He may well be right. I've seen both black and green mambas at large in Africa, but the most terrifying snake I ever encountered was a fat Breton viper coiled on a rock in the middle of the heath behind Cap Fréhel - spitting at me. It was that personal, too. It wasn't spitting at anyone else. It was looking at me. In the eye. Giving me a sort of come-here-sonny-boy look. Perhaps it knew I was English. But despite the possibility of anglophobic Breton vipers, we soldier on. Pluck, that's the thing. Keep your nerve up. And get the porters walking a few feet ahead.

Segal (age 2&¾) sits in yet another puddle. He looks pretty pleased with himself this time. Perhaps he reckons each puddle is an ocean. Either way, he appears to have acquired a taste for this puddle-sitting business.

As we approach the antenna, Samson (age 4&¼) decides he's frightened of the looming red and white mast. I'm not sure why. Perhaps he's got a hotline to the Front de Libération de la Bretagne. In any case, I can see that Roc'h Ruz (385.01 metres, maybe), which is a little way ahead of us off to our right, is surrounded by dense heath, the sort that would be just perfect for a viper, while Roc'h Trédudon (383.29 metres, maybe), which lies back to our left, has several narrow paths leading to the top. The view looks better, too. And even if Roc'h Ruz was further from the menacing antenna and more easily accessible, by the time we reached it, some meddling governmental body would probably have changed the hierarchy all over again, and there'd be a new number one. So we'll settle for Trédudon. I'm not proud. I can pocket pluck when required.

C'est très haute la montagne!

"*C'est très haute la montagne,*" says Samson (age 4&¼) once again as we struggle onto the 'summit'. I guess that's how the Bretons do it, persuade themselves from an early age by repetition.

"*C'est très haute,*" I murmur to myself, "*très haute, très haute . . . .*" I'm not sure I believe this yet, but it's worth trying, at least for the purposes of research.

"*Tire toi de la, je peux pas passer dans la montagne*" -move yourself from there, I can't pass in the mountain- says Segal (age 2&¾), then promptly sits in a fourth puddle.

There are no snakes, as it happens. Just a baby salamander and a view that's really rather fine. It is, of course, essentially the same as the view from the car-park, but now that I think about it, having laboured up plenty of thousand-metre climbs in my time, it's actually quite pleasant to go 'up' a 'mountain' so very easily. These mountains of the mind have much to recommend them. They're certainly ideal for introducing kids to the life-enhancing euphoria that is the essential defining ingredient of any mountain worthy of the name. And if you repeat the native porter's wise dictum often enough (*C'est très haute la montagne*), you may well come to believe it yourself. It's addictive this, so addictive we 'climb' two more 'mountains' on the way 'down'.

As Samson (age 4&¼) says: "*On s'amuse bien dans la montagne.*"

Indeed, we do, even, perhaps especially, when it is an imaginary mountain.

9. Thin Tuesday: This Sporting Life

ACCESS - **Guerlesquin** is on the border between Finistère and Côtes d'Armor. Access via the N12 and D42.

This sporting life

Mardi Gras - what do those words suggest? Tropical gaiety? Sun-kissed beaches? Waving palms? Beating drums? Buxom girls dressed in a bit of string and a spray of feathers? Lithe-limbed young men with six packs in the most improbable places? How about grey skies and a bunch of old blokes from the north of a village confronting a bunch of old blokes from the south of the village for a game of bowls?

The gamut of Breton games is not immense, but given the limitations imposed by climate, toil, time and poverty, they've done as well as could be expected. The best known sport is *gouren*, or Breton wrestling, though in fact it's not strictly 'Breton' as it also exists in Scotland and Cornwall. Originally a martial art in the truest sense, *gouren* began as a military discipline practiced by medieval nobles and even kings: Arthur, Henry VIII, and François I were all said to be notable wrestlers, though I suppose people weren't exactly queuing up to tell Henry VIII he was a flabby butterball who couldn't wrestle his way out of a paper bag; that said, François I implied as much, since he won a *lamm* (the act of pinning your opponent's shoulders to the ground) against the English monarch. The sport's patrician pretensions have long since disappeared, but there are still certain chivalric rituals to be observed before a match (or at least as chivalric as you can get about dumping somebody on his back), and large-scale, team-based tournaments involve strategic considerations (concerning who challenges whom when) that are not so very far removed from the niceties of collective dueling.

Otherwise, there are various bowling and quoits games like *quilles* (the prototype bowling), *boul-ten* (the Breton version of *boules* or *petanque*), *palets, galoches bigouden,* and *birinic* which was originally a bar game determining who would pay for the drinks. The region's agricultural and labouring past is reflected in trials of strength, such as *ar men pouez*, that's "Chuck the rock as far as you can, Obelix", and *an ahel karr* AKA lifting a fifty kilo axle-rod as often as you can in a set time. In the general category of games measuring might, *ar voutelenn* is a sort of pole vault except, instead of jumping himself, the competitor pitches a sheaf of hay over a raised bar; *redadeg gant ur samm* is a relay race in which the 'batons' are fifty kilo sacks of grain; and *bazh-yod* is an elaborate version of a tug-of-war involving a plank, a big stick, and a lot of grunting and groaning.

Apart from the Breton version of hockey, *bazhig kamm,* there was only one real team game, and that was *soule*, the ancestor of rugby and Gaelic football. This deeply alarming 'sport' was the ultimate expression of the them-next-door-in-the-next-country mentality. In a match of *soule*, two villages, I mean entire villages, would vie to get a leather ball, variously filled with tow, bran, straw, sawdust, or horse shit (anything that came to hand really) back to their home-base. Why so alarming? Basically because the game had only one 'rule' and that was "anything goes". And anything did go, too. There was one notorious 'match' at Pont l'Abbé in which fifty men drowned! Academics trace *soule* back to ancient sun cults, the two communities competing for possession of the parturient god, but as far as I can see it was just a handy pretext for giving one another a good hiding. The 'game' (such words are horribly inadequate here) largely disappeared for obvious reasons after the Great War. It was revived under the aegis of the Nazis during the Second World War, presumably because the occupiers reckoned it better if the Bretons were hammering one another rather than their uninvited guests, enjoyed another brief, formalized revival in the sixties, and once again in 2003. Despite its them-next-door-in-the-next-country appeal, I somehow doubt it will become a regular event again, but if you do see a 'match' advertised on your travels, I suggest you buy yourself a crash-helmet and a white flag, inform your next of kin and get ready to run if it all turns nasty.

In the summer there are plenty of festivals and tournaments celebrating the less life-threatening Celtic sports, though from the reports I've heard, often as not the stars of these events are big-limbed Scottish men tossing their cabers about and getting the local women in a tizzy concerning their wildly flapping kilts and what, or what may not, be lurking about beneath them. Otherwise, there's a tour of bars offering traditional Breton games in Ille-et-Vilaine (www.jeuxbretons.org), and two centres dedicated to Breton sports, the Ti ar Gouren *Maison de la Lutte* at Berrien (www.gouren.com) and the *Maison des Jeux Bretons* at Saint Jean Trolimon (www.saintjeantrolimon.fr), both in Finistère.

Personally, I'm disinclined to have people chucking me on the ground (I don't flatter myself that I'd be doing the chucking), so the *Maison de la Lutte* is not for me. As for the summer festivals, I don't doubt the nether regions of big-limbed Scottish men are all very lovely if you like that sort of thing, but it's not a source of interest I've ever felt inclined to cultivate. No, what I want is something that is at once non-lethal and removed from the standard tourist circuit, a more eccentric but sedate sample of the Breton sporting life. Which is why we've opted to bump about the *Championnat du Monde de Boulou Pok*, which takes place every Mardi Gras at Guerlesquin.

Guerlesquin is a "*Petit Cité de Caractère de Bretagne*", the name of an organization set up in 1975 to promote twenty of the prettiest towns in Brittany. Yes, I know, sounds ghastly, doesn't it? One of those 'initiatives' that dishearten rather than stimulate. At best, a bit of mutual back-scratching and the publication of some banal little pamphlets, at worst, some bright bod dashing about with demonic energy painting everything with the same brush and insisting on a spurious uniformity. Branding, I believe they call it. In fact, it has been a great success and the participating towns are generally as full of character as the title suggests, so when you see a sign indicating a *Petite Cité de Caractère de Bretagne*, make a detour and take time to visit it. You won't be disappointed.

Guerlesquin is certainly a place of character. The annual *Boulou Pok* bash is not, for instance, the only world championship they've staged in recent years. In 2003, the town hosted the second *Championnat du Monde d'Insultes en Breton*. Sadly, this event seems to have disappeared from the calendar. Personally, I wouldn't have understood a word of it, but there's something rather heart-warming about the idea of a group of people getting together in all good nature for the express purpose of insulting each other.

Boulou Pok is not quite so eccentric, not quite, but this variant of *boules* intrigues me because it's not actually played anywhere else in the world, not even anywhere else in Brittany. In the circumstances, staging a Championnat du Monde is rather a nice touch, making the United States' allegedly 'World' Series look quite wide-ranging in its search for competitors. What's more, it doesn't actually seem to have occurred to anybody that having a non-contact game of skill that requires no unusual strength, yet sticking with the traditional rule that women aren't allowed to play, might seem the teensiest bit reactionary in the modern world, so I'll be interested to see what the atmosphere's like. Are there going to be a lot of scowling ladies lurking behind doors with rolling pins? Or gangs of rowdy young girls getting plastered and tossing the odd *insulte en Breton* at these unreconstructed blokes, even perhaps burning their bras to bounce Guerlesquin into the new millennium? Or does everybody think this is normal? To cap it all, the basic premise of team building for Boulou Pok is perfect for a region separated by so many conflicting customs and different orientations: it's the North against the South.

The men in the town are divided into two teams according to which side of the square they live on or, in cases of doubt, the orientation of their front door, the Southerners being those with a north-facing door, the Northerners with a door directed more toward the south. I'm sure you'll have spotted the flaw in this. It's highly unlikely that you're going to get equal numbers on each team and entirely possible that one team will so outnumber the other that the minority side will end up worn to a frazzle. Nobody seems to worry about this, though. The Bretons know life isn't fair and see no point in trying to construct a game that so manifestly runs counter to everyday experience.

Apart from a handful of manorial homes and the eighteenth century *Présidial*, a fortified gaol and court-house which dominates the central square, there are no major monuments in Guerlesquin, no single site that lures the tourists in, but it wins out over many better known towns due to the harmony of its architecture. Once an important market town and still home to a weekly cattle market, it centres on what is essentially a long tripartite square, the lower third being a public garden, the middle part a car-park, and the upper third a tree-lined oblong of well-trodden dirt, which is where I presume the festivities are to take place. And judging by the town's website, the festivities are going to be considerable.

The day begins with a Mass in memory of former players of Boulou Pok, after which there's a break for elevenses (*un café bien arrosé*, according to the website, literally 'well-watered', figuratively 'laced with something strong'), after which the match takes place, followed by the *gwin bian*, or 'small wine', in which the two teams make up over a glass or three, and the *gwin bras*, or 'big wine' banquet involving the whole town. With so much *gwin* going about, I'm sure this must be a grand event, and my first concern as we approach is whether we'll be able to park or not.

As we drive into the square, though, nothing seems to be happening. There's plenty of parking room, the usual moderate amount of through traffic, and no sign of anything very festive whatsoever. Then we see it. It's not very festive, but about fifty people are gathered in the upper half of the square, on the nearside of the *Présidial*. This is not precisely what I was expecting. I had a vague notion there'd be jostling crowds and hundred-strong teams. There's no mistaking it, though. The crowd . . .

The présidial at Guerlesquin

perhaps I should say the crowdette is clustered together to form an impromptu, fan-like alley, at one end of which players are taking turns to lob the Boulou Pok 'ball', a lead-weighted, yo-yo shaped lump of wood.

The two teams are identified by badges, gold for the North and red for the South, and several old guys are wearing traditional costumes - clogs, black waistcoats, and black hats with a broad upturned brim. In fact, nearly all the people here are old guys. There are one or two younger blokes, loudly joshing their elders in an attempt to stage an impromptu World Championship of Insults at the same time, a few, very few women, but for the most part, they're all men, the average age must be about seventy, and it's blindingly obvious that, far from being an eagerly anticipated event involving the entire town, this is a largely marginal activity. So very marginal, it's clearly never occurred to the womenfolk that they might protest at their unholy exclusion from the game. The few women in attendance watch the contest with bemused interest and occasionally pat their menfolk on the shoulder when they've done well, much as one would a successful child on prize-giving day. Meanwhile, the rest of Guerlesquin is carrying on as normal, going about its daily business, buying baguettes, digging holes in the road, delivering letters, devising ways of earning a mite, and so forth.

Nonetheless, those who are participating are doing their best, making up with enthusiasm what they lack in numbers, and the shouts and compliments on good shots are loud and excited. The raucous compliments maybe because another symptom of the enthusiasm is that the flat-sided ball has to be lobbed high to reach the half-sphere that serves as a target, and is frequently flung so wildly that those gathered at the target end need to move fast if they don't want to be knee-capped or get an impromptu nose job. In the circumstances, a well-aimed shot is eminently praiseworthy. But despite all the shouts and nimble footwork, there's no denying that this World Championship is not exactly the talk of the town. They may have been playing the game for five hundred years, but it's hard to believe the website's claim that the annual match is the subject of sustained speculation for the preceding six months and intense dissection for the ensuing six months.

I guess we're having an Asterix moment here. Remember when we went to Erquy looking for Asterix and he wasn't there? So it is in Guerlesquin: not so much Mardi Gras as Thin Tuesday. True, there are a few old boys wearing funny hats, but they're not exactly the samba carnival queen with the feathers and the legs and the rest of the bits and the startlingly exiguous underwear. Yet I'm not entirely disappointed.

The word that comes to mind looking at the costumes and the ancient, obscure and apparently declining game, is that damning epithet of the modern travel industry, 'folklore'. It normally means something dead that's been dressed up and staged as a spectacle to divert the tourists for

What price a string bikini?

half-an-hour. Boulou Pok isn't dead. It's not very lively, I admit. But it persists. And it hasn't been dressed up and staged as a spectacle. These people aren't doing this for anyone else. There isn't anyone else apart from us. They're doing it for themselves, carrying on in their own sweet way because that's the way they've always done it. I don't suppose it will ever rival Rio, not even if they get the girls in and go for the feathers and string-bikinis. But as testimony to the tenacity of Breton culture and Breton customs, it is commendable. And there's always the *gwin bras* to look forward to.

10. Made in Brittany: The Typical Frenchman

ACCESS - **Roscoff** is in northern Finistère, just north of St. Pol de Leon. Once there, follow the signs for the **'Vieux Port'** and **'Gare SNCF'**.

Defining Image

Typical Frenchman, ten seconds, what do you see? Stripy T-shirt? Black beret? Denim work pants? Drooping fag? Bike? Baguette? Bottle of *rouge*? Strings of onions? Chances are at least one of those items appeared in your stereotype, and I wouldn't mind betting the bike, T-shirt and onions were in there somewhere. Yet these three accessories are parts of the portrait that ninety percent of the French population find utterly baffling. The baguette, bottle and tobacco, they can understand, the denims and beret are fine, even at a pinch the stripy T-shirt, but what's this business with the bike and the onions? Frogs' legs, yes; *escargots*, yes; the diseased liver of a gluttonous goose, OK; but onions?!

Stereotypes are tricky, of course. When my partner and I first met, I told her my French brother-in-law was a 'typical' Frenchman, meaning tall, elegant, witty, handsome and charming, a slightly more saturnine version of Sacha Distel. She immediately imagined a small, pinched little creature with tight lips, a prissy moustache, and a regrettable penchant for Jean-Marie Le Pen. Likewise when a friend, naively but sincerely trying to flatter her, told her she was 'typically Parisian', she was mortally affronted. There are dozens of French stereotypes ranging from the saucy to the oily, the debonair to the downright grubby, but that classic figure sketched in the first paragraph remains one of the most enduring. The funny thing is, it comes not from the-big-bit-stuck-on-the-hind-end, but from Brittany, and not from Brittany as a whole, but from a handful of towns and villages tucked into a headland facing Plymouth. The stereotypical 'Frenchman' was an economic migrant from Roscoff, Santec, Cleder and St. Pol-de-Léon in the northern extremity of Finistère, a man who had probably never visited the-big-bit-stuck-on-the-hind-end, and possibly didn't even speak French. In some cases, he was also illiterate and underage, and he came from a region that was in the grip of a puritanical fundamentalist faith. If the British media heard about him today, there'd be an absolute outcry.

Roscoff is, in many ways, a very English town. Indeed, it was built because of us. Not, it must be said, because the Roscovites wanted to be as near as they could to Good Old Blighty. On the contrary, they wanted Good Old Blighty kept as far away as possible, because Good Old Blighty was making rather too much of a habit of hopping across the Channel and burning Good Old Roscoff to the ground. So the locals decamped from the town's original setting in the wide, readily accessible bay to the southwest, and relocated to the present site, where the ring of rocks framing the headland made a natural fortification, a redoubt to which both Mary Stuart and Bonnie Prince Charlie were later pleased to beat a discreet retreat.

It is not, however, the productive potency of English aggression that gives Roscoff its veneer of Britishness. The lay-out of the place suggests it, too. On the fringes of the town, for instance, where the residential area leeches into the countryside, tiny lanes wide enough for a single vehicle -and that one pretty narrow- wind between pocket-sized fields, and all they need is a tweed-skirted Miss Marple or an immaculate half-timbered Morris Minor to send us back in time to a fantasy of 1950s Britain. There's a red double-decker bus parked beside a roundabout on the edge of town, one of the main hotels is the Hotel Angleterre, another is named Le Brittany, a Brit numbers himself among Roscoff's principal wine-merchants, the Auld Alliance is commemorated in the Pizzeria Mary Stuart and, as one approaches along the D769, a flurry of signs advertise 'Wine and Beer Supermarkets - English Staff'. Roscoff is, of course, a major ferry port for passengers traveling between Brittany and Britain, but the association between the two is far older than the ferry service, and far more pacific and positive than the usual Perfidious Albion prejudices would suggest.

Temperate and fertile, the band of farmland along the northern coast of Finistère is famed for its agricultural produce, notably the region's first and best new potatoes, which come from Ile de Batz, the 'sand' carrots of Santec, and above all the sweet *oignons rosés* or pink onions grown between the Baie de Morlaix and the Grève de Goulven. It ought, by rights, to be one of the wealthiest areas in Brittany, and for some it always has been, those lucky enough to own large tracts of land or belonging to the merchant class enjoying considerable riches. But affluent landowners and prosperous businessmen are rarely good news for those fluffing about trying to survive at the other end of the economic scale, whatever trickle-down theorists may claim, and high population growth has generally ensured the inhabitants of Léon included a large number of landless day-labourers and impoverished farmers dependent on credit and rented land. In 1828, the domestic food market in France was in crisis, so an enterprising young farmer from Santec, Henri Olivier, decided to take a chance on selling his produce abroad. With four friends, he chartered a boat, loaded it with onions and sailed for Plymouth. Within a week, he was back, the entire cargo sold. Yet it was more than a boatload of onions Olivier had exported. It was an image. Unwittingly, he had begun a process that would create the kind of instantly recognizable icon for which a modern corporation would give its eye teeth - or at least the eye teeth of several low ranking employees.

Make your way to the Ty Pierre café behind the Vieux Port in Roscoff and you will be at the heart of the place where all this inadvertent image building began. It was a development that would have a defining impact on Roscoff and its history. Indeed, to reach the bar you may well have passed through the Rue des Johnnies, named in honour of the onion sellers that set off from here and became, the onions they sold notwithstanding, Roscoff's most famous export. The canny Leonards quickly learned from Olivier's success and soon Companies of onion producers were sending shiploads of onions and onion sellers across the channel. So many word-of-mouth deals were done over a *petit coup de rouge* at Ty Pierre's, a register was kept at the café, and gradually an elaborate organizational superstructure evolved to maintain the blossoming business, including agents dealing with the more recondite aspects of licensing, finance, customs and excise.

Not that you'd know this from a casual glance about the bar, because it is another fine example of Breton business practice: a marketing opportunity ignored with magnificent disdain. The Leonards may like money, but they like to make it from honest toil, not by promoting some paltry image of the past. Dotted about the bar, there are a few sepia-tinted photos and enlarged postcards portraying old boats and scenes from the port, but there is no stripy T-shirted barman, no Burger des Johnnies on the menu, not even a single blessed onion hanging from the ceiling. It's just a nice little café that has ignored the chintzy makeovers the tourist trade so often entails and remains what it always has been, a local bar for local people with local tastes.

The Johnnies got their name as a result of British laziness and the fact that the Bretons have never been terribly inventive when baptizing their children. Until recently, names not on the calendar were not allowed in France, and in Brittany everyone has traditionally been called a variant of Jean, Pierre, Yves, Marie, and a handful of the other more popular saints' names. Go into a Breton bar to this day and shout "Pierre!" and the chances are half the men in the bar will turn to look at you. Well, don't, actually. You'd feel pretty silly afterwards, but you get my point. By the same token, everyone in Brittany will have an anecdote about phoning a friend and getting the wrong number:

- Allô, Marie?
- Oui, Jean?
- Oui, comment ça va?
- Très bien. Jean-Marie est un peu malade. Mais ça va.
- Et Jean-François? Il va bien.
- Oui. Et chez toi? Comment va Marie-Pierre?
- Très bien. Elle est avec Jean-Michel en ce moment.
- Et Jeanne-Françoise?
- Egalement. Elle et Yves-Marie sont partis en vacances chez Jean-Pierre. Mais, dis donc, Marie! Est-ce-que tu a quelque chose? Ta voix n'est pas la même. *Your voice isn't the same.*
- La tienne non plus, Jean. *Yours neither, Jean.*

They have, of course, being talking to complete strangers who just happen to have the same names and a family with the same names as that of the intended interlocutor.

Seeing all these foreigners called Jean-this-that-and-the-other, the Brits took the easy option and dubbed them all 'Johnnies', opting for the diminutive because so many of the onion-sellers were very young. It was not uncommon to start at ten years old, or even younger, and many would-be Johnnies came over with their father for a season to learn the ropes and help out while they were still small children. Some went to school in Britain, others didn't, nearly all returned to their mothers speaking an extraordinary pigeon, mixing Breton, French and English.

Look across the port from the Ty Pierre café and you will see another significant site: perched on a rocky outcrop overlooking the harbour is the tiny whitewashed Chapelle de Sainte Barbe, dedicated to the patron saint of onion sellers. The *pardon* of Sainte Barbe takes place on the third Sunday in July, when the main onion harvest is over, and it used to mark the departure of the Johnnies for Britain. Prayers would be said for a good season and a safe return, and thereafter the exodus would begin, with up to a dozen ships sailing on each tide for the next few weeks. Those left behind would walk to the Pointe de Sainte Barbe when their loved ones embarked, and sing songs of praise to secure the saint's protection as the schooners and dundees negotiated the straits between the headland and the camel-backed islet of Ty Saozon, The House of the Saxons.

The Johnnies needed protection, too. Not, I hasten to add, because the English were so bloody horrible. It's true, many Johnnies preferred to sell to their Celtic cousins in Scotland and, above all, Wales, where the language is very close to Breton, but for the most part they were no less welcome in England, and comparable ties of fidelity and friendship were built up over the years (a Johnny never changed his patch and the 'address book' of clients that they carried in their heads would be passed down from father to son). No, the reason they needed the saint's intercession was because it was such tough work. It may look very picturesque swanning about being a stereotype, but you try lugging around 100 pounds of onions strung from a stick on your shoulder - *and* keeping a ready smile with which to charm the housewives. Even when bicycles were introduced in the 1920s, they didn't make life that much easier, since the load was simply doubled or even tripled, and you still had to sell everything by nightfall or the master of your company would be sending you out without your supper (itself possibly no more than bread and onion), and telling you not to come back to your lodgings until you'd sold the lot. And what lodgings they were: leaky, often condemned buildings, in which the onions got the driest and best rooms, and the Johnnies frequently slept on bare, damp floors. And then, at the end of the six month stint, there was the trip home with all the customary perils of a sea voyage, even a relatively short one. There were frequent shipwrecks, most tragically the sinking of the Hilda in 1905, when over seventy Johnnies drowned, condemning whole communities to penury as well as mourning, since at that time the

Johnnies carried their season's earnings in money belts, so that an entire year's income was lost along with the principal breadwinner. Many of those who died succumbed to hypothermia in the freezing November seas, and one of the most abiding and horrific images of the disaster is that of sixty-nine bodies being washed up at Saint-Cast, bobbing ashore in their life-jackets, still upright in a ghastly parody of life.

The hardships did not stop when the Johnnies reached home, either, for to this day, being an itinerant onion-seller is not recognized as a *métier* by the French state, so that anybody who embarks for Britain knows he will get no social security cover in France. In many ways, the French social security system is the envy of the world, but it is an extraordinarily rigid affair, preventing for instance someone who has a certified micro-business from doing a different, intermittent job on the side. If your occupation isn't recognized at all, you're done for.

Doubtless the lack of official recognition was one reason why many Johnnies worked seven-decade careers, crossing the Channel year after year, pedaling and peddling their onions into their eighties. But want of a pension was not the only reason they kept working. The seasonal migration was also maintained by what I can only call loyalty to a way of life. For all the hardships, the Johnnies learned a genuine affection for Britain and British ways, and, even if they did retire, would often return to their former haunts to visit customers who had become friends, perhaps selling a few onions in a leisurely fashion for the sons who had taken over their patch, but otherwise indulging in the easy-going gossip and the invitations to take a jar that time and economic imperatives had obliged them to refuse during their working lives. Many were fond of a British pint and would badmouth French lager with all the fervor, verve and vituperative vitality of a CAMRA fanatic banging on about Watneys Red Barrel, while the afternoon *copotee* has become a Roscovite institution in its own right.

All this and much more will be detailed if you visit the *Maison des Johnnies et de L'Oignon Rosé* on Rue Brizeux in the centre of Roscoff, just west of the railway station. They are most emphatic about this being a *'maison'* rather than a *'musée'*, because the history of the Johnnies is not over yet and there are still twenty or so men (they were nearly always men, though there were a few 'Jennies', too) making the crossing each year. Visitors from  the-big-bit-stuck-on-the-hind-end are often puzzled by the notion of a 'Johnny' and the museum guide even pauses when she first mentions the name to make sure everyone knows what we're talking about - and talking about it is the key. There's a wonderful collection of old farm tools in the courtyard: ploughs, harrows, presses, churns, barrows, carts, tackle, lamps, pitchforks, hay rakes, axes, adzes, picks, planes, mallets, scythes ... you name it, they've got it, all jumbled together in a happy chaos of apparatus from which much pleasure can be taken puzzling out the purpose of individual implements; but as far as artifacts go, that's pretty much it. This is not a museum of objects that are no longer used and have lost their meaning through neglect, but a celebration of a way of life evoked in words and images based on the testimony of people, real people, who have known the culture from birth, or even lived the life of a Johnny.

The guide is excellent, explaining the marvellous properties of the *oignon rosé*, which not only tastes good and won't make you weep because of its low acidity, but, if the aficionados are to believed, is a cure-all, boasting antiseptic, diuretic and antidiabetic properties, preventing cancer and cardiovascular disease, and treating respiratory, digestive and urinary problems. Once you've heard the catalogue of everything it's good for, you begin to understand why your average Johnny always had a fag in his mouth: he was going to live forever if he wasn't careful. Some of them seem to have had a good stab at eternity because the highlight of the exposition (apart, perhaps, from the excellent leaflet they give you detailing tempting *oignon rosé* recipes) is a touching film of old Johnnies talking about their lives, followed by the chance to meet some of those who are, or were until very recently, still making the journey north. This is a story of people meeting people, not people using things, and it is all the better for that.

So, what about that stereotypical image? 'Allo, 'Allo? It's something the younger guys crossing the Channel are acutely aware of. They know they are selling themselves as much as their onions and they know that, no matter how good their English, it behooves them to cultivate the sort of lip-pouting pantomime and heavily mannered accents that helped Maurice Chevalier, Yves Montand, Sacha Distel and Charles Aznavour develop their careers overseas. A good Gallic shrug doesn't go amiss, either. They stick with the old sit-up-and-beg bikes, too, sometimes without a chain (occasionally without tyres!), but not always just as an ornamental prop, for when you're selling onions in London, the profit margins are too tight to allow for a market stall or even accommodation nowadays. Sleeping in their van with their onions, they emerge during the day to wheel their laden bikes about the crowded streets of the capital, and wherever they go, they are sure to draw an audience. And though they may wear baseball caps at home, the working uniform demands a beret, either the *beret rond* of northern Finistére or, if, as one Johnny points out, you're "not from round here" (i.e. he's from another 'country'), the big floppy beret of the south. Look back at the pictures of Johnnies from the past and you'll see that the berets, bikes, fags and, of course, strings of onions that established the stereotype are pretty well ubiquitous. The only thing that's missing is that stripy Breton T-shirt, the one sold in every tourist shop, chandlers and sports suppliers in Brittany. In fact, this was originally the T-shirt of French naval cadets, subsequently adopted by leisure sailors, then by the St. Tropez set, and finally by pretty much everyone. I can only suppose it entered the popular image because sailors were the other Frenchmen seen most often in Britain and it was subsequently conflated with the Johnnies, for they were farming not seafaring men, despite their regular cross-channel sailings.

It's something of a novelty when you're bumping about Brittany to find a community where people are actively fond of Albion despite all its perfidy, and you may be beginning to wonder whether this little corner of Brittany is exempted from the prevailing clichés about the region. Don't worry. The Léonards may have overcome their historic antipathy toward the English, but when it comes to near neighbours, it's business as usual. The residents of Santec and Roscoff both claim Henri Olivier, the first Johnny, as their own, and can get quite vexed about the matter. As it happens, both have some justification because though Olivier did indeed come from Santec, the village was at that time part of the *commune* of Roscoff. Go back a little further in history and you will find that the church of Notre-Dame-de-Kroaz-Braz in Roscoff was built in the sixteenth century for the express purpose of liberating the town from the episcopal grip of St.-Pol-de-Léon, on which the seaport had previously depended for its baptisms, weddings and burials. And as for St.-Pol-de-Léon itself, just look at the skyline. It is dominated by three steeples, the two smaller ones belonging to the cathedral, the taller one to the immense Chapelle du Kreisker. Conventional histories tell you Kreisker was rebuilt in its present form by Bishop Guillaume Ferron in the fifteenth century, but local legend holds it was the product of ecclesiastical rivalry, and is so very tall because the abbot in charge of it wanted a bigger steeple than the bishop! To be honest, I wouldn't be all that surprised to find that, if you started poking about and asking questions, everyone in the area would agree that the *oignon rosé* is the finest onion in the world, but each, when pressed, would claim the very best are to be found in their particular parish, not next door in the next country. They might well sell you a string of onions to prove it, too.

The Breton Johnnies were the most effective ambassadors of the entente-cordiale and became one of the few true 'French' institutions of Perfidious Albion. The great days of the mass summer exodus are past, but the culture they created continues to this day, not in some dusty museum peopled with waxworks and decked out with archaic relics, but in the minds and lives of real people, and in the recipes they developed. The names alone are enough to make your mouth water: *crème d'oignons de Roscoff et croûtons au gingembre*; *oignons rosés farcis au riz et au jambon*; *tourteau farci aux oignons de Roscoff*; *tarte à l'oignon de Roscoff et au lard*; *médaillons de lotte aux lardons et oignons rosés de Roscoff*; *fricassée d'ormeaux au plat;* the list goes on, but I'm sure you get the picture. Go, buy some onions. You won't regret it.

11. Flânerie at the 'End Of The World'

ACCESS - **Brest** is at the western end of the main east-west dual carriageway in northern Brittany, the N12. Parking is easiest around the **Place de la Liberté** in the 'Centre Ville'. Street plans are available from the Tourist Information Office on Place de la Liberté or can be downloaded in advance from www.cerv.fr/fr/docs/centre_ville_brest.pdf

La Place des Portes, Brest

In the last couple of centuries, western countries have devised various solutions to the novel problem of how one should go about walking for pleasure. It was a quandary quite alien to previous generations. In the past, people walked because they had to, because they were too poor not to, because there was no food or work or fun where they were, because salvation lay at the end of the pilgrim's path, because there was a bloody great army looming out of the wilderness and it was as well to get the hell out of there . . . for any number of reasons; but they didn't walk for pleasure. Confronted with unprecedented leisure and the puzzling notion that the body was more than a mere briefcase for carrying the soul about, modern man had to develop fresh rituals to keep his feet moving.

Thus the Great British Rambler cultivated a taste for roaming aimlessly, frequently incompetently, across open country at great length, getting hopelessly lost, entangled in brambles, taking absurdly roundabout routes, diverting down every dead-end and by-way, dropping off the odd cliff-face, following his own sweet, crooked way, and loving every minute of it. Outward Bound American Hikers, meanwhile, were busy-busy-busy energetically driving straight lines directly over mountains, across deserts, through great forests regardless of what was in the way, because everything was just so damn big that if they didn't make a beeline for whatever lay on the other side, they'd never get there at all. In Germany, the romantic *wandervogel* movement was all about bare knees, big shorts, blind obedience, lusty vitality and invading Poland. And throughout the Mediterranean, variations were developed of the *paseo*, a formal dance of vanity and mutual admiration, in which polite society paraded up and down a promenade or esplanade, assessing the talent and paying one another elaborate, ceremonial compliments. The French, however, were having none of this country-loving stuff favoured by their northern cousins, and precious little of the meeting and greeting that evolved in the south; instead, they invented *flânerie*.

The principal attraction of *flânerie* is that nobody can quite agree what it is, so it fits in nicely with the controversialist traditions of French intellectual life. The name comes from *flâner*, meaning to idle or dawdle about, but the term was refined by the symbolist poet Charles Baudelaire and the Francophile literary critic Walter Benjamin to mean a leisurely city stroll in which the walker hopes, through happenstance and watching the world go by, to understand something of the nature of urban living, becoming in the process "a botanist of the sidewalk". It is, then, an essentially urban phenomenon, touched by dilettantism and a desire to engage with the world through chance encounters and casual observation. That's one way of looking at it. Alternatively, you can take the vision of La Société des Flâneurs Sans Frontières who promote their website (www.the.flaneur.co.uk) as an "open forum for Anarcho-Absurdists, Revolutionary Sybarites, Alchemical Hazardistas and Urban Arcadians". You see what I mean about it being hard to define. It's urban, yes, it involves idling about, yes, but beyond that the concept is a misfits' charter, and can mean just about anything you want it to mean. Originally the preserve of Parisian boulevardiers, *flânerie* has gone global, so to get an idea of what it involves, we're going to bump about Brest.

Brest is a city with a dismal reputation. Discounting the estuary anchorages of Nantes and Bordeaux, it is France's only natural and above all its most westerly oceanic port, as a result of which it has been a vital naval base ever since Roman times. The history of Brest is in many ways therefore a history of war, one in which the English inevitably had their say, holding the town for over fifty years in the fourteenth century. But for once, we're not the principal villains, not quite, though we did conspire in the events that lead to the city's present poor reputation. In 1941, the Germans built a massive submarine base at Brest, making it a prime target for Bomber Command. At the end of the war, of 16,500 buildings, seven thousand had been destroyed, five thousand were condemned, and the rest had been damaged. The only unscathed buildings were the Vauban *château* and the U-boat base. Of 115,000 residents in 1940, only 2,000 were still there in 1944. The physical city no longer existed. All that remained was a site and what Jonathan Raban calls the 'soft' city, the place that is created by the way individual people relate to it, and which lives more in the imagination than the physical attributes of the 'hard' city. Brest had disappeared from the map, leaving behind a remembered city the refugees carried in their minds and hearts.

Post-war reconstruction didn't do much to remedy the want of an infrastructure to match the city of the mind, for whereas places like St. Malo were painstakingly rebuilt according to the original plans, creating a simulacrum of the past that is remarkably successful, the burghers of Brest had other concerns than aesthetics. This was a big commercial port and commerce demanded accommodation and fast. You couldn't ponce about making things pretty. You just had to get on with it. The first phase of building was of temporary Nissan huts, known locally as *baraques*, a few of which exist to this day. The next phase was the building of blocks of flats throughout the fifties and sixties. You've probably guessed the rest. Those two words, 'flats' and 'sixties', say it all. Add to that the fact that the Rade de

Brest is like a hungry mouth gobbling up all the weather the Atlantic cares to chuck at it, and you will have a fair idea of Brest's reputation. It's known to be a wet, grey place of unprepossessing tower blocks. That, at least, is the standard image, and it's one reflected in the most famous poem celebrating the city, Jacques Prevert's *Rappelle Toi Barbara*.

In the poem; to read both the original and an English translation, see "http://xtream.online.fr/Prevert/beauties.html

Prevert recalls a chance pre-war meeting of young lovers on the rain soaked streets of Brest, how they smiled and fell into one another's arms, happy and heedless even though "il pleuvait sans cesse sur Brest", it rained ceaselessly on Brest. Evoking the sights of the old city, the Rue de Siam, the sea, the Arsenal, the Ouessant boat, all of it drenched in a rain at once 'happy and wise', he turns the downpour into a celebration of love and life and youth, and the fact that "il pleuvait sans cesse sur Brest" only seems to add to the festive insouciance of the young lovers' encounter. But then the poem takes a darker turn and, though the refrain remains the same, "il pleut sans cesse sur Brest", another rain has intervened, the wartime rain of blood and steel and fire, and the young man who fell into Barbara's arms is perhaps no longer alive, and no matter how much it may pleut sans cesse sur Brest, there's no washing away the wounds of war because everything is broken and wasted and nothing is the same anymore. Il pleut sans cesse sur Brest. It's a wonderfully evocative work, but the burghers of Brest must have greeted it with about as much warmth as the City Fathers of Slough welcomed John Betjeman's wish that 'friendly bombs' would flatten the place. I said the poem celebrates the city, but in truth it is a lament for the city that was and will never be again.

No doubt about it, it's an evocative refrain, but though the assonance and sibilance sound very nice, all that stuff about *il pleut sans cesse sur Brest*, didn't help the town's reputation at all. Not that Prevert was concerned with reputations. I said the poem celebrates the city, but in truth it is a lament for the city that was and will never be again.

Even if the rebuilding programme had been a miracle of imaginative reconstruction, it is unlikely that Brest would have garnered the tourist trade that came to St. Malo. This was still a big, industrial port, a ship building centre, and home to France's nuclear fleet. It was never going to be the sort of place to pull in the tourists. Indeed, until very recently, visits to the Arsenal naval yard were restricted to French nationals. They didn't want anyone from Perfidious Albion snooping about in there. Moreover, Brest has always been a place apart, a secular military stronghold in a land of pious peasants, a city that was republican when everyone else in the region was royalist, and francophone when the rest of Finistère still spoke Breton. It is also, of course, a frontier town, out on the edges of things, part of the fringe where people take refuge when they no longer feel comfortable at the centre. It's a city of misfits. Perfect, then, for *flânerie*.

If you care to confirm Brest's eccentricity, check out www.allegrofortissimo.com, the site of Allegro Fortissimo, a Brest based organization that campaigns on behalf of fat people. They arrange outings, fashion parades, dance classes, gym sessions and social activities, all specifically aimed at the principal felons of the new millennium, The Obese; above all though, they militate against discrimination, promoting positive images of those literal misfits, the men and women who are merely wider and larger than is considered wholesome. Best of all, they stage *La Journée Internationale Sans Régime*. In a world so obsessed with weight loss you've got to be virtually transparent to achieve the prototype of beauty, a city that can initiate International Non-Diet Day has got to be worth visiting.

Flânerie developed in Paris during the 1850s and 1860s when Haussmann's reconstruction opened up broad boulevards and bridges, making the city accessible and visible to the dedicated idler, and though the results were less happy architecturally, that is effectively what has happened in Brest. It's a big city of broad thoroughfares with plenty of public spaces that ought to be perfectly suited to wafting about, frittering away the time, crowd watching, and playing at being "a gentleman stroller of city streets".

My introduction to Brest has been organized by Yves-Marie, a psychologist, psychoanalyst and indefatigable enthusiast for his city. When he set up practice there several years ago, some less than compassionate souls suggested he would have his work cut out for him, since there were "*beaucoup de fous là bas*", *plenty of loonies there*. In a sense they were right. Not that Brest is full of people babbling to themselves in the streets and shrieking at their big pink camels (at least, no more than any other city of a comparable size), but it is a place with a deeply troubled past, a city established to meet the needs of war, a city that was then destroyed by war, and finally reconstructed to service the industries engendered by the Cold War. Haunted by a ship building industry in which the shipwrights lived in an atmosphere thick with particles of asbestos, by the lurking spectre of a nuclear fleet, and the more distant ghosts of France's first penal colony, it is a place that is bound to provoke a psychological response that is complex, to say the least.

Yves-Marie believes Brest is only now beginning to emerge from a long process of mourning brought about by its destruction in the Second World War and the subsequent shadows of the nuclear age. One symptom of this tentative revival are the number of gaily painted houses. Only in the last ten years has the monotony of the drab grey and off-white that prevailed after WWII begun to give way to bright, primary colours, as if the city is blossoming after a period of hibernation. But not everybody is happy about this. In a recent court case, one householder was (unsuccessfully) prosecuted for having the temerity to paint his home red, as if this were an affront to the sober mood that should prevail if all is to be seemly and proper.

Yves-Marie is taking me to meet Xavier, a university librarian who was born and bred in Brest, and was formerly a student of fine arts and architecture. The moment he emerges from his small terraced house, clutching a plastic bag and two crumpled supermarket receipts with our proposed itinerary scrawled on the back, it is evident that Xavier is the perfect *flâneur*, very possibly of the anarcho-absurdist, revolutionary sybarite, alchemical hazardista, urban arcadian type. Bubbling over with enthusiasm, this is a man who has spent many happy hours botanizing on the sidewalk of his city, a Joycean character who has roamed his hometown, claiming it for himself through his peregrinations, inventing the soft city of the heart that is the private demesne of every citizen. And I mean 'inventing' it. With his architectural background, Xavier has been the source of numerous ideas for urban renewal, proposing projects designed to bring people into the city and give them access to its public places. Unfortunately, judging by what they have actually done, the authorities are rather more inclined to keep people out and control them once they get in than to create something 'open', so Xavier has been obliged to survive, like everyone in Brest, in the Soft City. He's just taken it that little bit further. He's even invented a couple of roads that don't exist on the ground and has named them after his friends.

If Xavier is the perfect companion for a *flânerie*, we've also got the perfect weather for exploring Brest. Remember: *il pleut sans cesse sur Brest*. It's absolutely barreling down, great fat angry gobs of water driven by a frantic wind billowing off the Atlantic. Later, I will be told that nobody can remember such a concentrated and prolonged rain storm taking place in twenty years. But I suspect this 'not remembering' is due more to the regularity of the occurrence than its abnormality. I don't remember the last time I took a breath, but I'm fairly sure it has happened recently and that it has happened pretty regularly over the years. Thus the rain in Brest. Live there long enough and you will become as heedless of the rain as of breathing. There are times in the course of the next couple of hours when I begin to wonder whether there isn't a gang of pranksters on the roofs of the buildings bunging buckets of water down on us while someone with an enormous fan blasts it horizontally. By mid-morning, we're soaked to the skin. Come lunch, I have a strong suspicion my companions have shrunk a couple of inches. It doesn't matter though, because this proves to be the most extraordinary guided walk of my life. Xavier has devised a tour of doorways into Brest. And nearly every one of them proves to be closed, bricked up, blocked off, or a dead-end.

Our first door is in the neighbourhood where Xavier lives, the Quartier St. Martin, and is the entrance to L'Avenir in Place Guérin. Formerly a popular cinema and music hall, L'Avenir is now boarded up and has a large metal gate sealing the doorway. Xavier can barely contain his amusement. *L'Avenir*: The Future is closed! His hilarity increases as he recounts how the local authorities are not content with merely closing the future down, but want to demolish it, too. The humour hides something harder, something sadder and angrier, but it is relayed through a positively gleeful delight at the absurdities of the world. And it's dawning on me that this is not going to be your regular City Tour. Forget about the open-topped bus and the daffy blonde burbling bland factoids into her microphone in a voice that's barely the right side of catatonic. This is a tour with a difference. Look at the ordinary guides and they'll tell you to visit the gardens at Stangalar, the Cours d'Ajot promenade, the pedestrianized Pont Albert-Louppe, and these are all very nice places, well worth an afternoon's *flânerie*. Indeed, Stangalar is a marvelous public park and botanical garden, one of which any city would be proud. But the Soft City inhabited by the Brestois lies elsewhere, not in their town's prettiest places, but in the places that best express their own humour and eccentricity. First port of call, the future; and it's closed.

For the present, it's raining. *Il pleut sans cesse sur Brest.*

At the end of WWII, some of the toughest fighting in Brest took place in the Quartier St. Martin when the local resistance took on the more tenacious panzer divisions of the German rearguard. Look closely at the older stretches of paving and brickwork, in particular at strategic corners like the junction of the Rues Duret, Danton and Conseil, and you will see that they are still scarred by blasts of shrapnel and pocked with bullet marks. It's a bit like being in the Monts d'Arrée, a place where history writes itself in the stones, except here the history is more concrete, in every sense of the word. That said, our next door, the Porte de l'Octroi at the intersection of Rue Saint Marc and Rue Jean Jaures, is an invisible one.

Octroyer means to grant or bestow and this was the location of an ancient toll gate into the old fortified city, the *porte* where travellers and merchants arriving from the hinterland were taxed before being granted entry to the town itself. When Xavier's parents returned to Brest at the end of the war, they were astonished to reach the Porte de l'Octroi and find themselves able to see all the way across the plateau to the Pointe de Petit Minou lighthouse. There should have been a city between them and the sea, but there was nothing, just a vast expanse of rubble and phantom buildings, eviscerated carcasses resembling nothing so much as a company of inebriated skeletons propping one another up after a particularly lively party. The town wasn't there.

It was the defining trauma of modern Brest. As Yves-Marie points out, when you read the history books, they talk about liberation. In fact, '*Brest libéré*' was a euphemism for '*Brest bombardé*'. Such double-talk is second nature nowadays, but few places in western Europe have been liberated by being quite so thoroughly wiped out. Nonetheless, some buildings must have survived, because as we descend Rue Jean Jaures toward what I take to be the centre of town, we pass a reminder of pre-liberation Brest. On the doorway of house number 70, just in front of the Espace Jaures, there is a fading stenciled logo of a double-headed ax, which was the symbol of the Vichy regime. I presume it dates from the war, at least. There has, apparently, also been a move to adopt the double-headed ax as a lesbian symbol, a counterpart to homosexuality's rainbow. I'd love to see Petain's face if he was able to hear about that.

I say 'what I take to be the centre of the town' because it soon becomes apparent that Brest is a city without a centre, a place that is in some ways still searching for its lost heart, which was excised in the course

Vichy or Sappho?

of the liberation. The city was rebuilt under the direction of the architect and town planner J.B. Mathon. The challenge he set himself and his team was to do the job faster than anywhere else in Europe. In the process, little thought seems to have been given to what sort of city people might want to live in. Speed was everything. The old street plan was retained, widened to accommodate new traffic requirements, and pushed through regardless of other considerations. This haste and the peremptory imposition of a modern city on an old town plan resulted in an urban space without any natural focal point, and the amorphous nature of Brest was only exacerbated when the surrounding *communes* where subsequently incorporated into a unitary authority.

If you had to pick one spot as the centre of modern Brest, it would probably be our next destination and the location of our next *porte*, the Place de la Liberté in front of the town hall. This is a double door for there is both an imaginary *porte* and a real one, albeit bricked up. The town hall itself is, putting it kindly, a pretty nondescript edifice that could do with a dash of the primary colour paint scheme being adopted by individual Brestois, yet being one of the larger and more prestigious new buildings, it took a comparatively long time to construct, and for many years was clad in scaffolding. In fact, it took so long that when Xavier was a child, he thought they kept knocking it down and starting again, as if his birthplace was destined for an eternal process of destruction and reconstruction, a city of deconstruction before its time. When, in the 1980s, the authorities decided that Place de la Liberté needed a makeover, Xavier and a group of his friends tendered a project featuring a large gateway that would serve as a connecting point between the upland site of the old town, '*Brest même*' as the locals sometimes call it, which lies behind the town hall, and the new commercial district on the slope descending toward the Penfeld, Brest's main river.

The winning tender was far less imaginative. Instead of the linking device of a symbolic door, they opted for a vast, featureless, faintly totalitarian sunken 'space' (that's the only world I can think of for describing it) sloping away from the *mairie*, as if to encourage petitioners and citizens thither, gently downhill, away from the centre of power. The rudimentary proportions of the square and surrounding buildings are not displeasing, yet it seems designed to intimidate, like a stadium or one of those vast modern airports, as if the last thing wanted here was a lot of people cluttering up the place, and it was thought best to scare them away. The suspicion is confirmed by the fact that the benches are all carefully placed to catch the full brunt of the prevailing wind and rain that comes howling in off the Atlantic, and where the square is crossed by Avenue Clemenceau, the pedestrians are squeezed into a subway under the road, rather than the traffic tunneling under them.

There's certainly no shelter from the rain as we stagger across the square, buffeted by a wild wind and lashing rain. *Il pleut sans cesse sur Brest.* Xavier wrestles manfully and not entirely effectively with his umbrella, which seems to have taken on a life of its own and is expressing a strong desire to take wing and fly off to sunnier climes.

When the winning project got underway, the workers uncovered one of the old doorways, the Porte Saint Louis, that had given access to the fortified city. It was almost exactly where Xavier's team had wanted to locate their door. The Porte Saint Louis was integrated into the new square, but not as an opening or natural passageway. It's bricked up and covered by a metal relief map of what the city used to be like. Xavier doesn't seem in the least bitter about this. In fact, he finds it hilarious. This, he seems to suggest, is the nature of life in Brest. You imagine something ideal, some facet of your Soft City, find that it corresponds to a hidden reality in the Hard City, then watch as the authorities efface it.

The door was not the only thing the workmen found under the square. About 75 metres from the entrance to the town hall, they discovered a nuclear shelter stocked with bottled water and tinned food. It had been built during the Cold War so that, in the event of the holocaust coming to Brest, the *mairie* could go underground and continue administering the smoldering ruins of the city. The nice thing was, nobody had the least suspicion it was there. Even the town council had forgotten they had a refuge.

Could have done with it today, though. *Il pleut sans cesse sur Brest.* Even at the best of times, the Place de la Liberté is a pretty inhospitable place, but in the present conditions, it's bit like being on the deck of an aircraft carrier in a gale. Xavier doesn't seem to mind this, either, though. He even abandons his madly bucking umbrella so that he can wave his arms about a bit more freely and better express his delight at the glorious folly of everything that has been done in the name of the Brestois. I half suspect he takes more pleasure in the failures of town planning than he would have in something better thought out, as if this rather grim sunken space in which there's no room for intimacy and no shelter and no human scale, is actually more conducive to creating and enjoying his Soft City than if it had been more welcoming. It seems to be a conclusion other citizens have come to, as well, making the best of what they've got and perverting it to their own purposes. Despite its intimidating totalitarian aspect, despite the fact that it's a policeman's crowd control dream, the people of Brest have learned to use Place de la Liberté as the focal point for their protest marches.

As we go round -round, not through- the Porte St. Louis, we leave '*Brest même*' and enter the new commercial district. Not far from here you can see traces of a blue line delineating the original limits of Brest. It was painted a few years ago by students from the Ecole des Beaux Arts. Appropriately enough for something that defines a town that was wiped out sixty years ago, the line is rapidly disappearing, worn away by feet, weather, and traffic, and being broken up piecemeal by successive roadworks. Beyond the imaginary line, Place de la Liberté feeds into Rue de Siam, which was named in honour of the emissaries of Siam who processed along this route at the start of a diplomatic mission to France in 1686.

On either side of the road, two shallow channels of water descend to a small fountain. These were originally meant to go all the way down to the Penfeld, uniting the town centre with its main waterway, but that proved impossible, so the channels simply stop at a token fountain after a hundred metres. I am told this is typical of Brest: conceive a grandiose scheme then cut it short. Xavier couldn't be more chuffed. Except when he explains that, in the course of rebuilding the city after the war, the town planners decided they wanted a nice clean modern shopping district, so they declared there should be no food retailers at the top end of Rue de Siam. Mucky stuff, food. Brings people in! Anyone who happens to live near a MacDonalds may sympathize, but in circumstances where so much else seems to have been done against people, it does seem a little ominous. Not that the Brestois were bothered. As with the Place de la Liberté, they didn't take to being planned against, and there is now an excellent food market at the top of Rue de Siam on Sunday mornings.

Il pleut sans cesse sur Brest. I've rarely been so wet and clothed at the same time. Xavier's glasses look like they could do with a couple of windscreen wipers. Yves-Marie is so drenched he has to buy a bag of dates to get his blood sugar levels back to a concentration that can withstand the soaking. We decide it's best to retreat to a café. First, though, we've got to visit the entrance to the Eglise St. Louis. The doors are astonishing. The building isn't pretty, but it is ambitious, soaring skyward, a great mass of stone and concrete, yet the main access is by a line of doors that, on first sighting, look like nothing so much as a row of public conveniences. What this says about the Brestois vision of divinity, is something about which I don't care to speculate, but I wouldn't mind betting it's been the cause of numerous mishaps among newcomers and tourists. Perhaps it's a ploy for luring drunken sailors into midnight mass.

In the café we enjoy a long debate about the ironies of the Place de la Liberté being a constrained, restricted place, and Yves-Marie points out that a near homonym for Mathon, the city's designer, is *maton*, which is slang for a prison guard. After half an hour, there's a faint risk that some small corner of us might be drying out, which is such an appalling prospect for the Brestois that we go bundling out into the rain again.

Il pleut sans cesse sur Brest.

Xavier opens his umbrella as we emerge into the lashing storm and is as pleased as punch when first one rib is snapped in half then the whole thing is whipped inside out. We start talking umbrellas. Get somebody from Brest onto the subject of umbrellas and it's like talking to a rambler about walking boots. If you need to know (and you probably will if you come here), umbrellas made in China simply give up the ghost and expire at the very sight of the weather in Brest, but Dialogues, the excellent book and music superstore on Rue de Siam, has a stock of umbrellas freely available to their clients that should at least get you back to the car . . . possibly à la Mary Poppins, but that's beside the point.

The inverted umbrella, exclaims Xavier, is the *fleur de Brest*. Certainly, a broken brolly could easily be the city's symbol. This is the only place I can recall seeing denuded umbrella canes that have been completely stripped of their impermeable paraphernalia. No ribs, no canopy, nothing but the truncated stick. They're as common as Styrofoam cups in other cities. You find them lying about in the road, on street corners, in the gutters, the discarded cadavers of dead umbrellas. From umbrellas we move onto the fact that Yves-Marie's pale cotton trousers get darker the wetter they are. They are, in a sense, pluviometric trousers. He's very pleased. Like Xavier's glee at the incompetence of the town planning, this is a measure of the Brestois mentality: you don't just endure everything the elements and city fathers dump on you, but take a positive delight them.

Their buoyancy is most remarkable. I mean, what we've got here is an experience that is literally that most depressing of things - a wet Sunday in the city. Neither Yves-Marie or Xavier have to be here. Nothing obliges them to spend their day off playing tour guides. They could both be at home, warm and dry with their families. But generosity and a genuine pleasure in sharing their city with an outsider makes such a retreat unthinkable. Also, I guess, buoyancy is a prerequisite of life in Brest. Otherwise, you'd sink.

Il pleut sans cesse sur Brest.

We cross the main road and head west. No great feat in itself, one may suppose, but it's worth noting that in many French cities, the sight of a pedestrian on a pedestrian crossing is considered to be an outrageous provocation, a singular and intolerable abuse of the motorists' personal space, to which there is only one appropriate response: floor the accelerator and go careering down the road in pursuit of one's prey. I exaggerate, but only mildly. In Brest it's notable that you only have to approach a pedestrian crossing on foot and motorists will slow down in anticipation. It's not just the weather, either. They're not only slowing down because anybody out in a storm like this must be a dangerous lunatic. Several days later, I return to take some photos. It's a bright, sunny day (yes, they do happen) and, if anything, the phenomenon is even more marked.

As we reach the eastern end of Boulevard Gambetta, which overlooks the railway line and commercial port, a wall of water rises out of the Atlantic and sweeps across the harbour, evidently intent on turning the city into a sort of anthropic version of the nearby Oceanopolis aquarium. The only other person in the street is a slightly fugitive looking man scurrying across the road like someone dodging bullets in a gun battle. There's a shattered umbrella pinioned against the seaward wall, limbs every which way, resembling something wild that's ventured out of the woods and been run over by a car. Every house has triple glazing. The wind is howling, the rain is horizontal.

"We're lucky", shouts Yves-Marie, clutching onto his hat.

"We're what?"

"We're lucky it's not January. It's cold then, too."

This takes the transformational Brestois mentality to new heights. It's not just a question of laughing at the absurdity of adversity, but pointing out that it could be worse, too. In fact, the Brestois have much in common with the English when it comes to stoicism. The dog's gobbled your dinner, there's no money to feed the metre, your wife's run off with the milkman, your kids don't like you, the boss has given you your notice, and there's something large, hairy and hungry lying in wait at the bottom of the stairs. Still, mustn't grumble. Or if you're Brestois, you point out that it could be worse - it could be raining.

Il pleut sans cesse sur Brest.

Our next destination is the Quartier Merle Blanc, once a place of ill repute, now a huddle of semi-gentrified houses with small gardens sandwiched between the railway line and the port. To reach it we cross a narrow pedestrian bridge that gives every sign of going nowhere. It's a bit like walking the plank. The weather (if that's not too weak a word for it) pummels us as if we're a line of old carpets strung out for a good beating. Personally, I don't think I've been so clean since I was born. It's like walking through a car wash. Even the dye in my boots seems to have been leeched away, though, like Yves-Marie's trousers, they're so sodden they look darker than usual. There's still no sign of anything at the end of the footbridge and I'm beginning to wonder whether all that stuff about the future being demolished wasn't more than a metaphorical conceit. But at the end of the bridge, a staircase descends to the relative haven of the narrow cobbled lanes in Merle Blanc. Our objective here is another of Brest's classic *portes*. Halfway down the Allée de Merle Blanc, there's a door marked "10 - 12 - 14 - 16 - 18 - 20". At first it seems to be locked, but eventually we get it open. Behind the door, to Xavier's boundless delight, is a blind alley.

This, however, is a mere *jeu d'esprit* compared to our next destination, Recouvrance, site of the naval shipyard, l'Arsenal. To get there, we make our way along the celebrated promenade of the Cours d'Ajot. Midway along there's a ruddy obelisk, a monument to American soldiers who lost their lives fighting in Europe. Raised in 1932 to commemorate the forces that disembarked in Brest during the First World War, the memorial was razed by the Germans in 1941, then raised again in 1958. The surrounding gardens have been ceded to the United States and are officially American territory. Unusually, given current sensibilities, there are no border guards ringing this bit of America, no eagle-eyed patriots on the lookout for dubious types with dark designs. It would be interesting to know what would happen if you declared war and 'invaded'. The transition between France and the USA is marked by small placards along the garden's perimeter portraying a squatting dog and proclaiming: *'Pollution Interdite'*. Given that there's a nuclear fleet on the far side of the Rade, that the old shipyards churned out tons of asbestos that is still taking its toll to this day (3000 deaths per year), and that the commercial port just behind us is chock full of industrial chemicals, this seems a bit hard on the dogs. Possibly though, they were obliged to put the signs here, not anywhere else along the promenade equally suited to relieving a dog's bowels, because the Brestois went out of their way to have their dogs crap on America. Either way, if you want to visit the States without crossing the Atlantic, here's your chance. Just don't let the dog do his business on the other side.

At the end of the Cours d'Ajot, we head toward the towers of the famous bascule bridge across the Penfeld and make our way onto the right bank of the river into Recouvrance. If you happen to be following this itinerary and are in need of sustenance at this stage, carry straight on up Rue de la Porte (what else?), then take the second road on the left, Rue de Vauban, where you will find La Bigoudène, which may well be the best *crêperie* in Brittany. Galettes and crêpes like mother made - and mother made 'em good!

Otherwise, bear right and head upriver along the Rue de Pontaniou toward the abandoned shipyards and the former women's prison, the Prison des Femmes de Mauvaise Vie. We're in a narrow road, high walls on either side, several with doorways. All the doorways are bricked up. One has *Prison Maritime* painted in fading letters on the lintel. There's a plaque commemorating the Jews who were held here prior to deportation to the camps. Invisible but just beyond the riverside wall is the site of the old *bagne*, the penal colony before the French authorities decided being sent to Guyana was even worse than being sent to Brest. It shows how the big-bit-stuck-on-the-hind-end regarded Brittany.

At the end of Rue de Pontaniou are the gates of the Porte de Carpon. They're closed, like most of the Arsenal to which they gave access. Opposite, at the head of a rough stairway is the Bar Grappe Fleurie, better known as Le Trou. Now derelict like nearly everything else round here, this was where workers from the Arsenal would come to slake their thirst between shifts, and according to legend they had thirsts that required a lot of slaking. We'll be looking in detail at the culture of drinking in Brittany later, but it's worth pointing out here that the traditions of hard drinking from the days of the Arsenal persist in Brest today. A few years ago, concerned at the degree to which the population was dependant on alcohol and how drinking was such an integral part of Breton social life, a professor at Brest university's Faculté de Médecine launched the '*Defi Brestois*', challenging people to go three days without alcohol. The consequence of this annual dare? More alcohol is drunk in those three days than at any other time of the year. Mind you, it should be said that such schemes invariably go awry when the Gauls get their hands on them. Twenty odd years ago, breathalyzers were installed in select bars across France as an experiment in reducing drunk driving, the idea being that drinkers would test themselves, take note of the alcohol levels, and prudently stop drinking before they were over the limit. What actually happened was that a new bar game developed to see who could get the highest score.

The Arsenal is a legendary place in the culture of Brest and for decades its routines established the pattern of life throughout the city, but the people who worked there did not always have a good reputation. Some referred to them as the *arsouille* or blackguards, claimed they were the fastest men in the world, able to get home even before the clocking off bell finished ringing, and a joke of dubious taste but neat humour is told about a rape victim who knew her attacker came from the Arsenal because he made her do all the work.

There was, of course, another side to the story, a different almost romantic vision of the shipyards. It was a kind of hell the shipwrights worked in, a cacophony of panel beating and jackhammers, the atmosphere thick with asbestos dust, blast furnaces turning the air febrile, showers of sparks spitting from a thousand soldering irons, yet work in the Arsenal was highly valued, with ten applicants for every job, and, as in mining communities, there was a family tradition, a pride in the fact that you worked where your father and grandfather had worked before you. It was a convivial and cooperative place with a strong esprit de corps, and there was opportunity, too, fitters and sheet-metal workers often progressing to become technicians and engineers and, in one instance, the head of the shipyard. The Arsenal was at once the making of Brest (the city literally would not have existed without it, and it was said that one in two Brestois lived off shipbuilding while the other depended on it) and the unmaking of Brest, for along with the submarine base it was the principal target of the allied bombers during the war.

The staircase behind Le Trou descends into a pit between the prison and the naval yard, a ramshackle cobbled alley flanked by ruins, abandoned buildings and a couple of brightly painted squats. This is Brest's oldest road, Rue St. Malo. Apart from putting up a small explanatory panel, the authorities have done little to celebrate the place, but again the people have seen fit to make good the oversight, establishing the co-operative association Vivre La Rue, which aims to reanimate the area and create a kind of temple to conviviality, in which past and present blend in a continuous urban festival. It is a very Brestois response to blight. You're squeezed between an industrial wasteland, a vacant prison, and the site of a former penal colony, and what comes into your head? Let's have a party!

At the end of the lane, Porte St. Malo should give onto the river, 'should' because, of course, it's bricked up and the only sign it was ever there is the arch of the lintel stones. Xavier's effervescence falters momentarily here and again, later, as we pass the high walls topped with barbed wire defining the military property on the left bank. Understandably enough. A river ought to be the artery of a city, its life blood, defining the spirit of place, in the way that the Thames does in London or the Seine in Paris. The Penfeld is a smaller river than either of those, but it is Brest's river, and you could adapt the Bretons' defensive line about the Monts d'Arrée to describe how the people of Brest regard the Penfeld: *peut-être elle est petite, mais elle est notre rivière à nous et on l'aime bien*. Except it's not *à nous* because the Penfeld is separated from the city, just as the sea is separated from the city by the vast commercial and military docks, and it is again as if the heart of Brest has been excised, forcing the people back into their Soft City. Many Brestois see huge potential in this tract of riverside land. Reclaimed by the city and its people, it might be used to reposition and regenerate the entire community, to make soft city dreams a reality. But for the present, it's abandoned, barely used by the navy, but still kept apart behind high walls, barbed wire and countless bricked up gates, as if to say we're hanging onto it, just in case. Some local residents welcome this, knowing that a certain world, a certain way of life, a certain source of prestige is finished, yet fearing to let go of the military past. Like those people who protested against the brightly painted houses, they are comforted by what they know, and fear change as they move toward an uncertain future.

Our final *porte* is the gateway into the Jardin des Explorateurs, which overlooks the dry docks and military harbour on the seaward side of Recouvrance. There's a raised walkway here, a kind of catwalk. Nobody else is in the garden apart from a solitary man clutching the tip of a dead umbrella so that the hooked handle holds his hat on in the howling wind. From the walkway we can see all of Brest's history, what remains of its military past, and a token of the detritus from that past. It's all theoretically visible from the Cours d'Ajot, too, but when *il pleut sans cesse sur Brest,* you may have to get a little nearer. The walkway shadows old walls that once dropped directly into the sea, but which now descend to a road accessing the reclaimed land of the port. Walls and walkway are separated by two barriers, one a standard green metal fence, the other an elongated egg-slicer of electrified wires. Slightly to the left is the Vauban *château.* From the rise at the end of the garden we can see the U-boat base that led to Brest being bombed. Fort and submarine dock were among the few buildings undamaged by the bombing, unlike (to Xavier's undying chagrin) the town's two breweries, which were mistaken for parts of the Arsenal. On the nearside of the harbour are the dry docks, only one of which is currently in use. On the far side of the Rade we can see the nuclear submarine base of Île Longue. And moored on the quay between the dry docks and the Rade, is a rusting aircraft tanker, the Clemenceau, a vessel that recently inspired the sort of farce that is the delight and the despair of the Brestois.

Decommissioned, the Clemenceau was sailed off to India to be decontaminated and have the asbestos stripped out of its interior. Cue outrage on the part of Breton ecologists and protests from their Indian counterparts. What was France doing sending 20,000 tons of rusting metal to India? Bad publicity loomed like an Atlantic weather front, bad publicity the President of the Republic could readily do without since he was due to visit the subcontinent. So they did a Grand Old Duke of York job and, having sailed it out there, they sailed it right

The Vauban château

back again. The price tag for this little jaunt? About three million euros all told. Considerably more than what it would have cost to decontaminate the ship in France in the first place. Xavier doesn't know whether to laugh or cry.

Looking back at our *flânerie*, I get the distinct impression Brest has been designed against its people: the future has been dismantled, public spaces made as unwelcoming as they can be, food proscribed, the river and the sea cut off from the people who live beside them, doors and gates that should be ways into places have been bricked up or go nowhere, the gardens are hemmed in by electric fences, domestic pets are deemed sources of pollution . . . it's as if its position at the end of the world has been incorporated into the city's design. And yet the people take a perverse pleasure from subverting what has been done against them and are genuinely fond of their city. *Peut être elle est foutue, mais elle est notre cité a nous et on l'aime bien*. This, I suspect, is the true *defi Brestois*. Having learned to retreat to a city of the mind after the place's destruction during the war, the Brestois have come to understand that cities of stone are all too ephemeral, and that anyone who relies on architects and town planners to make them a city is onto a hiding to nothing. Better claim the town as your own and make it your own almost regardless of what exists on the ground, so that the Soft City of the mind becomes more real than the Hard City of concrete, tarmac, metal and stone. Estranged from their city, they turn its shortcomings into a source of laughter and approach each challenge with immense good humour and gusto. Told to drink less, they drink more; given a boulevard without food, they set up a market; surrounded by images of slenderness, they develop anti-diet day; confronted with countless closed doors, they imagine their way into their city. Whether they will one day be able to reclaim their link with the various bodies of water surrounding them, remains to be seen. But in the meantime, they have mastered the art of living in the Soft City. This is not a city you visit in order to admire the stones, though it does have some nice stones dotted about in unexpected corners. It's a city you visit to admire the warmth and humour and resilience of the people and to try and find your way into the Soft City they have created between them. If you like beautiful buildings, go to Paris. If you like people, come to Brest.

But, by God, you'd better be ready to get wet.
Il pleut sans cesse sur Brest.

12. Extremities

ACCESS - Cap Sizun is the most southerly of Brittany's western headlands. **Douarnenez** is northwest of Quimper on the D765.

Douarnenez, Port de Rosmeur

Brittany is a land built from stories, many so fantastic that the line about the Monts d'Arrée being the *royaume de l'imaginaire* might be extended to the entire region. Yet, no matter how far-fetched, these stories are often based on more than mere fancy, embodying a metaphorical truth about events otherwise obscured by the passage of time. A good example of this is the legend of the Ville d'Ys, or *Ker-Is* in Breton. Described by one observer as "a dream wrapped in a phantasmagoria of a chimera" (now there's a man who's been tucking into his mushrooms) it is, in all probability, actually an account of an authentic historical event representing a wider conflict that took place throughout ancient Brittany. Hugely improbable story, though. Goes like this.

Gradlon, fifth century king of Cornouaille and rapacious sea-going gadabout, is left high and dry when his sailors tire of doing the royal thing, sailing about pillaging such pillageables as can be reached by boat, and bugger off home leaving their monarch to get by as best he can. Along comes Malgven, Queen of the North, captivating beauty with long blonde locks and a bent for unbridled passions, suggesting Gradlon get himself northward in order to dish her husband, after which he can have a rare old time with hubby's gold and her unbridled passions. Husband duly dished, Gradlon and Malgven grab the loot and mount Gradlon's magical seafaring horse, Morvarc'h, with a view to paddling off to Cornouaille and enjoying their ill-gotten gains. Storm blows up, the fugitives are blown off course, and end up bobbing about the high seas for a year, at the end which Malgven dies giving birth to a daughter, Dahut, whom we've already met in Huelgoat. Father and daughter return to Cornouaille, daughter grows into a captivating beauty with long blonde locks and a bent for unbridled passions, in short the very spit of her mother, turning grief-stricken Dad soft in the head. Dad builds daughter a beautiful city in the Baie de Douarnenez, the Ville d'Ys, which, being below sea level, is protected by a gigantic dike, the single bronze door of which is opened by a key Gradlon keeps on a golden chain round his neck. Dahut turns Ys into the party capital of Cornouaille, taking a new lover every night, who is persuaded to wear a silk mask that turns into a clawed helmet at dawn, or is boiled alive after Dahut's had her way with him, or is simply strangled at first light, whereupon his body is dumped in the sea.

Saint Guénolé turns up and inveigles his way into Gradlon's good graces, installing himself in the traditional druidical role of royal adviser and all round bigwig. Tells Gradlon Dahut's antics are decidedly unchristian and that Ys will be punished for the debauchery into which she is seducing the city unless his daughter mends her ways. But Gradlon's besotted and Dahut is disinclined to mend ways she finds thoroughly congenial, so she simply carries on phantasmagoriating her chimera, dismissing these gloomy Christians as a lot of killjoys who just want to make Ys sad and boring.

Disgruntled God gets Satan to go along dressed as a seductive knight in red. Knight in Red beds Dahut, persuades her to pocket Dad's key, opens the big bronze gate, whereupon a bloody great wave rises out of the seas and engulfs Ys. Gradlon saddles his seafaring horse and sets off for the mainland with Dahut clinging to the croup.

"Dump the girl!" cries Guénolé, who has his own waterborne steed. "She's the devil's own work and must be disposed of forthwith".

"Never shall I abandon my beautiful daughter," says Gradlon, hanging on all the tighter to Dahut, albeit dimly aware that the magical seafaring horse isn't making much progress against these particular seas.

"Dump the girl!"

"I cannot abandon my beloved only daughter, apple of my eye, captivating beauty with long blonde locks and so forth, and the very spit of her mother. Go on, Morvarc'h, boy. Why are you sinking? You're meant to be a magical horse. Get magical. Swim!"

"Dump the girl, Gradlon, or you'll drown and your bones will be fish bait".

Third time lucky. Family's all very nice, but fish bait is something else. Gradlon dumps the girl, Dahut sinks, Morvarc'h finds his sea legs, and the only people to survive the inundation of Ys are Gradlon and Guénolé, Dahut being transformed into Ahès, the Mother of all Sirens who sits about at strategic locations on the Breton coast, combing her long blonde locks and luring sailors to their death.

Feeling peckish after his narrow escape, Gradlon bumps into the hermit Saint Corentin, and asks for food. Corentin dips his hand in a spring, pulls forth a fish, and slices off a tasty fillet, but instead of thrashing about and expiring, the fish is popped back in the spring only to re-emerge unscathed. An easy trick if you're gifted at sleight of hand, but Gradlon has never seen the like of it before, magical horses and captivating beauties notwithstanding. Mightily impressed, he takes Corentin with him to the site of the new town he is to found, the place where two rivers come together between seven hills, that is to say a confluent, or *kemper* in Breton, in other words modern day Quimper. Corentin becomes Bishop of Quimper, Gradlon gets by as best a man can once he's dumped his daughter in the briny, and the rest of Brittany laments the lost city of Ys, so lovely that the next most beautiful city, Lutece, was renamed "Par-Is" (or Pareil à Ys), meaning "Like Ys".

Nowadays, Bretons comfort themselves by saying the bells of

Ys can still be heard below the waters of the Baie de Douarnenez and repeating the adage that "*quand Paris sera englouti, la ville d'Ys resurgira*" (when Paris is engulfed, Ys will rise up again), and that when it re-emerges it will be more beautiful than ever. The deluge is commemorated in many paintings, notably E.V. Luminais' *Fuite de Gradlon*, which was the sensation of the 1884 Paris Salon; the legend is the subject of an opera, Édouard Lalo's *Le Roi d'Ys*, and a Debussy Prelude, *La Cathédrale Engloutie*; it is also commemorated in an annual son et lumière at Argol on the Presqu'île de Crozon; and I believe there's even a video game, than which there is no greater guarantor of immortality. So far, so conventional. You tell a tale, turn a penny, wax romantic, and peddle a bit of folklore to pull in the tourists. Dahut gets a different ending from that recounted at Huelgoat, but every myth-maker has to make do with the materials to hand. Except that here it's all true. Well, not all true. Doubtless we can make allowances for the magical horse and the submarine bells and the immortal mermaid, and I don't suppose much is going to be re-emerging from the seas after fifteen hundred years, but according to most accounts the Ville d'Ys probably did exist, was perhaps the victim of a fifth century tsunami, and the story of its flooding is the narrative of one of the defining periods of Breton history.

Venture out on any of Brittany's *presqu'îles* and you will find dozens of idyllic beaches, coves, and creeks, but among the most enchanting is Cap Sizun, the peninsula on the southern side of the Baie de Douarnenez that terminates in what, symbolically at least, is continental Europe's most westerly headland, the Pointe du Raz. I say symbolically because the shallower Pointe de Corsen is actually a little further west and the Pointe Saint Mathieu was the one that gave Finistère it's name, but as we will see, the Pointe du Raz is in many ways the most extreme of these extremities.

Nowadays Douarnenez is a busy fishing port that is well worth visiting to stroll round the lovely lanes and admire the sea views. For the most part, it's free of trippers' tack and, even in Summer, you still get a sense that this is a real community not solely dependent on the tourist trade. Rather than tourism, fish is what has defined Douarnenez, from Roman times when its wealth was based on the production of *garum* (a fermented fish sauce like the Vietnamese *nuoc-mâm*) to the nineteenth century when it was a sardine fishery with twenty-four canneries. I recommend following the main road in past the irreverently named Bar Vatican, getting a town plan from the extremely helpful and friendly tourist office, then just strolling around and admiring the attractive buildings dotted about the backstreets. Afterwards, make your way down to Port du Rosmeur and one of the seafront bars (La Trinquette is good) from where we can see the Trezmalouen and Ris beaches to the east, also accessible via the Sentier des Ploma'rch.

It's not the best view in Brittany, but it's interesting because this is where the Ville d'Ys is said to be located. At low water on the *grève du Ris* a fragment of Roman masonry is visible, half buried in the sand, and further along toward the *grève de Trezmalouen* there's a cluster of pickets, said either to be the remains of an ancient palisade, or the vestiges of an oak and yew forest. More significantly, several Roman roads converge at this point, disappearing into the sea in the direction of the old brick wall. Of course, nobody can categorically identify these remains with Ys. Some sources claim the legend dates back even further, perhaps over three thousand years, to the start of a long period of geological and climatic change during which the seas around Brittany were constantly rising and reclaiming low-lying coastal land, a theory that would fit with the name Ker-Is, which is thought to come from the Breton word *izel*, meaning 'low'. But on the whole it seems likely there was something there at about the time when Gradlon was King of Cornouaille, something that has since been swallowed up by the sea.

Further inland on the B143 to Lanudec is Pouldavid, previously Poul Dahut, where the princess is said to have been shoved off Morvarc'h, who left his own mark in the form of a hoof-print in a rock (a trace we failed to find, but maybe we're too literal minded), 'proving' that Gradlon made good his escape. As proof, this is a bit feeble, but Pouldavid is undoubtedly a place with a talent for spotting things that are going to end up at the bottom of the sea: in the late Middle Ages the inlet was still a broad bight and an important commercial centre, named in the trading accounts of ports as far away as Cadiz and Seville; its main stock in trade was linen; its most famous client . . . the Spanish Armada.

Head west along the course of the old Roman road that is now the D7 and you will find settlements that have taken heed of the story of Ys, for all the houses are built on high ground and they are all oriented away from the sea. In part, this is a result of meteorological imperatives. Nearly every old house in Brittany was built facing south and the windmills dotting the fields suggest anyone doing otherwise would have had a very airy time of it indeed. But even discounting the sun and wind, you couldn't blame the locals for turning their backs on the sea. No matter how balmy the weather, the waters along the northern cape are a turmoil of waves and conflicting

currents, and they certainly look like they're inclined to swallow up significant portions of the earth. Glance across the Baie des Trépassés and you will see the thin smudge of the Île de Sein looking unbearably fragile, as if the houses grow directly out of the sea. On occasion, they do. Three times in the last century, the island was inundated during storms, and in 1919 the inhabitants were compelled to clamber onto the church roof to save themselves from flood waters. Seen from the mainland, the lighthouse appears to be the only place you could guarantee dry feet.

Very airy, indeed.

There's no archeological justification (the Roman finds end at Trouguer behind Pointe du

Van), but for a long time amateur mythologists located Ys in the Baie des Trépassés, inspired by the howling winds and ceaseless surf rolling in unchecked by anything very much between here and Newfoundland. No surprise then that it was here the legend claims Dahut ditched the bodies of her discarded lovers. The name Baie des Trépassés translates as The Bay of the Dead.

On the southern side of the peninsula, we reach the magnet that draws most tourists to Cap Sizun, La Pointe du Raz. Like many places, La Pointe du Raz is preferable out of season as it can get horribly crowded, and even when comparatively empty, the infrastructure installed to cope with the summer influx can be a little off putting, with serried ranks of car-parks giving onto

Cap Sizun

concrete walkways, cafeterias, and gift shops. But this grim gateway serves to preserve what really is a very spectacular site, so if it's not absolutely heaving, it's worth persevering. If it is absolutely heaving, retrace your steps to the Pointe du Van and stroll down to the Chapelle de Saint They. The views are almost as dramatic and it should be a little less crowded. In fact, if a heavy sea is smashing against the rocks, just about anywhere on Cap Sizun has enough drama to make an Italian opera look uneventful, and when there's a high wind, the *sentier cotier* round the Mouillage du Vorlenn to the south of the Pointe du Van is reputed to be quite dangerous.

However, if it's not packed to the point of suffocation, take the Pointe du Raz Visitors' Centre for what it is, a necessary evil to be passed as promptly as possible. Avoid the main, paved walkway leading directly to the lighthouse, and head south onto the coastal path, where you'll soon understand why this has become the iconic if not the factual western 'end of Europe'. It's a grand, ungodly place, crumbing cliffs dropping into roiling seas, waves going every which way at once, as if unsure what makes them more angry, this impertinent patch of land protruding into the ocean or one another. At the very tip of the headland a blade like line of rocks points toward the Gort Greiz islet (another putative site for Ys, the rocks being mistaken for the remains of a ruined city) and the Île de Sein.

An engaging multilingual warning sign on the nearside of the promontory reads as follows: *Au dela de cette limite vous vous engagez a vos risques et perils dans un espace accidenté qui present des réeles difficultes de progression. Beyond this point you proceed at your own risk over uneven land where your progress will prove extremely difficult.* Then, with admirable brevity, as if anyone foolhardy enough to learn a Celtic language is beyond securing from danger, *Diaes tre mont dreist.* As it happens, there's a perfectly good path for anyone accustomed to scrambling about mountains, but rather more alarmingly than the signs, halfway along the rocks there's a lifebelt. I for one wouldn't want to be floating about in these waters, lifebelt or no. I wouldn't even want to be in these waters in a boat for that matter. This is not just pusillanimity on my part. Even accomplished sailors fear the Pointe du Raz. There's a mariners' saying, "*Qui voit Sein, voit sa fin*" (he who sees Sein, sees his end), and the wild waters and treacherous currents of the channel between the island and the mainland have been key to defining the reputations of both the *pointe* and the Sénans.

One glance at the Raz de Sein and you won't be the least bit surprised to hear that it is yet another gateway to hell. There's no escaping hell in Brittany. It's everywhere, in Huelgoat, in Yeun Elez, and now at the tip of Cap Sizun. The only excuse for this ubiquity is that it's so very different each time, being variously composed of rock, bog or water, depending on where you are. This particular manifestation would certainly be some sort of hell in a storm. The actual 'gates' are at the end of the path, midway along the line of rocks, but even from a safe distance, it all looks pretty hellish - and, of course, rather marvellous, inspiring that 'horrid fascination' that so pleased the early Romantics.

Another transition into the underworld is said to take place from the beach in the Baie de Trépassés where the souls of the dead embark for their final voyage to *l'autre Bretagne au-delà de la mer* (I believe they mean the underworld, not the United Kingdom), though the souls of those who drowned and were washed up on the beach had to make their own way to the Îlot de Tevennec if they were to catch the boat of the dead. Boats of the dead were a feature of this area, for the people of Sein weren't in the least bit worried about the *karriguel an Ankou* creaking about their island. You'd be a fool to even dream of progressing by chariot on an island that measures less than one square kilometre. No, what worried them was the *ar vag noz,* The Night Boat, skippered by the first person to die in any given year, sight or sound of which announced a forthcoming death. It is suggested that all these tales about dead bodies, beaches, and night boats are not merely a sample of how preternaturally gloomy the Bretons can be, but a hangover from pre-Christian times when the corpses of druids were taken from the Baie de Trépassés to be buried on Sein.

If you have the time, Sein itself is worth a visit (boats leave daily from the Sainte-Evette wharf near Audierne), so long, that is, as the legend of Ys, hasn't put the wind up you. With an average altitude of 1.5 metres, prone to flooding, subject to weather that can keep the fishing fleet in port for up to four months at a stretch, and lacking any upright vegetation, Sein is a place for people who can cope with big seas and big skies and big horizons. The land itself is an altogether provisional arrangement. It's certainly not for the faint of heart and the people who lived there in the past were anything but faint of heart. For centuries, they have regularly taken to the seas to help foundering ships (though some snide souls suggest the ships were foundering because the Sénans hung lamps from their cattle's horns to simulate lights and lure ships onto the rocks) and were until recently exempt from taxes in honour of a seventeenth century rescue, when Louis XIV admitted that the islanders were already so heavily taxed by nature, a fiscal levy was entirely superfluous. They were also singled out and honoured for the part they played in the Second World War. In 1940, 126 men, the entire able-bodied male population, were among the first to embark for England to join de Gaulle, forming a quarter of the first Free French volunteers, prompting the general to observe that the Île de Sein was a quarter of France.

Wild waters and recurrent floods notwithstanding, all this might seem a little distant from the legend of Ys, were it not for the fact that two of the earliest recorded residents of Sein were the saints Guénolé and Corentin. Though no trace remains, both founded monasteries on the island, and Guénolé had a tussle with the devil over the place. The story goes that Guénolé took a bucket of salt water, blew on it and conjured up an ice bridge between Sein and the mainland. The devil ventured onto the bridge, melted it with his red hot hooves and toppled into the sea, from which he was rescued by Guénolé on condition that he never set foot on the island again. The devil really ought to have known better. As it happens, Guénolé was Breton born, but most of the region's saints came to Brittany from Britain aboard granite boats, and you just don't mess about with a man admitted into a confraternity of fellows capable of sailing overseas in granite boats.

There's been much speculation about the Breton tradition that would-be saints given the call simply hopped on a rock and trusted to God to get them to their mission. Some claim they arrived in leather coracles or currachs that the locals mistook for stone; others suggest the flimsy leather boats embarked with a large rock as ballast, on which the migrant monks would sit or kneel in prayer. But such fanciful interpretations are not to the Breton taste. Bretons know their saints got here in granite boats and they aren't about to let historical revisionism give the lie to their convictions. In 1998, the Breton sculptor, Jean-Yves Menez (see http://jymenez.free.fr) built a three-and-a-half ton, four-metre long granite boat that can carry eight people. The Maen Vag has since happily pottered about numerous Breton harbours and rivers, and it hasn't sunk yet.

Transport systems aside, it's the presence of Guénolé and Corentin that is the link between Sein and Ys, for this is not simply a yarn about decent dads doing the best they can with disobedient daughters, but a story of whose god is going to be boss, and of the evangelization of Brittany back in the Dark Ages. Look a little more closely at the story of Ys and it transpires Dahut may have been portrayed in a light she did not necessarily deserve. Obviously, we'll never know just how fatal her attraction was, but it seems likely that her real crime was not bedding too many gentlemen in red, but being rather too fond of traditional ways and thus becoming an obstacle to a missionary doing what missionaries have always done, targeting the head of state on the assumption that once the king was converted, his people would follow suit. You only need to look at what Gradlon did next to get an idea of this. He was, after all, 'saved' (nudge-

nudge) by a saint, a saint reputed to have also banished the devil from the ancient burial place of the druids; he survived a deluge sent to punish a sybaritic society that had strayed from the path of righteousness, was fed on magical fish, and then settled in a city where two rivers converged like merging cultures, a city with seven hills to boot, corresponding to the mystic seven of the Breton church. All those Christian tropes aren't there by accident but to point the way to the future. Indeed, some accounts barely mention Dahut's debauchery, emphasizing instead her attachment to pagan rites. There's even a suggestion that Ker Is gets its name not from the Celtic word for low, but from a contraction of Isis, whose cult may have been brought to this important trading settlement by Phoenician and Egyptian sailors. Dahut's demonization is an example of history being written by the victors and the story of Ys is the story of a clash of cultures, of a new religion supplanting the old, and of the inevitable resentments and quarrels that entailed.

There are no martyrs among the Breton saints, but though they had the advantage of already speaking the language of the people they sought to convert, they weren't always well received by the local population. Accused of being a child-killer, Saint Ronan was chucked in a dungeon and had wild dogs set on him; evicted from the Bois du Gars by an unfriendly landlord, Saint Conval declared it would henceforth be so badly deforested there wouldn't be enough timber to fashion a tiller; Saint Jacut was so irked by his reception on an island in the Baie de Lancieux, he attached it to the mainland, creating the Presqu'île de Saint Jacut; in a fit of pique, Saint Quay afflicted all the girls of a hostile village with curvature of the spine; and St. Herbot had such a bad time in Berrien he condemned its people to harvest nothing but stones. In short, you didn't cross a saint lightly. He told you to dump your daughter in the sea, you dumped your daughter in the sea sharpish. Call him a boring old fart and you'd end up going down in history as a lewd little floozy with a penchant for topping her playmates.

If you care to see something of Dahut and her dismal end in a more domestic setting than that offered by Cap Sizun, you should follow the itinerary suggested in our next chapter and visit Quimper, where Luminais' *Flight of King Gradlon* is on display in the Musée des Beaux Arts, and a statue of Gradlon dominates the facade of the great Gothic cathedral. But that, of course, is another story.

13. Shooting the Parrot:
Old Customs & Modern Art in Quimper

ACCESS - To reach the start of our itinerary in **'Place de la Résistance'**, follow the 'Office du Tourisme' signs through **Quimper**.
An interactive town plan is available on www.quimper.fr/83283987/0/fiche__pagelibre/#. To reach **Les Vire Court** take the D20 toward **'Plomelin'**, then turn left just north of the km6 milepost to reach the **'Kerambleiz'** car-park.

Quimper's most famous son

Picasso's godson

Tourism doesn't get much more classic than pottering about a medieval town then popping into the museum, but things become classics for a reason and it would be a pity to visit southern Finistère without seeing the city of Quimper. Tucked away in the haven of the River Odet and located at a crossroads of ancient trading routes, Quimper is the natural capital of Cornouaille and has existed in one form or another since Roman times. It was, however, only in the middle ages that the city really developed, becoming famous for the great fairs that were staged on the third Sunday of every month, before establishing itself in the aftermath of the Revolution as the capital of the new *departement* of Finistère.

To explore Quimper, I propose two short itineraries, one bumping about the heart of *les vieux quartiers*, the other visiting the most famous stretch of the River Odet. An essential part of bumping about is following your nose, so to allow your nose a little liberty, we'll get the directions out of the way now: Tourism office, Place de la Résistance, head upstream on Boulevard Dupleix, hang a left in front of the *préfecture* and cross Pont Ste. Catherine into Rue du Roi Gradlon. Nip into the Musée Departementale to see the yard of the bishop's palace, visit the Cathédrale Saint Corentin, then take Rue Keréon to the River Steir. Double back to the right on Rue des Gentilshommes, staggered crossroads into Rue de Sallé, pass the Place du Beurre, right on Rue Elie Fréron, right again into Rue du Guéodet, then back to the Odet via the Rues des Boucheries and Saint François. Got it? No matter if not. Just walk. It's a small city and the chances are you'll bump into everything we mention anyway.

Place de la Résistance isn't much of a *place*, but in view of the city's limited parking facilities, it has the inestimable advantage of being surrounded by car parks. It was not, however, always somewhere to simply leave the car, since in 1793 this was the site of a more traditional form of

French combustion, the *brûlis des saints* when local republicans asserted their claim to be the *departemental* capital instead of their rivals, Landerneau, by burning the cathedral statuary. Behind Place de la Résistance lies Mont Frugy, a modest hill (what else?) with fine views over the heart of the old city. Until the great storm of 1987, the *Chêne Papegault* or Parrot Oak stood at the foot of the Mont, commemorating an eighteenth century custom in which a bird was placed at the top of a mast on one of the ships moored at the nearby quay and the townsfolk took potshots at the poor thing. The person who shot the parrot successfully (and honourably - the victor had to swear he'd loaded his gun "loyally and without fraud", though how a gun can be loaded disloyally and fraudulently, I wouldn't know) was proclaimed 'king' for a year and exempted from certain tolls. The custom was inspired not merely by mercenary motives or a collective seizure of pollyphobia, but was an attempt, copied by local authorities throughout Brittany, to compensate for undermanned garrisons by encouraging the citizenry to learn to fend for themselves.

With its medieval trappings and air of bourgeois respectability, Quimper can seem like an old fashioned place, and yet it has strong links with modernism. Opposite the Tourism Office is the Pont Max Jacob, named after the city's most famous son, the art critic, poet and painter who was among Picasso's associates in the early days of Cubism, notably during the painting of the *Demoiselles d'Avignon*, and who went on to become an avatar of literary modernism. The son of a Jewish tailor, Max Jacob was dismissed as the token 'clever Jew' by many of his classmates (he came of age at the time the Dreyfus affair exposed the virulence of French anti-semitism), but the dull-witted, narrowing mindset expressed by *isms* of the token and semitic variety was never going to trouble a man who subsequently counted Cocteau, Apollinaire, Modigliani, Braque, Derian and Picasso among his friends. Jacob had his eyes set on more distant horizons and the only *isms* he cared for were those that expanded perception. Yet, despite rejecting the provincial limitations of his hometown, he never escaped the charm of its streets, which figure in many of his works, notably the roman à clef, *Le Terrain Bouchaballe*. As a result of two visions in which he claimed to have seen Jesus, Jacob converted to Christianity in his forties, Picasso standing in as godfather, and many of his later works are meditations on religious themes or sketches of biblical scenes. But faith, no matter how genuine, provided scant protection against the insanities of the Second World War. Once a Jew, always a Jew, was how the *ism*-mongers saw it. Jacob was tagged with a yellow star, saw his siblings disappear into the maw of Auschwitz, then died of pneumonia at Drancy, the deportation camp to the north of Paris. Nowadays, the Jacob shop at 8 Quai du Parc, opposite the Boulevard Dupleix, is marked with a commemorative plaque.

The Cathédrale Saint Corentin was one of the first gothic cathedrals in Brittany and is a very fine building, so fine it's hard to believe that such harmony of form was achieved over the course of three centuries (they were still fiddling with it in the nineteenth century, some seven hundred years after they'd started the thing), and was largely financed by subscription, parishioners paying for the construction with a levy known as the *sou de Corentin*. Glance up at the bridge between the steeples and you will see the statue of Gradlon, which dates from the 1850's when the original was struck by lightning, incidentally putting an end to another curious custom. Until then, every 26th of July, a stable lad would scramble up the steeple and install himself on the horse's crupper. After offering Gradlon a glass of wine, he would wipe the king's mouth, then toss the glass to the waiting crowds below. Whoever caught the glass without breaking

Saint Corentin Cathedral

it, or having it broken for them by jealous neighbours, would win one hundred *écus*. The glass invariably smashed and nobody ever got the gold.

The cathedral itself is famously twisted, shifting its axis between the choir and the nave. Various theories have been put forward to explain the bend, some suggesting it's due to unstable foundations and the proximity of the Odet, others that the masons had to build around a tomb that was already in place, or that it symbolizes Jesus' drooping head as he hung on the cross. More likely, it's the consequence of incorporating the foundations from two earlier buildings, a chapel and a Roman church, into the new cathedral. Thanks to the *brûlis des saints,* the interior is relatively poor in decorative detail, its principal appeal being the dappling of light on the flagstones from the stained glass windows. Nonetheless, there are several statues of Saint Corentin with his miraculous self-repairing fish, the latter looking pretty sour on the whole, which is understandable in the circumstances, and on the right just short of the chancel there's a seventeenth century statue of Yannick (Little John), also known as Santik Du (Little Black Saint), Jean Discalceat (John Shoeless) or Yann Divoutou (John Clogless).

Yannick was a Breton-born Franciscan who dedicated himself to alleviating poverty in Quimper until his death in 1349 after he had contracted the plague from the people he had been nursing. Pretty much the common lot of your average saint, you may think, but Yannick is, in many ways, a singularly Breton saint. First there's his name. The use of diminutives is a tradition that persists to this day in Brittany, inspired not by size or maturity, but by one's situation within the family. Thus one may meet middle-aged men of grand stature, large girth and wide responsibility, who are still distinguished from fathers or uncles by the name 'Petit Jean', and they will remain 'Petit Jean' until their dying day, no matter how big they get or how long they live. Yannick is also typically Breton because, like virtually all the region's saints, he is unrecognized by Rome, being sanctified instead by popular acclaim - *vox populi, vox Dei*. As we've seen in the Monts d'Arrée, this is a very Breton way of going about things. You want a mountain, you go ahead and make it up. You reckon the local good guy ought to be a saint, you don't wait for the ecclesiastical lawyers to drag themselves through the rigmarole of beatification while a committee of cardinals examines your man's record on the miracle and apparition front; you just call him a saint and have done with it.

Also typical is Yannick's relic, a thick cap of bone which I take to be a portion of his cranium, though I'm not absolutely sure about this. Anatomy never was a strong point, the relic isn't mentioned anywhere else, and it really is very thick. There again, the Breton's are famed for their obstinacy, so perhaps the thickness of this skull is pertinent to Yannick's Breton identity. The business of relics is one the Bretons embraced with a passion in the middle ages, and there are fragments of saints scattered all over the place. Saint Corentin's arm is lurking about somewhere in Quimper cathedral, as well as three drops of Jesus' blood. Elsewhere there's St. John's finger, St. Jacques' blood, St. Pol's arm, St. Gildas' leg, St. Yves' head and I don't know what else, St. Peter's pinkie, probably. Sometimes the relics are deemed so important, they are taken as the defining merit of a place. St. Jean du Doigt, for instance, was not home to a specific John who did some special trick with his finger, but is the lodging place of the saint's phalanx.

Selecting architectural highlights in the old quarter is a bit pointless since the real appeal of the place is its ensemble impact, but it is worth pausing at the junction of Rue Keréon and Rue des Boucheries to admire the timbering on the corner houses. Time was when the entire town was composed of half-timbered houses crowded together in narrow lanes, and some locals still refer to the Rue Fréron as Rue Obscure, recalling the confined passage that existed here until the nineteenth century, a passage that was 3.7 metres wide at street level, but narrowed to 55 centimetres between the eves. Half-timbering was prohibited after a devastating fire in 1762, but there's still a medieval air about the granite buildings that prevailed thereafter. This is particularly notable after we double back into

La Maison des Cariatides

Rue des Gentilshommes, away from the River Steir, which was the dividing line between the ducal and episcopal sides of the city, a division that reflected a predictably Breton rivalry between contending power bases. The most striking stonework, though, is in Rue du Guéodet.

The road gets its name from a contraction of *guet de l'Odet*, literally the Odet look-out post, because there was once a chapel here housing a well with an underground canal leading to the River Odet, and it was said that Gradlon, a man with an understandably uneasy conscience, would visit the well and listen to Dahut whispering from the distant sea soft words of reproach or invitation or whatever mermaids whisper to fickle fathers. Midway along Guéodet is the Maison de Cariatides, named for the heads decorating the entablatures. They're very merry heads, all giggling away as if the spectacle on the street is a glorious and unprecedented refinement on the human comedy. Some say their mirth stems from the building's sixteenth century origins as a tavern (it's still a bar to this day), but others claim the gaiety is an unseemly celebration of a successful battle during the Wars of Religion.

You'll have noticed that most of the streets are named after the professions that used to congregate in them, butchers obviously in the Rue des Boucheries, cobblers in the Rue Keréon, dairymen around the Place du Beurre, and pork butchers in the Rue du Sallé. The butchers, in particular, were restricted in where they could work and what they could do, being obliged, for instance, to reserve all marrow bones for the Seigneur du Cludou in recompense for a somewhat onerous duty with which the aristocrat was charged: when a new bishop came to Quimper, it was Cludou's job to carry the newcomer into the cathedral! Whatever advantages it may have had in terms of regulation, concentrating trades in restricted areas was not without its negative results and an eighteenth century report complains that the entire town was permeated with the stench from the Rue des Boucheries abattoir, the smell being so bad that it's thought the airy upland of Place Mesgloaguen got its name because it was the only place free of the cloaca enveloping the rest of the town.

Another big stink surrounded Quimper's second most famous son, Elie Fréron, an eighteenth century journalist and polemicist who took issue with the Enlightenment Encyclopédistes. Voltaire was so vexed by this opposition from a fellow author that he wrote several vicious satires against Fréron, including a play traducing Fréron's annual literary review, *L'Année Littéraire* as *L'Ane Littéraire* (The Literary Donkey), and numerous epigrams, amongst them a quip that has often been repeated in less literary terms:

L'autre jour au fond d'un vallon,
Un serpent piqua Jean Fréron;
Que croyez-vous qu'il arriva?
Ce fut le serpent qui creva.

Even if you don't know French, you've probably guessed the outcome: a snake bit Fréron and the snake died.

After bumping about the streets of Quimper, I recommend visiting the excellent Musée des Beaux Arts in the Place Saint Corentin behind the cathedral. Small enough not to be overwhelming, but rich enough to be engaging, the collection includes works by Dutch and Flemish old masters and classical French artists, but the most interesting sections are those related to local themes. The first picture we see when we enter is the *Légende de Kerdeck* (1890) by Fernand Le Quesne, an adaptation of the Washerwomen of the Night theme, described a bit sniffily as being 'academic and Parisian'. It's certainly not your traditional image of terrifying hags wringing out their winding sheets, but a distinctly salacious painting of a shadowy Breton peasant being lured into the sea by a lot of luscious young nymphs romping about in the foaming waves - what Freud would have made of it all, I hate to think. It's a very Victorian piece of work, at once titillating and moralizing, with the girls adopting various attitudes of abandon and doing the come-hither bit, while the hapless peasant is looking decidedly haggard, as if he knows it's all going to come to a sticky end. In the far corner of the same room, there's a *maquette* of the Gradlon statue by Amédée-Renée Ménard that adorns the cathedral, and beside it Luminais' *Fuite de Gradlon*. In the painting, Gradlon is emphatically shoving Dahut off his horse, while Saint Guénolé, a bit dubiously for a man of God, is galloping along clasping a bejeweled box of valuables, as if his very life depended on it. He is also, apparently, giving the finger to someone out of frame on our left.

Upstairs, the regional theme continues with some Botrelian images of Brittany by Charles Cottet (1863-1925) (a bit too keen on dead babies for my tastes) and the realist painter Lucien Simon (1861-1945), men who managed to live through Impressionism, Post-Impressionism, Expressionism and all the other artistic revolutions of the late nineteenth and early twentieth centuries without taking a blind bit of notice. To be fair, rather than being a simple case of negligence, this was a conscious decision to set themselves against the trends of their time, both in treatment and, to a lesser extent, subject matter, creating what became known as *La Bande Noire* in contrast to the light-infused works of the Impressionists. Some paintings, like Simon's *La Recolte des Pommes-de-Terre* (1907), give the lie to the group's dark name, but it all looks a bit dull once we move into the next room, which is dedicated to the Pont Aven school. We'll be bumping about Pont Aven later, so apart from advising you not to miss what's on display in Quimper and drawing your attention to the 1906 sculpture, *Les Fumeuses de Plozavet* by Renée Quillivic, we'll return downstairs, back to Quimper's most famous son and the Salle Max Jacob.

Jacob's own -Cubism influenced if not strictly Cubist- works are on display here, alongside slightly disappointing sketches by Picasso and Modigliani; there's another Gradlon statue, this time by Giovanni Leonardi; a much reproduced portrait of Jacob by Christopher Wood, the Cornish based artist who worked alongside Ben Nicholson before committing suicide at the age of 29; and various works by another Quimpérois artist Pierre Belay, notably the *Pardon de Saint Guénolé* (1943) and *Buvette en Bretagne* (1928). But by far the most interesting works in historical terms are the sketches by Jean Moulin.

It may not spark any instant recognition in the Anglo-Saxon world, but Jean Moulin is a household name in France, yet few people associate him with artistic endeavour. In the course of a twenty-three year career as a civil servant, Jean Moulin became the youngest *sous-Préfet* (in charge of an *arrondissement*) at the age of 26, the youngest *Préfet* (in charge of a *departement*) at the age of 38, and served in various ministerial postings, notably as *Ministre de l'Air* in the Front Populaire government, in which capacity he was instrumental in sending covert aid to the Spanish Republicans. In June 1940, the occupying forces ordered Moulin to sign a document blaming French Senegalese troops for massacring civilians who had actually been killed by a German bombardment. He refused, was thrown into jail, and tried to commit suicide by cutting his throat with a piece of broken glass. His captors saved his life, but he was dismissed by the Vichy government, after which he established contact with the nascent French Resistance. He then went to London to report to de Gaulle on the state of the Resistance and the resources they required, whereupon de Gaulle set him the task of unifying the movement's disparate elements, a major challenge given the political rifts between the various groups. He spent the next two years in and out of France, orchestrating the Resistance, until he was denounced and detained in 1943. He was tortured by the henchmen of Klaus Barbie, the notorious Butcher of Lyon, then again by the Gestapo in Paris, before dying en route to Berlin, where he was due to undergo further 'interrogation'. After the war, his ashes were transferred to the Panthéon and he was apotheosized as a symbol for the heroism of the French Resistance.

Moulin is not wholly untainted by controversy: as de Gaulle's representative, he was mistrusted by many at the time who saw no good reason why an absent right-wing general financed by American money should be issuing orders to the people fighting on the ground, many of whom were almost as wary of the Americans as they were of the Germans; and after the war Moulin himself was accused of being a crypto-communist; but there's no questioning his heroic stature. This was a man who, more than anyone, knew names, dates, addresses, networks, contact points, codes, plans, strategy and tactics. He was tortured by Barbie's men for three days. He didn't talk. He was tortured by the Gestapo in Paris. He didn't talk. He was due to be tortured in Berlin. He probably wouldn't have talked there, either. Whatever else may or may not be true about him, his heroism is humbling.

All this is well known. What is less well known is that he was an accomplished draughtsman and that when he was *sous-Préfet* in Chateaulin in Finistère, he was part of Max Jacob's artistic circle, drawing cartoons for local periodicals and illustrating a collection of poems by Tristan Corbière. It was clearly a period that marked him, for during his time as a clandestine organizer of the Resistance, his front was an art gallery called Romanin, the *nom de plume* he'd used as an illustrator, his messages to London where prefaced by lines from a poem by Corbière, and his undercover pseudonym was Max.

Among Moulin's most remarkable works are his drawings for Corbière's *Armor* collection. In terms of pure draughtsmanship, they're not particularly noteworthy, but their prescience is astonishing. Shot through with images of hunger, death and suffering, they are drawings that can only really be described as 'haunted', except what haunts them is the future rather than the past. Eschewing both the complacent appeal of the picturesque that Breton customs evoked in so many artists and the pornography of suffering that seduced others, his drawings still retain a raw power comparable to Goya's black paintings, above all the illustration for Corbière's *La Pastorale de Conlie*, a poem recalling one of the more infamous episodes when Breton peasants were employed as cannon-fodder by a nation that was otherwise content to keep them out on the fringes of things. Set against a field of crosses, a rough pit is filled with the emaciated corpses of naked men and women piled indiscriminately on top of one another. It was drawn in the early 1930s, but could easily have been

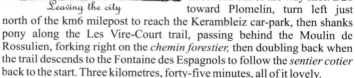

Leaving the city

inspired by a newsreel from the mid 1940s.

All this may seem a bit grim, so to escape the darker doings of mankind, I suggest leaving the city behind and visiting the countryside that was the refuge of both Moulin and Jacob. Again, we'll get the directions out of the way first: D20 toward Plomelin, turn left just north of the km6 milepost to reach the Kerambleiz car-park, then shanks pony along the Les Vire-Court trail, passing behind the Moulin de Rossulien, forking right on the *chemin forestier,* then doubling back when the trail descends to the Fontaine des Espagnols to follow the *sentier cotier* back to the start. Three kilometres, forty-five minutes, all of it lovely.

Some claim the Odet is the most beautiful river in France, which is pushing it a bit, but it is a lovely patch of water and Les Vire Court is one of its most attractive stretches. Literally 'the short bends', it's a sharp, narrow meander where the fast current used to pose problems for large ships bound for Quimper. The passage is so tight that legend claims marauding Spanish pirates got as far as what became known as the Pointe des Espagnols, decided the river ended there, took on fresh water supplies (hence the Fontaine des Espagnols), then turned around and sailed out to sea again. They must have been pretty hopeless pirates because it wouldn't have taken much initiative to poke their noses round the bend in the river, but Pugwashism notwithstanding, Les Vire Court earned themselves a fierce reputation. When the *chemin forestier* climbs steeply to a bench, look back upriver and you will see, below the Château de Kerambleiz, a waterside house known as *La Maison du Pendu*. It got its name from the fact that several of its proprietors hanged themselves, cursed, it is said, because previous residents had profited from their strategic location by imposing an illegal levy on boats negotiating the tricky passage to Porz Meillou and Porz ar Gwin.

The Porz ar Gwin creek is named after the Breton word for wine, since merchant ships on which the crew had been a bit too bibulous were said to stop here and take water from the spring to top up the barrels they'd illicitly tapped at sea. Opposite Porz ar Gwin is the Rocher du Forçat, a flat rock where a fugitive convict or *forçát* escaped his pursuers by doing a Reginald Perrin, leaving his clothes on the bank as if he'd thrown himself into the river, then hiding under the rock while plod scratched the collective noggin and concluded the man must have drowned. Another rock, La Chaise de L'Eveque on the left bank of Les Vire Court, is said to be where Quimper's bishops liked to sit back and contemplate the scene, a scene that includes a third rock, Le Saut de la Pucelle or The Maiden's Leap, after a girl who jumped to safety when menaced by the attentions of a randy monk. The monk jumped, too, but weighed down with concupiscence, he sank without trace.

There are countless lovely corners along the course of the Odet, places like Benodet, the homebase of France's most famous yachtsman, Eric Tabarly, or the chapel of St. Cadou, the patron saint of wrestlers, or the Anse de Toulven, source of the clay used in Quimper's potteries, or Sainte-Marine where Emile Zola became one of Brittany's first tourists in the Summer of 1883, and some of the finest châteaux in Brittany are hidden away in the woods overlooking the river. We've taken a day and have just touched on what the area has to offer. Take a week and you will continue to find extraordinary places and eccentric histories. Who knows, you may even spot a parrot perched in the treetops. Probably best not to shoot it, though. The taxman won't take any account of your prowess whatsoever and having a lot of holidaymakers taking potshots at the local fauna wouldn't do the reputation of the English any good at all.

14. The Man From Far Away

ACCESS - **Pont Aven** is between Quimper and Quimperlé, just south of the N165 on the D783. To reach **Port Belon**, take the D783 east toward Quimperlé then turn right on the minor road passing through 'Coat-Pin'.

Quick word association: what images are conjured by the name Gauguin? The chances are you'll think of tumultuous times in Arles with Vincent lopping off his ear, or picture some Polynesian paradise freighted with *deshabille* native girls and big metaphysical questions. In some ways, though, the most influential period in the artist's career were the thirty-two months he spent at Pont Aven in Brittany between 1886 and 1894, when he more or less invented Modern Art.

The Pont Aven School was a loose association of like-minded painters whose experiments synthesizing form, colour and motif proved to

Gaugan's Christ Jaune

be an essential bridge between Impressionism and the artistic movements of the early Twentieth Century. When Gauguin, whom Van Gogh described as "The man who has come from far away and who will go far", first arrived in Pont Aven, the former tide-mill town was already a thriving artistic colony, and had been for several decades. In a world that was rapidly becoming industrial and urban, Pont Aven was a haven of tradition and tranquility that attracted artists from far and wide, the best known of its earlier residents being the American painter, Robert Wylie. Granaries were converted into studios, lofts turned into cheap lodgings, artists' cafés sprang up, and the town adapted itself to accommodating a bucolic variety of the

Bohemian life - to a degree, at least: in 1883 the municipal authorities were obliged to forbid the sale of alcohol after 10pm, because it was all getting a bit too Bohemian! There was, therefore, nothing pioneering about Gauguin's presence in Brittany. But whereas previous painters had pictured the region in a realist, academic, and historical vein, portraying with conventional piety a conventionally pious society where everyone knew their place and God was in his heaven, Gauguin was seeking something else, something at once displaced and discrete. In 1888, he wrote: "*J'aime la Bretagne, j'y trouve le sauvage, le primitif. Quand mes sabots résonnent sur ce sol de granit, j'entends le ton sourd, mat et puissant que je cherche en peinture.*" I like Brittany, there I find the savage, the primitive. When my clogs resound against this granite ground, I hear the dull, dark, powerful tone that I'm searching for in painting.

Not that we should get too misty eyed about the reasons he came to Brittany. He liked it, all right, and his work is full of Breton images,

Breton models, Breton light, and even, I'd hazard, the Breton penchant for the *royaume de l'imaginaire*, for one of the defining precepts of the Synthetism or Cloissonism that evolved in Pont Aven was a symbolism in which dream, mystery, fantasy and oneiric visions were primary; anyone who has bumped about the Monts d'Arrée can tell you that's a very Breton appraisal of what's important. Nonetheless, his main motive for coming to Pont Aven was money. Gauguin didn't have any and his creditors felt he ought to be doing something about finding them some. Lodgings, booze and food were all cheap in Pont Aven, it was full of kindred spirits, and none of his creditors lived there: ergo, the perfect place to invent Modern Art.

Pont Aven may not be the first spot that comes to mind when you mention Gauguin, but it's famous enough to have become a major tourist attraction, and first impressions are not good. Approach it on a holiday weekend and the town looks like it's sick with money. There's no denying that it's very pretty, even when swamped with coachloads of tourists, but nearly every building houses an alleged art gallery and those that don't are either selling more commonplace souvenirs or the butter biscuits for which the region is also famous, a hangover from the town's flour-milling traditions. The business of arts and crafts is so prevalent, a sign I initially take to be an indication that dog owners should clean up after their pets proves to be an advert for a glassblower's workshop! 'Heritage', dread word, dominates the place, even the surrounding fields are full of rape, as if in homage to those big, blocked yellows Gauguin liked so much. My first instinct is to tell you to get in there, get your packet of Traou Mad biscuits (they're very good), get into the museum, then get the hell out of there. But it's worth persevering. This maybe a conventional tourist destination, but as with Quimper, what's conventional is not necessarily to be condemned. Behind the facade, there's still a real community, and if you can get past the initial shock and don't choke on your biscuit when you see the price tags, the private galleries are worth visiting. Admittedly, two thirds of them could be replaced by a chocolate box factory and you wouldn't miss a thing, but there are some interesting artists here, not least some of the most derivative imitating techniques refined by Gauguin, Maurice Maufra, Paul Sérusier, and the Émiles Bernard and Rocher. I guess if you're going to imitate someone, best imitate the masters. There are, however, some symptoms of the malaise of money. Landowners with property fronting the estuary of the nearby River Belon argued, unsuccessfully, that the waters weren't salty enough for the *loi littoral* to be applicable, so there was no preemption right for the *sentier cotier* to cross their land! But in contrast to such nimbyism, Pont Aven itself is a welcoming place and not everything is geared toward fleecing the transient custom.

So what's to be done when you visit Pont Aven? Well, you do buy your biscuits and you do visit the Musée des Beaux Arts, but before making a break for the countryside, have a look at the private galleries, too. True, there are sixty of the things and, for a permanent population of less than 3000, that's got to be about fifty too many, but it's by no means all painting by numbers, and there's some pleasure to be had from sifting the chaff from the wheat for yourself. Beforehand, though, set the standard by taking a turn round the Musée des Beaux Arts, which incorporates part of the Hotel Julia, one of the artists' resorts in the early years of the colony. The permanent collection isn't a match for that in Quimper, but it's still a miniature treasure trove, and the front rooms are reserved for excellent temporary exhibitions of individual painters associated with Pont Aven.

Once you're sated with art in enclosed spaces, it's time to take to the woods, the Bois d'Amour to be precise, to visit the sites that inspired Gauguin and his contemporaries. There are several pictures of the Bois d'Amour in the *musée* and it might seem a bit naff to visit the 'real' thing that inspired the painting, as if you were missing the whole point of the art, the very artifice that has been deployed to render an artistic truth beyond what is visible to untutored, untalented eyes. All I can say is that it doesn't feel gauche once you're there. The magic of the waymarked trail is unmistakable as we stroll alongside the River Aven between the woods and the water, our path spotted with wildflowers, the steeply sloping hillside spangled with tumblings of mossy rocks, and all the while the water whispering and chattering at our feet, shifting back and forth between babble and susurrus, susurrus and babble according to the various obstacles in its course. And then there are the paintings. Oh, yes. You don't escape painting at Pont Aven, even when you get out into the countryside. Both within the town and in its immediate vicinity, ceramic reproductions of the Pont Aven School's most famous works have been installed in front of the scenes that first inspired them. Another invincibly naff idea? Not really. Again, it's done with such discrimination and the original paintings are so very good, it works. This is not a theme park and the people of Pont Aven haven't painted themselves into a corner.

Moulin du Bois d'Amour

The first reproduction we pass lies upstream of the local Chaos on the right bank of the river, and is the product of perhaps the most famous and certainly one of the most influential painting lessons in history. Paul Sérusier was another painter with a passion for Brittany, which he described as his true homeland, the place where his spirit was born. Quite apart from any intrinsic merits it may possess, Sérusier had good reason to like the region, because, without greatly exaggerating, it was the work of one afternoon in Brittany that secured his place in the history of art. All those involved in the Pont Aven School denied it was a 'school' in any conventional sense, insisting it was rather a 'school of nature', a coming together of artists, ideas and subject matter that subsequently inspired movements as diverse as Symbolism, Fauvism and even, to a degree, Cubism. But much of that inspiration can be traced to an isolated 'lesson' when Gauguin stood behind Sérusier as he painted, advising him not to copy nature too closely, but to dream in front of it, prompting the younger artist with a series of rhetorical questions: *How do you see that tree? It's green, isn't it, really green? So make it green, the loveliest green you have on your palette. And that shadow, it's more blue, isn't it? So don't hesitate to paint it as blue as possible...* Such advice may seem banal nowadays, but in a period that was still, despite the impact of Impressionism, dominated by the burden of academic realism, the notion that an artist should bring out the immanent, abstracted truth of colour was revolutionary.

Maurice Denis articulated the underlying principle best when he said: "*La Nature, j'ai voulu la copier; je n'arrivais pas. Mais j'ai été content de moi lorsque j'ai decouvert que le soleil, par exemple, ne se pouvait pas reproduire, mais qu'il fallait le représenter par autre chose - par le couleur*"; in short, you can't copy nature, you can't remake the sun, but you can represent it through colour. Even more baldly, he explained that it was as well to remember that a picture, before being a battle horse, a nude, or an anecdote, is essentially a flat surface covered with colours assembled in a certain order. If the world cannot be reproduced and colour is pre-eminent, you're only a short step away from abstraction. And Gauguin knew what he was doing, too. He later said: "*Vous savez depuis longtemps ce que j'ai voulu établir: le droit de tout oser. Ceux qui, aujourd`hui, profitent de cette liberté me doivent quelque chose*"; *I always wanted to establish the right to dare/risk everything. Those who profit from this liberty today, owe me something.*

There's certainly something daring, something verging on the abstract about the picture Sérusier painted under Gauguin's guidance and which is reproduced alongside the Aven, the *Paysage du Bois d'Amour*'(1888). But the importance of this painting was not simply personal, for Sérusier subsequently returned to Paris, showed the picture to friends like Pierre Bonnard and Edouard Vuillard, spoke about Gauguin's ideas, and thus inspired the group that came to be known as the *Nabis* or 'the prophets', named for the ancient prophets of Israel who had revitalized Judaism in the same way that these young artists sought to revitalize art. That's one theory, at least, though I've also read they got their name because they were desperately earnest, bearded Jews. Either way, the *Paysage du Bois d'Amour* was a talismanic painting for the group and is to this day still better known by the title *Le Talisman*. Not bad for a sketch on the back of a cigar box.

Shortly after the reproduction of The Talisman, we reach a picture perfect mill-cottage, the timeless aspect of

The Talisman in situ

which is marred only by a satellite dish. The footbridge in front of the cottage leads to the main Bois d'Amour car-park and features another reproduction, Gauguin's *La Baignade au Moulin du Bois d'Amour* (1886), but to see the inspiration for a painting that has been even more influential and pivotal in art history than The Talisman, we need to continue on the waymarked circuit. Upstream, the left bank of the river is dominated by some rather grim industrial warehouses, but somehow even these don't spoil the charm of the woods. Doubtless, they'd be a bit more disagreeable if they housed a lot of rackety machinery belching out clouds of black smoke, but in context they barely take the edge off the prettiness and help prevent Pont Aven becoming the museum city it might easily be. After climbing away from the river, the trail curves back to a road just above the town, at which point we turn right to visit the Chapelle de Trémalo, which houses what is, in many ways, the holy grail for fans of the Pont Aven School.

The road is drivable and doubtless much driven, but if you're early enough, it's infinitely more pleasurable and fitting to approach the chapel on foot, almost in a spirit of pilgrimage. The other advantage is that you're more likely to get waylaid by the retired sailor who lives in the rundown farmhouse just before the chapel. I swear, this garrulous old salt lays in wait for tourists, whom he will bushwhack with any observation that comes to mind, so long as it's enough to ensure you'll tarry along the way. In our case the trigger is our Pyrenean Mountain Dog: "Look-at-that-for-me-will-you, look-at-the-size-of-that-thing, bet-you-get-a-stiff-back-walking-a-beast-like-that-don't-you, got-a-stiff-back-have-you, what's-it-weigh, must-weigh-fifty-kilos-a-dog-like-that, you-got-a-stiff-back-have-you, I-bet-you-have, look-at-that-for-me-will-you, look-at-that-woman-there, she's-got-back-problems, she's-got-to-have-back-problems, big-dog-like-that, that-can-give-you-back-problems-a-dog-like-that-can . . ." He then regales us with a colourful evocation of his forty year career at sea: "Come-back-to-bury-myself-in-the-earth-here, you-go-to-sea-you-can-walk-round-the-boat-fifty-times-and-it's-all-the-same, all-water, water-as-far-as-the-eye-can-see, nothing-but-water, just-water, water-everywhere-I-tell-you, water-water-everywhere-and-not-a-drop-to-drink, when-I-go-to-town-now-I-really-hang-one-on, really-I-do, I-really-hang-one-on", this last sentiment expressed via the picturesque maritime expression for getting drunk, *prendre une bordée*, which is analogous to if not quite the same as 'going overboard'. Despite all the tourism, the people of Pont Aven haven't changed all that much since Gauguin was here. Always presuming you get away from this agreeable old Cerberus, you will find at the Chapelle de Trémalo something else that hasn't changed much since Gauguin's time.

The oaks in front of the entrance, for instance, are old enough to have provided the painter with a bit of oxygen and not a lot has been altered in the chapel itself, but what is most extraordinary is the crucifix that hangs inside, a seventeenth century carving that moved Gauguin so deeply he took it out into a field and painted the most famous of his Cloisonnist works (the term comes from the *cloisonné* enamelling technique developed by Émile Bernard), *Le Christ Jaune* (1889), which is reproduced on another panel outside. This painting with its bold blocks of colour and idiosyncratic take on perspective is regarded as a turning point between two types of art, dispensing with the post-Renaissance pretence at realism and liberating, as was Gauguin's avowed intent, other artists to 'dare everything'. And the original crucifix, which would probably be worth a small fortune to an unscrupulous collector, is still there, the chapel is open, and anyone can go in and see it; this in a region where places of worship have regularly been stripped of their art works - even our local church in a relatively obscure corner of Brittany, well off the tourist track, was burgled and the statuary later surfaced in an antiques shop in the south of Italy. Doubtless alarm bells would go off if you tried to prise the thing off the wall, but in an age when any sorry peck of memorabilia is fenced off and turned into a fee paying attraction or whisked away for its own protection to the sterile vaults of a museum, the fact that such a potent icon is still in its original place and is freely accessible to all, is greatly to be admired.

If, by the by, you still have any doubts as to the impact of what went on at Pont Aven, or suspect it was a matter of one famous artist and a lot of hangers on, another anecdote. When Gauguin went to work with Van Gogh in Arles in 1888, he took with him Émile Bernard's recently completed *Bretonnes au Pardon* to decorate their shared studio. Van Gogh was so taken with the painting, he said he just had to have a copy, so he sat down and promptly reproduced it in watercolours. Any group that can move an artist of the originality and stature of Van Gogh to become a mere copyist, is not some little local phenomenon.

By the 1890s, Pont Aven was developing as a tourist resort and was getting too crowded and too costly for the likes of Gauguin, so for his last visits to Brittany, he retired to the coastal hamlet of Pouldu in Clohars-Carnoët and the seaside bar of Marie-Henry, which he decorated with murals during one idle and indigent Summer. Planning this excursion, I decided we would do the same. Not that

Chapelle de Tremalo

we'd be knocking out a lot of infinitely valuable murals, but we would escape the crowds of Pont Aven and end our day bumping about peaceful Pouldu. Alas, no! We went there, all right, but I wouldn't recommend you go out of your way to do likewise. I'm sure it's a nice enough place for a summer holiday. The beaches must be lovely and the customs path to Doelan is reputedly very pretty. And doubtless the dedicated Gauguinophile will go there regardless of what I say. But whereas Pont Aven's prettiness already existed in bricks and mortar before Gauguin's time, and was thus readily preserved, the principal appeal of Pouldu was its untenanted wildness, a wildness that has now been lost, and the dunes for which it was famous have all but disappeared under charmless second homes. I was so upset, I just turned around and drove away.

There is, however, another option for escaping the crowds if you're visiting at the height of the season and even the Bois d'Amour is overwhelmed, and that is to drive out to Port de Belon, famous for the brackish waters that give its oysters such a distinctive flavour, and infamous for that spat about when is a coast not a coast. Happily, the *sentier cotier* is gradually being pushed through and very nice it is, too, winding its way alongside the picturesque estuary, shaded by woodland that need feel no shame when compared to the better known Bois d'Amour, and lined with a lovely array of wildflowers. This is very much a working estuary and there are places where patches of the path are so densely encrusted with the spoil of oyster shells that they appear to be paved with mother of pearl. After your stroll, you can sit beside the river and indulge in a dozen *huîtres de Belon* washed down with a bottle of white wine. Even if, like me, you don't quite see the point of oysters ("They taste of the sea", claim aficionados, but then so does the sea and it comes a lot cheaper than oysters), it's still a perfect spot to sip a drop of wine and make a toast to the man from far away who did, indeed, go far.

In some ways, Gauguin may not have done the region many favours, putting it a little too firmly on the map, but there's enough magic here to carry the burden, and give you a sense of somewhere special, somewhere privileged, somewhere that might be full of personal meaning for each and every visitor. Indeed, sat on the banks of the Belon with a glass in hand at the end of a good day's bumping about, one can even begin to fancy there's a peculiar quality to the light bathing this patch of southern Brittany: a brightness and depth, a true lucidity; evanescent but so evocative it would be worth striving, no matter how vainly, to capture it on canvas ("Another glass? Don't mind if I do"); the sort of light that might inspire you to dabble in paint yourself, the sort of light that brings everything out in sharp relief, makes everything more real, the sort of light that was bound to get the artists crowding in. A peculiar quality? Probably not. The illumination is likely rather nearer to that of an *illuminé*, the derogatory French word for a visionary. As I say, Gauguin's reasons for coming here were more down to earth than the quality of the light. But fancy never did anyone any harm. Not in the *royaume de l'imaginaire*, where dream, mystery, fantasy and oneiric visions are primary - or perhaps that should be oenic visions. Another bottle? Why not?

15. Also Made in Brittany:
Le Pape, Le Pen, et Le Maire

ACCESS - **Ploërmel** is in eastern Morbihan at the intersection of the N166 from Vannes and the N24 from Rennes. **Trinité-sur-Mer** lies to the west of Vannes between Quiberon and the mouth of the Golfe de Morbihan. **St. Coulitz** is in Finistère just west of the N165 between Quimper and Brest. The simplest way to get there is to go into the centre of **Chateaulin** then follow the minor roads to the east (signposted 'St. Coulitz') along the left bank of the River Aulne/Canal de Nantes à Brest (i.e. the southern side).

Big Bronze Pope

Travel between England, France and Spain, and you will notice that there are distinct techniques for keeping a conversation going. In England, talk is passed from person to person, like a small and delicate parcel that everyone must touch but nobody must snatch and which can only be unwrapped if each person peels off a sheet of paper in turn. Doesn't matter if you have no opinion about the subject. Everyone must have their say and recalcitrant talkers will be chivvied into making their contribution, no matter how banal it maybe. In France, conversation better resembles a brawl in which everyone starts bawling at once and he who bawls loudest and longest is begrudgingly listened to by everyone else until a new subject crops up and the skirmish begins again. In Spain, everyone shouts all the time, nobody listens, and everybody's happy. But there is, in France, another, less well known and far more diffident technique wherein every attempt at eliciting a conversation is killed stone dead by a monosyllabic interjection: "*Bof!*"

There's no translation for this word. In some contexts, it echoes the Anglo-Saxon variant of testes, but it's far more versatile than your average male reproductive organs. It incorporates something of the traditional 'Gallic shrug' overlaid with a more pessimistic sense of I-can't-be-arsed. It's indicative of dismissive, slightly cynical fatalism. It's not the sort of thing you'll hear the President of the Republic saying, though it would be fun if you did. Instead, it's part of the language of adolescence, admittedly an adolescence that can be arrested well into early middle-age, but none the less adolescent for that, a sort of halfway house between childhood's defiant "Yeah? You and whose army?" and the self-deprecating "I'm afraid I'm passed all that sort of stuff now" capitulation of advanced maturity. Used in response to a question or suggestion, it implies that the person who asked the question or made the suggestion should have known better and that their interlocutor is not going to stoop so low as to respond in detail.

I like this word. French, after all, is a language in which the translations of Don Quixote and Moby Dick each run to two substantial volumes rather than the usual single volume editions in English. It's famously precise, but it does take up a lot of space. That such a complex and multi-layered concept as I-can't-be-arsed-it's-all-going-to-fall-apart-I-don't-think-much-of-that-what's-the-point-what-a-lot-of-cobblers can be reduced to a monosyllabic puff of air is a considerable achievement. In fact, there's nothing else quite like it in French.

Bof! can be used to answer interrogative suggestions: "Why don't you try something else, I'm sure you could?"

"*Bof*!"

It can be used to respond to unwarranted optimism: "Let's look on the bright side."

"*Bof*!"

It can be used to curb enthusiasm: "Did you hear what the President said? That's really rather interesting, isn't it?"

"*Bof*!"

And it can be used as a substitute for a disparaging comment you can't be bothered to make but still want to communicate: "I do admire politicians."

"*Bof*!"

This is a chapter of two *bofs* and an *unbof*, bumping about three villages in Brittany that have earned fame or notoriety for reasons that have little to do with the criteria of ordinary tourism.

***

Ask anybody in France who doesn't live in the immediate vicinity of Ploërmel in Morbihan if they've heard of the place and the chances are they'll say, "Ah, the pope!" This may come as a surprise to the casual visitor. Popes in Rome, we know, popes in Avignon we may have heard about, but popes in Ploërmel? Well, one pope, actually. Jean Paul II. Nine metres of him.

In September 2005, Ploërmel was rocked by scandal. The right-wing mayor, Paul Anselin, a man of such authoritarian instincts his political opponents nicknamed him 'Pol Pot', announced that a nine metre statue of the pope by the Russo-Georgian sculptor Zourab Tsereteli would be placed between Ploërmel's College du Sacré-Coeur and the Ecole St. Joseph. Cue local and national outrage.

First, the statue was free, but the town council had voted 130,000 euros for the plinth and an opening ceremony, 130,000 euros a lot of taxpayers felt might have been better spent on local services than on glad-handing a big bronze pope.

Second, if public art was required, there were plenty of good Breton sculptors just itching for such a commission, so what was all this business with Russo-Georgians?

Thirdly, it was widely disputed that Tsereteli was a 'good' sculptor. A favourite of the Muscovite mega-rich oligarchs and the grandees of the Kremlin, Tsereteli specializes in colossal statues that make up in bulk what they lack in subtlety. Frequently accused of heavy-handed academicism, he has been scattering giant bronzes about Moscow ever since the disintegration of the Soviet Union (including a 96 metre Peter The Great!), but not satisfied with that, he's started giving the things away abroad, too. Unfortunately, not everyone wants a Tsereteli. His Balzac got shunted about France for dark ages before it found a home, Manhattan politely turned down his 175 ton commemoration of 9/11, and the people of Ploërmel were none too sure they wanted a statue at all.

Fourthly, people wondered why they were getting it. How come the mayor of an obscure Breton commune was chummy enough with a high-flying Russian sculptor to be getting free statues out of him? 'Services rendered', said Anselin, and refused to elaborate. Journalists started digging and it transpired that Anselin had links with the French arms dealer, Pierre Falcone, who is in turn linked to the billionaire Russian businessman, Arcadi Gaydamak. Nothing was proven, but there was a widespread suspicion that there was a bad smell in the room and it wasn't coming from the pope.

Above all, though, it was the fact that the statue was of a pope that got people's backs up. Balzac may have been obliged to haul himself about the country before finally finding a berth at Agde in the Herault region, but whatever else he may have been, Balzac was no pope - not to the best of my knowledge, at least. And the 1905 law concerning the separation of church and state specifically forbids the placing of religious symbols in public places. This is hard to understand for the British who have happily muddled along for several centuries with intimately interlinked political and religious authorities, and the only time anybody talks about it is when debating whether disestablishmentarianism is the longest word in the dictionary or not. But secularity is one of the lynchpins of French republicanism and people can get very heated in its defence. Very heated. The Ploërmel pope rapidly became a *cause celebre*.

"*C'est grotesque!*"

"*C'est n'importe quoi!*"

"If he wants a statue, let him have it in his garden."

In fact, Anselin had offered the statue to the local friary, who've got a nice big garden and might have been supposed to be quite keen on the pope, but for some reason the brothers had declined this kind offer, so he was stuck with nine metres of pope and nowhere to put the thing and he couldn't very well stick it in the shed.

"You got nothing better to do with your money than put up a statue to a dead pope?!"

"A Stalinist statue for a Stalinist administration!"

It all got quite intense. Protests were made, petitions were signed, websites set up, demonstrations staged, but all to no avail. Anselin was adamant. The Pope stays!

Clochemerle? Never heard of it.

I don't know whether it has anything to do with the pope or not, but there seem to be an uncommonly large number of houses for sale as we drive into Ploërmel. And there he is! Can't miss him. Big pope. Well, biggish. Jean Paul II, standing on his plinth, framed by a bronze scaffold topped with a dirty great cross. To be honest, it's a little hard to see what all the fuss was about. True, the statue isn't very pretty, but then neither is Ploërmel. More to the point, all those reports about nine metres of pope were a bit disingenuous. The bulk of the statue is plinth, frame and cross. You only actually get about three metres of pope for your money, three metres too many for French republicans, but still several metres short of nine, which it must be said, would have been a pretty scary prospect. Three metres is big for a pope, but it's not that large for a statue. And the sculpture itself is not really as Stalinist as we'd been lead to believe. Competent town-hall bust stuff, no better, no worse. Certainly looks like the pope. True, the bright shining bronze is a bit vulgar, but come in search of a Sino-Soviet-Saddamite-North-Korean monumentalism, and you'll be disappointed. Apart from us, there's a couple of middle-aged bikers, all belly and leather and too many business lunches, posing for a photo in front of the plinth, and an old boy gazing at the pope's backside with dazed admiration muttering something along the lines of "Now that's what I call art". The Pope appears to be smirking. Perhaps he's pleased with the message inscribed below his feet: "*N'ayez pas peur*", have no fear. One lapsed catholic, seriously lapsed, demands what that's all about.

Momentarily disappointed in our search for schlock, we stroll into town. They're busy digging up the road. There's a rather jaunty cock atop the war memorial. Behind the church there's a locked door with an A4 sheet in the frosted glass window saying, "Everything English". In one sense, that's a fair description of Ploërmel. There are security cameras everywhere. This may not shock someone coming from the UK, where I believe there are more surveillance cameras per head of the population than in any other country in the world, but the definition of civil liberties is a very mutable thing and what exercises one nation will be of not import to another. The British are up in arms about identity cards as a potential infringement of their freedom, but are perfectly happy to have cameras recording their every public move. In France, ID cards are so integral to daily life it's actually illegal to go out without one, but surveillance cameras are considered a bit iffy, especially in a quiet country town like Ploërmel. This is the smallest *commune* in France to have installed CCTV. The message is - There may only be 8,500 of you, but We Are Watching You!

What's really sinister, though, are the loudspeakers. They're everywhere, fixed to walls beside the cameras, burbling piped music like those sound systems councils put up at Christmas to regale the weary shopper with jingle bloody bells and Noddy Holder's bid for immortality. Except here the piped music is interrupted every thirty seconds or so by a mincing voice promoting the local entrepreneurs and encouraging the idle *flâneur* to stop wasting his time and to get in there and buy something, you bloody waster! It's really rather nasty and the longer we stay, the more uneasy I become. Maybe I'm over-reacting, perhaps I'm having some sort of panic attack. It's perfectly possible. Get stuck inside a shop too long and I begin to believe I'm never going to get out again. It's very distressing. Perhaps the impression that the shops are now getting proactive and coming after me is enough to tip me over the edge. But I still think there's a distinct whiff of Big Brother about Ploërmel. Forget about the pope. *N'ayez pas peur!* There's something gone badly wrong here and it's been going badly wrong since long before Jean Paul II got himself done up in bronze. Ploërmel is the antithesis of a *Petite Cité de Caractère*. It's got no charm, no focus, no character and gives the impression of having being put together with willful incompetence, as if this were an experiment in making all the wrong town-planning choices that were possible and just sort of jamming stuff together to see what it looks like. And it's this very awfulness I recommend you go and see. There are more pleasing sites all around Ploërmel, but when you're bumping about, you don't want everything to be too conventionally pretty. You want things to be a bit off the wall, too. And Ploërmel is very off the wall with its CCTV and disembodied injunctions to buy! buy! buy! And there's always the pope - and his friends . . .

Didn't I mention that?

That Paul Anselin, he must have been chastened by the way his statue was received, eh? He wouldn't be wanting to make that mistake again, would he? Er, well . . . By the time this book goes to press, a winged lion by a local sculptor should have been installed in Ploërmel. Then it's back to our boy Tsereteli for a St. George and The Dragon and -wait for it- a nineteen metre General de Gaulle.

Clochemerle? Never heard of it.

***

Nineteen metres of General de Gaulle might well be the defining nightmare for the personality that inspires our next visit in this triptych. It was de Gaulle after all who 'gave away' Algeria, wherein the rot began.

Trinité-sur-Mer is an estuary port that would probably be no better known than any other seaside resort were it not for the fact that it was the birthplace of a national figure who is deeply attached to his roots and wants everyone else to be deeply attached to their roots, too. Head of the extreme right-wing Front National and presidential candidate for the party until 2007, Jean-Marie Le Pen was born in Trinité-sur-Mer in 1928, the son of a fisherman of Italian stock, and a girl from the farming hamlet of Kerdaniel at Locmariaquer.

When he talks about his childhood, Le Pen's reminiscences are only a shade this side of that *We-had-it-hard/Call-that-hard!* Monty Python sketch. His home was a two room cottage with a dirt floor and an attic full of fishing gear. There was no electricity or running water, the privy was a thunderbox at the bottom of the garden, and the eggs were sold at market, never eaten by the family, except on Easter Day. "*C'était très pauvre. Pauvre, mais hônnete*". The poverty only got worse when Le Pen was 14 and his father was killed after his boat hit a mine, an accident rather than the result of fighting the Germans as has sometimes been suggested. At sixteen Le Pen volunteered for and was turned down by the French Resistance.

Arriving in Paris as a student, he earned a reputation for being munificent with his mouth and even more munificent with his fists, and in 1949 was elected president of the radical right-wing student union at the

University of Paris Law School. After serving in the army, he joined the populist movement of Pierre Poujade, a former stationer who blamed France's postwar economic turmoil on tax-collectors, intellectuals and Jewish big business. The movement fell apart after 1958, but not before Le Pen had become France's youngest ever member of parliament at the age of 27. Following a second stint in the army, this time in Algeria, he lost his seat and became presidential campaign manager for Jean-Louis Tixier-Vignancour, former Vichy minister and defence lawyer for the OAS leaders who had, among other things, conspired to assassinate de Gaulle. In 1972, Le Pen formed the Front National and in 1974 stood for president, getting one per cent of the vote. In 1977, a wealthy admirer left him a fortune, securing his financial future. By the 1990s, his share of the vote had risen to 15 per cent. In 2002, the socialist presidential candidate, Lionel Jospin, was knocked out in the first round, forcing French left-wingers to don the blindfold, pinch their nostrils shut with a clothes peg, grit their teeth, cross their legs, curl their toes, tie a knot in their craws, plaster their necks with deep-heat cream, and vote for the widely despised incumbent, Jacques Chirac. The spectacle was extraordinary. It was as if an entire nation had been obliged to scrape their nails across a blackboard and pretend the sound it made wasn't particularly unpleasant.

The outpourings of Le Pen, both physical and verbal, are well documented and are far too distasteful to be detailed here, including as they do comments most people regard as racist, anti-Semitic, xenophobic, and homophobic - there are a lot of phobias in Le Pen's discourses. Rather more interesting, though, for the purposes of bumping about is the question of what impact Le Pen has had on his hometown.

Trinité-sur-Mer is nowadays a popular yachting centre and the quayside is defined by the usual yachtie paraphernalia of restaurants, bars, chandlers, and shops selling stripy T-shirts. But behind this veneer, the old fishing village has remained intact and is largely untouched by the big business of moneyed leisure. It's a strikingly charming place, too, with narrow peaceful alleys and tiny paths snaking their way between picturesque old cottages.

There are no statues of Le Pen, though his father's name does appear on the war memorial in the church square. The inscription, 'J Le Pen', is one that would also have served for Le Pen *fils* before he entered politics, when he changed his name from Jean to Jean-Marie, allegedly on the advice of his wife, who reckoned it a better device for pulling in the conservative Catholic vote. A little way behind the church, opposite the Impasse de Farfadets, is the cottage where Le Pen was born, now turned into a holiday home to which he returns every year at All Saints. Locals are understandably cagey when asked about the town's most famous son. Trinité-sur-Mer is a conservative place, but not that conservative and, like elsewhere in Brittany, the Front National has traditionally scored poorly in elections. Some of Le Pen's contemporaries hint at dark secrets they'd rather not tell, others are openly hostile, but the comments are by no means all negative. He is still regarded as *'un enfant du pays'*, even if most people disagree with his political views, and virtually everyone will tell you that when he's in residence he expects no favours and assumes no airs or graces.

As tourism goes, this trip was all a tad furtive. You can appreciate people must get a bit miffed at snooping journalists turning up before every election and they probably don't need some sardonic Englishman sticking his oar in, too. After we'd glanced at the cottage, we strolled down the Impasse de Farfadets which leads into a lovely flower-lined path winding between the back gardens of houses before emerging on a private driveway overlooking the seafront. I was quite pleased by this; it seemed only right that a foreigner visiting Le Pen's birthplace should engage in a little light trespassing. Better still, the night before, there was a crescent moon rising above Trinité-sur-Mer.

The shock of Le Pen making the second round of the 2002 presidential election was a profound national trauma and it was in no small measure thanks to that shock that there was such a record turn out for the 2007 election, in which Le Pen was roundly shoved back into fourth place. In that perhaps, he was a good thing for democracy. Nonetheless, he still got ten per cent of the national vote, and the extreme right is far from a spent force in France. Le Pen has played the politics of opposition so effectively that opinions once considered marginal if not actively deranged are now aired without shame, and he will for a long time represent something that many people want represented, a consistent strand in French politics ever since the days of the Dreyfus affair, reappearing in the Vichy regime, the Poujadist movement, and the candidature of Tixier-Vignancour, and doubtless to be embodied by someone else in the future. Dismal it maybe, but dead it ain't.

Trinité-sur-Mer war memorial

It's a facet of France most French people prefer not to contemplate, but it's there nonetheless, and is not above suggesting France is full of "invaders who want to sleep in my bed with my wife" (*sic*). Perhaps somebody should point out to the Front National that there are around one and a quarter million French people living abroad, nearly 300,000 of them in the UK. What are *they* doing, I wonder. They can't all be flogging arms and scouting about for freebies from dodgy Russian sculptors. Whose jobs are they taking and whose wives are they sleeping with? Hm? Answer me that! Questions must be asked.

So what else has Trinité-sur-Mer got to offer apart from a handful of pretty lanes lined with some nice stone houses? Well, there's the coastal path, which is always worth exploring. There's the port with a plethora of yachts to spark the imaginations of the fantasists amongst us. More tellingly, though, this is the heart of menhir land. The majority of the most famous megalithic alignments are just next door to Trinité-sur-Mer. It's all a bit antediluvian, really. Primeval, if you know what I mean.

***

Head west from Morbihan into Finistère and you will find the tiny hamlet of St. Coulitz, home to a man who could not be further removed from Le Pen. St. Coulitz is the smallest and best preserved of the three *communes* featured in this chapter, untouched by tourism, and far and away the hardest to locate both on the map and on the ground. Our approach was not helped by the fact that the main road from Chateaulin was closed, as a result of which we began by driving across a peripheral tongue of land framed by a couple of *communal* boundary signs and thinking that was St. Coulitz in its entirety. But even without roadworks, you could easily miss the place if you weren't actively looking for it.

A scattered farming hamlet set amid attractive rolling countryside, this is a peaceful, lost corner. The web of lanes holding it together are signposted with local names, but there's scant indication of any way out toward bigger places, as if, once here, no one would ever want to leave. They've got a point. I could quite happily settle down in St. Coulitz and vegetate, though vegetate is hardly the word to describe the career of its most famous resident.

We spent a very pleasant half-day there pottering about, visiting the sixteenth century church, the seventeenth century Chapelle Saint Laurent, the bucolic little Fontaine de Troboa, and above all strolling along the canal linking Nantes and Brest. This is a particularly lovely inland waterway and wherever you happen to touch upon it, you can guarantee an idyllic stroll. At St. Coulitz it's lined with majestic plane trees, the towpath is spotted with orchids, and the odd clump of arum lilies form islands in the bankside shallows. And there's plenty of wildlife, too. As we strolled along the left bank, there was a staccato splashing as a scattering of frogs dived for shelter, shattering the still surface of the reflected plane trees - mind you, the frogs are always a bit jumpy when the English are around. Later, a plump coypu rolled lazily off a log into the rust coloured waters of the canal; coypus

are illegal immigrants, of course, brought to Europe for their fur, then dumped when fur became unfashionable, but that would probably be no excuse for the likes of Monsieur Le Pen. In the vanguard of our progress was the flashing electric blue dart of a kingfisher, which seemed fitting, since in some ways the whole thrust of this chapter is fishing after kings or would-be kings, those who have been touched by some ambition for power. We also saw a fisherman wading across a weir, again fittingly enough, for the people hereabouts know how to bridge a

Fontaine de Troboa

divide. The thing is, delightful though all this may be, none of it explains why St. Coulitz is so celebrated. Left to its own devices, nobody would ever have heard of the place. But they have, for amid all the exotic flora and fauna there is nothing quite so colourful and heartwarming as the career of the man who was St. Coulitz' mayor from 1989 to 2001.

For the present, we'll call him KY, not for the gel, but after his initials. In short, the career of KY goes as follows: born 1945, studies mathematics in Brest during the sixties, marries 1969, settles in St. Coulitz 1973, and begins working for the local authority, given special responsibility for public works of art; qualifies as a civil engineer in the late seventies and returns to work for the *Direction Départementale de l'Equipement*, where he becomes 'Monsieur Ponts', charged with building Finistère's bridges. Elected mayor in 1989, he creates France's first *Conseil des Sages*, an advisory council composed of local elders. In 1990, he receives the *Prix National du Civisme* and is voted Breton of the Year by the monthly periodical, Armor. And then his career really takes off: 1991, appointed Secretary of State for *Affaires Sociales;* 1992, confirmed as *Secrétaire d'Etat à l'Intégration*, elected *Conseiller Régional de Bretagne* and made a Knight of the British Empire; 1993, sets up the *Fondation pour l'Intégration Républicaine*; 1994, elected *Conseiller Géneral du Canton de Chateaulin*; 1995, elected *Président de la Communauté des Communes du Bassin de Chateaulin* and made *Chevalier dans l'Ordre National de la Légion d'Honneur*; 1997, elected to the national parliament; 2002, named a member of the *Haut Conseil de la Coopération Internationale* ...

Perhaps that's enough. You get the idea. Big career and doing good stuff. Just look at the words: a bridge-builder, civic duty, social affairs, integration, co-operation . . . It's a remarkable CV by anybody's standards, but in some ways that first step into public office when he was elected mayor in 1989 was the most remarkable of all and the one that made his name. KY is Kofi Yamgnane, a Togolese immigrant known throughout France as *Le Celte Noir* and famed for being the only black mayor to have been elected by a population that was otherwise entirely white. Witty man, too. One other award: in 1992 he got a prize for political humour after announcing, "*je suis un Breton d'après la marée noire*", alluding to the black tides of the oil spills that have regularly despoiled the Breton coast. I bet Le Pen was hopping mad when he heard that.

Kofi Yamgnane is often mistakenly said to have been France's first black mayor. In fact, that honour goes to Raphaël Élizé, a vet from Martinique who, in 1929, was elected mayor of Sablé-sur-Sarthe, a post he fulfilled by all accounts with considerable verve and skill. Demobilized in 1940, he sought to resume public service, but was told by the local Feldkommandantur that it was "incomprehensible for German sentiment and the German sense of rectitude that a man of colour should be dressed in mayoral authority". Understandably peeved, Élizé joined the resistance. He was denounced in 1943, arrested and deported, and died during an allied bombardment of Buchenwald in 1945.

Despite the fact that we live in an allegedly more enlightened age,

Kofi Yamgnane's election was in some ways the more extraordinary. As a Martiniquaise, Élizé was already a French citizen. He was not an outsider as such, not one of the 'invaders sleeping in somebody else's bed'. When Kofi Yamgnane came to study in France, he was the only black man in Brest and he had no intention of staying. His aim was to return to Togo and build bridges there. As it happened, they needed someone to build bridges in Brittany, so he stayed, married a local girl, and the rest is history. He has clearly been more fortunate than his predecessor, yet his story is not one of unadulterated optimism. When interviewed, he says that his elevation from foreign scholarship boy to minister of state would simply not be possible nowadays because institutional racism would not allow it. He claims he wouldn't even get his residence permit, though I guess he might improve his chances by changing his name to Jean-Marie Le Blanc or somesuch. The business of names is significant. Time and again, highly qualified people from French minorities report that not only do they not get job offers, they don't even get interviews. A foreign sounding name or the wrong postcode are all it takes. It's not just a question of not reaching the highest rungs of the ladder, but of not even getting off the ground.

Kofi Yamgnane lives in one of St. Coulitz' satellite hamlets. Originally nothing more than a calvary, a crossroads, and a farm overlooking Chateaulin, Pennaros is now a scattering of modern suburban houses, all very unassuming, modest, family residences. It's a pleasing setting for a man whose ambitions have never got the better of him, but who has achieved so much. He was voted Breton of the Year for the second time in 2005.

So that's our triptych: three Breton villages, three Breton figures who've made international headlines. Whether any of this tells us anything about Brittany, I haven't a clue, but it does seem to indicate a place much like anywhere else in the modern world, a place where identity is in flux and people react to the uncertainty in their different ways, variously embracing and lamenting change, looking out and looking in, getting by as best they can in complicated times, or clinging to a fantasy of a past when everything was simple and as it should be and all was for the best in the best of all possible worlds. Like any place in the developed world, France is a crowded room. There are people that want the door open and people that want the door shut; some fancy a bit of fresh air, others fear burglars would climb in an open window; some reckon the burglars are already in the room and you'd better keep your hand on your ha'penny if you don't want to have a very nasty surprise indeed.

So what was all that business about *bof* at the beginning of the chapter apart from a bit of fun with the French language? Well, as I suggested, *bof* is a pithy way of declaring partiality. Everyone will have their own perspective on this, but I know which boxes I'm ticking off.

Nine metres of pope? *Bof*!
Jean-Marie Le Pen? *Bof*!
Kofi Yamgnane. *Unbof*! Very *unbof*.

16. Big Stones

ACCESS - **Monteneuf** is in eastern Morbihan, southeast of Ploërmel on the D776 between Guer and Malestroit. **Les Pierres Droites** are on the same road just northeast of the village.

Les Pierres Droites

That's what Flaubert said after visiting Carnac. He'd seen nothing but a lot of big stones. *Bof*! Big deal. Big stones. So what? So quite a lot in Brittany, where nothing tickles the *royaume de l'imaginaire* nearly so much as the region's big stones, a literal translation for the 'megaliths' that provoked Flaubert's withering comment.

Spend any time in Brittany and you might get a bit blasé about big stones yourself. They're absolutely everywhere. You can barely turn around without bumping into one, which suggests Obelix's little business was not so little after all, but an enterprise on an industrial scale, with thousands of Polish stone masons chipping away day and night, heedless of the burgeoning immigration debate, and getting on with the stuff immigrant labour generally gets on with, to wit, getting the job done. To be perfectly honest, there are so many big stones, I was at a loss where to go for this chapter.

The obvious illustrative visit would be the main concentration of megalithic monuments around Vannes. Carnac, for instance, where they've got three alignments, two with more than a thousand menhirs each. Or one of the megalith studded Islands in the Golfe de Morbihan, like Gavrinis with its Grande Dolmen and cryptic inscriptions, or the less well known Ilot Er Lannic. What about Locmariaquer, which has three of the most important megalithic structures, the Tumulus d'Er Grah, the Table des Marchand, and the Grand Menhir Brisé - the biggest menhir in the world before it was felled and broken, topping twenty metres and weighing 300 tons. Or maybe we should visit Eredeven and the second largest alignment, or Crucuno and the world's biggest dolmen. Why not head north to Barnenez and the biggest cairn? Or west, to Le Conquet and the biggest standing menhir? Maybe we should investigate Plouarzel to see if couples still rub their tummies against the stones, the blokes to ensure a male heir, the women to keep their husbands in order. Or we could pay our respects to Les Demoiselles Piquées on the Landes de Cojoux in Ile et Vilaine, a gang of girls petrified in punishment for dancing when they should have been at vespers. Or the Roche des Fées at Essé, or the Allée Couverte de Mougau near Commana, or the end of the world alignments near Camaret-sur-Mer, or that funny looking boulder down the bottom of the garden . . . How to choose one representative trip among so many? Maybe it would be simpler to just stick a pin in the map, drive wherever it indicated, get out and set off on foot till we bump into a big stone, which shouldn't take too long. There are 6000 menhirs in Brittany and 1000 dolmens. Start walking pretty much anywhere and you'll stumble upon one sooner or later.

OK, forget the where for now. Let's look at the what first and clarify the vocabulary. The abundance of big stones in Brittany is such that when nineteenth century academics, piqued by the dismissive comments of people like Flaubert, got round to classifying the things, they naturally turned to Breton and Gaelic for their technical vocabulary. A menhir is a long, upright monolith of the sort Obelix carries about on his back, examples of which can be seen within easy striking distance of any village in Brittany. An alignment is a rectilinear constellation of menhirs, such as those found at Carnac. A cromlec`h is a circle or semicircle of menhirs, like Stonehenge or Avebury. A dolmen is (in rather approximate Breton - those who know say it's a double solecism, which is pretty impressive for a two syllable word) a stone table formed of smaller menhirs and a coping slab, and generally sealed at one end. An Allée Couverte (the French option, presumably to escape the fable making implications of the Breton *hent korriganed*) is the same as a dolmen except longer and roofed with several slabs. A cairn is a large dolmen or series of allées couvertes capped by a pile of rocks so that it resembles a dry-stone dwelling. And a tumulus (Latin name but a Neolithic barrow) is basically the same thing with an additional layer of earth. But what are they for and when were they built and how on earth did the people who built them do it? This is where the *royaume de l'imaginaire* really kicks in.

The Breton *hent korriganed*, literally Korrigan Street, speaks directly of the interpretation put forward by traditional superstition. The megaliths, it was said, were the work of *korrigans*, a word that can mean both fairy or dwarf; so in fact all these stone superstructures were the homes of dwarves, a theory some maintain to this day, suggesting that when the Celts rolled up in Brittany they were a lot bigger than the indigenes, hence the natives were 'dwarves'. The enlightenment couldn't be doing with dwarves, though, they wanted a more intellectually rigorous explanation, and come the late eighteenth century, the *Celtomane* craze emerged, in which everything was ascribed to the Celts. Dolmens, said the *Celtomanes*, were the altars of the ancient druids, a theory that engendered countless nineteenth century paintings of bearded high priests on storm-swept moors making human sacrifices at their stone tables, preferably waving their daggers over a female victim displaying a lot of palpitating chest. Less frenzied imaginations suggested Arthurian remains or Roman ruins or Gallic cemeteries.

In fact, it's now known that the megaliths predate all these suggestions, save perhaps for the *korrigan* hypothesis, as they are Neolithic monuments that existed long before Obelix fell in the magic potion, and therefore had nothing to do with the Gauls or the druids, though doubtless these late-comers were as taken with the things as we are. If, like me, you're a bit hazy about your prehistory, the Neolithic period was at its height between 5000 and 3000BC, and covers the era when our ancestors worked out that if you buff up a stone it cuts better, as a result of which they settled down, planted gardens, polished axes, and passed the winter evenings inventing pottery, weaving and wicker-work. It's also widely accepted that, rather than being homes for little people or tables for displaying the palpitating breasts of sacrificial maidens, dolmens, *allées couvertes*, cairns and tumuli, were sepulchres or ossuaries, either communal and reusable or dedicated to an individual Neolithic big cheese, and that they were largely abandoned during the Bronze Age.

So, that's the megaliths sorted then. Well, no, actually. Speculation is a hardy plant and you can't uproot it with a bit of carbon dating and a few airy assertions about funerary chambers. It's all very well and good burying the dead, but raising over a thousand stones at a time, that's pushing grief a bit far. In fact, that's downright morbid. So what was the occult significance of menhirs and alignments?

Solitary menhirs are sometimes interpreted in anthropomorphic terms, since they stand upright like men and occasionally have carved features, suggesting they're a place of residence for a departed soul, a sort of keep in which to lock up the dead and stop them wandering round the countryside scaring the children. Other carvings bring to mind an ophiolatrous cult (no, I didn't know what it meant either; snake worship to you and me), though squiggly sticky up carvings could equally be phallic symbols, or just conceivably a bit of Neolithic graffiti done by randy adolescents. More down to earth commentators point out that nearly all of these big stones, especially cairns and tumuli, are built on promontories or uplands and are visible from far away, implying they were wayposts on trading routes or territorial boundary markers asserting the claims of one tribe against another. Ah, but what about the telluric currents? What about the solstice? Yup, things get weird again. The dwarves idea begins to look refreshingly simple, the sort of notion to have you whipping out Occam's razor.

The thing is, the underlying rock that defines Brittany produces an awful lot of ambient radioactivity and is laced with an uncommonly tight network of telluric lines. Isolated menhirs are generally placed at points where telluric currents branch into two or three. And dolmens and allées couvertes are often aligned either with these currents or with subterranean watercourses. And the alignments are, now famously, placed to point toward the sunrise at key moments of the agricultural year, in particular at equinoxes and solstices. Houses for little people? Get on with you. These were astronomical maps. Or cosmological maps. Or subterranean maps. Or subterranean cosmological astronomical maps.

With so many theories, you can understand why people might get confused as to the purpose of Brittany's big stones. It's even reported, probably apocryphally, inspired more by anti-Americanism than anything else, that when the Yanks landed in Brittany during World War Two, they thought Carnac was one vast German anti-tank trap. In a way, this is not so far fetched. Just look at the things for a moment. Putting aside the question of purpose, it's hard to imagine how anyone without heavy-duty machinery and a lot of whizz-bang engineering know-how could have erected such tall and multitudinous monuments - you certainly wouldn't see modern roadmakers putting up 300-ton signposts with their bare hands, that's for sure. That, of course, is the other part of the mystery - how *did* they do it? Not only did some of these stones weigh several hundred tons, they often had to be transported up to ten kilometres from the quarry.

Logs and levers is the general theory, though not everyone buys it. Surely levers would have snapped when placed under a 300-ton rock and tree trunks would have sunk into the ground under the weight? And even if the logs didn't sink, how were you going to get the thing rolling? It's been calculated that to move the heaviest blocks you'd need manpower covering several hectares, or be able to get 500 oxen all pulling in the same direction at the same time. OK, so if they didn't lug it and shove and roll it, what did they do with it? Again, theories abound.

There are legends about Stonehenge recounting how Merlin moved great weights using magic. It was psychic energy! No it wasn't, it was the magnetic currents; they harnessed the earth's telluric power and . . . No, it wasn't, it was solar power. No, no way, the menhirs were a sort of giant acupuncture needle arousing and focusing the earth's energy . . . No, no, no, no! It was electricity. I'm not joking. Some claim Neolithic man had electricity.

The theosophists, meanwhile, aren't fazed by any of this. It was giants what done it, the third sub-race of the fifth Aryan root race of the three astronomical dynasties of the third sub-race of the Fifth . . . no hang on, I think I got a bit lost there. Anyway, there were these big people, fifteen foot tall, and when you're fifteen foot tall planting a three hundred ton rock in the ground is a lot easier than when you're a dwarf - apparently. I like this theory. It conjures pleasing images of harassed giant mothers telling tardy giant toddlers to hurry up because the picnic's over and they've got to stop playing with those bloody stones since we've got to get back and feed the cat. "All right, mum, I'll just put this one on top of this one, then push this one over here, and . . ."

So it wasn't the dwarves, it was the giants. Or if it wasn't the dwarves and the giants, it was the Little Green Men . . . oh, yes, the Erich von Danikens of Brittany have their theories, too. Or it's all to do with Atlantis and the hierophantic priests of the Solar Dragon, each of whom personally placed his stone in the given alignment as a sort of memento of his own isthisisiasissinic pongo wongo dongo doo-da . . . oh, that's enough.

There's a lot of fun to be had from these theories and, apart from being fairly certain the big stones are about burying people and bigging it up with whatever god they believed in back then, we'll probably never know the full story. Still, without indulging the more deranged speculations, I see no good reason why several purposes might not have been served at the same time or variously according to location. The Christian cross, after all, has been used to mark burial places, sites of battles, places of worship, prominences, promontories, intersections, sacred sites, and serves as waypost, boundary marker, icon and memorial. By the same token, it seems reasonable to suppose menhirs might have been used to harness dead spirits, calculate calendars and eclipses, mark sacred heights, keep travellers on the right path and in the right territory, commemorate victories, possibly even to produce some sort of ionization phenomenon in the earth. Maybe if we all went out and started rubbing ourselves up against big stones, we'd discover a cheaper high than the one normally purchased from the local bottle merchant. As for the larger alignments, it does seem pretty obvious that they delineated a ceremonial space . . . unless of course it was that troublesome giant toddler with his building blocks: "And I'll just put this one here . . ."

The number of theories though is not nearly so baffling as the number of possible daytrips. Faced with such a multiplicity of potential outings, I eventually opted for a visit to an alignment that is at once extensive and obscure, thus relatively free of the crowds and the queues and the ice-cream vans and the waxwork Neolithic men and the plastic hand-axes and the

Somebody's Playground?

megalithic baseball caps and souvenir T-shirts. I'm exaggerating the risks of encountering a sort of Neolithic theme park, but it has to be said, some of the menhirs at Carnac are so popular they've been fenced off to stop them falling over from the impact of all the shuffling feet, while other sites have been closed entirely for years on end to let the vegetation recover. But it will be a long time before that happens at the Monteneuf Pierres Droites.

Located alongside the D776, the Pierres Droites alignment consists of 420 menhirs, the largest of which is five metres high and weighs about 38 tons. They date from between 4,300 and 2700BC, and shards of pottery show that they continued to be used throughout the Bronze Age and into the Gallo-Roman period. Carbon testing indicates that they were knocked down about a thousand years ago, probably by the church, after which only three were left standing. This was not uncommon. The church's relationship with the megaliths was always an ambiguous one, often co-opting them as Christian symbols (many menhirs used to be topped with a cross and there's still a stone cross at Batz-sur-Mer on which the carved image of a Neolithic axe is visible) or cautionary tales (as per Les Demoiselles Piquées mentioned above), but equally often destroying them to discourage pagan superstitions. All it took was a particularly puritanical clergyman in the parish. Menhirs were widely regarded as the IVF treatment of the day, and women would rub their tummies against the rocks to ensure pregnancy, or even go the whole hog and do a bit of al fresco *kof a kof* with their partners on the site. You can imagine how a pious, fresh-faced young medieval cleric would feel about that. Some stones were associated with curing ailments like arthritis, but generally fertility was the problem, and it has been suggested that these peasant beliefs show a better understanding of the stones' original purposes than the supposedly more educated guesses of latter-day academics.

It wasn't just the church that indulged in such casual vandalism. It's estimated that up to half the region's megaliths have been destroyed one way or another. Until the nineteenth century, the Dolmen de Crucuno was fronted by a long corridor of giant slabs, but they were subsequently borrowed for building the village, a common fate for many megaliths. Other menhirs got broken during the building of modern infrastructure projects, like roads and canals, and many disappeared during the industrialization of agriculture in the 1970s because they made ploughing inconvenient. Perhaps most notorious is the case of the cairn at Barnenez, the largest in the world, which came within a hair's breadth of being dismantled in the 1950s by a road-building contractor who reckoned it a handy stock of hardcore. The cairn was only saved when the man sent to dig it up thought it a bit strange that the stones were so regularly tailored and reported the fact to a friend on the local paper.

In the case of the Pierres Droites, though, the church's vandalism saved the site from more permanent damage, since the megaliths were soon overgrown and therefore couldn't be nicked for building or mucked about by having a lot of barren women and druid hunters swarming all over them. Locals knew there were some stones there, but nobody suspected how many, and it was only thirty years ago that the scale of the alignment was revealed by a forest fire. Realizing the importance of the site, the mayor of Monteneuf, Joseph Orhan, bought the land for the *commune* to preserve it from further depredations. A series of digs ensued and, thanks to the fact that the stones had lain untouched for a thousand years, it was possible to re-erect them in their exact original alignment, which has not always been the case at Carnac. According to the site's chief archeologist, Yannick Lecerf, the six parallel lines of stones were arranged in an East-West orientation not because of some arcane cosmological imperative, but because that's the orientation of the local seam of schist. So apparently topography and geology were more important to Neolithic blueprints than astronomy. Just dig it up and set it up, that's all. Life's complicated enough without calculating which way the magnetic field's blowing or where the sun's coming from on a given day. He also confirms that, as well as their religious function, the stones served as boundary markers for tribal territory, citing as evidence for this the similarities between the Pierres Droites and other sites in Paimpont and at Saint Just. Perhaps, too, in an oral culture, they commemorated an important event or a famous man, a theory that would fit with the legends that later oral cultures constructed about them.

Compared to the relatively nondescript land lying behind Carnac, the countryside around Monteneuf is particularly lovely, a patchwork of pretty hamlets, rolling hills, verdant pasture, and spacious birch, beech and oak woods. It really is idyllic and, if you get there reasonably early, the chances are you'll have the prehistoric site to yourself.

It's worth making the effort because there's a real atmosphere among the Pierres Droites, one that's best savored alone or in the company of an intimate friend. I'm not suggesting you get down and dirty and start indulging in pagan fertility rites or anything like that, though each to his own, and if pagan fertility rites are your bag, you could do worse than practice them here. But tummy rubbing aside, there's a spirit of place at Monteneuf that really is very special. Visit a megalithic monument in the right conditions and all that guff about blood sacrifice, little green men, giants and dwarves suddenly seems eminently plausible. There's a real sense of mystery, of something other, something beyond our ken. It's the telluric current, the phreatic nappe, the psychic energy, the hoodoo-voodoo doodly-doodly-do . . . I'm a teapot!

Dangerous stuff this, so before I became totally unhinged, we took to the woods, following one of the waymarked walks outlined on a mapboard in the car-park. These are all lovely and highly recommended, but even if you don't do a walk, it's worth poking about on the fringes of the main site, picking out the remains of the paved Roman road that's still discernible amid the trees, picturing life in the reconstruction of a Neolithic hut, and visiting the clearing 100 metres to the southeast where there are a couple of mock ups showing how the menhirs got there. Not content with merely uncovering the alignments, Lecerf's team conducted experiments to see how the stones were quarried, transported and erected. I'm sorry to say they were generally rolled on logs or, when necessary, floated down rivers or across bays, then slid into a hole, levered up, stabilized with tightly packed pebbles and soil, and bingo, there's your menhir. No psychic powers, no telluric magic, no Neolithic Powergen, just a lot of sweat and what must have been some very compelling authority figures: imagine how you'd respond if the local mayor invited you to come and prop up a hundred ton rock commemorating his all round wonderfulness; those Neolithic architects must have been awfully persuasive people. And clever, too, for we still don't understand how they were able to make such fine mathematical calculations, getting the centre of gravity so perfectly balanced that a stone several metres high could remain upright in a shallow trench often only a few centimetres deep. Presumably it wasn't trial and error - "Ooops! It's fallen over. Right, pull Bert out from under there and we'll try again".

If you're disappointed by the bad news about the magic, don't worry. These megalithic sites really are such evocative places everything might be true and they can carry a burden of fancy far greater than the probable reality of their original purpose. You want dwarves, giants, and little green men, well, why not? On the spot it all seems perfectly reasonable. You don't actually have to go to Monteneuf if you want to see a big stone. As I say, just turn around and the chances are you'll bump into a menhir or dolmen in your back garden. But the Pierres Droites are big stones that I, for one, will be visiting again. I'll be taking my little-green-man detector, too. Dibbley-wibbley-ibbley.

17. All At Sea

ACCESS - **Quiberon** is midway between Lorient and Vannes. **'Port Maria'** is signposted throughout the town. The ferry service is run by the Societé Morbihannaise de Navigation (0820-056-000 www.smn-navifation.fr). If you want to stay overnight on Houat, call the Hotel-Restaurant Les Iles on 0297-306-802, or the town hall (0297-306-804) for the campsite and B&B options in private homes.

If you really want to get to know Brittany, you've got to get out of it. Not administratively or even, in a sense, physically, but emotionally, for there is little your average Breton loves better than boarding a boat and heading for one of the islands that are spattered around the peninsula like a pointillist fringe beyond the fringe

Beg ar Vachif, Houat

It's still Brittany, though, one might protest, you don't actually leave Brittany. True, but the people living on these islands have a strong sense of difference, referring to the mainland as *l'autre côté*, 'the other side', as if the translation from one pocket of earth to another entailed a definitive spiritual transformation. And the way some people talk about the islands, you could be forgiven for believing they really were enthusing about a trip to another dimension; except, of course, the transformation is not definitive, and can be repeated time and again. And it is, again and again and again: by Sunday sailors and Ocean-going yachtsmen; by professional fishermen and pappies pottering about with an outboard; by lone swimmers on occasion (not recommended!) and less reckless visitors like ourselves taking the commuter boats that ply the channels day in, day out, taking the essentials of modern living to the islanders, and bringing mainlanders in search of something indefinable but equally essential that is missing from modern living. For no matter how the transition is completed, all those who head for the islands share a desire for displacement, to get away to some place different, somewhere 'other', somewhere all at sea. And in Brittany the love of islands is not merely a coastal phenomenon. To appreciate just how deeply imbued it is in the Breton psyche, one need only look at the town of Belle-Isle-en-Terre, a place that, as its name suggests, is perfectly landlocked, but is nonetheless proud of being a 'beautiful island'. Get your head round that one if you can.

The Breton islands are collectively called the Îles du Ponant, of which there are between seven and eight hundred depending on who's counting. Naturally, the Bretons disagree fiercely with one another about how many islands there are, justifying their sundry reckonings by different definitions of what an island is, some including islets only exposed by the falling tide, others totting up outcrops that can be reached on foot at low water, purists rigorously sticking with those that are permanently surrounded by sea. If something in the region of eight hundred islands sounds a little daunting for the casual visitor, do not despair. For the purposes of what might properly be considered a tourist destination, there are only really a score of islands, though wherever you find yourself on the coast, you can double that number by counting the islets that are accessible on foot at low tide.

Many *îles* are associated with famous names: Lindbergh had a home on Île d'Illiec, Milliau was the Summer retreat of Aristide Briand, Sarah Bernhardt was a regular visitor to Belle-Île-en-Mer. Others are known for environmental or geographical peculiarities: Groix is a natural museum of geological history, Batz is renowned for producing the first and finest new potatoes in Northern Brittany, the Glénan archipelago is frequently compared to a tropical paradise. But for bumping about, we've chosen an island untouched by celebrity and that has few physical peculiarities, but which is the name most often cited with far away looks in the eye. Speak to anyone who has spent a lifetime island-hopping round Brittany and the chances are that, when asked for a preference, they'll plump for Houat. It's got no single claim to fame, but it is one of the wildest and most otherworldly of the inhabited islands, and when Bretons recommend it, they do so with a faintly abstracted air, gazing off into the distance, already there in the mind's-eye, murmuring, "Yes, that's it. That's The One". It also happens to be about the right size (5km by 1.3km, though the tortuous coast bumps the pedestrian circuit up to 15km) to walk round in its entirety on a daytrip, without busting a gut or ending the day kicking your heels on the wharf waiting for the boat back to the other side.

Even as you approach the embarkation point for Houat at Port Maria in Quiberon, the 'other-worldly' sense begins to assert itself, for this stretch of the southern coast seems to belong to a different region altogether, and initially the difference declares itself in a negative sense. Gone are the rolling hills, wooded valleys, winding rivers, and rugged granite cliffs. Instead, it's all sand and sky and flattening white light, better resembling the flatlands of the Vendée or the Landes de Gasgoine or, God forbid, one of the grimmer bits of the Spanish *costas*. An array of hoardings, so multitudinous they're almost hallucinogenic, proclaim the services of a host of professional leisure providers, a promise that's not disappointed when you reach the tourist heart of Quiberon with its seaside cafés, restaurants, rental emporiums, and shops selling buckets and spades and multifarious beach fun paraphernalia. It's not terribly appealing if you've grown accustomed in the preceding days to the tranquility of the Breton hinterland, but take it as a kind of purgatory preliminary to reaching somewhere heavenly and you'll get by well enough.

The high speed passenger ferry is a bit brisk, too, certainly not the ideal way to reach a haven of peace, but these are day trips, so unless you're schooling around in your own yacht, needs must. After twenty minutes, you'll see off to the East the Teignouse lighthouse. Brittany's 100 lighthouses are almost as important to the Breton sense of identity as islands, imaginary mountains, and being done down by the Big-Bit-Stuck-On-the-Hind-End, and an evocation of their names (Jument, Île Vierge, Les Pierres Noires, Ar Men) can become almost incantatory when a group of Breton sailors get together, as if they're chanting themselves into a trance-like state, taking flight on wings of fancy to soar overseas and circle about their favourite *far*. I'm no sailor myself, but I can see how these isolated towers have taken on a legendary status. There's a classic photo of the Jument lighthouse that says it all. The base of the building is embroiled in an enormous angry ruff of boiling surf from an immense wave breaking against its weather side. And on the nearside, standing casually in the open doorway, hands in pockets, peering across the green balustrade that rings the narrow walkway, looking very, very tiny, is the lighthouse-keeper. Judging by the photo, you'd think the wave is about to come piling round and pluck him from his doorstep, pulling him down somewhere very deep indeed. I presume it didn't. I presume he knew what he was doing. That this wasn't the ultimate in foolhardy photo opportunities, after which the authorities concluded they'd better automate. But every time I look at it, the picture takes my breath away and I can appreciate why the Bretons are so attached to their lighthouses.

As we approach Houat, a spur of islets off the northwestern headland gives a hint as to why so many lighthouses were required. Compared to the notorious Fromveur (literally 'grand torrent') channel between Sein and Ouessant, where the Gulf Stream runs at a speed of seven or eight knots, the waters around Houat present relatively few nautical challenges, but even so, you wouldn't be all that chuffed to see these nasty, ragged little rocks if you were being tossed about by a storm in a small boat, or even a large one for that matter. Look at a map of the shipwrecks dotted about the Breton coast and it resembles a Jackson Pollock painting - and not all of them are marked, the whereabouts of some kept secret to prevent treasure hunters or prying divers disturbing wrecks that are now officially tombs for the drowned sailors. Happily, the further east you come along the southern coast, the further you remove yourself from the really dangerous waters, a fact attested to by a famous adage:

Nul n'a passé Fromveur sans avoir peur,
Qui voit Ouessant, voit son sang,
Qui voit Molène, voit sa peine
Qui voit Sein, voit sa fin
Qui voit Groix, voit sa joie

Nobody's passed Fromveur without fear,
He who sees Ouessant, sees his blood,
He who sees Molène, sees his grief,
He who sees Sein, sees his end,
He who sees Groix, sees his joy.

Sure you still want to go bumping about the islands? Perhaps we should stick with Belle-Isle-en-Terre. Anyway, too late now. And at least Houat is nearer the sanctuary of Groix than any of those islands whose names rhyme with woe of one class or another.

The boat docks in Port Saint-Gildas, which gets its name from a Scottish monk who took refuge on the island in the sixth century. He was not the first resident of Houat, which has been occupied off and on for some 12,000 years, though its existence was not officially recorded until 56BC, when the Roman invaders sank the fleet of the natives, who were curiously unwilling to participate in the Latin prototype of European union. Succeeding turmoils were not behindhand when it came to giving Houat a good poke in the eye. It was virtually deserted for the next five hundred years thanks to repeated pillaging by the Saxons, and was subsequently invested by the Normans, the Spanish, the Dutch and, of course, the English. Like the Channel Islands, we thought the Îles du Ponant were ours and kept on occupying them just to make the point, notably doing dastardly English things to the entirely innocent and unsuspecting French fleet at the Battle of the Cardinals in 1759. Nature was no less kind to the island, decimating its population with typhoid and yellow fever, and so isolating the survivors that, in the nineteenth century, the local clergy concluded there was little point pretending they were part of a distant and negligent republic, and duly set up a theocratic government in which the priests wielded both temporal and spiritual authority.

Though rarely enacted in an official charter, the ubiquity of priests in island life has been a common thread in the history of the Îles du Ponant. Even in the 1960s, there were islands where the priest was still the principal contact point with the mainland. Mass would feature a slightly surreal distribution of letters among the parishioners and, at the end of the sermon, the priest, who often had the only telephone on the island, would conclude his homily by advising Madame X that her brother was ill in hospital, but his condition wasn't life-threatening, Monsieur Y that his son was coming home for Christmas, but couldn't stay for New Year, and Mademoiselle Z that cousin Jean had announced the banns and wanted her on the other side sharpish.

Houat means 'duck' in Breton, presumably after some fancied resemblance between the shape of the island and the bird, because its smaller, sister island, is called Hoëdic or duckling. It could, though, as easily have been because the island and its inhabitants have stayed afloat in the turbulent waters of the Atlantic and history. Despite plague and pestilence, despite penury and want (despite the English for God's sake!), the people of Houat have soldiered on, getting by on fish and a little subsistence agriculture until tourists discovered the beauty of the place and a new chapter in their history began.

Tourists 'discovered' it, though you wouldn't know it from appearances, for Houat, like most of the Îles du Ponant, has clung onto its original face. The modest port is still dominated by the island's fishing fleet, the smaller boats belonging to the *ligneurs* who fish for bass and conger eels, the larger to the *caseyeurs* who catch prawn, crabs and lobster. There are a couple of bars on the lane up to the village, but otherwise the place shows no sign of providing for an influx of visitors that can number 4000 a day during the height of the season, and the lime-washed cottages with their brightly painted shutters, suggest somewhere that is sufficient unto itself, somewhere that needs nothing from the other side. This is an illusion, of course. The island was autonomous within living memory, every household had its own allotment where they grew greens, wheat, potatoes, possibly some flax and grazed a cow, and there was always plenty of fish. But all that ended with the Second World War and when we asked one old boy if there was any livestock left on the island, he said he thought there might still be one sheep, but he was none too sure that hadn't died, too. Just how dependent the islanders are is indicated by the municipal rubbish bins that are transported back and forth by the ferry boat, and by the fact that the postmistress doesn't actually turn up for work until after the first boat has arrived.

You can join the coastal path directly from the port, but prompted by a social worker we met on the boat who had recently directed a group doing community service on the island, we opt to head inland, doubling round the mini-market to visit a newly rehabilitated dirt track. As tracks go, it's nothing exceptional, but it is an oddity, for it was originally a cart track constructed by wayward monks doing penitence for misdeeds on the mainland. Our informant seemed uncommonly pleased that the route his team had unearthed should originally have been the work of a sort of sacerdotal chain gang.

Heading northwest toward the Beg ar Vachif headland, we traverse a landscape dominated by gorse before joining the coast path behind one of the island's myriad bite-sized bays, a haven for a solitary yacht. The headland itself features the first of several forts dominating strategic locations (the English, remember), and is backed by a touchingly crenellated interior wall, 'touching' because it's so low in places you could step over it with relative comfort. I find it hard to picture anyone mounting a very serious defence against an attack from the interior, but then that's in the nature of island life: the menace and the adventure are all on the outside, living is governed by the fact that you're all at sea. The fort is private, but readily explored if no one's in residence, and a spur of the coastal path skirts its ramparts to reach the tip of the headland. It's worth the detour. At sea level, the rock is rimed with seaweed and clumps of mussels, and ornamented with a crust of embedded oyster shells, while the more commanding heights are splashed with white gulls, beadily eyeing the waters, waiting for something edible and imprudent to show its head. The rusting guns trained on our backs are a bit intimidating, but the location is so lovely, the fort so well integrated into the landscape, it would captivate the most militant pacifist.

Heading south we come to the first of the island's really great beaches, the Plage de Tréac'h er Venigued, framed by the islets of Guric and

Séniz. This is a beach that would make Robinson blush with shame for trying to pass his shabby Pacific island off as a tropical paradise. Houat isn't precisely tropical, but if ever a photographer for a promotional brochure needed a beguiling stretch of deserted sand backed by an azure blue sea and didn't have the wherewithal to head somewhere warm, he need go no further than Houat. Better still,

Waiting for something edible.

unlike many of the more westerly islands, surrounded as they are by steeply shelving seabed and deep oceanic waters that are heart-stoppingly cold, the sea around Houat is swimmable from Spring to Autumn. Parenthetically, I should point out that the weather was particularly fine the day we visited and chuntering on about tropical paradises might sound like so much guff if you happen to be here on a less balmy day. No matter, though, for experience suggests the Îles du Ponant are magical places whatever the weather, and I still have fond memories of a day many years ago when we strolled round Ouessant shrouded in a heavy shifting mist. It was another type of magic, but no less enchanting for that, the veil intermittently parting to reveal an unsuspected outcrop of rock or sweep of sea, repeatedly breaking and closing in so that the landscape kept discovering itself and disappearing again, like some capricious phantom coquettishly luring us on with glimpses of hidden charms.

As the path veers southeast, we see Belle Île, the largest and most populous of the Îles du Ponant, so large (84 square kilometres) and populous (nearly 5000 permanent residents) it even managed to cultivate some them-next-door-in-the-next-country rivalries within the confines of the island itself, villagers from different Belle Île settlements rubbing along well enough with one another because island living demanded it, but doing their utmost not to intermarry, lest the particular identity of a given village be vitiated by some interpolator from five kilometres up the road.

If the bays to the north and southeast of Houat are the demesne of yachtsman, the tiny creeks along the wild southern shore are the preserve of those approaching on foot, and given fine weather, the chances are that this stretch of the walk will be interrupted by long spells bathing from your own private beach. There are other diversions, though. It is here that we pass the Eclosarium, a biotechnology centre dedicated to the study of microscopic marine

Your own Private Beach

organisms, and also housing a small museum of island life, and behind it, there's another fort, this one built by the ubiquitous Vauban. It's not one of his best efforts (from a distance it resembles a couple of concrete storage tanks), but seeing yet another Vauban fort makes me feel there was something a tad sinister about this man. He's a bit like Melville's white whale or that Woody Allen character, Zelig, he's absolutely everywhere, and one wonders whether he was a discrete personality at all; judging by productivity, it seems more likely he was a team of people masquerading as one energetic individual.

At the southeastern end of the island lie the biggest beaches of all, Tréac'h Salus and Tréac'h er Goured, the latter pincered by two fat fingers of dune-land. Superficially a bit barren, these dunes are actually the most interesting part of the island in botanical terms, featuring helichrysum, sea pinks and sea bindweed, and above all sea *lis*, which are thought only to grow here, in the Algarve, and in Galilee.

Wherein lies the magic then? It's not something readily conveyed by a narrative of sights and sounds, but resides rather more in the simple sense of being there, somewhere else, somewhere other. If you go to one of the Breton islands looking for something apart, if you want to spend a little time in a world that at least gives the illusion of being preserved, if you seek, no matter how exiguous it may seem, a smidgeon of the Robinson experience, if you want to get away from it all and immerse yourself in an ethereal world of water and light, then you won't be disappointed. Even if the sense of displacement isn't strong on the island itself, returning to Quiberon, you realize that have you have after all been on 'the other side'. I know I did. In the short time we'd been away, they'd inflated a bouncy castle on the beach beside Port Maria! Nothing could have been more alien to the experience we'd had on Houat. I've got nothing against bouncy castles. They look rather good fun and, if I wasn't forty-six years old and trying to simulate the dignity I believe is meant to befit my age, I might well be queuing up myself, sweaty little paw tightly clutching a couple of euros. But compared to Beg ar Vachif, bouncy castles beggar belief. This has got to be the other side.

An addendum. The premise of this book is to describe repeatable daytrips that are hopefully as digestible at home as on the ground. But sometimes you've got to go beyond your brief. So, a word to the wise: if you are to appreciate the proper magic of insularity, a daytrip is not enough, it's essential to stay overnight. There's a small hotel on Houat and a campsite or the option of staying with one of the locals. Only then, when the last boat has left, when quiet cloaks the small sea-bound world and the big starry night sky seals the island in a dome of silence, can you really begin to understand the appeal of being all at sea. Sojourning overnight on an island, one realizes that those who have returned to the mainland and their bouncy castles have missed something, that you in some obscure way have stolen something from them, something they didn't know they had, something unique that you in turn will have to surrender when you finally embark, but which, for the moment, however briefly, is yours and you are

18. Frenchified

ACCESS - **Nantes** is at a confluence of major motorways at the extreme southeastern corner of the Breton peninsula. Follow the signs for 'Centre Ville' then 'Chateau'. The castle is on the **Place Marc Elder**. An access map in PDF format can be downloaded from the 'Practical information' page on www.chateau-nantes.fr.

A Beast

of different stripe

'Castle' is not an abstruse technical term or a word liable to inspire much debate among lexicographers. Everyone's pretty much agreed, you say 'castle' and you mean something big and solid and crenellated and probably Norman, a thumping great stone war machine employed by the French invaders to intimidate good Anglo-Saxon peasants like you and me. A 'château', though, is a beast of an entirely different stripe. Stress the first syllable and big it up on the *'Allo, 'Allo* accent, and you have the French label for a multitude of architectural phenomena, ranging from buildings that are little more than fortified manor houses to colossal lumps of conspicuous consumption like Versailles. There is, however, another way of pronouncing 'château'. Stress the second syllable and elongate it with a diphthong and you will have the French falling about in the aisles, tickled pink by an English interpretation designating a building that is not manifestly defensible but which is big and romantic, possibly with a lot of high white walls, probably with pointy black turrets, and almost certainly a few lofty balconies of the sort from which imprisoned princesses can lower their tresses to facilitate the alpinism of passing princes. The object of today's bumping about is a stronghold pitched somewhere between a castle and the second, anglicized pronunciation of 'château', the Château des Ducs de Bretagne in Nantes.

Nantes is a dynamic, youthful city (according to one source 35% of the population is under the age of 25) with a reputation for being one of the more livable provincial capitals, drawing in young professionals with its lively cultural life and frequent festivals, and enchanting families with its broad boulevards freshened by sea breezes, its readily accessible countryside and coastal resorts, and a green belt that is for once most emphatically what it claims to be. For all its qualities though, the city fathers are not above jumping on a bandwagon, and when we arrive in the city, we are greeted by posters promoting the recently restored and newly reopened château depicting a small child wearing a wizard hat, à la Harry Potter, with assorted objects spinning dizzyingly about her head. It is an entirely unnecessary contrivance as the château is quite magical enough of itself.

Nantes is no longer part of Brittany administratively, but for centuries it was at the heart of the struggle for Breton autonomy, since it was the seat of the dukes who sought to keep Brittany separate from France, and there are still strong currents of Breton nationalism to be found here. Independent since the defeat of Charles the Bald by Nominoë in 845, the strategic location of Brittany ensured it was the object of constant incursions by the English, the Spanish, and the French, and by the fifteenth century France was increasingly vexed by the existence of this capricious excrescence spoiling the perfection of the hexagon. Much plotting and intrigue ensued, and many Breton barons were suborned by murky deals involving French coffers and mutable loyalties. Acutely aware of the menace and hampered by the lack of a direct male heir, François II, the duke of Brittany, sought to fend off the French and avoid the forthcoming dynastic crisis by deploying the principal diplomatic cards at his disposal, to wit, his daughters, Anne and Isabeau, whom he regularly promised in marriage to pretty much anyone who would lend him a squad of pikemen. Unfortunately though, his options were limited, not because nobody wanted to wed Anne and Isabeau (on the contrary, suitors were queuing up in droves), but because François made the mistake of betrothing Anne to the Prince of Wales, the future Edward V of England, in exchange for an allegedly perpetual alliance with the boy's father, Edward IV.

Nothing piques the French like an alliance with the English and there ensued the First War of Breton Succession, AKA La Guerre Folle, which ended in 1488 at the Bataille de Saint-Aubin-du-Cormier when the ten thousand strong French army of Charles VIII, backed by 5,000 Swiss soldiers, defeated 12,000 Bretons supported (somewhat meagrely for a 'perpetual alliance') by 300 English troops, 800 Germans, and a handful of Spaniards. 'La Rencontre', as it is known, is still described as a tragic day in Breton history, for the loss of 6,000 men in less than two hours obliged François to negotiate with Charles, conceding that his daughters would not marry without the consent of the French monarch. This was enough to mortally wound the *amour propre* of an independent-minded man like François and he accordingly died the following year, precipitating an unseemly rush among the minor powerbrokers of Europe to wed the 12 year old Anne - and if you think that's a bit young, I should point out that her hand had first been promised when she was only four!

Despite the earnest efforts of assorted jongleurs, troubadours, minstrels, and bards, marriage in those days was a mercenary rather than a romantic business, but Anne was a headstrong child and, having seen off the suit of the ageing, boorish Alain d'Albret, 'settled' for Maximilian of Austria, who was handsome, charming, attentive and, as it happened, the Holy Roman Emperor. Handsome, charming, and attentive he may have been, but the press of affairs meant Maximilian could not attend his own wedding, so he sent an ambassador, Wolfgang de Polham, to stand in his stead. On the 19th of December 1490, bride and 'groom' were duly wed and the marriage was symbolically 'consummated' by Wolfgang literally slipping his leg into the bridal bed. There's an hysterical sketch of this ceremony, in which the pompous looking Wolfgang is piously baring a bony knee, while Anne lies abed, looking hugely peeved, as if wondering where this old fool learned the facts of life and whether nobody had told him 'getting your leg over' was a largely figurative expression.

Polite and not so polite society across Europe was creased with hilarity when word got round of this wedding by proxy, but Charles VIII didn't find it at all funny. Not only did it expressly contravene the Traité du Verger signed by François at the end of the Mad War, but calmly accepting a dirty great empire to the east and its satellite to the west was obviously strategic insanity. Cue the Second War of Breton Succession. Charles laid siege to Rennes. Handsome, charming, and attentive was still busy elsewhere. Begged by the starving population to put an end to their suffering, Anne capitulated. After a bit of dexterous footwork on the part of the resident theologians (well, not so dexterous when it came to Maximilian, there was, after all, only that leg between them), Anne's union with Maximilian and Charles' own marriage were annulled, and the Duchess and the King were wed.

Compared to handsome, charming, and attentive, Charles was no catch, a mere king rather than an emperor, and ugly, deformed and dissolute into the bargain. Yet a genuine affection seems to have evolved between the couple, albeit of brief duration, for seven years later Charles banged his head on a lintel and died of his injuries. Anyway, you know how it is with these things. Marrying kings is like eating Chinese takeaways. You have one and then a couple of hours later you want another one. Anne promptly married Charles' successor, Louis XII, who was also a libertine, but not a man to shirk his marital duties, as a result of which Anne spent the greater part of her short adult life (she died at the age of 37) pregnant.

I must say, I'm full of admiration for the resolution of the Second War of Breton Succession. Imagine if every war ended with the compulsory wedding of the principal heads of states. The nuptials might not be pretty, but you can be sure governments would be a lot more wary about going to war. In terms of Breton history, though, the settlement is significant because the union (Anne was sometimes called 'La Dame Union' after her third marriage) brought Brittany into the big-bit-stuck-on-the-hind-end. And it was in the preceding resistance to this union that the Château des Ducs de Bretagne was built by François II and his daughter.

The building's external aspect reflects the turmoils of the time and is very much a 'castle' castle, with neatly moated walls of schist and granite, but once inside the courtyard, we are confronted with what can only be

Château des Ducs de Bretagne moat

called a château (English pronunciation), a turreted renaissance palace built of dazzling white *Tuffeau* limestone. It might be a bit too white for some tastes and there are patches where the 15-year, 52-million-euro restoration programme has given the building an almost aggressive glare. The whiteness, though, is not the result of some over-zealous sand-blasting or indiscriminate scouring with a high pressure jet, for the stone has been meticulously restored to its original state by a process closer to the works of The Body Shop than a body shop, painstakingly sponged with compresses of rockwool to swab up the corrosive saltwater that had permeated the delicate stone (all those sea-breezes, remember), then washed with a fresh coat of lime to preserve the surface. The whiteness is appropriate for a building representing independent Brittany, for it echoes the Breton flag, the *gwenn-ha-du* or white-and-black, and is also a reminder of the winter coat of the ermine, the duchy's symbol and subject of what has become the anthem of modern Breton nationalism, *La Blanche Hermine* by Gilles Servat.

Some features are 'new', like the seventeenth century campaniles that had disappeared and which have been completely reconstructed according to the blueprint of eighteenth century sketches, and there are places where the restoration is so immaculate it looks like a modern building. Doubtless purists will balk at the doors widened to meet modern safety regulations, at the mesh lift-cages installed to allow disabled access, at the immaculately pointed stonework, but purists always balk at something, and I for one think the combination of old and new works well, a lot of thought having gone into integrating the two.

After buying our tickets for the museum and admiring the wrought iron crown capping the colossal courtyard well (you could drop a small train down it if you were so inclined), we take to the ramparts, access to which is free, and stroll round the castle's 500-metre circumference to enjoy the views over Nantes. The first thing we see on the anticlockwise tour is the blue cupola of the tower that dominated the former LU biscuit factory. This is perhaps more evocative in France as a whole than the château itself, for LU says to the French what McVities does to the British, and the petit-beurre biscuit they developed in 1886 is The French Biscuit by default, in much the same way that the digestive used to be The Ubiquitous British Biscuit. The firm got its name from the initials of the founding Lefèvre-Utile family and there are plenty of exhibits in the museum attesting to the importance of this company in the local economy, including art-deco ceramic adverts, LU memorabilia and several paintings, notably one depicting the prize-winning LU factory with a garland wielding angel hovering overhead, and a portrait of Lefèvre père, resembling nothing so much as a nineteenth century Anglican clergyman.

When the factory opened in 1885, it was in the context of a thriving economy, for after the development of techniques for refining sugar-beet and the abolition of the slave-trade in 1815, a trade on which Nantes' wealth had been founded, the city turned to foundry work, shipbuilding, and food production for its living. It was in this period of booming industrialization and the development of the international docks that Nantes' most famous son was born. Jules Verne lived here for the first twenty years of his life, and it was the ever more ingenious mechanization of labour seen in his hometown combined with the mariners' tales of exotic, colourful places heard on the quayside and in his uncle's ship-fitting yards, that first inspired the deft blending of science and fantasy in the novelist's work. The knack for reinventing itself according to the demands of new technology is not one that Nantes has lost, for after the demise of the shipyards in the 1980s, it turned its hand to modern service industries and its economy nowadays is based on IT, telecommunications, and insurance.

The château is in many ways the heart of Nantes and the integration of the two is mirrored in the permanent exhibition, which is not merely an illustration of what went on within the precincts of the ducal seat, but a history of the city itself and how it has evolved in relation to its geographical location. The first exhibit is a thousand year old dug-out canoe reflecting Nantes' situation at the confluence of three rivers, as a consequence of which it is dubbed "*ville port/ville pont*". Thereafter, we are taken on a journey through the commercial, revolutionary, industrial and post-industrial development of the region.

Relatively few of the items on display are of outstanding artistic merit in themselves, but taken as a whole they form a potent narrative, a little too potent as we progress, of which more anon. It's the sort of exhibition, sufficiently varied in tone and materials, to ensure everyone will come away with a different impression and fasten on different items as the highlight. For what it's worth, my attention was caught by several disparate exhibits, including a tapestry celebrating the union of France and Brittany with intermingled motifs of fleur de lys and ermine, a busty nineteenth century figurehead (naked women reputedly exercising a calming influence on turbulent seas), a remarkably elaborate wind vane, a vast poop lamp, various sea chests, and a cabinet display neatly juxtaposing the tools for navigation and the tools for killing whatever you found whenever you'd reached wherever you were going. There's also a rather jolly poster from 1910 reminding us that, though nowadays peripheral to Brittany proper, Nantes is very much a part of the *royaume de l'imaginaire:* promoting the city's summer festivities, it extols the virtues of *"La Bretagne a travers les ages: héroïque, fantastique, mystique".*

The most emblematic item, though, is a gold casket that once contained the heart of Anne de Bretagne. When she died in 1514, worn out by husbands who, mindful of posterity, had ensured she got pregnant on average every fourteen months, Anne was buried in the royal mausoleum in Paris, but her heart was returned to Brittany and kept in this casket until it was desecrated during the revolution. The reliquary itself is small, but it's pretty big for a heart, and that, essentially, is the message Breton nationalists have sought to cultivate over the centuries: Big Hearted Anne, the Queen in Clogs who sought to defend Breton rights and who, like the duchy itself, was married by force to the French state. There is some truth to the politics of this, but the image of Anne as a simple woman of the people is fanciful. Apart from anything else, she had a gammy leg that, according to the Venetian ambassador, she disguised by wearing high heels - anyone who has ever tried on a clog can tell you, you wouldn't want to be hobbling about with a high heel on the thing. Reputedly a vivacious and engaging woman (no pun intended), Anne also learned a sincere liking for the husband who had literally laid siege to her, so even if she was the woman who defended Breton rights against the rapacious big-bit-stuck-on-the-hind-end, she was herself a part of that big-bit.

In many ways, though, the principle exhibit is the château itself. There's no shortage of loggias and recesses and dormer windows and pillars and posts and towers, but the most intriguing architectural features are the minutiae, notably the bestiaries carved into the window frames and cornices. Even more captivating though, is the graffiti. I'm not talking dirty words and scatological ditties, but intricate carvings worked into the stone by prisoners when the château doubled as a gaol. We first see these in the Tour des Jacobins behind a maquette of medieval Nantes, where an entire wall has been decorated by incarcerated soldiers, among them an English sailor William Crisp, who was captured in 1746 during The Wars of Austrian Succession - you'd have thought these people might have succeeded without going to war all the time. Thereafter, though, it becomes apparent that this wall to which the curators have drawn our attention is notable only for the number of tags. In fact, there are dates, names, images, and messages carved in corners and on columns throughout the château. Given how elaborate much of the graffiti is, how long it must have taken, one has to conclude this was a fairy relaxed gaol that let the prisoners while away their time digging holes in the masonry.

Of the original architectural features, I'm afraid nobody's enthusing over the vast vaulted ceilings and immaculately calculated staircases. Instead, it is, as usual in these places, the stone plumbing that pleases most (note the sniggering crowd round the rampart privy in Room 16), as if nobody's much fussed about the wars their ancestors fought, or the architectural challenges they confronted, but are very excited to see how they went to the toilet. Perhaps it's understandable. Lofty spaces filled with God and great thick walls designed to prevent your neighbour inserting a cannonball in your head are things of the past, they no longer speak to us; but the business of bowels, not *that's* something we really understand, *that's* something with which we can identify.

At the heart of both the exhibition and the history of Nantes there lies the dark shadow of slavery. At first, it seems as if this dismal episode is to be glossed over, evoked by nothing more than a couple of friezes of carved negro heads and a solitary set of shackles. "He can't have moved much in them," observes a middle-aged, middle-class woman, grimly satisfied it seems. Not much, no; only 3000 miles and into a story the consequences of which are still not concluded 300 years later. I'm mildly surprised that an exhibition of such modern sensibility should duck this issue, but then, as we pass into Room 12, a tiny pocket book in a glass case attracts my attention. It looks inoffensive enough, but take a closer look and you will see that this little book, the size of a slimline cigarette pack, is "The Black Code", incorporating the regulations governing the French slave trade. You could slip it in the back pocket of your jeans, yet it speaks volumes. And what it announces is even more sinister.

Some years ago, I happened to stopover in Carcassonne, where so many Cathars were taken to be 'relaxed' out of their heresy during the Albigensian Crusade. It's a lovely medieval city, but an appalling place because the torture chambers have been turned into tourist attractions with pushy barkers trying to bounce you into visiting the delightful horrors of the dungeons. Perhaps I'm being a bit po-faced here, but the commercialism seemed utterly crass, even grotesque. By contrast, the unshowy display in Room 12 of the Nantes museum is a

The Black Code

damning indictment of what people can do to one another. There's nothing didactic about it and precious little moralizing because the objects on display say it all: there are small metal hand clubs, like delicately made pestles, 'pacifiers' designed to hurt but not maim, and riot spikes, like large metal jacks from some nightmarish 'game', and, in some ways most sinister of all because it attests to the banality of the whole enterprise, an inscribed shaving bowl presented to a captain to mark the end of a successful voyage, much as an insurance salesman might have won a plaque in 1950s corporate America for selling more policies than his colleagues. Later on there's a statue that was commissioned to commemorate the 150th anniversary of the abolition of the slave trade. It was vandalized within days of going on display, though whether by some dimwit who wished the trade had never been abolished or somebody who didn't think much of Europeans complacently patting themselves on the back for their magnanimity isn't specified.

As a whole, this is a very minimalist exhibition. There's no clutter, everything is presented discreetly and discretely, well spaced out with a carefully judged balance of old artifacts and modern interactive installations. You might think they had spread themselves a bit thin, that they didn't have enough stuff to fill the space. Don't be fooled. The curators had to choose from a staggering 50,000 potential exhibits. They whittled that down to a shortlist of 1500 from which they selected 850 items spread through 32 rooms to avoid detracting from the architecture itself. But despite such discrimination, you can really only take in about half of it. My legs have happily walked the length of the Pyrenees from the Atlantic to the Mediterranean, and would gladly do so again, but present them with one cabinet of curiosities too many and they just sort of curl up and die on me. By Room 14, I had pretty much had my fill, my legs were starting to wilt, my eyes were glazing over, and I had the feeling my hair was falling out faster than usual. The pity of it is, there's plenty to see in the remaining rooms, but this is not necessarily a problem; entrance to the museum is relatively cheap, so if you suffer a similar lassitude, you could always go back the next day. If, however, that's not an option, you have to plan ahead, studying the map of the museum and pacing yourself so you see what really interests you, or just accept that after a while you'll have had enough and will miss something. I for one missed the painting of Nantes done by Turner in 1826 when he toured the châteaux de la Loire, though an obsession with Moby Dick did mean I lingered in Room 19, caught by the Ambrose-Louis Garneray whaling scenes and the massive cast-iron try-pot for rendering blubber. If you do crack and find yourself hurrying through the last rooms, whatever else you miss, don't skip the diorama by Pierrick Sorin. There are a couple of seats here if you're quick off the mark, but even if they're already taken, make your legs hang on just a little bit longer. It's a wonderfully witty, slightly surreal résumé of everything seen in the exhibition so far, worth the entrance money in itself, neatly integrating the narrative of a thousand years and juxtaposing oddly contrasting images: silly and touching, light but never trivial, it's a must see.

The symbolic importance of the Château des Ducs de Bretagne for Brittany's uneasy relationship with the-big-bit-stuck-on-the-hind-end is obvious, and is acknowledged, perhaps unconsciously, in the official brochure, on the cover of which the 'des Ducs' part of the title is written in lower case letters and a less bold font, as if this was really The Castle of Brittany, a metonym for the region itself. Taking the long view, the self-sacrificing marriage of the Duchesse Anne was not the end of the story of Breton independence. Uxorious despite his excesses, Louis XII ratified the duchy's autonomous rights, which were confirmed in the marriage of Anne's daughter Claude de France to another French monarch, François I, and again in the 1532 declaration of perpetual union between the duchy and the crown. However, the shift from Anne *de Bretagne* to Claude *de France* was significant, and for all the hagiography that later accumulated around her, the image of Anne as the last bastion of Breton independence expresses a version of the truth that has only been lightly massaged. Autonomy did not really end until the French revolution, but by marrying Charles VIII, Anne brought Brittany into France and the stronghold of the Ducs de Bretagne became the Breton residence of the French kings, reduced from a 'castle' on the front line of a long-standing struggle to a royal 'château' - English pronunciation.

19. Gwenn-Ha-Du

ACCESS - The Brière regional park is due north of St. Nazaire at the mouth of the Loire river. **Rozé** is on the D50 north of Montoir-de-Bretagne. Our itinerary follows the D50 and D33 to **Herbignac**, then heads south along the D47 before taking the D247 to **Guérande**, the D774 and D32 across the saltmarsh, and the N171 onto the **Pointe du Croisic**.

The white and the black of the Breton flag, the white representing the sees where Breton was spoken, the black the Gallo-speaking dioceses, are so integral to Breton identity that they're often echoed in place names like Pouldu (black mud), Kerdu (black house), Guingamp (white field), and Guendol (white heights), but this Manichean toponymy is rarely made so manifest in topography as in the area around the Parc Naturel Regional de la Brière, encompassing as it does the black peat bog of the Brière itself and the glistening white salt marsh of the Golfe de Guérande. This is vexillology writ large in the very land itself.

Guérande City Walls

      The second biggest marsh in France after the Camargue, the Brière, from the Latin *brica* meaning earth or mud, occupies an ancient subsidence basin that was inundated by the sea several million years ago. The sea withdrew, man moved in, forests flourished, the sea returned, man moved out, the sea decamped again, man moved back and discovered a marsh defined by a talus of alluvial deposits from the Loire. Reeds grew in abundance, died in abundance, and decayed in abundance, stacking up a stockpile of peat that became the defining matter of the marsh. Thereafter, a distinct lifestyle developed, fuelled by peat, sheltered by thatch, transported by flat-bottomed punts, fed by wildfowl, pike, *pimpeneaux* (a type of silver bellied eel) and livestock raised on reclaimed land, and funded by the manufacture of wax flowers and work in the nearby shipyards.

      The Golfe de Guérande, by contrast, began life as a standard stretch of coast, open to the Ocean and most decidedly wet. But silting slowly built a land bridge to the west of modern day Pouliguen, eventually linking the Île de Batz (not to be confused with the island of the same name opposite Roscoff) to the mainland and its future as the holiday resort of Batz-sur-Mer. Behind this dyke, the shallows of the former gulf, still subject to the influx of the tides thanks to a narrow channel opposite Le Croisic, gradually turned into the salt marsh of Guérande, which gets its name from the Breton *gwen* and *rann* meaning white-country. Thus the black and the white or, as the Bretons will have it, the white and the black.

If you happen to have been bumping about Nantes beforehand, I recommend approaching the *parc naturel* along the backroads north of the Loire via Coueron, Bouée, and Dongées. This attractive rural no-man's land between the commercial and industrial hubs of Nantes and St. Nazaire is being integrated into a coherent coastal-cum-cultural capital in the image of Barcelona, and if you stray down to the water's edge en route, you may be in for a surprise. To bring together the estuary's long-time rivals, *Nantes-la-bourgeoise* and *Saint-Nazaire-la-prolétaire*, the local authorities have inaugurated a biennale of contemporary art for which the 'gallery' is the sixty-kilometre estuary itself. Among the wittier installations commissioned for the first biennale was a reproduction of a posh townhouse planted in the middle of the estuary near Lavau-sur-Loire, a 'melting' yacht perched on the quay of the Canal de la Martinière, its prow dipping waterward as if wanting to take the plunge but worrying about the temperature, and a twenty-five metre tall plastic bath duck bobbing about near Île de Nantes to remind us that, in a post-industrial world, this is our playground.

Our tour, however, begins in the inland port of Rozé, which is a good place to start exploring the canals that bisect the Brière marsh, the core axis being formed by the Canals du Rozé and Bréca, Le Vieux Canal and the Canal du Nord. The main tourist attraction in Rozé is the *Maison de l'Éclusier*, the lock-keeper's house, an *eco-musée* that, along with the *Parc Animalier,* provides an overview of the marsh's natural and historical evolution. But since main tourist attractions aren't necessarily the objective of this book, we simply stroll along the Brivet, the watercourse accessing the Loire and a good way of getting a feel for the marsh before heading for its more frequented heartland.

How to describe it? Well, in a word flat. I mean really flat. There are places where you can set off walking with no visual clue whatsoever that you will ever reach anywhere, places so flat that a cow is a landmark, places where you suspect that if you walk far enough you might well tip off the edge. And it is this absence of anything against which you can measure yourself or your progress that is so refreshing about the Brière, as if there is infinite space into which you might expand should you so choose. You're not going to be doing a lot of grandiose landscape photography here, but there's a definite magic about the place, a more subtle appeal that cannot be captured but simply has to be soaked up. La Brière seeps into the eye rather than springing it open with a staggering display of stunning contours. There aren't any contours. Nothing but us, the distant silos of St. Nazaire, and a tranquil waterway, lined on its left bank with gardens, each with its own private landing stage and personal punt, a few with spidery frames for dipping fishing nets into the river.

The most accomplished literary evocation of the region is 'La Brière', a bestselling novel from between the wars (609,000 copies sold, winner of the Grand Prix de l'Académie Française, and much admired by fellow writers) by the Breton aristocrat Alphonse de Châteaubriant. A melancholy romance recounting a very Breton history of a jealous father's opposition to his daughter's marriage to a man from 'another country' (i.e. 'the village down the road'), the book is impregnated with a sense of place, matching the shadowy half-lives of its characters with the misty, mysterious shadowland they inhabit, but its literary merits are largely forgotten nowadays thanks to the lamentable political history of its author. A volunteer paramedic during the First World War, Châteaubriant was so horrified by what he saw, he concluded that France and Germany must never go to war with one another again. Unhappily he was so fervent in this belief that he embraced a mystical variant of National Socialism, proclaiming Hitler a new messiah, extolling "*la beauté morale de la capitulation*", and so thoroughly compromising himself as a collaborator, he was condemned to death in absentia at the end of the war and died in disgrace in exile six years later, all of which inevitably took the shine off his literary achievements.

From Rozé, we head north, detouring onto Île de Fédrun, home to the *Maison de la Mariée*, the House of the Bride, dedicated to the cottage industry that supplemented many local incomes, the composition of bridal bouquets from wax orange flowers. There are dozens of mini-museums like this dotted about Brittany commemorating all manner of obscure and marginal craft activities, but personally I can't cope with more than one indoor visit in a day, so we skip the wax flowers and just take a turn round the island. It's pleasant enough, perhaps a little too densely populated for my tastes, but its principal appeal lies in the fact that, for those approaching from the south, this is the first place where the Brière's traditional thatched roofs have not succumbed to the cheap Spanish slate that caps the newer houses on the edge of the marsh.

Some of the thatching is ancient and mottled with moss, elsewhere it has been redone and is so tidily trimmed, it's hard to believe it's not machine made. Best of all are the roofs where one end has been re-thatched and the other left as it was, the raggedy patchy reeds deemed to have a few more years in them yet, even if they look a bit shabby beside their pristine new neighbours.

Old Thatch, New Thatch

uniformity is not an issue

Pulling over at an inlet alongside the D50, we are serenaded by frogs (amphibian variety), reminding me of a wonderful film following the misadventures of a couple of indigent frog catchers in another marsh, *Les Enfants du Marais* by Jean Becker, which featured a cameo by Eric Cantona of all people. It's a warm, witty, moving film governed by the philosophy of its principal character, the affable wistful drunk, Garris, played by Jacques Villeret, who proclaims: "*On est des gagnes misères, mais on n'est pas des peignes-culs*" - basically, we're at the bottom of the pile, but we don't comb our arses! Such pragmatic humility touched with pride might as easily have characterized the *enfants du marais* in La Brière, too, for though few grew rich from their environment, the Brièrons are deeply attached to their marsh, and it is their marsh, too, most of it being common land granted to the local residents in the fifteenth century.

Egrets and heron flap overhead with ungainly grace and nonchalantly stalk the shallows, searching for fish and admiring their own patrician reflections in the still surface of the water. Cormorants and moorhen scull industriously about the canal, diligently ducking and diving and dipping and turning, looking infinitely busy beside their lanky aloof neighbours. A dozen punts are moored in the inlet, some waterlogged and clearly abandoned, others new and ready to be taken out tomorrow when the fishing season opens. It is while inspecting these boats that we decide we want to get out onto the water - on our own.

There are plenty of waymarked walking and cycling routes in the Brière, and those who find the flatness oppressive can always climb the pink church tower (ecclesiastical architecture is not the strong point of the Brière) at St. Lyphard; the marsh would probably make a very pretty pattern seen from above, a sort of poor man's Mekong Delta. But, to my mind, you should embrace the defining feature of any given landscape. Get into the mountains and it's a good idea to get onto as high an elevation as energy, vertigo and weather allow; go somewhere flat and you should get as deep into the flatness as you possibly can. In La Brière, you've really got to become a part of it by taking to the water. In fact, it was always my intention to take to the water one way or another. There are dozens of guides in the marsh's ports offering outings in punts (*chalands*) and horse drawn carts (*calèches*), but when I was doing the preliminary research for this excursion, I got the impression you couldn't just do the boat trip but had to take the combined package. Trundling around in a horse drawn cart seemed a little too close to sitting in a tourist train tooting about a theme park, so I was hoping to find someone who would take us out in a *chaland* without exposing us to the experience of a *calèche*. On the spot though, even that seems too conventional. Doubtless the guides are good and can give an insight into the workings of the marsh you won't get from bumping about on your own, but if you're searching for the spirit of place, it's best to accept a little ignorance and even embrace your own limitations: "*On est des gagnes misères, mais on n'est pas des peignes-culs*".

First, though, we visit the Château de Ranrouët to the south of Herbignac. I don't know what your take on castles is (and this is a 'castle', not an anglicized 'château'), but I'm irredeemably contaminated by nineteenth century romanticism. I know a man who lives in a ruined castle in the south of France, and it really is a ruin, and when people come to visit him, they look around, awestruck by the crumbling walls and gaping holes in the roof, and say how wonderful it is, then ask when he's going to start restoring it. But he has no intention of 'restoring' it. It is what it is, a ruin. He bought a ruin and it is his intention to live in a ruin. Quite right, too. It's all very well prettying up a renaissance palace like the Château des Ducs de

Bretagne, but your big stone jobs with arrow slit windows and chutes for pouring boiling oil on unwanted guests really shouldn't look too clean. They're rough old war horses and they should look like rough old war horses, all beaten about and duffed up.

Rough old war horse

Happily, Ranrouët has been thoroughly beaten about. Built in the twelfth and thirteenth centuries to control the salt trade, it was dismantled by Louis XIII in 1618, then burned during the revolution - any more beaten about and it would be a heap of rubble. Nonetheless, enough of the castle remains intact to function as a 3D history lesson, explanatory panels describing how the building developed, how to 'read' a résumé of military architecture between the 13th and 17th centuries from its six towers, and elucidating puzzling details like the protruding stones representing the armorial emblazon of the Lords of Rieux. But the history per se is perhaps less interesting than the atmosphere. Basically, anybody who likes a good ruin will glory in this precarious pile of stones. And kids love it. If you're really lucky, you may even catch a play or a concert in the grounds.

Thereafter, it's back to the business of the punt. Pretending DIY is the only proper way to approach a marsh is all very well, but it's easier said than done. First, though it turns out plenty of guides offer the *chaland* outing alone, relatively few rent out boats without a guide - possibly even fewer after the experiment of our outing. It takes us some time to find someone willing to let us out in a boat on our own, but we eventually track down the nice people at L'Arche Briéronne operating from the popular embarkation point at Port de Bréca. Nobody seems the least bit troubled by our sniffy dismissal of their *chaland-calèche* service. They even have a waymarked circuit round the marsh that, for the most part, avoids the routes followed by the guided punts - for the most part, whereby hangs another tale and the second 'difficulty' of the outing.

Still smiling broadly, the people manning the L'Arche Briéronne stand take one look at me and promptly hand over a couple of paddles. Clearly, only professionals get a punt pole, a precaution I soon realize is entirely justified. Even the paddles prove a bit of a poser. The more meaningful part of my education took place on the lam rather than on the Cam, as a consequence of which the only experience I've previously had of being in a flat-bottomed boat was messing about in a West African lagoon: the key feature of West African lagoons is that they're big and wide and there's nothing much to bump into. I manage to get into the boat without overturning the thing or tipping myself or anyone else in the water, and we even back off from the bank and round the corner into the first channel without ramming anything - not that anyone is there to see this as the young

Don't give that man a pole!

man from L'Arche Briéronne has wisely walked away, leaving us to get on with it as best we can. Our preliminary success does not last long, though. To start with at least one of us begins by pushing the water the wrong way and, even when we're both pushing it backwards with a view to getting ourselves moving forward, our notional wake (notional because we really aren't moving very fast) resembles a football manager's tachogram at a particularly delicate instant in a vital match. It isn't exactly Last of the Mohicans.

Zigzagging along, we emerge from the first channel, manage to hang a left, get ourselves into the second, considerably narrower channel, and there, slap bang in front of us, are met with the looming prow of a big fat punt carrying a dozen or so tourists, all smiling at us fixedly while the punter prattles on about some goats grazing in the meadow off to our left. I'm not quite sure what happens next, but somehow we manage to broadside the big fat punt. I say 'broadside', but rather than drawing alongside our intended target and letting him have it with all guns, we develop a new technique for 'broadsiding' whereby you place yourself side on and then paddle edgeways directly into your foe's bow before shooting off to his leeward side and ploughing into a bank of reeds. It's not an easy manoeuvre to master, but if you want to alarm a few tourists and make yourself look like a complete idiot, it can't be bettered. As for the man with the punt pole, he is imperturbable and doesn't even acknowledge us, as if having some clown broadsiding him is a professional hazard he encounters every day of his working life. Perhaps it is.

Despite this unhappy early encounter, we soon leave the other boats behind (or, more likely, word gets around and they leave us behind), and begin to make reasonable progress. We aren't exactly scything a straight line down the middle of the channel (there are probably not quite so many clumps of reeds along the fringes of the mud banks as when we first ventured onto the water), but it's all really rather agreeable, and the instinct that prompted us to avoid the guided tour proves sound. In your own boat, you get a real feel for the marsh, can even believe you've got the place to yourself as you plough through the black, turbid water between reeds, silver birch and yellow iris. Languid looking herons embellish the mud banks, so perfectly posed you half suspect they were placed there by the tourist board, busy little dragonflies skitter hither and thither, a profusion of hunters' hides are scattered about the drier islands to feed the fantasies of the paranoiac, and several coypu swim casually across our bows - poor fools, they little know the risks they are running.

The meandering course of our itinerary is so convolute, I begin to wonder whether somebody hasn't inverted a few strategic waymarking arrows, or whether the whole thing isn't some elaborate practical joke, designed to take us ever further into the middle of the marsh until we don't have a clue where we are. All things considered, I wouldn't much mind. Getting lost is always the best way to get to know somewhere and La Brière is a very pleasing place in which to lose yourself, a real escape from the clatter and clutter of modern living. It's worth taking a picnic if you're not in a hurry (there's no time limit on the boat's rental, just a flat fee of 20 euros) and really making a day of it, but even if time is short, stop once in a while and clamber onto the firmer mud banks (don't let go of the boat!), in order to be still and let the atmosphere sink into you - and, of course, the damp if you've chosen an island less firm than it looked.

Eventually, we round the bend into the home stretch. If you are a novice and are still having difficulty maintaining a straight line, get your paddling technique sorted out here because the last furlong ends in a comparatively narrow chicane and, instead of friendly clumps of reeds waiting to bump you back on track, the chicane is lined with overhanging boughs and banks of brambles. Apart from nearly taking a dive into the water as we moor, we disembark unboughed and unbrambled, and feeling curiously chuffed with ourselves. It may not seem like a very great adventure, getting in a punt and paddling about a marsh, and I should warn you there's plenty of potential for initiating divorce proceedings ("You paddle this side." "I am paddling this side." "No, this side!" "I am, I am!" "Harder, harder!" "I'm paddling as hard as I can." "Watch out, there's a heron." "Do you think he can still fly with one wing?" "Mind those reeds!" "Oh, bugger!"), but I recommend it wholeheartedly.

Leaving the black country behind us, we move onto the white country and the medieval city of Guérande. Guérande is not one of the great walled cities, but it's good enough, and definitely worth stopping off en route to the salt marsh itself. We visit the Musée du Pays de Guérande, which is housed in the tower of the main gate into the city, the Porte Saint-Michel. Far from being an exhaustive and exhausting interactive, high-tech, modern museum like in Nantes, this is very much a municipal museum, a collection of items in glass boxes, the only interactive pursuit a short stroll along the ramparts. It's the sort of place that used to render me catatonic when I was kid (there's even a display of waxworks wearing traditional costumes), but there are a couple of school parties here today and the five year olds seem to be having a whale of a time, banging on the glass cabinets, swinging from the curtains and so forth - I guess everything's interactive when you're five years old. Like all such collections, the Musée du Pays de Guérande is a pleasingly promiscuous rattle-bag of objects, jumbling together all manner of items that are only marginally linked by their common local origins, a clock mechanism standing beside a loom, the region's traditional red furniture crowded together in a corner, the walls festooned with enlarged *fin de siecle* postcards of locals doing folkloric *fin de siecle* things, clay pipes beside an eighteenth century child's clay bath (the latter strangely moving because so simple yet clearly so tenderly conceived), and various tools of the salt maker's trade.

The main street leading into the city is a little off-putting, rather too many gift shops and boutiques dedicated to designer underwear for my tastes, but it's worth persevering because the backstreets are charming and the Church of St. Aubin is very impressive, particularly the capitals of the gothic pillars, which are decorated with friezes depicting scenes that, to the untrained eye, look decidedly pagan. As with the Brière though, the indoor attractions are secondary here, so we skip the *Musée de la Poupée* (I ask you!), and head for the heart of the salt marsh and the capital of salt, the island settlement of Saillé. The *Maison des Paludiers* and *Terre de Sel* offer professional insights into the history of the salt marsh, but again we go for the unmediated experience, simply driving west, opting for the least promising minor roads each time, preferably those with no names and no direction panels, until we fetch up at the western rim of the marsh, just short of the sea defence wall.

In season, the salter or *paludier* irrigates the salt pans every fortnight, spreading the sea water across a gently sloping reservoir and feeding it through successively shallower basins, gradually concentrating the brine as the sun and wind evaporate the water until the salt crystallizes in the harvesting pan or *oeillet*, a word that translates literally as an eyelet, grommet, or carnation. The floral image is appropriate because during the summer harvest (June to September) the *oeillet* yields two types of salt, the fine *fleur de sel* creamed off the surface and the coarser *gros sel* or *sel gris* that gathers underneath. Each *oeillet* produces three to five kilos of *fleur de sel* a day and 40 to 70 kilos of *gros sel*, and in a good year the *paludier* can harvest up to three tons a day. It's a delicate business though and it's essential to calculate the flows of water correctly, since if you let in too much or too little, you'll get less salt. Little wonder then that the *paludiers* traditionally sought divine aid, one superstition that persisted into the twentieth century recommending stoning a local statue to guarantee a good harvest. Nowadays famous for its flavour and high levels of oligo-elements, *sel de Guérande* is a selling point for quality foodstuffs, featuring in upmarket butter, biscuits, and crisps. These are available in most Breton supermarkets, but the local shops also stock more specialist products from the salt marsh, like *salicorne*, a type of glasswort eaten in salads or served as an aperitif or garnish.

Given its present celebrity, you'd have thought *sel de Guérande* had always been a gourmet item, yet the traditional craft nearly died out during the 1960s and it was only a rearguard action by a handful of *paludiers* that saved it from industrialization in the 1970s. Some modern techniques are employed, they no longer, for instance, simply toss a potato into the brine to test its salinity (if the spud floated it was time to harvest), but a *paludier* from a thousand years ago would not be at a total loss if he was brought back to life today. The solar technique for refining marsh salt seems to have evolved in the early dark ages, prior to which salt had been extracted since the Iron Age through the *'briquetage'* technique of artificially heating sea-water, and before that . . . well, before that you just kept munching on your mastodon and hoped for the best. The first record of salt-making in Guérande dates from the ninth century, though many claim it was already being produced here during the Gallo-Roman period. Like most craft industries, salt making has known its ups and downs. For obvious reasons, Guérande is vulnerable to pollution, particularly the *marées noires* from shipwrecks, and working here has always been a punishing business. Time was when the *paludiers* rented their patch of marsh from wealthy landowners on a sharecropping basis, turning over half their harvest as rent, and in living memory the drudgery of transporting salt to market was such that one veteran remembers receiving his first wheelbarrow with the sort of joy a modern teenager greets his first moped.

The salt marsh itself is less immediately beguiling than the Brière marsh, which is fair enough. This is a business, after all, a working landscape, not a place for fluffing about communing with coypu and playing at waterborne dodgems, and you can understand if it looks a little scruffy. Moreover, an unusually wet Spring means the *paludiers* have postponed harvesting to repeat their winter cleaning of the salt pans, so it doesn't look particularly white today either. But even in such unpromising circumstances, the deeper you get into the marsh, the more entrancing it is. The eye gradually grows accustomed to the rough cracked dykes and all you see is the perfect symmetry of salt pans stretching away into the distance, a pristine grid catching the bright white light from the big sky and setting up a hypnotic pattern of neatly framed reflections. It's an unforgiving place, though, and I pity the people who work here in the heat of high summer. Strangely, they are not dried out or pickled by their labours, but are for the most part warm and approachable. One or two holdings have 'private property/no entry' signs, but most *paludiers* are welcoming and don't mind visitors strolling along the dykes, so long as you don't descend into the salt pans themselves. Even so, it is hot and it is dry and there is no shelter and after a while the proximity of the sea makes a swim seem like a fairly imperative conclusion to our outing.

The Guérandaise coast is dotted with holiday resorts, the most famous or infamous depending on your point of view, being La Baule. Alternatively, fans of Jacques Tati may wish to head further east to visit Saint-Marc-sur-Mer, the location of Monsieur Hulot's Hôtel de la Plage - fans may, I don't. I've never really seen the point of Jacques Tati. He always reminds me of a laboriously unfunny uncle being consciously 'funny' for the children, hamming it up, terminally aware of his own 'funniness', despite the fact that by the age of three the children have long since outgrown his clumsy attempts at humour. The gags are clearly intricately structured, but they're often so carefully thought out and beautifully conceived they forget that they're meant to make you laugh. So rather than visiting Saint Marc, we head for La Côte Sauvage beyond Batz-sur-Mer. By Breton standards, this is a relatively tame *sauvagerie*, but those are unusually exacting standards, and the peninsula has some excellent rock pools, notably at the Port au Rocs bus stop on the western tip of Pointe du Croisic.

Between the black country of the Brière and the white country of the salt marshes, the landscape is not typically Breton, but it is more than a mere echo of the Breton flag. It's a place where poverty was common and survival meant working with elements that were not always clement. It's a place where unpromising raw materials prompted ingenious solutions to the problems of making a living, a place trapped between the sea and the land, the glare of the sun and the shroud of the mist, a betwixt and between land of subtly shifting colours, and a very particular, very private, very local lifestyle in which pride and humility mingle in equal measure. These are generalities, but they wouldn't be valid everywhere. And yet they are true of most places in Brittany, where it's always as well to remember: *On est des gagnes misères, mais on n'est pas des peignes-culs.*

20. Tideland

ACCESS - To find somebody else's 'secret' hidey-hole, head for **Locmariaquer** at the mouth of the Golfe de Morbihan near Vannes, then follow the headland road round **Pointe de Kerpenhir**. Wherever you see cars lined alongside the road at low tide, you can be sure that this is a good spot for *la pêche à pied*.

If you want to warm the cockles of the Breton heart, I use the time advisedly, two words suffice, *grande marée* or 'big tide'. Much of Breton life is governed by tides from the best, like the fabulous beaches that expand and shrink and sometimes disappear altogether in sync with the moon, to the worst, like the *marées noires* that pollute the coast whenever some flag of convenience founders

A Bucketful of Fun

between the Bay of Biscay and the North Sea. But it's the *grandes marées* that really set the heart fluttering, for it is then that the Bretons take to the tideland for *la pêche à pied*, fishing on foot.

It's a passion that was not always so comprehensive as it is today. Not so long ago, Bretons were baffled by Parisian holidaymakers collecting such unsavoury items as winkles, limpets and razor-fish, and were frankly disgusted when the same holidaymakers took to the fields after a rainstorm to gather snails. By God, life must be hard in the city! Bretons were fond of a fish, they relished the larger crustaceans, but you wouldn't catch them swallowing some slimy lump of sea slug. They might be poor, but they weren't that hungry. Nowadays, though, they've acquired a more expansive palate and are ready to eat virtually anything that comes out of the sea, and it's all to the better if that something has been scraped off the rocks or plucked from a tide pool or dug out of the sand with their own hands.

So a session of *la pêche à pied* seemed essential to a book that purports to be a thorough bumping about Brittany. The only drawback was that I knew zilch about *la pêche à pied* and there wasn't much point wandering aimlessly about the beach hopefully showing the sea an empty plastic bag on the off chance that something might leap into it. What we needed was an expert to show us how it was done. This didn't seem too tall an order. We know plenty of people who go fishing on foot and they're always boasting about what they've caught. All we had to do was ask someone to take us with them the next time they went. They'd be delighted to enlighten us and be immortalized by a big time writer in an international bestseller, right? Wrong. Apparently they weren't persuaded by the big time writer and international bestseller bit of the equation. In fact, the first person we asked nearly fell off his chair with fright. Once he'd caught his breath and we'd fanned his sweating brow and patted his wrist for a few minutes, he stammered out something about it being very difficult, and you couldn't just read about it and then go out and do it, and nobody would find anything, and there really wasn't any point.

After several similar demurrals, it dawned on us that, no matter how many people you see *pêching à pied* (and there are places where they number in their hundreds at a really *grande marée*) this is not necessarily a gregarious activity. Convivial, communal, collective, all those nice words of togetherness, just don't figure when it comes to *la pêche à pied*. Your inveterate *pêcheur à pied* would sooner cut off his right arm (or at least his wife's right arm, he needs his own right arm for *pêching à pied)* than share his know-how, because the key to *la pêche à pied* is knowing your terrain. Going out year after year on their local ground, *pêcheurs à pied* build up an intimate mind map of the precise points where their prey can be found, and this insiders' knowledge is guarded with the same jealousy that a land-bound forager protects a patch of fungus-rich woodland. Even when we found a couple willing to show us how it was done, the same phenomenon pertained.

"Yes," they said, "there's a fairly big tide in a fortnight."

"Great," we said. "We'll come and see you then."

"Oh," they said. "Er, no. No, don't do that. We'll come and see you."

"No, no," we said, airily. "No trouble, we'll come to you. It's for our book, after all. We don't want to bother you."

"No," they protested. "No bother, no trouble at all. We'll come to you."

Now these are old friends, people with whom formative experiences have been shared, people with whom holidays have been taken, people with whom we hold common values and beliefs, people who have gone out of their way on more than one occasion to help us, people with whom we might well trust our lives. But they weren't having us round their place so we could see all their secret hidey-holes stuffed with abalone. No way! Even when we agreed that they would visit us, the complications weren't over. My idea was that we would go on a nice simple bucket and spade excursion, something that anyone reading this book might repeat during their own holiday, something that required no special equipment, but could be done on a whim, with maybe a penknife, perhaps a shrimp net if you were pushing it, but otherwise simple, straightforward, easily repeatable. That was my idea. There was a long silence on the other end of the phone, followed by the whistling sound of air being sucked between teeth.

"But what do you want to catch?"

"Anything we can really apart from a cold."

"Yes, but . . ."

"I know, I know, it's very difficult."

"You can say that again."

"Once is enough. Look, all we want is to spend a bit of time messing about in rock pools - and hopefully have something to eat afterwards. Something we've caught, that is. Not something we bought down the market."

"Yes, but it depends what you want to catch. We've got lots of equipment. You've got to have the right equipment."

It was at this stage that I started having visions of them turning up with an articulated lorry and of myself crawling across the sands weighed down with harpoons, stun guns, and drag nets. Surely it couldn't be that complicated? Oh, yes it can. Got to have the right equipment depending on what you want to catch. Eventually, we settled on abalone, prawns, and clams. At least, I reasoned, that wouldn't involve me massacring or being massacred by anything large and more at home in the water than myself, tangling with a giant octopus say, or being dragged out to sea by an irate whale. Even so, I was sufficiently concerned to buy a book entitled *'La Pêche à Pied'* by a Monsieur Lagenette. This obviously wasn't going to be such an easy business as I'd anticipated, not some idle outing laced with infantile fun, but a real expedition of the kind undertaken by men far more virile than me, the sort of men who like having the heads of big cats eyeballing them from the library wall. It was as well to prepare myself. Otherwise, I'd end up looking like a right prawn.

At first, Monsieur Lagenette's words were encouraging, outlining the gravitational forces behind tides, the *vive-eau* of big tides and the *morte-eau* of small tides, and the peculiarly French system for calculating the difference between them with a coefficient of amplitude rather than the simple high and low water tide-tables that are good enough for the rest of the world, which didn't surprise me in the least, since *l'exception Française* is always expressed by having an entirely different system from everybody else. A small tide coefficient is forty to seventy, average tides are around eighty, and big tides, the ones we want, are over a hundred.

His next chapter, though, was titled "*Bien s'équiper pour bien pêcher*". Here we go, I thought. Two pages were dedicated to what you ought to wear on your feet, ranging from a pair of espadrilles to chest high waders. Slopping about in rope-soled slippers didn't recommend itself to me, but neither did I fancy slipping under the seas dragged down by a pair of elongated Wellington boots full of water, and yet I read this chapter with some attention because it mentioned *'les piqûres des vives'*. If you've ever stepped on a weaver fish, you'll appreciate why this phrase leapt off the page hollering Danger! Danger! Danger! The poisonous dorsal spines of weaver fish can cause quite excruciating pain, and there are only three cures for a sting that, if not treated immediately, can cause problems for months. This is worth noting if you're swimming, too, as weaver fish are endemic on large, flat sandy beaches in Brittany. Cure number one, you piss on the afflicted portion of your anatomy. I've not tried this and, given that the afflicted portion is generally the underside of your foot, it can't be an easy cure to affect, but if you do happen to be stung when you're on a remote beach, this maybe your only option. You will, at least, soon find out who your friends are. Cure number two, douse it in vinegar, so I'm told at least, and I suppose this remedy is coherent with the urine. Cure number three, the most common and the one of which I have personal experience, is to plunge your foot in a bucket of scalding water, or at least as hot as you can tolerate, and keep it there till the pain subsides, which can take an hour or more depending how quick off the mark you are getting your hot water. Anyway, the upshot of all this when it comes to *la pêche à pied* is to go well shod. Quite apart from the weaver fish, there are sharp rocks and splintered shells and slippery seaweed and possibly broken bottles out there, all of them potential hazards.

As for clothing, that's much as you would expect of any outdoor activity, basically 'protect yourself from the elements', though the book also cites an old saying: "*La meilleure façon de pêcher, c'est de mettre la main dans le trou*" - the best way to fish is to put your hand in the hole. Good idea! Haven't these people read any Greek myths? This may be the best way to fish, but it's also the best way to get yourself pinched or stung or bitten or to touch something distressingly slimy, hence Monsieur Lagenette's next piece of advice, take an old garden glove. Fair enough. So far, so good: well shod, well covered, and with a glove, just the one, à la Alvin Stardust.

We then moved onto the tools of the trade and this is where it all started to get a little surreal. Monsieur Lagenette says you don't want to be cluttered up with lots of equipment, then goes on for five pages about hampers, buckets, baskets, haversacks, capacious sidepockets, rakes, nets, pursenets, hooks, knives, and screwdrivers (better for prizing limpets off rocks than your average penknife), the catalogue of which conjured images of me staggering about the beach looking rather more like a porcupine than the feared prawn. Perhaps looking like a prawn would be easier. At least you don't need any special equipment for that. Instinctive ignorance and native incompetence will do the trick all on their own.

I was 26 pages into the book and all I really knew was that I was going to look pretty daft whatever I did, what with my one glove and so forth. Happily, where to fish was a simpler matter, since every marine environment has its own treasures, so the best thing to do is find a beach with as many different features as possible (sand, silt, rocks, stones, seaweed etc.) and just get on with it. Getting on with it, though, was one thing I found hard to envisage as the next seventy pages detailed the finer points of fishing for everything from winkles to conger eels. Now with the best will in the world, there's no way I'm going out to grapple with a thirty kilo conger eel with teeth in its head simply for the purposes of producing a chapter in a book. I've got things I'm very attached to, fingers and arms and things like that, and I don't intend offering them up as bait to a conger bloody eel, the fishing of which requires a gaff hook on top of everything else - one more spine for the porcupine.

I don't really have the space here to detail seventy pages of fishing lore, but in brief, when *pêching à pied,* you can find the following creatures in the following places with the following techniques: winkles, half-tide, in amongst the weed and under the rocks, eminently collectable with no special equipment required (this is my sort of fishing); limpets, half-tide, rip 'em off the rocks a bit quick with your screwdriver or else they'll stick like . . . well, like limpets really - and don't be embarrassed by sneering experts who regard this particular gastropod as beneath them; shrimp trapped in tide pools, scoop 'em up and try not to feel guilty about eating something so tiny; abalone, rare and therefore restricted by a quota per person (the quota varies depending on where you are), but still found, generally in hush-hush hidey-holes at very low water; cockles, razor-fish, and more types of clam than I could count let alone find translations for, are caught by grubbing about in the damp sand with a rake, a spade or an old spoon (two more spines for the porcupine), or in the case of certain varieties of bivalve, dropping your spade on the damp sand, whereupon the mollusc will spit a jet of water into the air, hence the nickname *pisseurs*; in the case of razor-fish, if you find the twin holes they leave in the sand where they bury themselves, the holes so close together they resemble a figure of eight, don't bother digging because they can dig quicker than you, just pull them out with an umbrella rib (yet another spine) or sprinkle salt on the holes so they surface of their own accord, then grab 'em quick before they start digging again;

All this and more is to be found on the falling tide, but the real specialists have barely begun because as the lower rocks are exposed, there are, to be taken from very clean waters and only very clean waters, oysters and mussels, the former levered away with knife, screwdriver or chisel (another spine, are you counting?), the latter 'requiring no particular technique' though a fork might come in handy

Digging for Victory

(do individual tines count as spines?). By this time the sea's just about withdrawn to England and your confirmed *pêcheur à pied* is beginning to get really excited because now there's a faint hope of finding a scallop, either big (*Coquille Saint-Jacques*) or small (*la pétoncle*), the former sculling about the sand, the latter fixed to the rocks, both betraying their whereabouts by 'clacking' their valves, always presuming you can hear anything clacking above the racket of the cutlery clinking in your pockets. If there are a lot of loose rocks on the beach, turn them over with your jemmy (spine #94) and you can find crabs, the diminutive green *crabes enragés* (I'd be pretty cross myself), the ruddy (in every sense of the word) swimming crab, the Big Daddy of them all, *le tourteau* (handily translated by my dictionary as 'edible crab') and, much prized because it doesn't travel well so is hard to buy, the spider crab. Key information here is to replace each stone precisely as you found it to preserve the micro-ecosystem it shelters, and to be careful how you pick up your crab, especially the swimming crab, who is sufficiently gymnastic to pinch you no matter where you hold him, in which case your best bet is to get him to grasp your jemmy then shake him off into your bag, basket, hamper, haversack or capacious pocket or wherever it is you're storing all these things.

I confess, I began to have my doubts about Monsieur Lagenette at this stage, for we are surrounded by kindly neighbours with boats and crab pots who, in season, regularly bring us spider crabs. *Araignées* may well by prized by gourmets, but if you tend more toward the gourmand end of the scale, they are hugely frustrating, involving a good forty-five minutes of strenuous wrestling to extract a handful of meat that would barely fill a Shippam's paste pot. By the time Monsieur Lagenette got round to the King of the Coast, the lobster (tickle it with your gaff hook then slip it into the net - yeh, right), I was beginning to conclude this entire enterprise was going to be a large waste of time, no matter how well equipped we were. My suspicions were confirmed when he got his gaff hook out again for a titanic battle with a two-metre long conger eel (oh, please!), as a result of which, his advice about the wrist action required when you're wading about netting brands of prawn (*bouquet, crevette*) and squid (*seiche, calamar, chipirons*) largely passed me by. And when he started going on about sole (find it under your foot and you've got to stamp on it a bit quick and hope you haven't misidentified a weaver fish), he lost me altogether. It's very difficult, you won't find anything, there's no point - maybe our first informant was right and the friends who had agreed to act as our guides had only done so thanks to the sort of imperishable optimism that had maintained the friendship thus far.

A few days before Jacqueline and Michel were due to arrive, my partner mentioned that she used to go fishing for abalone when she was a kid.

"They've got to be scraped out of their holes", she said.

"Scraped out of their holes, you say?" I didn't recall anything about scraping. What about my glove?

"Yes, you run a piece of metal along the line of a crevice . . . . "

"A piece of metal?! What sort of a piece of metal?"

"Well, any piece of metal will do. Something long and flat is best. We used to use an old garden sickle."

I had a quiet cry then. Not even Monsieur Lagenette mentions sickles. I was going to look like a combination of a prawn, a porcupine, a glam rocker, and the grim-reaper. Great.

The trauma wasn't over yet, though. We mentioned to another friend, Mireille, that we were going *pêching à pied* for, among other things, prawns.

"Prawns!" she exclaimed, hands pressed to her cheeks as if she'd just seen a prawn herself, a big bald one with a beard and a book contract. I don't think she meant it personally, but she was clearly troubled. "Prawns?!"

"Yeh, you know, little pink things with wafty red feelers. Big shrimps. Cocktailed, canapéd, curried, scampied, potted, pied, pasted . . . in a word, prawns."

I tried impersonating a prawn, but I'm not sure it helped.

"But you won't catch prawns", she said. "You need a tide with a coefficient of at least a hundred to catch prawns. The next big tide's only eighty-nine".

It's very difficult, you won't find anything, there's no point. Back to the drawing board: *Prawns, the fishing and viability of in relation to a coefficient of eighty-nine. Discuss.* Well, according to both Monsieur Lagenette and our guides, you *can* catch prawns on a relatively modest tide since they follow the flux of the waters. The good news about prawns notwithstanding though, our guides *were* having second thoughts about abalone.

"But we said we were going to catch abalone", I protested. "With a sickle and a piece of metal and a double-headed axe and a pitchfork and a small waterproof cannon".

"Yes, but it's not really the season. Winter's best for abalone. And we really need a bigger tide".

After some complicated negotiations that were only marginally less convolute than attempts to persuade the American government that Cadillacs may have some distant connection to climate change, we decided to replace the abalone with cockles. So it was settled then: prawns, cockles and clams - and I wasn't telling anyone else about it in case they started objecting that the prawns were all on holiday at this season or that the cockles had decamped to Nova Scotia or that the clams were shut so tight they weren't communing with anyone, no matter how heavily armed.

The preparations weren't done yet, though. You may recall that cockles and clams require . . . actually, you may not; I had to double check myself. Cockles and clams require nothing more than something to scrape up the sand, unless you want to provoke the *pisseurs*, in which case you need one spade for the dropping thereof. I was keeping quiet about this technique, though. Knowing my luck, I'd have the *pisseur* pissing all over me for the greater amusement of the assembled Frenchies. I'd already had a near escape with the one glove, which we wouldn't be needing because we weren't going to be putting our hands in any holes, so it was as well to keep mum about arcane methods for provoking *pisseurs* or I'd end up wielding a jackhammer. Prawns, however, require a net and, despite their vast array of equipment, our friends only had the one net, so my partner went to purchase another. Transpires that the real McCoy when it comes to catching prawns is a net so vast it could be used by the municipal authorities for waylaying stray dogs. Reasoning that we would look pretty silly with an enormous net if we didn't catch anything, my partner chose instead to buy a little tiny net that would be a lot less obtrusive. I wasn't entirely persuaded of the logic behind this (presumably the smaller the net, the less likely you are to catch anything), but I appreciated the urge to avoid looking like a fool, so again I held my peace.

Before we get down to our practical experiment though, another handy hint from Monsieur Lagenette. If you're out on the sandflats in a place you don't know and you reckon you've got loads-a-time before the tide turns and you happen to see a lot of excitable French people hurrying toward the high water mark, don't just shrug your shoulders and think, "Hmph! Typical French pusillanimity. It's like with the rugby. Wonderful when things are going their way, but as soon as the tide turns, they just give up. Not like us doughty Brits". This is not a moment for shoulder shrugging and belittling French valor. If all the locals are hurrying home, it means something wet is going to happen in the near future, and it's probably going to happen faster than the locomotive power of a doughty Brit.

When Jacqueline and Michel turn up, they've got more rakes and spades and spikes piled in the back of their car than an out of town garden centre, and Michel's asking about market day so we can sell our surplus catch. I still have my doubts, though. I'm even wondering whether we shouldn't have invested in another staple of Breton fishing expeditions, a tin of pâté Hénaff. Sold in every supermarket in Brittany, pâté Hénaff isn't exactly a *fines herbes* and truffles job, but a plain pork pâté that would probably horrify connoisseurs. To be fair, it's perfectly edible, but it really isn't the sort of delicacy that earned French cuisine its preeminent position in world gastronomy. Nonetheless, in the past, no Breton sailor or fishermen would venture out to sea without a tin of pâté Hénaff in his pocket, just in case, and after all I've read and heard, 'just in case' seems like a very wise dictum. This is a time for the Precautionary Principle. Especially when Michel goes on to confess, quite proudly it seems, that he knows nothing about fishing for prawns.

In theory, we're due to set off an hour-and-a-half before low water, but it's been raining since the early hours of the morning, so we settle down in the living room to watch the sky and discuss strategy, in the course of which a few more handy hints emerge: Jacqueline says prawns are most plentiful when the tide's moving, either up or down but not at slack water; Michel repeats, in case we missed it first time round, that he knows nothing about fishing for prawns, but admits he's a dab hand with a clam, which are easiest to find when the tide is rising, when they'll either surface or poke their feeding tubes through the sand, leaving two tell-tale holes side by side.

The clouds get darker, the rain gets heavier, but the wind begins to blow, which is good news because it means there's a chance the sky will clear. However, according to Jacqueline, it is not good news for fishing since prawns don't like wind and choppy waters, and tend to stay tucked away in their holes.

"I don't know anything about prawns," says Michel, as Mireille arrives for coffee.

"Prawns!" she exclaims, looking at me again. I do wish she'd stop doing this. "You said we're going to The Beach of Bad Weeds, didn't you? You won't find any prawns there".

This triggers another strategy conference about what we should fish for first and where. Clams are better on a rising tide, but cockles can be taken anytime. Personally, I don't dare mention prawns anymore, but I gather they are most plentiful on sandbanks, which we don't have, or flat weedy areas, which we do have. Mireille's still doubtful, but according to her we will find winkles, cockles and clams in abundance on The Beach of Bad Weeds, so we more or less agree (more or less, this is Brittany after all) to look for the shellfish first then try our chances with the prawns once the tide has turned.

Meanwhile, though the rain has ceased and the wind continues to blow, the sky is getting lower and darker by the minute, so very low and dark it instigates a debate about catching lance-fish by moonlight. There are various techniques for this, but all basically boil down to one person raking up the sand and somebody else clobbering or clutching the twisting flashing fish as they squirm across the moonlit sand like streams of quicksilver.

The weather continues to twist and flash like the lance-fish, one minute darting out a few rays of sun or silvering the sea with a broad beam of bright white light, the next coalescing into big black clouds and spitting gobbets of rain at the window pane. It's way past the time when we were meant to leave, but the spectacle across the bay is so changeable, we can't quite bring ourselves to head doorward. Instead, we engage in yet another debate, this time about the length of trouser leg desirable for *pêching à pied*. Should we wear short shorts, normal shorts, knee-length shorts, pedal pushers, or long trousers?

"It depends how deep we have to go for prawns", says Jacqueline.

"I don't know anything about prawns", says Michel.

"You won't find any prawns", says Mireille, peering at me sideways.

"Sometimes you have to go calf deep", says Jacqueline, "sometimes waist deep".

The shorts debate spirals into extended deliberations about how many layers of clothing we should wear, what sort of shoes are best, whether socks are desirable inside the shoes, and how (apart from staying at home on the sofa) to avoid damp buttocks. In the course of these discussions, it becomes apparent that the party is torn between optimists (Jacqueline: "look the sun's shining - we're going to catch loads - the wind's chasing the clouds away") and pessimists (Mireille: "we could always go to the shops - there's a very good museum in town - the wind's bringing more rain"). After several changes of clothing (since there are five of us, we've covered all bases concerning the appropriate length of leg covering), the rest of us decide to make a dash for the beach while Mireille decides to make a dash for the bakery and join us later. So, forty minutes past the planned starting time but beneath a promising patch of blue sky, we reach The Beach of Bad Weeds.

Unloading the car is such a major operation I begin to wonder whether I haven't missed something vital in the preceding debates and we've actually decided to go hang-gliding instead. I'm assured though that we're going fishing, to prove which I am given the smallest, rustiest rake in the pile, but I don't object since at least it's discreet and, if I don't catch anything, I've got an excuse. I'm not trusted with a mesh hamper or anything of that nature, but I do get a ten-litre yogurt bucket salvaged from the local food processing plant. Quite how I'm meant to fill a ten-litre yogurt bucket, unless with a sludge of sand and sea water, I do not know. Anyway, we traipse off onto the beach, each with some variation of a rake, a shrimp net, and bucket or plastic hamper. It's not at all bad on the porcupine front, but even so, we do faintly resemble a bunch of Victorian entomologists.

There are three other people on the beach, one guy poking about in the sand, two others picking their way through the seaweed mantled rocks along the water's edge. The four of us split up and head our separate ways. This, apparently, is the convention. In our case, we split up because we don't know the lay of the land in terms of *pêching à pied*, but Michel says it is even more imperative when you do know the lay of the land because nobody wants to share their hidey-holes with anyone else. He tells me of occasions when friends have taken him to sandbanks or outcrops of rock in their boats and then hurried away the moment they landed, leaving him to get on with it as best he could with no hint as to where he might find anything. This culture of secrecy is so acute that even fathers conceal their hidey-holes from their sons, sometimes taking the secret to the grave with them. Such suspicions are only exacerbated by a long-standing tradition of people with boats who, unwilling to pay for a permit, go out in the early hours of the morning to poach the lobsters and crabs from other people's pots. And if there happens to be an oyster park in the vicinity, everyone's out on the sands after a big storm, as the professionals' sacks, each of which holds 150 oysters, are considered fair game if ripped away from the beds by heavy seas.

I still only have the haziest idea what I'm meant to be doing, so after strolling about a bit peering at the sand trying to look intelligent, I start digging in the hope that something will turn up, even if it's only a rusty tin of pâté Hénaff. At first progress is slow. I find a crab the size of my thumbnail, inadvertently do some serious damage to a tiny jelly fish, scare the living daylights out of some small fry buried in the sand, and get quite excited when I unearth what proves to be a pebble. As far as I can see, I'm doing what everyone else is doing, except that whereas their digging is punctuated by the regular tock of shells dropping into the bottom of their buckets, mine is so pristine you could still keep your yogurt in it. Then I find something very small that I suspect might be edible. Michel confirms that it's a cockle, a very small cockle, very very small, but fearing this might be the sum total of my catch for the day, I pop it in the bucket anyway. It's not quite a 'tock', more of a 'tick' really, but it's a start. At least I now know what I'm looking for and before long I find two more cockles of a more respectable size and even chance upon a clam. I'm beginning to enjoy myself, it's certainly quite amusing grubbing about in the sand, but then the wind blows up, topples my bucket and my first mini-cockle disappears.

Mireille arrives and starts feverishly searching through the rocks for winkles, clearly persuaded the heavens are about to open. Michel strolls over, casually pokes the patch of sand I've been scratching at without success for the last few minutes, and instantly finds five cockles and a dead *crépidule*. The *crépidule* is a migrant from America that is now widespread in Breton waters, to the despair of ostreiculturists and mytilculturists since it eats the same food as oysters and mussels, is multiplying like mad, and really doesn't taste very good. Helpless in the face of this thriving invader, name-calling is the only revenge the locals have been able to take. Political Correctness doesn't have the same grip on France as it does on the Anglo-Saxon world. True, due to the gender conventions of French vocabulary, politicians are compelled to employ laborious circumlocutions to make it clear that they're addressing both female and male voters, but in other spheres the French still happily talk about people with Downs Syndrome as 'Mongols', don't have any hesitation about identifying those with origins in sub-Saharan and North Africa as *'noirs'* and *'beurs'*, and, most breathtaking of all, call homosexuals *pédés*, a diminutive of paederast, as if same-sex orientation implied one was more inclined to leap upon the underage. It was perhaps inevitable then that, when the *crépidule* turned up displaying a propensity for mounting on the back of its coevals, often as not in an orgy of gastropodic extravagance, it should have been nicknamed *pédé*. Scientifically, this slur is at once justified and invalidated, justified

Gastropodic Orgy

because the *crépidule's* Latin name is *Crepidula Fornicata*, so the French weren't the only ones with dirty minds, invalidated because when three *crépidule* form a stack, the top one is male, the bottom one female (*plus ça change*), and the middle one hermaphrodite. In English, the *crépidule* is known with becoming modesty as the Slipper Shell. There's no escaping stereotypes, is there? The Frenchman loves his *Hong-hee-hong*!, but the Englishman will opt for his slippers every time.

Still scratching about, I suddenly find three large cockles in the space of thirty seconds. This proves to be a pattern, the 'Rule of Three', as in the course of the next couple of hours, I never find more than three shellfish at a time and know that once I've found three in quick succession it's time to move on, as if cockles live singly, in pairs or in *ménages à trois*, but never band together in a group bigger than the nuclear family. After thirty minutes, I have four decent clams and half a dozen cockles. Clearly, at this rate I'm never going to fill a ten-litre yogurt bucket, but I'm not doing too badly, especially given that I've got the smallest rake on the beach. Even so, that I should have found clams on a falling tide by simply grubbing about in the sand would horrify your more puritanical *pêcheur à pied*. Given that cockles are nearer if not actually on the surface and, apart from the pissing variety, do little to betray their whereabouts, aimlessly grubbing about for them is tolerated, but blindly digging for the more deeply buried clams is a definite breach of etiquette. Remember, a rising tide and those two tell-tale holes if you want to look like you know what you're doing. Otherwise, you can always try the Davis Manoeuvre.

But before I detail the Davis Manoeuvre, a word of advice. You will recall my resolve to steer clear of *pisseurs* for fear of making the Frenchies laugh. The thing is, if you want to steer clear of something, you've got to know what it is you're steering clear of, and since I can't tell one clam from another, avoiding the *pisseurs* is beyond me. I discover this when I'm peering into my bucket admiring my catch and something at the bottom of the bucket, evidently taking exception at my complacent satisfaction, spits a jet of liquid skyward. This is clearly intended maliciously as my face is between him and the sky, but happily it's a puny piss and doesn't catch me in the eye or anything. Nonetheless, the realization that I've got a *pisseur* in my bucket also makes me realize that I need to be a *pisseur* myself. Absorbed in the hunt, I've ignored the growing pressure in my bladder, but now relieving it is a matter of some urgency. No great dilemma, you may suppose, given that we're out in the wilds and everyone pisses in the sea once in a while, but when you're surrounded by people collecting their lunch, it seems a bit infra dig to start urinating on what might turn out to be their starter. I end up traipsing miles across the beach to reach somewhere sufficiently remote to double as a *pissoir*, so remember when you go *pêching à pied*, if you don't want to let the side down, take a pee before you find yourself in the middle of a featureless expanse of sand with nothing but a bucket to shield yourself.

I pass Mireille on the way back and see that she already has nearly a pint of winkles despite the fact that she only arrived fifteen minutes ago, whereas I'm working at the rate of about one clam every ten minutes. It's at this stage that the Davis Manoeuvre starts to evolve. Digging alongside the channels of water striating the beach, I find that the running water washes the sand away making it easier to spot a clam. Following the water channels, I approach the water's edge, but here the sand is so full of stones it's almost impossible to distinguish a shellfish from a pebble, so I head back to the half tide mark where the sand is softer and deeper. Before long I've got upwards of a dozen shellfish and I'm delighted to realize that one can go *pêching à pied* as I had originally envisaged, with nothing more elaborate than a child's bucket and spade. Indeed, the winkles need no equipment at all, so if you get stuck with a Monsieur Lagenette kitting you out in waders and single gloves and what have you, remember that this really is a simple activity that can be conducted with the minimum of equipment. At this stage, I get so carried away that I inadvertently develop the Davis Manoeuvre. Dispensing with the rake altogether, I get down on all fours in the deep wet sand and start digging like a dog, and discover that my fingers are considerably more sensitive than the tines of a rake, so that I'm soon tocking away with the best of them. I know this is incompatible with everything I said about weaver fish and broken glass, but by the time I start digging I'm so engrossed by the task I forget about such considerations. Happily, the most disagreeable thing I come up with are a couple of lugworms. I'm so pleased with the Davis Manoeuvre that, when the others go to look for prawns and clams on the rising tide, I carry on tocking up the cockles and the occasional clam.

I can see, though, that there maybe reasons why not everyone will want to be on all fours digging like a dog, so if dignity is your thing, I'll let you in on another secret imparted by Michel and apparently unknown to even Monsieur Lagenette. The reason the spade dropping technique needles the *pisseurs* is that it increases the pressure on the sand. At St. Jacut near St. Malo, the women have traditionally practiced a more refined version of this provocation, walking backwards along a shallow watercourse, feet slightly ajar, stamping lightly on the wet sand, whereupon the agitated cockles and clams rise to the surface and can simply be pocketed. Mind you, you may not wish to look like a duck in rewind, in which case, dig like a dog.

As you will have gathered, *pêching à pied* is a fairly labour intensive way of filling your tummy. I certainly wouldn't want to have to earn my living like this and the principal merit of relying upon *pêching à pied* to feed oneself is that it would be a good way of going on a diet. But there's no denying it's really very agreeable, certainly a healthier way of satisfying the hunter-gatherer instinct than trawling round the supermarket with a trolley. Less efficient, I grant you, but I can't think of many activities that are such an effective way of cutting yourself off from the outside world. Blackberrying is comparable, perhaps climbing a mountain, but that's about it. *Pêching à pied* is almost a meditative process, the perfect way to pack up your troubles and forget all those quotidian cares and petty compromises that inevitably beset anyone engaged in the busyness of modern living. Moreover, the pleasures do not diminish with repetition. I had worried that the whole outing would be a bit of a bore for the others. They do this all the time, after all. But when I begin to wilt and start muttering about heading home for a beer, I can hardly tear them away from the beach. *Just fifteen minutes more*, they beg. *The tide's turned. Look those are the clam holes.* I think they find me a bit dilettante to tell the truth. The passion of the hunt holds Mireille so strongly, she refuses point blank to leave and stays behind on the beach so long she gets faint with hunger and has a dizzy spell.

By the time we drag the others away, not quite kicking and screaming, but near enough, lunch doesn't actually happen till late in the afternoon, and I am able to confirm another of Monsieur Lagenette's precepts, that you need to be fit for *pêching à pied*. I'm not saying this an activity reserved for manic athletes with bulging biceps, but spend three hours on your knees in the sun and the wind, and you'll know it. I'm shattered.

Between us, we have gathered a good two litres of cockles and clams, and a handful of tiny prawns. True, the prawns are so tiny several have slipped through the mesh hamper, but they aren't too tiny to escape being tipped into boiling water, something for which you must prepare yourself if you want to become a real *pêcheur à pied*. A large part of French cuisine appears to be premised on a desire to outrage English sensibilities, what with their partiality for horse meat, their penchant for boiling things alive, and their tendency to eat raw that which ought to be cooked and cooked that which ought to be raw. There are enough prawns to justify an aperitif supplemented by Mireille's winkles, which are as easy to cook as they are to catch, simply being boiled in salted water. The cockles and clams are marginally more complicated since you've got to leave them standing in salt water for a couple of hours, either sea water or, if you don't fancy lugging a heavy bucket back from the beach, water salted to a comparable salinity (60 grams of salt to 2 litres of water). The clams are then cleaned and opened and prepared according to size and taste: the small ones eaten alive and kicking (another outrage, I know), the large ones stuffed with butter, parsley and garlic, and then . . . well, then, if you're French, you engage in a heated discussion as to whether they ought to be briefly baked then finished off with a flash of the grill, or just briefly baked, or just briefly grilled, a conversation that, encouraged by appeals to gender solidarity, should take you through to midnight, when it will be time to go out looking for lance-fish. Cockles are less controversial as you just have to stick them in a hot pan for a few minutes, stirring occasionally until the shells have all opened.

In brief, experience suggests the proper procedure for *pêching à pied* is as follows:

a. sit about for two hours watching the showers scudding across the bay and discussing whether it's going to clear or not;

b. if you happen to exhaust the topic of the weather before it's time to move, cultivate an argument about appropriate clothing and *pêching à pied* techniques;

c. consequent upon the changing weather and the clothing debates, change clothes half a dozen times before settling on what you were wearing before;

d. go fishing;

e. everyone who went fishing gathers to eat the catch, congratulate one another on how well they did, and reminisce about marvellous fishing grounds found in the course of the last thirty years - and have a heated argument about how long each crustacean and mollusc should be cooked and precisely what source of heat it should be subjected to.

f. drink large quantities of wine.

And that's about it really. Perhaps, though, you're wondering where to find The Beach of Bad Weeds? You don't really think I'm going to tell you, do you? I've been bumping about Brittany far too long for that. The Beach of Bad Weeds is my secret hidey-hole. You find your own spot. Or consult the access details at the start of the chapter which direct you to a famous *pêching à pied* beach far away from me. There are some things in life that you've just got to keep to yourself.

21. BANDITS, BUSINESSMEN AND ROMANTICS

ACCESS - To reach the **St. Malo**-Dinard ferry, follow the signs for the main ferry port then cross the bridge to **'Gare Maritime de la Bourse'** and the **'Esplanade Robert Surcouf'** parking area below the city walls. Street plans of St. Malo and Dinard can be downloaded as PDF documents from www.annuaire-emeraude.com. **Combourg** is southeast of St. Malo at the intersection of the D794 and D795. The château is open to the general public between April and October, and to pre-booked groups in March and November. See www.combourg.net for details.

Bumping about one inevitably bumps into something conventional once in a while and, in terms of tourism, it doesn't come much more conventional than St. Malo, the walled city that is also one of Brittany's principal ports of entry. However, our excursion involves a somewhat eccentric take on the city whereby we get to where we're going only to get out of it again before getting back to it by other means. Rather than visiting St. Malo itself, we're taking a boat across the bay to Dinard then following the coast on foot back to our starting point, an eleven kilometre amble through the history of St. Malo and the Rance estuary.

Château de Combourg

The ferry for Dinard leaves from between the Gare Maritime de la Bourse and the foot of the city walls, and already the principal theme of St. Malo's history is announced, for the quay is below the Esplanade Robert Surcouf and the boat belongs to the *Compagnie Corsaire*. If there's one thing every Englishman knows about the Malouins, it's that they're a bunch of bandits or, more specifically, corsairs. Now, some may protest that the English aren't exactly behindhand when it comes to a cavalier attitude to wealth creation (the French are convinced of it to this day, and can, and will, at the slightest provocation, cite chapter and verse from the history of the European Community to prove their point), but you and I know that when John Hawkins and Francis Drake went gadding about lifting whatever was liftable on the high seas, they might, technically, if you were being a bit pernickety, have been what we like to call 'privateers', but really they were Noble National Heroes, otherwise they wouldn't have been knighted. The corsairs, on the other hand, they were just a bunch of bloody pirates, right? Rightish. The thing is, this business of shiplifting is a bit like freedom fighters and terrorists: one man's piratical, buccaneering, sea-roving bandit is another man's licensed privateer building the fortunes of the nation and God bless his heart.

Words for piracy have many origins, ranging from Dutch *vrijbuiter* or freebooter which morphed into filibuster, to the buccaneer's *boucan*, a type of grill used for curing meat at sea, but the source of corsair really gets to the heart of the matter. These were not men who were uncommonly coarse, but specialists in the *guerre de course*, a war of racing or pursuit, that is to say 'My boat and my wits are quicker than yours therefore your boat is mine'. The Malouin tradition originated in the ninth century, when the Vikings were being so disagreeable along the coasts of western Europe, obliging the locals to get out there and repel the Northern hordes. Having acquired a talent for fighting at sea and occasionally even coming home richer as a result, the Malouins perfected their techniques during the Hundred Years War and became so very good at the business of robbing foreign ships that, by the time France was battling with England and Holland in the seventeenth century, it was only natural that Vauban should incorporate the Guerre de Course in the general campaign. Codifying the system, he issued *lettres de course* allowing French sailors to rob English ships without suffering any of the inconveniences (like hanging for example) inherent in the pirate's trade. The loot was subsequently divvied up, a fifth for the king, a tenth for the Admiral of France, two thirds for the owner of the boat, and the rest for the crew. The most famous corsairs were René Duguay-Trouin (1673-1736), *Terreur des Anglais*, and Robert Surcouf (1773-1827), *Le Tigre des Mers,* after whom the Porte de Dinard esplanade is named.

The exploits of these two men are legendary. After being captured early on in his career by the English, Trouin escaped from Plymouth, and went on to take more than three hundred merchantmen and twenty warships, getting himself ennobled in the process and celebrating his new status by seizing Rio de Janeiro. Surcouf, meanwhile, only took forty-seven ships, but made up in quality what he lacked in quantity, famously defeating two much larger English ships, the Triton and the Kent, when he was hopelessly outmanned and outgunned, and ought, by all reasonable estimations, to have simply sailed as far away as he possibly could and hide his head in a bucket in the hope that they wouldn't notice him.

Feats like these suggest buccaneering in every sense of the word, yet neither of these men were disorderly outlaws having riotous fun cocking a snook at society, and not just because they had *lettres de course*. Trouin was the scion of a wealthy shipping family, while Surcouf, whose ancestry went back through generations of naval officers to an Irish king, began his career on the slave boats, and ended it as a wealthy shipowner, the first Malouin to be awarded the Légion d'Honneur. The juxtaposition of piratical exploits and professional respectability was typical. For centuries, the ships of St. Malo were at once privateers and merchantmen, and the corsairs were as much businessmen as bandits. Indeed, the business tradition runs so very strong in St. Malo that it was an eighteenth century Malouin economist, Vincent de Gournay, who coined the maxim underlying economic liberalism, "*Laissez faire, laissez passer, le monde va de lui-même*", a creed many French people now consider typically Anglo-Saxon.

The *Compagnie Corsaire* boats leave St. Malo for Dinard every forty minutes, except at lunch time when there's a two hour break in service. It's a brief but pleasant crossing, passing some lovely old schooners and giving us a glimpse of the open sea that tempted countless generations of Malouins to try their luck in foreign waters. Reaching the far side of the Rance estuary, we disembark below the Grand Hotel which, in architecture and name, is a suitable emblem for the chic resort of Dinard, a town that resembles an upmarket Torquay, all palm trees and grand Grand Hotels and hardly less grand grand villas.

Crossing the Bay the Old Way!

In fact, Dinard as we see it today was developed by an American promoter in the middle of the nineteenth century as a continental rival to Brighton, not the seedy Brighton of Graham Green, nor even the Brighton of charabancs, motor rallies and massed bike rides, but a fashionable bathing hole for people with pots of money, and it still has a reputation as a resort for people with pots of money. I generally steer clear of anywhere known to be a ghetto of the wealthy, not just because my wallet won't stand the strain, but because such places are often crippled by their own success, stultified by preciosity and snobbery. Dinard, though, does not have that deadening impact. Perhaps this is because we stay on the fringes of the town, following the celebrated Promenade du Claire de Lune to the south and thence onto the *sentier cotier* proper. Or perhaps it is because, when we visit, *il fait un temp de chien* in the engaging French phrase for foul weather, so that we have the promenade and coastal path to ourselves. But I suspect there's more to it than that. Often as not the sort of edifice that merits the title 'grand' looks absurdly pompous when you try to picture anybody actually living there, but the grand villas of Dinard appear for the most part to be very livable places, many with private access to secluded coves that can otherwise only be reached by hiking along the coastal path. And Dinard is that rarity in Brittany, an anglophile town, celebrating its mimetic origins with an annual *Festival du Film Britannique*.

There are more predictable mementos of the era when English aristocrats regarded Dinard as a little patch of England overseas, such as *Le Brighton* bar, the *Au Chic Anglais* women's outfitters, and the *Rue Winston Churchill*, but it is the festival that suggests the most interesting aspect of the attachment. In a recent interview with the Daily Telegraph, the festival's artistic director, Hassam Hindi, praised the humour, vitality and relevance of British films, contrasting them with the mind-numbing navel-gazing of French cinema. It's most heartening to hear this from a

Frenchman (albeit a Palestinian born Frenchman), since it confirms my own prejudices. There are plenty of great French film-makers bucking the trend, or taking the trend so far they come out the other side with something genuinely interesting, but for a long time I was firmly persuaded that the typical French film featured someone young, beautiful and rich living in a luxurious Parisian apartment with someone else young, beautiful and rich, and suffering exquisite existential angst as a consequence. "In Britain," says Hindi, "you have ordinary-looking people achieving the extraordinary". This is a refreshingly clear-eyed perspective for a festival held in a place premised on loads-a-money, the sort of place you might expect to have a strong antipathy to ordinary-looking people achieving extraordinary things. The Best Film award at the *Festival du Film Britannique* is the Hitchcock d'Or, for it was in Dinard that the master of avian revolt and malicious crop-dusting spent his summers.

The route we follow round the estuary is well waymarked with the red-and-white stripes of the GR, so you don't need to worry about getting lost in the next three hours. After following the Promenade du Clair de Lune with its strategically located benches sheltered by majestic cedar trained over the walkway, we skirt a rocky promontory via a submergible causeway then climb onto a corniche snaking along a narrow band of woodland below luxury flats and more villas. From here we have fine views across the bay toward St. Malo. When you arrive in St. Malo by car, the urban sprawl appears seamless and, apart from the *intra-muros* area, that's to say within the city walls, it's hard to work out where one section of the city ends and another begins, but from our present perspective it's clear that St. Malo and St. Servan were once naturally distinct entities, divided by a couple of

wooded headlands. St. Servan was
the site of the *Cité d'Aleth*, the
original settlement at the mouth of
the Rance and capital of the Celtic
Coriosolites when St. Malo itself
was little more than a windy bit of
rock stuck out in the sea.
Unfortunately for the adepts of
Aleth, the Franks, Saxons and
Normans displayed a distressing
tendency to roll up and pillage the
place, and the less chauvinistic

Promenade du Clair du Lune

citizens, the bishop among them, gradually removed themselves to the
more readily defensible St. Malo, named after a Welsh monk, also known
as Maclow or Maclou, born in Gwent in 487 and bishop of Aleth around
541. What man began, nature confirmed. Sea levels rose, swallowing the
sandbanks Aleth had used as landing stages and on which its commercial
success depended, while at the same time improving sea access to St. Malo.
By the thirteenth century, Aleth had become so marginal it rebelled against
its burgeoning neighbour and the exponentially burgeoning taxes the
Malouins felt compelled to levy on the declining mother city, but the revolt
was promptly suppressed. In the fifteenth century, an earthquake further
modified access to the two cities, again to the advantage of the Malouins,
and Aleth/St. Servan was reduced to little more than a fort defending its
former rival, a satellite status that was not really remedied until
comparatively recent times when the growing population and the cost of
housing *intra-muros* persuaded people that St. Servan wasn't such a bad
place to live after all.

Looking back at their history, you can begin to appreciate why
the people of St. Malo are so proud of their city's motto: "*Ni Français ni
Breton: Malouin suis*". A renegade people forced to fight for several
centuries to secure their survival, they were bound to be a bit prickly about
being lumped in with outsiders, and it was only natural that once they had
built themselves some solid walls to hide behind, they should go out and do
unto others as had been done unto them, to wit, grab what they could and to
hell with the hindmost: "*Laissez faire, laissez passer, le monde va de lui-
même*". It's a spirit that has persisted into modern times, the legendary
Malouin fishery captain Fernand Leborgne often being described as a
contemporary corsair for the part he played in the cod wars off the banks of
Newfoundland.

After a little over four kilometres, the GR detours through an
estate of suburban housing then drops down to the Barrage de la Rance, just
upstream of which there is a charmless but conveniently located bar. The
dam was the first successful tidal electricity generating plant in the world,
opened in 1967 and equipped with reversible turbines to harness the ebb
and flow of the sea. Doubtless it has long since been superceded by more
recent plants, but it is still an impressive piece of engineering. Some

alarming little whirlpools can be seen in the water on the seaward side as we stroll across the dam to recover the coastal path, which then contours round the Briantais estate, the seventeenth century manorial home of a family of Malouin shipping magnates. This business of shipbuilding, ship-fitting, ship-owning, and shipping in general is omnipresent in the history of St. Malo, and it's striking that when you check the biographies of famous Malouins, the first line nearly always reads *"fils d'un riche armateur"*, *"d'un père armateur"*, or *"issue d'une famille d'armateurs Malouins"*, even when the person in question, like de Gournay, is renowned for something that has nothing to do with shipping. In St. Malo, everything and everyone comes from the sea if you go back far enough.

Probably the most famous Malouin mariner is Jacques Cartier. In three voyages between 1534 and 1541, initially intended to find a northwest passage to Asia but rapidly accommodated to the more pressing requirements of "discovering lands where it is said that a great quantity of gold and other precious things are to be found" (*Laissez faire, laissez passer, le monde va de lui-même*), Cartier 'discovered' Canada (i.e. stuck a flag in it, hollered 'finders keepers', and named the place after the Iroquois word for 'village' which kept cropping up in the conversation), established camp on the site of what would become Québec, visited the village that would blossom into Montreal, purloined a native remedy for scurvy concocted from the white cedar tree, explored Newfoundland and the St. Lawrence River, and pocketed what he thought were diamonds and gold, but which transpired to be quartz crystals and iron pyrites, giving rise to the expression "*faux comme les diamants du Canada*". Like most explorers, Cartier was not averse to the odd moral compromise when dealing with the indigenes and his achievements as a 'discoverer' are limited, given that the Eastern seaboard had already been visited by Norse, Basque and Breton fishermen, but he was far from being the most brutal of the bunch and his technical facility is remarkable, for he never lost a ship, despite sailing in dangerous, uncharted waters, and exploring scores of unknown harbours. There again this was a man from St. Malo. If you claim to be Malouin and can't sail a ship across an unfamiliar ocean into troubled waters and come back again, you don't really merit the name at all. After his third voyage, Cartier retired to a fortified farmhouse in the hamlet of Limoelou behind Rotheneuf, now a part of greater St. Malo. The Manoir Jacques Cartier, as it is now known, is a charming, surprisingly modest pad, still surrounded by countryside but within sight of the sea

Immediately after the Briantais estate, we pass a nice walled pond, a good spot for a picnic if required, and then embark on the dreariest stretch of the walk, following minor roads and lanes into the suburban sprawl of St. Servan. There are some good views over what we've walked already, including the startling sight of the large but, on the ground, largely invisible buildings overlooking the path between Dinard and the *barrage*. Compared with these, much of the housing traversed in the next twenty minutes is decidedly dull, and yet these are considered highly desirable residencies. Nowadays, local people are hard pressed to find affordable accommodation in St. Malo, and if you want to live *intra-muros*, well . . . an apartment below the top of the walls without a view costs an arm and a leg; go up a storey so that you can see over the walls and you can forget about shoelaces and tying your own tie unless you're octopus rich. Thus the exodus of the Malouins to the outlying areas and the revival of St. Servan's fortunes. As we make our way between blocks of flats and modest townhouses, I am surprised that the generally bullish agents of the *loi littoral* haven't obliged the local landowners to cede the necessary land for the *sentier cotier* to follow the coast, but it all becomes clear when we return to the seafront and find this long diversion has been a detour round the grounds of the *Gendarmerie Maritime* - only the government is immune to the laws that constrain everybody else.

The principal landmark in St. Servan is the Tour de Solidor, a fourteenth century Martello tower that was restored in the seventeenth century and which formerly served as a gaol. Again, the maritime theme persists, for this is now the *Musée International du Long Cours Cap-Hornier* because, of course, the first French sailors to round Cape Horn were from St. Malo. When it comes down to it, anything to do with the sea and the chances are that the Malouins were the first Frenchmen to do it: in the seventeenth century, Frotet de la Bardelière and François Grout opened the sea route to India, in 1698 Gouin de Beauchesne did the same for the South Seas, and in 1737 Moreau de

Tour de Solidor

Maupertuis confirmed that the earth was 'flat' at the North Pole. Nor was that an end to the polar explorations, for St. Malo was the adoptive home of Charcot, the French Scott, by whom he was dubbed "the gentleman of the poles". In a series of boats called the *Pourquoi Pas?*, a name still used to this day by oceanographic research vessels and local lifeboats, Charcot mapped thousands of kilometres of previously uncharted polar waters, became the first Frenchman to reach the east coast of Greenland, and was still exploring at the age of sixty-nine, when his last *Pourquoi Pas?* foundered in a cyclone with the loss of all hands bar one. And whilst we're on the subject of exploration, have you ever wondered why everyone else calls the Falkland Islands the Malvinas? I'd always vaguely supposed it had something to do with Bad Vines, but not a bit of it. When Gouin de Beauchesne rounded Cape Horn in 1698, he bumped into a handful of windswept rocky islands and duly baptized them the 'Malouines' in honour of his hometown.

There is another facet of the Malouin seafaring tradition we have barely touched upon yet. As you stroll along the seafront, picture if you will a scruffy, hungry-looking eighteenth century peasant patrolling the quayside and peering hopefully at the ships anchored in the estuary. After a while, he is picked up by a prosperous looking gentleman with whom he repairs to a nearby tavern for a bowl of cider or three. Later, we see the same peasant resplendent in oilskins and carrying a brand new blanket and palliasse. The transaction that has taken place has nothing to do with rough trade and shady liaisons (though the prosperous looking gentleman may have been less than transparent in his dealings), but is one that was familiar in ports all along this stretch of coast from the sixteenth century until modern times, as impoverished peasants seeking to improve their lot signed on with an *armateur* for a voyage to the cod fisheries of Newfoundland. It was a punishing life and the contracts signed by the neophyte sailors, many of whom would have been illiterate, often included nasty surprises, stipulating for instance that in the case of shipwreck, if the sailor happened to survive, it was up to him to find a berth on another boat and he could forget about any remuneration since his pay depended on a lay of the catch. Driven by the demands of the fish-on-Friday fast and the rarity of fresh fish in the hinterland, this was a major industry, as definitive of St. Malo as the business of banditry, and there are descriptions of the city that make it sound like one vast fish-stall, with salted cod suspended from every available wall, lintel, table and sideboard.

We end our walk along another corniche trail, this time skirting the remains of the *Cité d'Aleth*, actually an eighteenth century fort that was transformed and reinforced by the Germans during the Second World War, a fact attested to by the spectacularly pock marked gun emplacements that line the corniche. When the allies invaded, Colonel Andreas Von Aulock, the commandant of Saint Malo, was told to defend the city to the last man. He didn't quite do so, surrendering after a week of ferocious bombardment, but by then St. Malo *intra-muros* had effectively been destroyed. The story here, though, is the antithesis of that in Brest. As we have seen, being an industrial city, Brest was not lovingly reconstructed. But St. Malo was already an acknowledged heritage centre and so was painstakingly rebuilt precisely as it had been before the war. To give an idea of the scale of this work, the first task they undertook lasted eighteen months and consisted of removing 750,000 tons of rubble from the ruins, sorting it out stone by stone, and numbering each stone with a view to piecing together the puzzle of the vanished city in the coming years. The result is a spectacular success, as we see when we round La Cité and look across the curve of Les Bas Sablons to the perfect proportions of this most immaculate of walled cities, a very Breton city, despite what the Malouins say, since it is often described as a "*carrefour des mondes, entre le réel et l'esprit*".

So that's it then. We've 'done' St. Malo. Well, no, not quite. But to finish doing it, we're going to go away from it again. Bandits, businessmen, and romantics, remember. We've had the bandits, though the Malouins won't thank me for saying so, we've had the businessmen, but what about the romantics? Doubtless there were some broken hearts about what with all that sailing off to unknown foreign parts, but when all is said and done, duffing up the Dutch and the English, nicking the Iroquois' land, and fishing for cod, no matter how desirable of themselves, are not exactly romantic activities. We have, though, yet to speak of St. Malo's most famous son, a man more influential even than Jacques Cartier, François-René de Chateaubriand, who was born there in 1768 and is buried on the Île du Grande Bé at the mouth of the Rance estuary. Grand Bé, which is accessible at low-tide, is the conventional visit honouring Chateaubriand, but true to the perversity of our principles, we're bumping about elsewhere, a short drive or train journey to the south, in the Château de Combourg, where Chateaubriand lived for several years during his childhood and which he immortalized in his posthumously published autobiography, *Les Memoires d'Outre-Tombe*.

In brief, Chateaubriand's career runs as follows. Born into impoverished aristocratic family, Dad mends family fortunes (ships, of course), buys Château de Combourg, where the boy endures a gloomy, solitary childhood. François-René joins the army on the eve of the revolution, is alienated by the Terror, decamps to America, has wild times traveling in the backwoods with trappers and Indians, hoping to find the fabled Northwest Passage. Passage unfound, returns home with sackloads of raw material and writes a trilogy of passionate, poignant novels depicting lavish, lush nature in a lavish, lush prose style that pioneers the French Romantic movement. Marries, joins the Royalist army, gets wounded, retires to England, scrapes a living teaching and translating. Returns to Imperial France, writes a Christian apologia, catches the eye of Napoleon, but resigns from the ensuing diplomatic posting in protest at Napoleon's tendency to execute people he doesn't like. Does a bit of writing and travelling, criticizes Napoleon, gets kicked out of Paris, and begins writing his memoirs. Empire falls, Chateaubriand joins the Bourbons, is appointed a Peer of France, but proves himself notably undiplomatic again, this time criticizing Louis XVIII. Briefly disgraced, he joins the ultra-royalists supporting the future Charles X. Bounces back to the Bourbon cause and embarks on a political career, including stints as Ambassador to Britain (where his cook invents the thick cut tenderloin fillet topped with butter, parsley and béarnaise sauce that is now known as a Chateaubriand steak) and Minister of Foreign Affairs. Sacked as a consequence of political machinations largely not of his own making, turns toward the liberal opposition and populist causes such as Greek independence and press freedom. Briefly resumes diplomatic duties under Charles X, resigns once again, then really queers his pitch with Louis-Philippe by refusing to swear allegiance to the House of Orleans, effectively putting an end to his political career. Retires from politics and dedicates himself to the literary life, and therefore dies in poverty in 1848.

I only have the haziest notion of the convolute politics of this period, but one thing that stands out from the above summary is that Chateaubriand wasn't afraid of pissing off people you would have thought best left unpissed off, people like emperors and kings and what have you. And his strong stands of principle in politics and literature appear to have elicited equally strong and divergent opinions as to his qualities. In his nonage, Victor Hugo exclaimed, "*Je veux être Chateaubriand ou rien!*", I want to be Chateaubriand or nothing! Talleyrand, meanwhile, (a man so inscrutable that, when he died, Metternich is reported to have observed, "Now I wonder what he meant by that") said, "*Monsieur de Chateaubriand croit qu'il devient sourd car il n'entend plus parler de lui*", Chateaubriand thinks he's going deaf when he no longer hears anybody talking about him. That snide little backhander might explain all those grand-standing resignations and going so far out of his way to get on the nerves of people in power, people with nerves I for one would strenuously avoid getting on. Apparently, though, Chateaubriand was not immune to such commonplace qualms. The solitude and phantom terrors of his childhood (of which more anon) left him with a lifelong propensity to fear others were plotting against him, a tendency some describe as paranoid, though if you've aroused the enmity of three kings and an emperor, I would have thought a little anxiety was entirely justifiable. Certainly, you can't help but admire the man's courage. I mean, Napoleon wasn't just any old dictator. As these things go, he was pretty much the prototype in the modern age. And he wasn't exactly a famously laid-back, easy-going character. His was a temperament more in the prickly line. So resigning 'in disgust' when the tyrant topped the Duc d'Enghien was tantamount to standing on the rooftops and shouting, "Oi, you, tiny! Woddjerfinkyerdoing, ya little . . . "

The town of Combourg is a classic small country town, pleasant but nothing special by Breton standards, save for the fact that it's got this whacking great château planted in the middle of it. Originally a part of the defensive line built along the Breton marches to keep the French out, it is an austere building, very continental in its conception, but sturdy and serviceable enough to tend toward the 'castle' end of the scale. Just the ticket then for a romantic sensibility. That said, the woman at the reception desk isn't terribly romantic, treating with withering disdain the perfectly reasonable query of an Australian couple who want to know if the guide can speak slowly. *No, she can't. She's very busy. She's on her own. She's got other groups to guide after you.* Perhaps it's dyspepsia. Lunch is not long finished.

Waiting for the busy, solitary, fast-talking guide, we stroll around the grounds, which are pleasingly unfussy, a great expanse of simple, unmediated green framed by alleys of trees, not at all what you would expect of a French château. As it happens, the park was designed by English landscape gardeners after Chateaubriand's time, but you can still see the stone cross he described in the *Memoires* where his sister, Lucile, with whom he was unusually, perhaps unhealthily close, would sit and read devotional works as dusk was falling: "*Lucile aimait à faire seule, vers le soir, quelque lecture pieuse: son oratoire de prédilection était l'embranchement de deux routes champêtres, marqué par une croix en pierre et par un peuplier dont le long style s'élevait dans le ciel comme un pinceau. Ma dévote mère, toute charmée, disait que sa fille lui représentait une chrétienne de la primitive Eglise, priant à ses stations appelées Laures*". Even if you only have an approximate understanding of French, the romantic atmosphere should be clear with its suggestion of simple rustic pleasures evoking echoes of a distant, almost prelapsarian past.

François-René subsequently immortalized Lucile in the novel *René*, in which 'a sister' gets herself to a nunnery rather than give way to a disproportionate passion for her brother, the eponymous hero, who spends the rest of his days roaming North America, wracked with guilt.

The castle itself is yet another grand building, grander than anything in Dinard, and it's worth spending a bit of time strolling round the outside before the official tour begins, in part to get an idea of the lay out (the interior is quite a maze), but also to look at some of the architectural details. The plumbing is particularly impressive and I recommend you check out the guttering pipes at the side and behind the main building. With its looming grey walls, imposing turrets, and narrow windows, you can appreciate how a gloomy, impressionable youngster could be carried away by his imagination. Get inside a place like this and you might never get out again. There's a nicely disarming touch to the west of the building, though, a link between business and romanticism, for there is a sign revealing that Combourg is now a SARL or *société à responsabilité limitée*, that's to say a limited company. This is a statute more commonly seen on the sides of white vans belonging to jobbing builders or families of peasant farmers. In the present context, it's a bit like discovering Newstead Abbey is run by Byron & Son, or Chanter's House by Coleridge & company

When the guide turns up, she doesn't look too promising. She's not as terse as the receptionist, but she's clearly not a bundle of laughs either, a bit prim and proper, and after sending us up the main staircase, she disappears for a few minutes, leaving everybody shuffling about in front of the firmly closed main door waiting for something to happen. Apparently she isn't trusted with a key to the front door and has to go through the servants entrance, but eventually there's a creaking of hinges and the door opens from the inside. The first thing you see in the hallway is a boar's head poking out from the wall, showing off his tusks like he's hamming it up for a toothpaste advert. At least he's smiling.

The guide asks what languages we speak and, for a moment, I'm impressed by what promises to be a fairly remarkable linguistic range, but in fact she's not checking what languages *she* has to use (a tour in English, Flemish, German and Swedish would have been quite a feat), rather who's going to need which plastified leaflet filling them in on the details they miss when she's talking too fast. At first, her manner is a bit crisp and, in the course of the next forty-five minutes, she displays enough schoolmarmish qualities to be faintly comic. We are reminded on at least four separate occasions that this is a private house in which the descendants of Chateaubriand's elder brother still live, the implication being that we're a lot of nosey, intrusive sods who really shouldn't be here poking about in this intimate family milieu. In keeping with this precept, she gets very upset when someone tries to take a photo after she's expressly forbidden photography inside the very private house and there's even a bit of irate finger wagging when one old boy starts fondling a brass doorknob. She's none too keen on questions, either, not at least until the designated question and answer session at the end of the tour, by which time everybody's learned their lesson and nobody dares ask anything. But for all that, she is proficient, well-versed in her subject, knows how to smile, occasionally, and compared to the receptionist her comportment is positively uproarious.

At first, I find the interior a little disappointing compared to the imposing exterior. The château was sacked during the revolution and restored in the nineteenth century, so what you see inside bears little resemblance to the austere interior Chateaubriand knew. The small hallway, the damp and lugubrious side-chapel where his mother whiled away her hours in damp and lugubrious contemplation of the almighty, and the *grande salle* from which Chateaubriand is said to have spotted the first of what proved to be many loves, don't really cut the romantic mustard now, cluttered as they are with busy motifs, sombre paintings by wannabe Old Masters, Studies In Brown Varnish 'from the school of', and a muddle of Victorian knickknacks. The only thing that's really simple and unelaborated is the very modern looking dinner service dating from Chateaubriand's days as ambassador to London. The weather's missing, too, for though the heavens have opened and are doing their best to conjure an atmosphere of romantic turmoil, there is a covered stairwell in the courtyard now, which wasn't there in the eighteenth century when, to get from one room to another, you had to cross the open quad, bombarded by whatever the gods chose to bombard you with.

It seems a pity that the original atmosphere has largely been dispelled, but as the tour progresses, the rooms become simpler and less ostentatious, letting us imagine something of what it must have been like to be a small child here in the eighteenth century. The *salle des archives*, for instance, is decidedly scruffy and has some genuinely romantic cobwebs lurking about in the high corners. It now houses a collection of Chateaubriand's belongings, nothing very evocative (bed, chair, diplomatic document wallet and so forth), but there's always a slight frisson about these things (Did the great man's bottom really polish that wood?), and there's a nice sketch hanging beside the door jamb depicting a black cat and (a little difficult to make out if you don't know the story) a disembodied wooden leg.

The leg belonged to the Marquis de Coétquen, a previous proprietor of the château, whose own peg had been blown off at the Battle of Malplaquet fighting the English. Since the demise of Coétquen, the surrogate leg had taken to patrolling the corridors of the castle in the company of a cat, its distinctive tap-tap-tapping echoing off the bare stone walls. Granted, it sounds a bit silly, but remember François-René was only eight and was an impressionable, imaginative child. In the circumstances, the notion that there was a detached leg perambulating (or hopping or whatever it is a detached leg does) about the family home, ought to have been enough to turn the boy totally doolally. Come to think of it, perhaps that was why he was so courageous in later years. Once you've overcome a locomotive wooden leg, confronting kings and emperors is child's play. Nothing more can frighten you.

We then stroll round the ramparts to the tiny, remote room where

Chateaubriand slept and which he describes in some detail in the *Memoires*: "*J'étais niché dans un espèce de cellule isolée en haut de la tourelle de l'escalier qui communiquait de la tour intérieure aux diverses parties du château. La fênetre de mon donjon s'ouvrait sur la cour intérieure; le jour, j'avais en perspective les créneaux de la courtine oppossée ou végetaient des scolopendres et croissait un prunier sauvage. Quelques martinets qui, durant l'été, s'enfonçaient en criant dans les trous des murs étaient mes seuls compagnons. Relégué dans l'endroit le plus désert à l'ouverture des galeries, je ne perdais pas un murmure des ténèbres. Quelque-fois, le vent semblait courir à pas légers; quelquefois, il laissait échappers des plaintes; tout à coup, la porte était ébranlée avec violence, les souterrains poussaient des mugissement, puis ces bruit expiraient pour recommencer encore*".

With its isolation, mysterious murmurings, rumblings, moanings, mumblings and things that go bump in the night, this could be taken as the opening paragraph for countless nineteenth century ghost stories and, apparently, Chateaubriand Sr., who seems to have had some rather harsh educational principles, chose this room for his son expressly to test the boy's mettle (really, Napoleon had no chance). After accompanying his mother and sister to their respective rooms and checking in all the wardrobes and behind the curtains and under the bed to reassure them there were no ghosts lying in wait, Chateaubriand would make his way along the gloomy corridors to his tiny room at the top of the most remote tower, and then lie there listening to the soughing and sighing and creaking and crying and groaning and muttering that issued from all corners of the castle. Tell him there was a dead cat immured in the wall and it would have tipped him right over the edge into the screaming abdabs. I'm not being frivolous here. There *was* a dead cat in the wall, though it hadn't been dead when they put it there. Its desiccated corpse, discovered in the course of later restoration work, is in a glass case in the corner of Chateaubriand's bedroom now, but it was originally bricked up while still alive, a custom designed to ward off the evil eye. The Australian couple, who are apparently fond of cats, are a bit upset by this, and I'm beginning to get a few shivers up the spine myself, but the visit is over, so we shuffle downstairs, taking care not to touch any doorknobs or inadvertently point our cameras at anything private.

Nowadays, Chateaubriand's reputation is muddied by changing literary fashions and over-exposure as one of The Greats (it's not quite the Shakespeare industry, but not far off), being foisted on generations of unwilling teenagers. Moreover, if you want to be mean about it, his track record as a Romantic can be questioned. Diplomacy, after all, is hardly the most romantic calling, and when you learn that he married for money then buggered off to Belgium after he'd discovered there wasn't any and didn't see his wife again for ten years, you begin to wonder - in all fairness, it should be added that he did elope with the girl, carrying her down a ladder from her bedroom window, and then rescuing her from a nunnery after her uncle had grabbed her back. But when it came to lugubrious musings and lost causes, he was up there with the best of them. He was, like Byron, a passionate advocate of Greek Independence, he also struggled for most of his adult life to revive popular religious faith by celebrating the poetic and artistic appeal of Christianity, and he campaigned for freedom of the press, which can't have been an easy task in an age of dictators and kings.

Personally, though, I do hold one slight grudge against the man. His entry in the Encyclopaedia Britannica says he "began the Romantic vogue for world weary, melancholy heroes suffering from vague, unsatisfied yearnings". Anybody who has undergone adolescence knows how that feels, but you don't necessarily want it elevated into a narrative model. I say this because 'world weary, melancholy heroes suffering from vague, unsatisfied yearnings' are the very stuff of those French films I was complaining about earlier. And get this, from his Christian apologia, *Le Génie du Christianisme*: "*On habite, avec un coeur plein, dans une monde vide; et sans avoir usé de rien, on est désabusé de tout*". In those words, I can hear the solemn harbinger of breaking Rolexes and the inexpressible misery of living in a well-appointed apartment in the *17eme arrondissement*. If all those films about self-indulgent poor little rich people suffering *le Mal du Siècle* can be laid at Chateaubriand's door, the man's got a lot to answer for.

But by far the best epitaph for Chateaubriand's brand of romanticism (and that brand of egoism suggested by Talleyrand's jibe) comes from his own words in the *Memoires d'Outre-Tombe*: "*Quand la mort baissera la toile entre moi et le monde, on trouvera que mon drame se divise en trois actes . . . Dans mes trois carrières successives, je me suis toujours proposé une grand tâche: voyageur, j'ai aspiré à la découverte du monde polaire; littérateur, j'ai essayé de rétablir la religion sur ses ruines; homme d'Etat, je me suis efforcé de donner aux peuples le vrai système monarchique représentatif avec ses diverses libertés. Des auteurs modernes français de ma date, je suis quasi le seul dont la vie ressemble à ses ouvrages: voyageur, soldat, poète, publiciste, c'est dans les bois que j'ai chanté les bois, sur les vaisseaux que j'ai peint la mer, dans les camps que j'ai parlé des armes, dans l'exil que j'ai appris l'exil, dans les cours, dans les affaires, dans les assemblées que j'ai étudié les princes, la politique, les lois et l'histoire . . . . Si j'ai assez souffert dans ce monde pour être dans l'autre une Ombre heureuse, un peu de lumière des Champs-Elysées, venant éclairer mon dernier tableau, servira à rendre moins saillants les defauts du pentre: la vie me sied mal; la mort m'ira peut-être mieux*".

A very Breton sentiment that perhaps death will suit him better than life.

22. GOD BESIDE THE SEA

ACCESS - **Rotheneuf** is northeast of St. Malo on the coast road, the D201. The **'Roches sculptées'** (AKA **'Rochers Sculptés'**) car park is signposted from the centre of the village. The Molinié and Tesnières polders can be reached via the D90 from **St-Georges-de-Gréhaigne** or the D478 from **Beauvoir** and following the signs for 'Bas Coin', 'Camus' and 'Saincey'.

Seafaring and religion are natural bedfellows in Brittany, much as they are any place the sea is large and man is small and the margins are closely cut, and in this chapter we visit two works of religious art for which the sea is an essential foil. First, *Les Roches Sculptées de Rothéneuf*, the work of a nineteenth century priest driven to art by a misfortune posterity can only count as serendipity.

Born in 1839 and ordained in 1863, the Abbé Fouré was a big man with big hands and a big heart, a muscular sort of Christian, who distinguished himself by defending striking metal workers at Paimpont against their English bosses. But in his early fifties, he suffered a stroke that robbed him of the power of speech. Deprived of more conventional means of conversing

Lost, One Monument

Last seen in Normandy

with the world, he engaged in a dialogue with stone, retreating to a remote stretch of coast near St. Malo, where he began sculpting the rock along the seashore. Taking for his theme the story of the Rothéneuf, a clan of smugglers, pirates and shipwreckers who controlled the area in the sixteenth century and whose name survives in the nearby village, he spent the next twenty years chipping away at the granite, conjuring from the rock's natural contours a medley of phantasmagoric figures depicting the lives of the Rothéneuf and their grisly end, massacred by rivals after supporting the wrong side during the revolution, then devoured by sea monsters lured by the gore.

It all sounds a bit grim and, hearing that many of the carvings are badly weathered, I did wonder whether the visit would be worthwhile, but seeing some intriguing photos of what remains, we decided to risk the very modest entry fee. A wise decision. A lot of it is grim, but whatever else his stroke deprived him of, the Abbé did not lose his sense of humour and there are plenty of witty touches leavening what might easily have been a dour morality tale of unchristian souls getting their righteous comeuppance.

The site itself is magnificent (if you had to spend a couple of decades on your hands and knees with a chisel and hammer, this is the sort of place you'd want to do it) with the flowing grey rock plunging into surf-rimmed emerald seas and a broad span of windswept water stretching away to the horizon. Better still, the sculptures are not fenced off and neither are the spectators. Rather than being corralled like so many sheep, we are allowed to roam at will, even trampling over the works themselves if so inclined, presumably since natural erosion is bound to efface the sculptures in the next fifty years or so, and the occasional stray philistine isn't going to make a huge amount of difference in the long run. Instead, we are simply told to take the right hand staircase and given free rein to follow the internal logic of Fouré's art, picking out the miscellaneous characters that made up the Rothéneuf clan, their loves, their lives, their ill works, their diverse rivalries, and their final destruction.

Distressingly for the modern age, the most popular scene is the Punch and Judy frame in which 'Gargantua' (real name Durand) Rothéneuf (pirate-in-chief and head of the family) boots his wife up the backside because she has been receiving advice that is a little too intimate from her intimate adviser, Jean de Caulnes (dubbed the Egyptian after a stay in Alexandria); to add insult to injury, Gargantua's own lover looks on chuckling. Elsewhere, Lucifer puts in an appearance, as do *les cinq clowns* (five cunning crewmen with a penchant for whooping it up), and there are more conventional homages to Saints Budoc, Sylvain and Urbain. The highlight, however, is the central tableau depicting the demise of the Rothéneuf, with the last of the clan being devoured by a cold, clammy sea monster with long claws and many teeth. Hollywood couldn't have done it better.

A Marvellous Obsession

Some sculptures are so badly eroded they're virtually indecipherable and one or two busts appear to have been liberated, but there's more than enough to make the trip worthwhile. In some places the carving is quite elaborate, elsewhere the contours of the rock have been adapted with a few modest lines to bring out an image that was innate in what the wind and waves had already achieved. Fouré wasn't just a Sunday afternoon artist. He was a real sculptor with a real talent, and rather than simply imposing his vision on an inert lump of rock, he sought the shape that lay within, contriving something closer to midwifery than golem making.

Go see. It is the work of a marvellous obsession.

A still greater marvel though, lies thirty miles to the east, just over the *departemental* border, for the most famous monument 'in' Brittany is actually in Normandy. *Le Couesnon dans sa folie mit le Mont en Normandie*, the mount in question being Mont St. Michel, the Couesnon the river that marked the boundary between Brittany and Normandy, and which perfidiously changed course, giving this glorious place of pilgrimage to the Normands. That's the myth, at least, and one to which the

Bretons cling dearly, for which reason alone it would be worth including the Mont in a bumping about Brittany book. Unfortunately, it seems to have little bearing on reality. First, though the Couesnon has regularly changed course over the centuries and, as we will see, is due to do so again in the near future, it is not and, so far as I can find out, never has been the official frontier, the famous dictum about its *folie* apparently being a fabrication on the part of fanciful historians during the Romantic period. Second, when the Carolingians ceded Normandy to the Vikings in the hope that it would stop them sailing up the Seine and sacking Paris, there was no question but that the see of Avranches and the Mont, at that time little more than a modest chapel, were part of the new duchy, no question at least in the minds of the Carolingians and the Vikings. The Bretons, on the other hand, were full of questions, for they had controlled the area for some fifty years previously and, though they hadn't done anything about developing the Mont (all the great building took place after their tenure), they had been in the habit of pocketing the stipends from the pilgrims that already visited the shrine, and were in no wise willing to have a bunch of bloody pirates from up North taking over this nice little earner. The dispute rumbled on for another fifty years before being settled in favour of the Vikings, as were most disputes involving swords, and the Mont has been Norman ever since. Yet many Bretons feel aggrieved to this day and you only have to mention the river or the Mont to have them quoting the Couesnon dictum. The silly thing is, while historical precedent and the vagaries of rivers are irrelevant, they could make a perfectly valid claim on geological grounds, since the Mont is within the Massif Armoricain, which largely corresponds with Brittany and has very little to do with Normandy. Anyway, if you're bumping about somewhere it's best to identify with the natives and, if the Bretons want to think Mont St. Michel really ought to be in Brittany, I'm prepared to go along with it and give them a helping hand. So we're bumping about Brittany - in Normandy, right?

Clearly this is not an off the wall, eccentric visit, since after the Eiffel tower, there is probably no more instantly recognizable monument in France, but Mont St. Michel is such an extraordinary site, it really ought to feature in any book that strays within a hundred miles of the place. Most tourists (and at the height of the season that 'most tourists' can seem like an absolute definition, as if Most Tourists in the World are here) arrive by car or coach through the rather dismal gateway of 'Beauvoir', so called because a woman miraculously cured of her blindness proclaimed that it was beautiful to see again. Beauvoir is not beautiful to see. Given the volume of traffic (well over a million visitors every year) it's not nearly as bad as it might be, but even so, this is not the sort of place you endorse for a good day's bumping about - except perhaps to pick up a packet of the excellent Mère Poulard cookies, named after a former restaurateur on the Mount who was famous for her light fluffy omelettes. One way or another, you have to pass through Beauvoir sooner or later, but beforehand, I recommend negotiating the labyrinth of dikes lozenging the polders immediately to the west of the Couesnon in order to approach the Mont on foot. If you're feeling energetic, you could even start in Brittany from the Chapelle Ste. Anne at Cherrueix, but otherwise turn left in St-Georges-de-Gréhaigne and keep heading north till you pass the Camus farmhouses and reach the coast.

The polders are so immaculate and so seamlessly integrated with the salt-marsh and the bay beyond that it would be easy to believe they'd been here for ever and a day. Locals had long known about the fertility of the soil where freshwater silt mixed with sedimentary marine deposits, but it was not until the nineteenth century that the watercourses were sufficiently well canalized for the land to be properly exploited. The resulting maze of dikes has created a unique walking environment that won't be to everybody's taste (the flatness can feel monotonous), but which is still worth visiting, especially since it's possible these polders will not be here forever, some activists suggesting the reclaimed land has denatured the Baie de Mont St. Michel and that the dykes should be bulldozed, the marsh allowed to recover its proper dimensions.

To the north of the Camus and Saincey farms, a track cuts across the Molinié and Tesnières polders to the seaward dyke that stretches all the way from Cherrueix to Beauvoir. The salt marsh is easily crossed here and there are some great short walks along the outer dyke and on tracks leading to a channel carved out by a branch of the Couesnon. Hardly anybody goes there and you can get to within a few hundred metres of the abbey without being caught in a scrum, thus preserving the sense that this is a rare experience. Indeed, if you're short of time and shy of crowds, a stroll through the salt marsh is all you really need to get a feeling for just how fabulous Mont St. Michel is. You're only about half a mile away from the main causeway and the coaches and the cars and the crowds, but it feels like a million miles. It would be a particularly fine walk under a full moon.

I had feared Mont St. Michel was such a hackneyed image that bumping about there would be a large waste of time and that I'd be so upset by the crowds, I wouldn't even bother writing about it. But the instant you step onto the dyke and see the reeds stretching away to the sandbanks and the soaring form of a building that is rightly dubbed *La Merveille*, you know this is a sight that just has to be seen, no matter how many other people are there, and, if at all possible, not seen merely once, but revisited again and again until you're thoroughly impregnated with the place. In the unlikely event that you're unfamiliar with the image, what we see is a circle of rock ringed with medieval walls and turrets, above which the village clusters around the crowning glory of the abbey. From a distance, the silhouette resembles nothing so much as a janissary's helmet, but as you approach, details begin to emerge, and you see how the tailored stone complements and completes the natural form of the underlying rock, so that the whole gives a positively organic impression. Surging skyward, it's a poem in rock, a collective work that serves as a counterpoint to the solitary voice of the Abbé Fouré seen earlier. The Catalan architect, Gaudi, was no great traveller, nor a man to admire the marvels of a country other than his own, but even his chauvinism would not have been proof against this. He would have been green with envy, for though less delirious in its conception, the Mont achieves more or less the effect he sought in his unfinished masterpiece, the Sagrada Familia.

Beyond the abbey, the bay is so flat it looks like all the vital landmarks have fallen down or been surreptitiously removed overnight. It's a cliché to say it resembles a desert, but a cliché that was good enough for Flaubert and Victor Hugo is good enough for me. There's that same curious banding of light in the distance that you get in the desert, in this instance exaggerated by the shading of sand into sea into sky, the precise boundaries between each barely distinguishable - unless of course you're foolish enough to wander out to the water's edge when the tide's turning, in which case the boundary will become all too distinct. At *grandes marées*, the sea can retreat eighteen kilometres from the coast and, when it turns, it comes thundering in at a phenomenal rate, not quite the speed of a galloping horse as legend claims, but sufficiently fast for kayaking enthusiasts to surf across the sands on the breaking wave. The sky is immense and between the great flat expanse of the sands and the broad sweep of the heavens, the pinprick figures seen toiling across the bay look absurdly tiny. Even on horseback, human beings are dwarfed by the landscape. It's a natural place for pilgrimage. There's no mistaking where you're going, you can see for miles and, by the same token, you can walk for miles without apparently getting anywhere. Having visited the Brière and Guérande beforehand, it's striking that the northern and southern gateways to Brittany, which otherwise boasts a rough, rocky coast and hilly interior, should both be dead flat.

The best way to see any ancient monument is when nobody else is there, but in the case of Mont St. Michel, this would involve waiting till hell turns arctic and pigs start cluttering up the

Rare in Mont St. Michel - No People!

flight paths, so we've opted to see it by getting away from it, it and the crowds squeezing through the narrow alleys of the village, taking instead a guided walk across the bay to its smaller twin, the Rocher de Tombelaine. I'm no great fan of anything guided by anybody else, least of all a walk, preferring to follow my own sweet wayward path, generally getting hopelessly lost in the process, but the Baie de Mont St. Michel is notorious not only for its 'galloping' tides, but also for its shifting quicksand, so getting hopelessly lost doesn't seem like a terribly clever idea. There are two guided walks on offer and both seem painfully slow. The pace implicit in the long tour of the bay, taking eight hours to walk a mere 22km, sounds like it might well prove mortal, so we sign up for the equally leisurely (6km in three hours) there and back walk to Tombelaine. If it is tedious, at least it won't take so long, and we will see the abbey from the seaward side when it's illuminated by floodlights, since we happen to be here on a day when the short walk can be done in the evening.

The meeting point is inside the main gate of Mont St. Michel, which means we've got to brave Beauvoir and take the causeway linking the Mont with the mainland, crossing a lake of Dormobiles so broad and dense it resembles a caravan park or a car pound at the end of a massive assembly line. This is due to change, though. In Merovingian times, the full name of the Mont, for fairly obvious reasons, was St. Michel-au-Péril-de-la-Mer, but in the last century it became apparent that if something wasn't done soon, they'd have to rename the place St. Michel-au-Péril-de-la-Terre. After canalizing the Couesnon and creating the polders, the local entrepreneurs had acquired a taste for raising bulwarks against the sea and, around the turn of the century, the causeway was built, bringing an end to the Mont's insular status. The consequence, apart from the ranks of camping vans, was that the Couesnon silted up and came over all sluggish, and was no longer able to wash away all the accumulating sands, as a result of which the distinctive character of the Mont was menaced by a 'natural' polderization of the bay. You could argue that this process was a simple reversion to what pertained before, since sea levels were lower when the first records concerning the Mont appear and, prior to the fifth century, it was surrounded by the Forest of Scissy. But fifteen hundred years of pilgrimages and image-making have long since effaced this memory, and most people were appalled that the Mont should become just another bit of inland rock. At the time of writing, work is beginning on an ambitious project to widen the Couesnon and increase its flow by a factor of ten to clear away the rising sandbanks. At the same time, the causeway will be breached, the car-parks removed to the mainland, and anybody wanting to visit the re-insularized island who is not disabled or staying at a hotel, will have to reach it via a nine hundred metre footbridge. Needless to say, in our sedentary age, the Mont's restaurateurs are appalled by the prospect. Who on earth will walk 900 metres for a meal? A question that suggests they are none too confident of their culinary prowess.

Despite the silting, some of the present car parks can still be flooded at very high tides and we are subsequently told by our guide that every year someone will ignore the warning signs and come back to discover their pride and joy all at sea. He describes, with particular relish, the spectacle that took place the previous year when a German tourist was to be seen frantically splashing through the advancing sea to rescue his Mercedes while the assembled masses on the Mont applauded and cheered him on, encouraging him with laudatory catcalls and delighted hoots of derision. The car, our guide confides, was not a Vito. He thinks perhaps it was a Cynic.

There is no such tide today, which is just as well, since we're aiming to walk out onto the sands. Guide or no guide, time it wrong and you're in trouble out there. Mind you, we might be in trouble anyway judging by the way the guide is rigged out. Most companies offering tours of the bay recommend bare feet and shorts for walking on (and, as it turns out, in) the sand, but when we reach the rendez-vous point, I'm a little alarmed to see that our guide has got himself zipped up in a set of complicated waterproofs and impermeable bootees that suggest we're in for some serious exposure to the elements. Among the party there are several people wearing long trousers and trainers, and one bloke's even togged up in a pair of brogues. And there's a big black cloud off to the west.

Our guide congratulates us, first for being the elite, turning out when all the other tourists have hightailed it home, second for our good fortune, the last two walks having being cancelled due to rain. There's a bit of muttering at this stage and surreptitious glancing westward, but everyone is pleased at being part of the elite, the compliment even elicits a little cheer, so nobody mentions the cloud. Brogue puffs his chest out, lifts his chin, flexes his jaw muscles, as if to say he can take anything the

Inside the Mont

weather cares to throw at him. The guide then points to our two dogs, suggesting that the group is triply lucky since it will be accompanied by a couple of highly trained rescue dogs. I don't disabuse anyone. The best you could hope for from those two mutts if you got stuck in the quicksand is that they'd lick you to death in a frenzy of empathy before you sank below the surface.

It may simply be due to all the extreme weather gear he's wearing, but our guide appears to have a faintly game leg. It does not, however, impair his performance, which in pedestrian terms proves effortless. As for his guiding, he is the antithesis of both the Grande Gueule encountered at the Château du Taureau and Miss This-Is-A-PRIVATE-HOUSE! at the Château du Combourg, for he is a modest, educated man with a sly sense of humour and a ready supply of quiet chuckles for celebrating and disarming the absurdities of the world.

Apart from Brogue, the rest of our party seem fairly normal, but I'm a bit disturbed when I realize there are nigh on forty of us. This seems rather a lot for an 'elite'. As it transpires though, once we get out on the sands, there's no sense of being part of a crowd. Less easily resolved are Trouble and Brother Bother. There are several children in the group, but as somebody who spent far too many years in a classroom pretending to be a teacher, I have no difficulty singling out the two kids to steer clear of. Trouble is about eleven, Brother Bother nine, and they're prowling round the fringes of our party, grinning at one another and sniggering and larking about behind the backs of unsuspecting adults, among whom must be their parents, who are doing their level best to feign ignorance of their offspring.

We stroll round the western walls, on top of which there is a rampart mill (the only remaining example in western Europe apparently), and then our party comes to an abrupt and appalled halt. There's another group returning from a walk and they're fording the Couesnon, following a complicated route carefully trail-blazed by their guide. The guide is a distinctive figure with long straggly hair and a big beard, whom our own guide identifies as the Marquis de Tombelaine, named after one of the first and most famous guides taking parties across the bay in the nineteenth century. I believe his contemporary has earned the name because of their physical resemblance, at least I hope so, for when I later look up the details of the original 'marquis', I discover that, despite his celebrity, he managed to drown himself by getting drunk and falling over in front of a rising tide. However, it is not the appearance of the current Marquis that has alarmed our party, nor even our own guide's explanation of why they are following such a tortuous route (there's only a narrow sand bridge below the water, the quicksands shift, and if you get it wrong, you can disappear up to your chest quicker than you can call for a snorkel), but the fact that the other party are all thigh deep in water. Even Brogue has developed a slight twitch in the corner of his eye. Trouble and Brother Bother are fascinated and are following the progress of the other party with an almost predatory glee. Eventually, a rather pale looking woman, who is wearing pedal-pushers and appears to be shivering, plucks up courage and asks if we are going to do that. Our guide reassures us. We will cross elsewhere. Trouble and Brother Bother look vaguely disappointed, doubly so when the last member of the other party fords the Couesnon without mishap. The way clear, we proceed round the back of the Mont, where there is an outcrop of rock embedded in the sand with a diminutive chapel built on top of it. This is the Chapelle de St. Aubert.

Mont St. Michel was originally called Mont Tombe, from the Latin root *tu'm* (knoll, hillock, mound) which also gives us tumulus and, via the shared Indo-European roots, Greek *tumbos* and Gallic *dunos* (from which, Dunkerque); and it continued to be called Mont Tombe well into the Christian era, in the early years of which the Mont was the site of both pagan and Christian shrines, the latter dedicated to Saint-Étienne and Saint Symphorien. Legend holds that the bay was the site of a mighty battle between St. Michael and Satan in the form of a dragon, a battle that began on Mont Dol in Brittany and concluded, unhappily for the dragon, on Mont Tombe. Aubert, after whom the chapel is named, was Bishop of Avranches in the early years of the eighth century, and one night the archangel popped into the episcopal dreams, demanding a sanctuary be built to commemorate his victory. Aubert begged to differ, or forgot, or didn't trust his visions, even when the apparition recurred and the message was repeated. Thoroughly narked by such negligence, St. Michael poked the bishop's cranium, leaving a finger sized hole in Aubert's skull, which is now on display in the basilica in Avranches if you care to verify the story. Hole in head, Aubert finally got the message and set about appeasing the irate angel, hurrying off to the Mont where, as promised, a bull marked the spot on which the shrine was to be constructed.

Aubert began preparing the ground, but the summit of the Mont was crowned with a great granite rock, or a tailored megalith according to some interpretations, and no amount of heaving and sweating and cursing and beggaring about could move the thing because Satan, in no wise abashed by his archangelic duffing up, was underneath hanging on for grim death. St. Michael appeared again, this time to one of the labourers, telling him that if he went to work with all his children, the rock would move. The family duly clocked on and gathered round the rock, but nothing happened. Then Aubert remembered there was another child, a baby, whom the father had left at home in its cot since, even in those days, babies weren't employed on building sites. The babe was fetched and presented to the rock, which he tapped lightly with his foot, whereupon the rock tumbled off the summit. St. Michael got his shrine and Aubert built himself a chapel on the toppled rock, where, as with the finger hole in the episcopal skull, the babe's footprint can be seen implanted in the stone.

A stone stairway leads us across a spur of rock behind the chapel, beyond which there's a scattering of boulders, reputed to be the playthings of our old friend Gargantua, who is said to have been so tall he could stand with one foot on Mont Tombe and one on Tombelaine. Useful trick, as those who ignored the shorts and bare feet directive are now obliged to roll up their trouser legs and take off their shoes (Brogue's upper lip begins trembling slightly) in order to wade across a narrow channel of water. There's some mild shrieking and modest hilarity as the slick mud oozes through our toes and up over our ankles, and Trouble and Brother Bother are sloshing about with all the enthusiasm of a couple of topers pressing grapes. Thereafter though, the sand is dry and the walking easy, despite which, we proceed at a snail's pace, stopping every quarter kilometre so the guide can give us an additional gobbet of history, natural or otherwise, or tell another anecdote, while Trouble and Brother Bother playfully hurl clods of mud at one another.

The guide is good, he knows his stuff and tells it well, yet the best of being out here is not the narrative but the being itself. The atmosphere is extraordinary. We are surrounded by grand, flat lines: flat sands, flat sea, flat horizon, flat striations of the sky. . . You certainly wouldn't want to race anything like a tide out here. There's nowhere to hide, which is another reason why it must have been a good place for a pilgrimage. It's that desert feeling again. There's a sense of the numinous about the Baie de Mont St. Michel and you can appreciate the motive power that got the Old Testament prophets going. When it's just you and empty space and a big god-shaped hole, there's a definite urge to start inventing a religion. If the peoples of the Middle East hadn't already done the job, I can imagine the fishermen of the Baie de Mont St. Michel dreaming up monotheism - all that space confronts you with something else, something bigger than you that has to be addressed one way or another.

Meanwhile, the big black cloud to the west is limbering up to address us. It's moving nearer and there's nothing between us and it apart from a prayer and the faint possibility that it will be blown inland. I wish Trouble and Brother Bother could be blown inland. They're pulling faces at the dogs and eyeballing them from a distance of about two-and-a-half centimetres, apparently hoping to provoke a rash of barking. If they carry on like this, I'll be the one doing the barking. I might even bite.

There are places where the sand gets disturbingly soft and, as the Couesnon curves back from the west, veering toward Tombelaine, our guide points out a pocket of quicksand. To my astonishment, everybody rushes forward and starts stamping up and down in the stuff. On the flats above the waterline it's not as quick as the quicksand you see in the movies, the sort that swallows up baddies in the blink of an eye, but even if it's fairly slow quicksand, I'm not persuaded jumping up and down in it is really very advisable. There again, Trouble and Brother Bother are in the forefront of the stamping and I entertain a momentary vision of the pair of them disappearing altogether. Disappointingly, it seems that you really have to make an effort to sink. Later we discover there are places where no effort is required at all, but for the moment nobody disappears and there are no tearful farewells and promises of mended ways if only we'll throw them a rope. Still, perhaps even slow quicksand can get quick if you persist, because after watching the antics of his charges for about a minute, the guide suggests it might be wiser if we moved on.

Deprived of the quicksand, Trouble and Brother Bother are obliged to pull faces at the dogs again, at least for the next few hundred metres, though now they know what it looks like, they have an eye for quicksand, and are leaping in the stuff at every opportunity. At one point, Brother Bother gets stuck up to his knees and proudly proclaims that he's sinking. I briefly contemplate giving him a tap on the head to help him on his way and put everyone out of their misery, but decide it would not be charitable - not to Brother Bother, at least, though his parents, who continue to keep a low profile, might be quite pleased.

Halfway across the bay, the big black cloud concludes the power of prayer and the possibility of blowing inland are beneath it, as are we, and the heavens open, deluging us with a cold slanting rain. Most people have some sort of waterproof (I half expect Brogue to produce an Aquascutum mackintosh and James Smith & Sons brolly), but nobody's as well equipped as the guide, and by the time we reach Tombelaine, the tootsies are feeling decidedly nippy, and several women are overheard muttering "*Je n'en peux plus*", I can't take any more. Even Trouble and Brother Bother have quietened down, which suggests a bucket of chilled water might be a useful adjunct to standard classroom equipment. Personally, I don't find it too bad. The storm does pass, or at least diminish, and the shallow water we occasionally wade through is delightfully warm compared to the sand. Nonetheless, if you do a night walk, I recommend taking several layers of clothing, because it would be miserable out here if you got really cold and wet. It's worth noting that professional *pêcheurs à pied* in the Baie de Mont St. Michel were called *Pieds Rouges* for their violet tinged feet.

Tombelaine is only forty-five metres tall and looks insignificant from a distance, but once we draw near, it's a striking bit of stone (anything that protrudes from this flatness is striking) speckled with gulls and egrets, and, according to our guide, occasionally visited by wild boar that have followed the same trail between the mainland and the island since the middle ages. Tombelaine is commonly thought a diminutive of *tombe*, taking its name from *tumbellana* or 'little mount', though there are other, equally plausible explanations, most strikingly *Tombe-Belen*, the tomb of the 'brilliant one', that is the Celtic solar god of light and fire. Belen is sometimes said to have been Gargan/Gargantua's father and other legends claim Gargantua buried his parents either here or on Mont St. Michel itself. It's also thought that before Aubert's time, a Mithraic sun cult was celebrated on these rocky outcrops, which I'll take on trust, though given the weather we've got today, locating a sun cult here is a bit like staging a regatta in the middle of the Sahara.

At first glance, all these conflicting legends seem confusing, but the etymological and mythological muddle can be resolved syncretically. The Gargan/Gargantua legend appears throughout Europe, for the most part in simple tales about a mythical giant, but originally Gargan, like Mithras, Zeus, Belen and Jupiter, was a manifestation of the pre-Christian sun god, a god the early church habitually supplanted with the cult of Saint Michael, the heavyweight who threw Lucifer, the rebellious angel of light, out of heaven and into the underworld. It's even possible that the entire sanctification of Mont St. Michel was modelled on Mont Gargan in Italy, where Aubert had been on pilgrimage and which had been dedicated to Saint Michael through a similar process, the revelatory dream, the signpost bull (the bull being a sacrificial animal for the Mithraic cults) and so forth. Either way, the mish-mash of pagan and Christian myths is a symptom of the classic process whereby the new religion overtook and co-opted the old.

There's little visible on Tombelaine now, even if you visit out of the nesting season, when some parties stroll round the island itself, but time was when it had its own village - an English village. Naturally, this was not an English village in the sense of Miss Marple and the thwack of leather on willow, not with the French so near to hand, but one of 'Mister English to you' and the clash of steel, for we occupied the place for thirty-five years during the Hundred Years War when it was the base for an unsuccessful siege of Mont St. Michel. For much of its history, the Mont was a military stronghold as well as a spiritual stronghold, the abbot a soldier as well as a prelate, the last siege taking place during the Wars of Religion. As a result of successive conflicts, plus the impact of several fires and the general attrition of time, the Mont we see today did not actually take definitive form until the nineteenth century.

Despite the lateness of the hour, we see several other parties out on the sands and, judging by their behaviour, it seems the atmosphere affects different people differently. Some clown around, only a step up from Trouble and Brother Bother's comportment, splashing one another, pushing each other in the quicksand, but most people contemplate the emptiness and grandeur with awed silence. In retrospect, I think the clowning is a response to the same thing, an attempt to disarm the intimidating bigness of the place, to make light of something heavy and faintly oppressive, belittling what is in reality belittling us. It's hard to evoke the atmosphere, but it is perhaps best conveyed through the prevailing colour scheme, which is composed of shades of grey. Its a natural water-colour land really, possibly a gouache, a place where there are no clear boundaries between things, but a shading of the material into the immaterial, and the prevailing feeling is of something other-worldly.

In all, we see upward of a dozen groups scattered about the sands during the course of our walk, so the guided tours are clearly a thriving business, but you get no sense of being crowded into a tourist attraction. On the contrary, the lines of people inching along in the distance resemble nothing so much as medieval pilgrims, or figures in some post-apocalyptic landscape, like in a Kurosawa film. And the darker it becomes, the more atmospheric it is. From a distance, everyone seems small, huddled, hunched, exhausted, labouring along making slow progress against a backdrop of infinite nothingness, the timelessness of the scene marred only by the occasional flicker of an isolated camera flash.

After trudging through a field of mud, we return to dry sand and head back toward the mainland amid the gathering dusk, at which point the abbey starts to light up, not as one might expect in a sudden effulgence, but a slow creeping glow crawling up the walls from the foundations like some luminous lichen. It's subtly done, but compared to the palette of greys, it's a slight disappointment. That nacreous half light of dusk was the real magic, the reason in the end that we are here. The most attractive view of the illuminations lies a few hundred metres short of the Mont when we reach the watercourse we crossed earlier beside the Chapelle de St. Aubert. It's slightly deeper here and the still water mirrors a strip of the wedding cake Mont as if it's toppled into the sand and is sinking into the underworld.

The closer we get to the abbey, the brighter the lighting, the more wedding cake-ish it seems, like something conjured from a fairy tale. Despite it's organic character, La Merveille is also a very artificial confection, and you can almost understand why developers have got so carried away they wanted to complement it with a theme park or surround it with a simulation Venice. It's so fantastic, so improbable that it's almost Disneyesque, and yet it is saved by the austerity of the landscape and the sheer grandeur of the building. Moreover, its history is anything but Disneyesque, for as well as being a military base, the Mont was used as a gaol, first by the kings of France, who installed the horrible *cage de fer*, a tiny iron cage that was suspended in the air and swung to and fro whenever the prisoner moved, then by the revolutionaries who locked up refractory priests in the *Bastille des Mers*, and finally by the Imperial authorities who felt it a fitting penitentiary for revolutionary socialists like Blanqui (I hate to imagine what Blanqui thought about Brittany, for he was forever being banged up in the place, if not here then at the Château du Taureau or on Belle-Île-en-Mer). There was one celebrated escape in 1832 (a real Colditz job, with tunneling, debris disposed of in the latrines, and a rope suspended from the walls), but for the most part prisoners just rotted and went mad, and in one, probably apocryphal instance, got eaten alive by the rats. The prison wasn't closed until 1863.

Our walk is coming to an end. The brightly lit building soars above us. Meanwhile, we've got our feet firmly on the ground - well, in the ground, actually. Traversing the broad sandbank, the coating of mud and caked quicksand that encrusted our calves has dried and dropped away, but suddenly, some five hundred metres from the car-park, just three quarters of an hour short of midnight, when everyone's wilting fast, our guide announces that the dry walking is done and it's mud till the end, and off he goes, plunging across the watercourse and disappearing into the darkness, and we plunge after him and find that he really meant it. The mud is the deepest we've hit yet, and several people sink up to their knees and can't get out unaided, inspiring a few bitter comments along the lines of "Is he taking the piss, or what?". I don't think he is, but it's an object lesson in why it's best to follow a guide - if this is the easy, approved route, we might well be up to our necks elsewhere.

Despite my comments about slow walking and six kilometres being no distance at all, when we eventually get back to the car-park, we are exhausted, literally footsore from trudging on the hardpacked sand and plunging through the mud. Even the dogs are subdued. As for Trouble and Brother Bother, there is no sign of them, and I realize I have neither seen nor heard from them for some while. I wonder where they are? I hope nothing's happened to them. Nothing nefarious. Nothing nasty. Back there. In the mud. In the dark. Doubtless St. Michael's looking after them. Miracles do happen, especially when you're bumping about Mont St. Michel.

23. IF YOU GO DOWN TO THE WOODS TODAY

ACCESS - The **Forêt de Beffou** is in Côtes d'Armor in the triangle formed by Belle Isle en Terre, Callac and Plouigneau. The easiest approach is from the N12 via **'Loguivy-Plougras'**. Our walk starts at the intersection of the D11 and D119.

It was a dark and stormy night and a deed was about to be done that many would deem unspeakable, but whereof we will speak, for we are intrepid reporters of the truth, or something very like it. The tale we have to tell concerns clandestine organizations, splinter groups and rival factions. It is a story of subversion, dissidence, trespass, theft and, some would say, kidnap. It is not a narrative for the faint of heart.

Bill & Ben

Pre-Liberation

Not so long ago, a rambler in the Forêt de Touffou to the South of Nantes made a strange and disturbing discovery. There, secreted in the heart of the woodland, like hobgoblins gathered together to practice their occult magic, were 157 garden gnomes bearing the inscription, *"Libérés en 2000"*. The rambler had inadvertently stumbled upon the largest gnome dump in Europe. The gnomes were removed to the gendarmerie at Vertou, where they were arranged on the lawn in case the gnomes 'owners' wanted to claim them back, and there they remained, testament to a disquieting phenomenon that has periodically upset the tranquil world of garden ornamentation since the late 1960s, when the *Association Internationale pour la Protection des Nains de Jardin* (AIPNJ), also known as the *Internationale Vereinigung Zum Schutze der Gartenzwerge* (IVZG), was founded in Switzerland by Fritz Friedman, a man active to this day in the often shady world of the garden gnomes' rights movement and reputed to number over one thousand garden gnomes in his entourage.

The spectacle of 157 garden gnomes deployed on a gendarmerie lawn was not one I had the strength of mind to resist, so in order clarify the sketchy Internet report of the incident, I went to Vertou and tracked down the gendarmerie, which is located on a quiet residential street on the fringes of the village. Sadly, there wasn't a gnome in sight. And the gendarmerie was closed. At least, there was a big metal grill blocking the public entrance and all the gates were shut. But beside the main gate there was an off-duty gendarme walking his Tibetan terrier, which was at the time taking a leak on the lawn. I caught the gendarme's eye, no easy task, given that he was concentrating hard on his Shih Tzu's micturition, and, apologizing for disturbing his reverie, asked if he might be able to give me some information. No, he might not. The gendarmerie was closed and I had to come back in office hours. It was all a bit frosty, to tell you the truth. He probably thought I was a tourist who had managed to lose his wallet, a problem of surpassing inconsequentiality when one's Shih Tzu is pissing on the constabulary lawn. I hastened to assure him that this was not an official matter and I only wanted to ask if they had any gnomes secreted about the place, in a back room say, on a top shelf, a bottom drawer, a corner of the armory, or perhaps lurking in an unused cell. The man allowed himself a small smile, but confirmed the evidence of my eyes. They had no gnomes in the Gendarmerie de Vertou. There may, briefly, have been some gnomes on the lawn in the past, but they had long since been removed, doubtless sent to the *mairie* for 'disposal', a sinister euphemism suggesting the small band of fugitives had come to a sorry end. I thanked the gendarme. The Shih Tzu sniffed at a cluster of daisies then delicately shat upon the flowers and ambled away. This is the way of things when you're trying to track down the workings of the Garden Gnome Liberation Fronts (GGLF).

Of the many advocacy groups militating for the rights of garden gnomes, the most famous is the *Front de Liberation des Nains de Jardin* (FLNJ). The premise is simple: gnomes, like people and animals, have rights, too. Obliging gnomes to stand about in gardens for the mere purposes of ornamentation, against their will and without any proper or fitting remuneration, be it pecuniary, alimentary, medical or therapeutic, is unjust, immoral, and contrary to the egalitarian principles that have evolved in the context of the liberal-humanist tradition over the last three hundred years. You might get away with that sort of thing in some third world country, but in a liberal western democracy, it's simply not on.

Like most political movements, the GGLF is riven by competing factions disputing means, objectives, and the validity of one another's claims to represent the interests of their chosen constituency. There is a legitimate political wing, Free The Gnomes (FG), but like most legitimate political wings, this is a pretty dull organization, largely given to ringing declarations of principles and drawing up timetables for gnome liberation that never come to anything. There are extremists, like the Italian *Movimento Autonomo per la Liberazione delle Anime da Giardio* (the MALAG) who smash the gnomes' bodies so that their liberated spirits can fly away. Another type of flight is engineered in the Travelling Gnome Prank (TGP), whereby gnomes are abducted and taken off to see the world, sending their bereft owners regular photos of themselves posing in front of well known landmarks like the Kremlin or the Taj Mahal, before mysteriously returning from their travels several years later, often as not having acquired a spouse on the road. There is the *Mouvement d'Emancipation des Nains des Jardins* (MENJ), a pacifist organization that deplores such antics as 'liberating' gnomes into the wilds of the forest, claiming the poor creatures will be at a loss in this alien environment and wholly unable to fend for themselves, deprived of both their customary working tools (garden forks, wheelbarrows and so forth - *nanipabullus* is the technical term for a garden gnome with a wheelbarrow) and the protection provided by a secure and caring home. And then there is the very mutable and somewhat mysterious FTNJ, an acronym sometimes applied to the *Front de Torture des Nains de Jardins*, sometimes to the *Front de Tuerie des Nains de Jardins*; depending on your source and the interpretation of that 'T', the FTNJ is either a garden gnome equivalent to the RSPCA, providing a refuge for abused gnomes (there are some horrific pictures on the FLNJ website - go to www.flnjfrance.com and click on 'La Torture'), or a revolutionary cell inciting gnomes everywhere to rise up and rebel against their tyrannical masters, or a sort of anti-immigration campaigning group, warning innocent gardeners of the risks they are running letting alien life forms like gnomes indiscriminately colonize their gardens.

But by far and away the most active of these movements is the FLNJ. Members of the FLNJ, sometimes called 'Liberators', have no truck with the squeamish qualms of the MENJ concerning the 'natural environment' of garden gnomes. Just because they're called 'garden' gnomes, it is entirely fallacious to suppose that gardens are their ideal habitat. The qualifier is simply a convention reflecting our common experience of gnomes, not a determiner of nature, much as a house fly is not defined by a house, which is simply where we happen to see it most often, and field mice probably got along perfectly well in the wilds before we began demarcating fields. No, the FLNJ are having none of this wishy-washy, hand-wringing over mere words. That's just political correctness gone mad. Not, of course, that words aren't important. An elaborate vocabulary has developed within the ranks of the gnome liberation movement, ranging from easily interpreted terms like *nanomane*, *nanopathe*, *nanophile*, and *nanoprotecteur*, through more arcane words like *nanologue* (an academic specializing in the study of gnomes), *nosographie* (the science of determining a gnome's character from the shape of his nose) to the downright abstruse, such as *ananipabullofère*, an adjective describing someone who, through injury or innate incompetence, is incapable of carrying a wheelbarrow gnome. But for all this very necessary vocabulary (as everyone knows, no academic discipline is taken seriously until it has developed a lexis that is incomprehensible to laymen), the FLNJ and their Breton splinter group (the NFM, an organization so secretive that I haven't actually been able to find out anything about it apart from the initials) are not hung up on arid debates about words. They are militant organizations dedicated to direct action and they get out there and act on their principles, liberating gnomes wherever these blameless creatures are detained by inconsiderate gardeners for whom a simple shrub is not decoration enough.

It's inspiring, really, is it not? It inspired this friend of mine anyway, an Englishman who settled in a remote Breton hamlet several years ago. Most of the houses in the hamlet are holiday homes, but there is a small permanent population, with the majority of whom this friend of mine maintains cordial relations. There is, however, one neighbour with whom relations, if not uncordial, are at the very least cool.

Things began well enough. My friend would regularly pass the house of the man in question and at first his greetings were returned. But then one day, without the relationship ever having gone beyond the ritual exchange of *bonjours*, something happened and the neighbour took to studiously avoiding the eye of my friend and steadfastly refused any reciprocity of *bonjours*. There were no apparent grounds for this sudden *froideur* and the only reasoned supposition anyone could come up with was that the neighbour had suddenly realized that this friend of mine, with whom he had been so recklessly exchanging *bonjours,* was not a Good Breton like himself, but a bird of a different feather altogether, to wit an Englishman, and thus beyond the pale, certainly not deserving of a Good Breton Bonjour. Initially, my friend found this hard to believe and persisted with his own *bonjours*, but nothing came of it, and gradually the gross and unmerited incivility of the whole affair began to irk him. True, he was English, which in some eyes is crime enough, but he was otherwise a largely irreproachable individual who only wanted to maintain good relations with all his neighbours, at the very least to have them recognize his existence with the occasional *bonjour*. Well, you know what we English are like when irked. It can really get very ugly. Something had to give.

This friend of mine has shown me the neighbour in question, so I can describe the man in some detail. He's clearly a toughy, a macho man, always chewing gum to develop his jaw muscles, and given to wearing sleeveless T-shirts to display the modest development of his arms. The arms themselves can't quite hang straight for some reason and he has to keep his elbows bent outwards at all times, like a couple of jug handles, as if to accommodate bulging biceps. This makes his shoulders look rather round, suggesting they, too, are overburdened with muscle, or are permanently hunched into a wrestling posture. His legs are slightly bandy, as if decades of lifting heavy weights have bowed the bones as they built up the imaginary muscle. His ears stick out, his hair is cropped short, and his moustache, which is close clipped, curves round the corners of his mouth, like the moustaches favoured by body-builders and bouncers in the 1970s. You get the picture. He's All Man and, though not as burly as he fancies, burly enough to be the sort of bloke who might enjoy a brawl down the local bar of a Saturday night. Which is why his garden is so bizarre.

You'd have thought the garden of man like that would consist largely of tall trees festooned with sturdy lianas the better for swinging from bough to bough between bouts of slapping his pectorals, but not a bit of it. My friend made a point of drawing my attention to the garden. I've never seen anything so prissy in my life. It was surrounded by a low pink wall. The lawn was manicured to within an inch of its life. The flowerbeds were defined so meticulously, weeded and hoed so thoroughly, they looked like something simulated from synthetic materials, a sort of garden carpet that, once laid, wouldn't budge or upset the symmetry by doing anything untoward like growing. Every shrub was shaped and primped and pussy-footed about and firmly divided from its neighbour by a no-man's land of immaculately turned soil, as if the plants might get up to some funny business if allowed to fraternize. There was a water feature, a rock garden, a miniature landscaped hill, a proud cock weather vane, a little teeny weeny tiny pond ringed by sunken floodlights, and behind the little teeny weeny tiny pond a model lighthouse surrounded by garden ornaments in plaster, plastic and wood. Taking the lighthouse to set the scale, there was a mansion-sized windmill, a fake well as big as a bungalow, a frog that would in real life weigh about fifteen tons, a curlew that would be about nineteen metres tall (perhaps modelled by Tsereteli?), a duck the size of a Clydesdale horse, a handful of Great Dane ducklings, a tank-sized tortoise, and a toadstool as tall as a Georgian townhouse. The man maybe All Man, but at heart he is Rotomold Man. And there, on the window ledge, veritable giants beside the lighthouse, were three garden gnomes. I use the past tense because when this friend of mine, this other bloke, heard about the FLNJ, he really was inspired. Irked, as I say, and English, too. Piqued by his neighbour's discourtesy, he resolved to teach the man a lesson by freeing the gnomes.

It was a dark and stormy night when my friend turned liberator and stole toward his uncivil neighbour's garden. He was, he says, feeling pretty nervous, for though the neighbour was not nearly so burly as he fancied, he was nonetheless a little bit burly, and a little bit burly is all you need really when you get into a scrap, especially if you're incensed by the sight of someone nabbing your prized garden gnomes, and that someone an Englishman to boot. My friend had done his research, too. Your average *nain de jardin* doesn't come cheap, each one costing (we'll put aside, for the moment, questions about the moral legitimacy of 'purchasing' gnomes) twenty quid or more, so this garden clearly represented a considerable investment on the part of the neighbour. But my friend had made up his mind and he wasn't about to be put off by the prospect of a quarrel. He was a Liberator, an Irked Liberator, and he was going to go on the FLNJ website and sign up under an alias, a sort of *nom de guerre*, like the other Breton Liberators (Monk3y Le Fou, C4puccino, Martino el Loco, Pupuce, and Revolouchionhair), in order to record how many gnomes he had liberated. He'd even borrowed a black hoody the better to camouflage himself. And he had half a mind to form his own cell, a *Brigade Libératrice des Nains* (BLN). There was no going back now.

My friend approached the neighbour's garden, checked the surrounding houses were silent and shuttered, looked up the road, looked down the road, then peered over the garden wall for a final inspection of the terrain. All was quiet and propitious for the lifting of the gnomes. He braced his shoulders, took a deep breath, pulled his hood tight, and then . . . . Imagine his dismay when he glanced across the garden and there, where the gnomes had been, there were no gnomes! His gnomes had gone. They'd buggered off, absconded, scarpered, done a runner, taken a French leave, gone AWOL. Everything else was there, the ducks, the curlew, the frog, the tortoise and so forth, but of the gnomes there was no sign.

He never did discover what had happened to them, whether they'd already been liberated or his neighbour, suspecting something was amiss, had brought the gnomes indoors for safe-keeping, but there was no questioning this particular liberator's plight. If there's one thing pretty well essential to the practice of liberating gnomes, it's gnomes in need of liberation. Without gnomes, he was scuppered. He was a liberator without any gnomes to liberate. 'Liberating' a lighthouse didn't seem quite the same thing somehow and my friend was casting about, wondering what to do, when to his immense relief he saw that there were in fact two more garden gnomes he hadn't spotted during his previous recce trips and which had not so far been removed. The reason he hadn't seen them before was that they really were very small, in scale with the lighthouse and knee high to the frog, nothing like the giant gnomes he had had in his sights. Even for garden gnomes they were on the small side. But Hey! Who's measuring? This was no place for size-ism. They might be small, but they were as worthy of liberation as bigger gnomes, so he decided to proceed with his plan.

Now in these matters there is a certain protocol to be observed. You don't just go blundering in and nick . . . sorry, liberate the gnome. The procedure is outlined as follows on a French website dedicated to promoting the proper way of doing things when it comes to liberating gnomes:

1. Ne pas uriner sur la clôture électrifiée . . . ça fait mal . . . et puis il fallait faire ça avant de `partir en vadrouille;

2. ouvrir le portail sans se coincer les doigts dans la charnière;

3. éviter de se faire exploser la tronche avec les mines en glissant sur l'herbre mouillée;

4. libérer le nain de jardin;

5. faire demi-tour;

6. chemin inverse, toujours en évitant les mines;

7. balancer les tracts pour narguer Jean Culé;

8. fermer le portail car, après tout, on n'est pas des vandales.

Which is to say . . .

1. Don't urinate on the electric fence . . . it hurts . . . and besides, that should be done before going gadding about;

2. open the gate without pinching your fingers in the hinge;

3. avoid slipping on the damp grass and setting off the mines;

4. free the garden gnome;

5. about turn;

6. retrace your steps, still avoiding the mines;

7. chuck about a few tracts to taunt (an indelicate expression for an Everyman subjected to rectal insemination);

8. shut the gate since we are not, after all, vandals.

My friend had already relieved himself before leaving home, there was no electric fence or, as best he could ascertain, mines, and he didn't have any tracts, but for the rest of it, he followed the prescribed procedure to the letter, then hastened off, pursued by the gathering storm, carrying to safety his purloined gnomes, whom he had in the meantime christened Bill and Ben.

Simple. Except that it was, as I say, a dark and stormy night, and before my friend could safely stash the gnomes, the skies opened, and all three of them were drenched. The gnomes, being more accustomed to this sort of thing, shrugged off the soaking as a matter of course, but my friend caught a chill and was obliged to take to his bed. Housebound for the rest of the week, he couldn't help dwelling on the fact that Bill and Ben were shut up in his garage, and their presence there began to weigh on his mind. Not only was this no proper place for two liberated gnomes, but there was always the risk his burly neighbour might chance upon them, in which case he, my friend, could well be housebound for considerably longer than the course of a common cold. It was at this juncture that he called upon me to conclude the liberation process.

"You", he said from his sick bed, feebly clutching my hand and staring feverishly into my eyes, "you have got to get Bill and Ben into the woods. Their lives may depend on it. My life may depend on it. I'm trusting you to do this. I'd do it myself, but as you see . . . " whereupon he collapsed onto his sweat soaked pillows, worn out by his efforts on behalf of suffering gnomekind.

Now, normally I keep my nose clean, do things by the book, take great care to think inside the box, and steer well clear of blue skies, because I don't like being caught out and I wouldn't want some burly little bloke with an antipathy toward Englishmen in general finding me with his missing gnomes in the boot of my car. But given that the well-being of Bill and Ben was at stake, I agreed to help my friend. And so it was that I found myself bumping about the Forêt de Beffou to the south of Loguivy-Plougras in Côtes d'Armor.

Why Beffou? Well, first off, it's as nice a wood as any in Brittany and the beech trees, after which it is named, continue to flourish alongside oak, ash, birch and the odd wild cherry tree, so hopefully Bill and Ben will feel at home there. Second, topping three hundred metres, it's the highest wood in Brittany and, after a lifetime imprisoned behind pale pink walls in a prissy little garden, Bill and Ben have surely earned a tranquil retirement on a wooded eminence. Third, in the Allée Couverte du Brohet it has a Hent Korriganed, and it seems only fitting that Bill and Ben should be in the vicinity of a Little People's Street, just in case the academics and archeologists have got it hopelessly wrong. Fourth, it's nowhere near me, my friend or, above all, the burly little bloke, thus reducing the likelihood of disagreeable incidents. Also, and this is a strictly frivolous reason, but might well prove the most potent of all, especially for people idly bumping about, St. Émilion passed through this area before settling in Aquitaine and becoming a wine merchant, and the stream to the north of the forest still bears his name: so, please, before bumping about the Forêt de Beffou, buy yourself a bottle of St. Émilion so you can raise a glass to Bill and Ben.

We set off along the yellow waymarked circuit that starts from the junction of the D11 and the D119. Apart from a steep climb near the start, it's an easy, seven kilometre stroll using the two principal east-west axes of the forest, the Laie Sommière Nord and the Laie Sommière Sud, to loop round the main sights of the wood, including the Etang de Comprejou, a pond said to be the resort of otters, the *allée couverte*, and Le Pavé, an ancient Roman way that crosses the 322-metre culminating point of the forest.

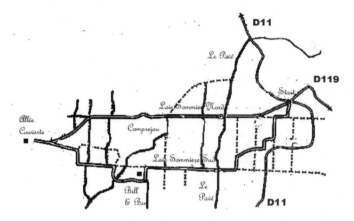

Naturally, I didn't just go wandering off into the woods with a couple of garden gnomes casually tucked under my arm. I've got my reputation to consider and I've no idea where the burly little bloke hangs out when he's not primping his garden. Bill and Ben were well wrapped up and secreted at the bottom of my rucksack, and there they stayed, apart from a couple of brief outings to see the sights, till I found an appropriate hideaway for them, well off the beaten path and out of sight of burly little blokes and casual passers-by who might be inclined to go poking their noses into places we want no noses poked in.

Crossing Le Pavé, the route descends to Comprejou, then climbs gently before forking left to reach a signposted turning on the right to the *allée couverte*. To be honest, as megaliths go, this one is eminently missable, having suffered considerable damage over the last three millennia, most recently in the great storm of 1987, but Bill and Ben insisted we check

Admiring the view at Comprejou

it out, so they would know where it was in case of emergency. We then retraced our steps to rejoin the yellow route and signposted turnings taking us right, left, right, then left again onto the main track of the Laie Sommière Sud. The track crosses a rivulet, immediately after which the waymarked route turns right again, then left at a T-junction to return to the Laie Sommière Sud. 60 paces after the T-junction and 50 paces short of forestry markers '36/37', there is a small boulder off to the left in the undergrowth in front of a tall conifer. Directly behind the conifer, 12 paces from the trail, the trunk of a fallen tree lies at the foot of a plane tree. Bill and Ben's new home is under the fallen trunk to the right of the plane tree. I know nothing of their sexuality, but they're a charming couple and would be delighted to see you. And if you happen to liberate any gnomes yourself while on holiday, I'm sure they'd be glad of the company. Be discreet about it, though. I wouldn't want you to attract any unfriendly attention, either to yourselves or Bill and Ben. Toasts made and respects paid, simply follow the waymarked route back to the start.

I appreciate that paces vary, so if you happen to have a handheld GPS receiver, the coordinates of the Bumping About gnome dump are 48° 29' 054 / -3°30' 376, though bear in mind that reception is not perfect in the woods and accuracy is reduced to ten metres. Bill and Ben are well hidden and it is unlikely anyone would stumble across them by accident, so if they are no longer there, it means somebody else has read this book and taken them home as a souvenir. If so, we can only hope that another BLN will free them again at some future date and return them to their natural state, for once liberty has been tasted, renewed captivity is intolerable, and Bill and Ben will surely pine away and die.

Vive le FLNJ! Free the gnomes!

And the British think *they* are eccentric?

24. MAGIC POTIONS

ACCESS - **Guimaëc** is in northern Finistère near the Côtes d'Armor border and lies immediately north of Lanmeur (D786 Lannion to Morlaix) on the D64 to Locquirec. The **Kervéguen** orchard is signposted from the centre of the village and from all the major approach roads, including the D786. **Vieux Tronc** is on the D17 between Huelgoat and the D764 from Carhaix. The *zone artisanale* is signposted and visible from the turning. The Brasserie An Alarc'h is the unit with all the beer barrels piled outside!

Un petit coup de Muscadet? Not so long ago, the offer of a small glass of the nearest thing Brittany has to its own wine (an offer generally made while the glass was being filled, refusal being unthinkable) was an essential component of every household visit, no matter how casual. Consequently, drunkenness was a professional hazard in jobs involving house-calls and many a postman concluded his working day in such a lamentable state it was little short of miraculous if anyone at the end of the round received a letter. It's no accident that the Breton gates of hell at Huelgoat precede a pub crawl of ninety-nine *auberges*. Serial drinking was virtually a vocation in Brittany and to this day St. Malo, Dinan and Rennes take a perverse pride in their respective Rues de la Soif or Streets of Thirst,

roads lined with up to thirty bars, the challenge being to drink a glass of calvados in each, at the end of which the last one standing is the winner - or is in hell, as the case may be. Brittany has long been a hard drinking culture and the man who didn't drink was no man at all. Nowadays, the range of drinks offered to guests may be more extensive than a *petit coup de Muscadet*, but as the popularity of the Rues de la Soif suggests, the essential truth remains: to the despair of health authorities, social services, law enforcement agencies, and anyone keen on clean living, booze is an integral part of the Breton way of life.

Un petit coup?

Apart from Muscadet, the archetypal Breton alcoholic drinks are cider and beer. There are several Breton whiskies, about which experts suggest the less said the better, while the lingering tradition of manufacturing mead is largely limited to the souvenir market, and quality home-made calvados is increasingly hard to find as the last generation granted licenses for domestic stills dies out; so, if you really want to identify with the Breton way of drinking (and I'm not necessarily advising you do, not if you're fond of your liver or anything like that), it is in the fermented beverages that the most authentically Breton experience is to be found. Muscadet, it has to be said, is not the most elevated oenological discovery to be made on the continent, or even, for that matter, in the Loire region where it's produced. It's a perfectly drinkable wine with a commendable tradition of being kept on the lees, and many Bretons swear by it, or because of it, but connoisseurs tend to be a bit dismissive, complaining that its acidity is heavy on the stomach. So for the purposes of bumping about, I propose concentrating on cider and beer.

To get an idea of just how integral cider has been to the Breton diet, we need only look back fifty years to the daily *working* intake of the average farm labourer. Arriving at the farm in the morning, he would be given a litre of cider to take with him to the fields. Mid-morning break, there was another litre of cider. Another litre accompanied lunch and another litre was taken to the fields for the afternoon. And then, when the day was done, he'd go home and begin drinking. Likewise, tramps stopping over at a farm to spend the night in the barn would surrender their matches to the farmer's wife, be given a bowl of soup in the kitchen, then retire to the comfort of the haystack with a bottle of cider. Cider, drunk from a shallow cup rather than a glass, was the standard accompaniment for a meal, and continues to be so in many contexts, strong dry *cidre sec* being recommended with seafood, *demi-sec* with dishes like *kig-ar-farz*, *cidre brut* with savoury *galettes*, and *cidre doux* with sweet crêpes. And on cold mornings in the not too distant past, certainly within living memory, kids would be sent to school with a tot of calvados inside them. Little wonder that the culture of drinking was also a culture of alcoholism. Much of it was alimentary alcoholism, drinking steadily throughout the day as a means of sustenance rather than binge-drinking to get roaring drunk, but it was none the less deleterious for that.

Like megaliths and Vauban fortifications, cider houses are absolutely everywhere in Brittany. Most ciders are made from a mixture of apple varieties chosen to get the right balance of sweetness, astringency and acidity, as well as the vital yeast spoors that are carried in the skin, but around Vannes they use a single variety (le Guillevic) to produce Royal Guillevic, a pale drink dubbed the 'champagne breton' and accordingly served in flutes. Elsewhere in Morbihan, the farmers make the less refined but no less feted Cidre du Terroir, which is much in evidence at Lorient's Festival Interceltique and reputedly very popular with the Irish. Other light, acidic ciders come from Redon and the Pays de Dol, while the Vallée de la Rance and Trégor-Goëlo regions are known for more robust, tanniny ciders.

Perhaps the most famous cider producing region is Fouesnant in southern Finistère, where they stage the Fête des Pommiers on the third weekend in July. The cider from Cornouaille (in particular the *pays de* Fouesnant, Bigouden, and Clohars-Carnoët) was the first in France to get an AOC, the recognition of a distinct regional tradition ordinarily reserved for wines, cheese, and the occasional oddity like the *oignon rosé* of Roscoff. Cornouaille was singled out for this honour because its cider-makers were particularly active and well-organized, making a conscious decision to add value to what was a languishing industry by establishing strict norms for the cider they produce, which can only be made from locally grown varieties of apple, like Kermerrien, Kroc'hen ki, Sac'h Biniou and the Avaloù Belein, *aval* being the Breton word for apple and the etymological root of Arthur's Avalon. We're not necessarily talking gourmet palates and *vins fins* here, but as is often the case, when discussing what you put in your mouth, French is the best language to use. This particular AOC is described as "*un cidre légèrement amertumé à la robe dorée-orangée*" - translate that into English and it sounds like tainted Tizer.

So, when it comes to cider, wherever you are in Brittany, you'll find the wherewithal to bend the elbow, debilitate the general stock of brain cells, and dismantle your liver. For the purposes of bumping about though, we've opted to illustrate the culture of cider with a visit to the Kervéguen orchard at Guimaec near Morlaix, where Eric Baron produces three types of cider (*demi-sec, brut* and *Carpe Diem*) from several varieties of apple, including the appetizingly named *peau de chien*. *Cidre à l'ancienne* is what it says on the label and *cidre à l'ancienne* is what you get: the apples are hand picked and left to ripen undercover for up to four months before being pressed slowly (go too fast and the juice is an insipid *jaune pipi*); the juice is then left to ferment and mature, not in the modern stainless steel tanks that are standard elsewhere, but in oak barrels that lend flavour and longevity to the cider. The trickiest part of the process is getting exactly the right bar pressure. To suit contemporary tastes for a moderately effervescent cider, the bar pressure must be between two and three. At one bar, there's not enough fizz for your average Breton punter, at four there's every likelihood the cork will take your eye out.

Baron describes himself as a *paysan*, though it has to be said, he's not exactly your typical *paysan*, and not just because of his surname. It all looks *paysan* enough as we approach the farm along narrow green lanes leading to a driveway flanked by a couple of wooden barrels, but thereafter doubts begin to creep in. There are, for instance, a couple of ponies and three indolent looking donkeys grazing in the orchard on our right, pack animals that apparently do no packing whatsoever to earn their keep. And on the orchard's website (www.kerveguen.fr), we see a photo of Baron cradling a soppy looking puppy that any ordinary self-respecting *paysan* would keep chained up in the farmyard. But if *paysan* is mistaken as a synonym for tradition, then I guess it's an accurate description. Not that Baron is a man who adheres very greatly to labels: he uses no chemicals and everything is done to an organic standard, yet he hasn't bothered to apply for the much coveted *bio* badge, a certificate for which many farmers invest heavily and go through years of labour.

Kervéguen is immaculate, too, and if you didn't know better, the ancient press on display in the car-park would suggest a gentrified second home or country hotel rather than a working farm. And there's a Tibetan flag in the courtyard, the significance of which is a little unclear, the only explanation offered being that "Buddhism has a meaning, it's a way of being, of living", a way of living that appeals to a man who practices no religion. When we arrive everything is open and untended, including the cash register, though there are a couple of rangy hounds lurking about (one of them apparently the soppy looking puppy grown big); they're friendly enough but that might change if they caught you with your hand in the till. A woman drives up to the shop and starts unloading crates of bottled mead from the boot of her car, at which point Baron emerges from the fifteenth century farmhouse.

"Ooh, he's in a bad mood!" she exclaims cheerfully, and it's true, he does look a little grumpy. As it transpires, he's not exactly unfriendly, but he's certainly on the *demi-sec* end of the scale. What's really striking, though, is the man's physique. Without wishing to go too far down the stereotype road, your average *paysan* comes in three sizes: there are the big broad ones, all belly and backside, the little squat ones built like wood burning stoves, and the wiry, grimy ones that look like they served an apprenticeship as pipe cleaners. Baron, by contrast, is a long, lean, finely muscled, softly spoken man, who looks nothing like any conventional image of a *paysan*. He hasn't even got red cheeks. Instead, in his sleeveless sweatshirt and baggy sweatpants, he resembles a busking acrobat or a laid-back athlete slumming it on holiday. But if he wants to be known as a *paysan*, *paysan* he is, and as a man of the earth, he clearly knows what he's about.

Kervéguen Pigeon Coop

While the kids whoop it up in the play area beneath the Tibetan flag, we're free to stroll around the orchard, visit the ancient pigeon coop with its honeycomb of nesting holes, and inspect the ranks of barrels in the long low shed where the cider is aged. The real business of the day though, is back in the shop where bottles line the counter for tasting and, apart from the cider, various other intoxicants are sold, including that mead mentioned earlier (*chouchen* in Breton) and the local firewater, *fine de Bretagne*.

So what about the cider? Well, it's a drink about which I profess no expertise, so rather than fluffing about trying to look intelligent and savouring the different varieties under the watchful and still slightly moody eye of the man who made it, I bought a bottle of each and sloped off for a leisurely tasting beside the home fires. I'm still no expert, but I can tell you that after three bottles of the stuff, I was so lightheaded I was ready to go out and give the fields a damned good thrashing, which suggests those old time farmers knew what they were doing when they kept their labourers tanked up on scrumpy. For what it's worth, the Brut (6%) was good but for my tastes on the verge of having too strong a flavour of the alcohol, the Demi-Sec (5%) was dangerously palatable (it was about halfway through this bottle that I had to quell a compelling urge to go out and do a little light hoeing), and as for the Carpe Diem (3%) . . . To be honest, I was in no state to judge by then, but the neighbours were hard pressed persuading me not to plough up their front lawn, and only narrowly avoided the complimentary landscaping by letting me hang about their necks advising them to seize the day. Good enough then to merit some more Latin quotes, say *Vive ut Vivas* or *Hoc Erat in Votis* Oops! *Disjecta Membra - Domine, Dirige Nos. Live to Live; This Was The Very Thing I Prayed For.* Oops! *Scattered Limbs - Lord, Direct Us.* Costs to the local turf notwithstanding, I'd say all three Kervéguen ciders are high quality tipples, because the only hangover they induced was a headful of Latin tags.

The best known of the three is Carpe Diem, which was developed in the early nineties by combining green and ripe apples, and is recommended by the Gault et Millau gastronomy guides. It's famous because in 1997 it was selected as the cider of choice for the cellars of the presidential palace. Now whether we're supposed to believe Jacques Chirac spent the next ten years knocking back this stuff by the case load is a bit doubtful. One only has to look at the By Royal Appointment logo to appreciate that stocking merchandise is not the same as consuming it: can you see our own monarch spooning down the Kellogg's corn-flakes between drags on a Benson & Hedges and gargling with Vat 69? Well, perhaps you can, I don't know, but you get my point. Being an official supplier does not necessarily mean the supplyee is addicted to what's being supplied. Nonetheless, the association was enough to secure Kervéguen national celebrity. Apparently, people frequently turn up and order a case of the Elysée cider without bothering to taste it first to see if they like it or not. I suppose there are worse ways of getting close to the seat of power. And even if we don't know whether Chirac actually drank the cider, *carpe diem* certainly echoes the life philosophy of a man famous for political expediency and being a bonviveur. Nicolas Sarkosy, his successor, is a strict teetotaller, so one might have expected Kervéguen to have lost its most prestigious client. Not a bit of it. The new regime continues to quaff, or offer its guests the possibility of quaffing, Carpe Diem, though whether they're quaffing as much as the *ancien regime* is unknown, since when it comes to quantities, the lips of the man furnishing the quaffables are sealed. Little matter. If you're bumping about Brittany and want a taste of power, try Carpe Diem. Drink enough of it and you might find yourself going places in politics. Brittany is, after all, known for its magic potions. *Pax Vobiscum.*

Beer drinking in France is not like beer drinking in Britain. Ask a visitor who turns up around 5 o'clock on a summer's afternoon if they would like a drink, and they will almost invariably remark on how thirsty they are and ask for a beer. This still shocks me. Perhaps I'm being unusually dissolute, but isn't a beer something you take as a precursor to a second then third and a fourth and so on with the intention of getting mildly tipsy if not totally plastered? If you're thirsty, you drink water. You don't abuse beer by turning it into a mere thirst quencher. I'm afraid you do in France. I once spent three hours drinking beer with friends of friends, until at about seven thirty our host clapped his hands and said, "Right, what do you want to drink?". I nearly fell under the table. I was half way there already. I could have sworn we'd been drinking since tea time. I certainly wouldn't have wanted to blow in a bag. But no, what we'd been doing was partaking of what I have come to refer to as 'a French cup of tea', that is a beer drunk at tea time as a pick me up prior to the serious business of getting smashed over dinner. Admittedly, the incident with the friends of friends was a little exceptional, we had had rather a lot of 'French cups of tea', an entire urn full probably, but the pattern stands, and the occasion remains relatively unremarkable.

The British generally treat the notion of French beer with derision, justifiably so given that the average French beer seems designed to make Watneys Red Barrel look like the acme of brewing quality. Indeed, for a long time, I maintained that the phrase 'a good French beer' was the perfect example of an oxymoron, except the French didn't take kindly to being associated with morons. As it happens though, this is a little unfair; not the crack about morons (in that department, France is no better nor worse than any other nation), but the blanket aspersion of French beer. There is a long tradition of good brewing in the north of France, where they produce *bières de garde* like Jenlain (winter brewed for keeping through the summer, when the heat and air-born wild yeast spoors used to make fermentation too unpredictable), and in the last ten years there's been a welcome surge in the numbers of small, independent brewers opening up to cater for local fans of unfiltered, non-pasteurized real ales. These are not beers you'll usually find in the supermarket and, when you do find them, they don't come cheap, but they are, by and large, very good.

At the forefront of this movement is Brittany (they are Celts, after all), where *cervoise* (the Celtic word that now survives only in Spanish *cerveza*, everyone else opting for the Germanic *bier*) was once regarded as a magic brew that opened the doors to The Other World (I'm sure we've all had that feeling once in a while), and where beer was used more recently as a source of nourishment for sailors who, despite the excellent, long-keeping *pains marins* some bakeries still produce, couldn't rely on their daily bread lasting a week or more at sea. At the start of the twentieth century, there were over seventy breweries in Brittany, but the number was gradually whittled down through takeovers and industrialization, and the last of the old breweries closed in 1980. Nowadays though, the revival of interest in artisanal beers has reanimated the sector, and there are nearly forty micro-breweries in Brittany, some serving only the bar they're attached to, others producing on a semi-industrial scale, and they are a very great comfort to an Englishman abroad.

Again, we're spoiled for choice when it comes to bumping about. I've spoken at some length about La Mutine, which is brewed at Portsall to the north of Brest, and will happily bang on about the stuff whenever we've got a beer drinking guest from Britain, so much so that my appearance in the local off-licence immediately prompts two declarative questions, "A crate of La Mutine?" shortly followed by "You've got visitors?". Another favourite is the Brasserie du Tregor near Treguier in Côtes d'Armor, which produces an excellent range of beers (above all the varieties of Dremmwel) that can often be found in supermarkets, as can Lancelot from the brewery of the same name at Roc St. Andre in Ille et Vilaine. Another widely available Breton beer is Coreff, much venerated for its pioneering work (it was the first of the new generation of breweries), but far from being the best of the bunch. Then there are the specialty beers laced with buckwheat, sea-salt, or extracts from seaweed. Ordinarily, I don't go a bundle on flavoured beers (the Belgians are particularly perverse in this matter, mucking perfectly good beers about with summer fruits and superfluous herbs), but the Breton varieties are never less than interesting and never leave you wondering whether the bottle wasn't inadvertently contaminated with something unspeakable. One of the most remarkable beverages (strictly speaking it doesn't actually qualify as a beer, but then there's plenty of less agreeable stuff sold in the supermarket as 'beer' that really oughtn't qualify either) is Lactiwel from the Brasserie de Brocéliande at Plelan Le Grand in Ille et Vilaine, a drink the like of which I'm fairly sure you will not taste anywhere else.

One problem with French brewers is that they often appear to believe a quality beer is synonymous with a specific gravity liable to smack you round the back of the head and have you crawling home after half a glass. Lactiwel, by contrast, is only 2.5% proof, an alcohol content that suggests it is made for babies or Americans or old ladies who've been hitting the tonic wine a little too heavily. The baby analogy is not that far off the mark in fact, the name giving the game away, for this is a 'milk beer'. When I first saw it in a small shop near St. Malo, I was delighted to find a new beer, but then I read the label and hurriedly put the 75cl bottle I'd been admiring back on the shelf. Milk beer! This was taking the French cup-of-tea analogy too far. Out of curiosity, though, I did buy a small bottle, which I was even ready to share, but the moment I'd taken my first sip, I knew I'd made a mistake when I replaced the big bottle on the shelf. This is a delicious drink, light, refreshing, but with plenty of flavour to give the lie to the low alcohol content. As it happens, it's not actually made of milk, but instead of using brewer's yeast it activates fermentation of the wort by using kefir, a lactic culture originally employed for fermenting milk in Mongolia.

You get the picture? Beer in Brittany is sufficiently varied and unusual to make this the perfect place for a tippler's holiday and, wherever you are in Brittany, there will be a local brewery somewhere in the vicinity, details of which can be found on www.bierbreizh.info. In fact, when the notion for this book was first mooted, I got terribly excited by the prospect of compiling a sort of brewery tour, a Breton counterpart to the classic circuits of châteaux in the great wine-producing regions, but on reflection concluded the spectacle of an aging drunk staggering from one brewery to another would not be a very edifying one. Instead, let one brewery stand for all.

The Brasserie An Alarc'h or Swan Brewery in the Vieux Tronc *zone artisanale* near Huelgoat is a one man operation run by Xavier Leproust, an English speaker and amateur of English beers, who in 1998 turned a passion for home-brewing into a profession. Before going any further, I should point out that the Brasserie An Alarc'h is not a prettified display of artsy-craftiness staged for tourists. It's a working brewery housed in a scruffy breeze block building with sacks of malt stacked outside, and barrels and bags piled higgledy-piggledy all over the place. The nearest thing to photogenic hardware are the wood clad coppers that have replaced the milk vats in which Xavier, like so many Breton brewers, began brewing. Otherwise, if you want picturesque, there's a big black dog lounging about outside, and Xavier himself with his pony tail and permanent roll-up.

The pony tail and roll-up are revealing as the interior of Finistère is pony-tail and roll-up country par excellence, the heartland of alternative Brittany, and a place of retreat for people who don't quite fit into conventional society or choose not to fit into conventional society, preferring instead to place the accent on a lifestyle and values that can loosely be described as cooperative rather than competitive. This general ethos is strongly present at the Brasserie An Alarc'h, which from the beginning has been a fair trade outfit and nowadays cooperates with Oxfam distributing a selection of local and fair trade drinks ranging from Beuk cola to rum and *aperitif* wines. The main objective, though, is to source raw materials locally and cultivate viable livelihoods for local suppliers. As far as I can see, it's a perfect marriage between traditional small scale craft and a modern sensibility.

Xavier possesses an encyclopedic knowledge of beers and brewing techniques, and anything he can't tell you about the brewing business in Brittany, probably isn't worth knowing. Apparently the complicity that prevailed among Brittany's micro-brewers in the early days has been impaired in recent years by increasingly intense competition, but Xavier still cooperates with several other *brasseries*, and doesn't hesitate to recommend the Brasserie de Pouldreuzic's Penhors Stout as the best stout in Brittany, despite the fact that he produces one himself. At 7% proof, Xavier's Kerzu stout is his strongest beer, brewed for longer keeping and maturing in the bottle for up to three years. His real dream, though, is to create a vintage ale like Dorchester's Thomas Hardy, to which end he is constantly experimenting with new malts and different hops. His hops all come from England because there's nowhere else with a comparable selection for balancing flavour against strength without resorting to spices to conceal the taste of the alcohol.

The Brasserie An Alarc'h's main beers are Hini Du (4.7%) a dark beer midway between an ale and a stout, *du* being the Breton word for black, Tantad (5%) a *bière blonde* named after the St. Jean firework night, Meleg (5%) a honey beer, and the *bière ambrée* Mallozh Ruz (5.6%), or red blasphemer, a name selected in the course of an impromptu straw poll at the Vieilles Charrues festival. There's also a summer beer flavoured with elderberry flowers and two specifically fair trade beers structured around quinoa (4%) from Ecuador and hibiscus flowers (5%) from Burkina Faso.

The Bumping About verdict? Kerzu stout is on the bitter side as stouts go and has a rather muddy head, but it's got a nice full flavour and, despite the strength, the taste is not dominated by the alcohol. It's got a kick, though. One large bottle and you'll have a muddy head, too. Hini Du is very *du*, so very *du* I was hard pressed to distinguish it from a stout, though in some ways it better resembles a winter ale without the sweetness or excessive alcohol; good without being great. Tantad is malty, hoppy, short on fizz, long on taste, and even tastier when you decant the dregs from the bottom of the bottle, in other words a pleasure from the first sip to the last. Meleg, *La Bière des Ours*, is described as a *cervoise* and is suitably other-worldly. There's a very faint aftertaste of honey, but otherwise it's a straightforward, high-quality lager-style beer with plenty of body - good enough to become one of life's bare necessities. Mallozh Ruz is a real Real Ale with a nice rich colour and subtle flavours, a beer that could hold its own in a CAMRA competition and that merits further exploration. The Bière d'Été is another 'drain to the dregs' job, an excellent light, fruity beer in which the elderberry flowers are nicely balanced by the other ingredients: the sort of drink that could easily move you to cultivate 'a French cup of tea' habit, indeed to go the whole hog and embrace alimentary alcoholism unreservedly. Despite being spiced with ginger and cinnamon, Kinoä is very, very light and a little bland compared to the other beers, though perfectly passable as a cup of tea. Finally, the only An Alarc'h beer that didn't inspire me to elaborate fantasies of topery was Hibiska, a "*bière au goût acidulé*" that was altogether too *acidulé* for this palate, to such an extent that I even committed the minor sacrilege of giving it a lemonade top.

In short, our favourites were Tantad, Meleg, Mallozh Ruz and the Bière d'Été, any one of which should be sufficient to dispel any lingering doubts you might have about the quality of French beer. So, if beer is your cup of tea, you could do a lot worse than pop into the Brasserie An Alarc'h. Otherwise, just check out the whereabouts of the brewery nearest your base on www.bierbreizh.info. Chances are, you won't be disappointed.

Quod bonum, felix, faustumque sit.
May it be right, happy, and of good omen.

25. SEVEN SAINTS:
A PILGRIMAGE FOR OUR TIMES

ACCESS - The **Hameau des Septs Saints** is in Côtes d'Armor, south of Lannion and just north of Plouaret and **Le Vieux Marché**. The hamlet itself is on the D74 and is clearly signposted from the D11.

In an age when it sometimes seems as if every profession of faith inevitably involves an overpowering compulsion to give people embracing different beliefs a good thumping, evidence of inter-religious harmony is worth celebrating. One heartening example of this uncommon phenomenon is the annual *pardon* that takes place on the last Sunday of July at the Hameau des Sept Saints near Vieux Marché in Côtes d'Amor.

A Breton *pardon* is not a diffident English-style apology for burping at table or a *Come again?* query when you didn't quite catch what somebody said, but an act of contrition on an epic scale, grappling with God and nature and hopefully casting a protective spell on the birds and the bees, not to mention the horses and cows and pigs. Celebrating the feast day of the saint

Seven Saints . . . and Friend

associated with the local chapel or church, Breton *pardons* beg indulgence of higher powers with a view to placating the disruptive spirits of an unpredictable and potentially malign environment. A sort of collective hail-Mary-hallowed-be-thy-name-touch-wood-cross-your-fingers-and-hope-not-to-die proto-insurance policy, their aim is to safeguard seafarers or livestock or crops or whatever the given theme of the day maybe, and generally promote the all round well-being of the celebrants.

The variety of *pardons* is remarkable. There are *pardons* for the poor, *pardons* for singers, *pardons* for the sea, the harvest, fire, birds, beasts with horns, beasts without horns, there are bovine, ovine, equine *pardons*, possibly lupine, porcine, feline and asinine *pardons*, too, for all I know, and most are closely tied to primeval fears of failure, hunger and annihilation. Many feature a blessing of animals or the means of making a living and surviving, and most include in one form or another an appeal to the elements, all of which suggests a pre-Christian origin in ancient pagan rites. Devout Catholics may well balk at such an idea and tell you this is a purely Christian ceremony, but given that nearly every *pardon* shifts in the course of the day from a sacred to a profane celebration, I have my doubts about the 'purity' of this Christian celebration. Some *pardons* even engage with subjects it's hard to see as anything but profane. On the 15th of August at Porcaro in Morbihan, for instance, there is the *Pardon de la Madone des*

Motards (yes, that's right, the Madonna of Motorcyclists) in which some twenty thousand motorcycles are blessed by the officiating priest, conjuring the beguiling image of a bunch of great big hairy bikers bending the knee and putting aside their six-packs long enough to have a quick prayer together. And on the third Sunday of May at the *Pardon de St. Yves* in Tréguier thousands of lawyers gather together to honour their patron saint, whose severed head they parade through the streets, as if to suggest legal advice will cost you more than an arm and a leg.

When you're bumping about Brittany, you should try to see at least one *pardon*. There's nothing quite like them anywhere else and they're such a long standing tradition that when the first Breton dictionary was compiled in 1499, the only French word to have found its way into the language was 'pardon'. The season begins in March and ends in October, but most *pardons* take place between Easter and Michaelmas. Quite what the Bretons have done to require such immoderate absolution, I couldn't say, but that's a question for the moral philosophers rather than the likes of us.

The seven saints celebrated at Vieux Marché are the seven sleeping saints of Ephesus, seven Christian brothers who declined to honour a decree by the third century Emperor Decius demanding everyone recognize the Roman deities. Given that they were imperial functionaries, Decius didn't take kindly to their lack of enthusiasm for the official gods and duly sent a delegation to 'persuade' them of the error of their ways. The brothers took refuge in a mountain cave, adamantly refusing to renounce their faith, whereupon the cave was walled up and they were left to rot. But instead of starving to death, they dozed off and slept for seventeen and eight score years, *seitek blaz ak eis unguen* in the Breton *gwerz* acclaiming the miracle, awaking to general astonishment, not least their own, 177 years later when the cave was reopened and they emerged into the newly christianized empire, firmly persuaded they'd only slept for a day and causing no end of havoc down the market by trying to pass coins from a currency that had gone out of circulation a century earlier.

The story spread rapidly, subsequently becoming a stand-by of medieval devotional literature, and was cited or retold in later works by writers as diverse as John Donne, Goethe, Thomas de Quincey and Washington Irving. The legend reached Brittany early, transported along trading routes by monks who debarked at Le Yaudet near Lannion and followed the River Léguer inland to the hamlet of Stivel, where the cult was installed on the site of a megalithic dolmen. So far, so conventional. Apart from its exotic origins, the *Pardon des Sept Saints* was a relatively unremarkable *pardon* resembling countless other *pardons* taking place all over Brittany. Enter Louis Massignon, a distinguished orientalist, one time friend of Lawrence of Arabia, and a man of such questing piety he changed his faith twice before settling on ecumenism as the most convenient resolution of his spiritual dilemmas.

In 1953, Massignon attended the *Pardon des Sept Saints* and was so astonished by the similarity of the stories told in the traditional Breton *gwerz* and Surah 18 of the Koran, known as *Al-Kahf* or 'The Cave', that he initiated the *pèlerinage islamo-chrétien*, by which name the *pardon* is better known to this day. That's the way it's recounted nowadays, at least, though you'd have thought that if Massignon was such a distinguished orientalist, he wouldn't have been that surprised. Quite apart from being the third pillar of monotheistic faith, Islam is well known for venerating Jesus and Mary and the Old Testament prophets, and sharing the Christian belief in bodily resurrection, so the fact that it also holds the Seven Saints in high esteem really ought not to have come as a bolt from the blue. But no matter how predicable the epiphany, the inspiration was a moment of serendipity that has since earned Massignon the enviable sobriquet of being the greatest Moslem among the Christians and the greatest Christian among the Moslems, a title that must upset modern bigots no end.

The *pardon/pèlerinage* begins on Saturday with a round table symposium in which representatives of the three monotheistic religions and an agnostic discuss a given aspect of interfaith relations, after which there is a communal mass, a procession, a firework display, and a *fest noz*. Sunday kicks off with the main mass of the *pardon*, after which there's a procession to the Fontaine des Sept Saints (a seven jet spring comparable to springs at other places where the cult is celebrated, such as Guijel in Algeria) and an imam recites Surah 18.

If all this sounds a little bit lovey-dovey, wishy-washy, wet-liberal, Jesus-wants-me-for-a-rainbow, hug-them-next-door-in-the-next-country, well . . . it is; and all the better for it, too. However, the organizers don't shy away from controversy or difficult topics. When we were bumping about, the subject of the Saturday symposium was a sober and powerful documentary, 'Le Testament de Tibhirine', about the abduction and murder of seven Trappist monks from a monastery in Algeria in 1996. At the time, the murders were blamed on the GIA (*Groupe Islamic Armé*) who were engaged in a vicious, fratricidal war with the military authorities, though it has since been alleged that the real culprits were the Algerian secret service, whose plans to stage a kidnapping and pull off a propaganda coup by 'liberating' the hostages went fatally awry. Either way, in the post 9/11 world, it's not exactly a cold potato, and there are potent symbolic overtones to discussing seven murdered monks at a shrine to seven martyrs

in a region that venerates seven founding saints; delicate, I'd say. Yet this was the central debate at the 53rd *pèlerinage islamo-chrétien*.

The title 'pilgrimage' is a bit of a misnomer, conjuring as it does images of large numbers of people traipsing across a lot of country, as happens in the Tro Breiz. Apart from the people who travel from distant places to celebrate the occasion, the most extensive progress of the weekend is the 250-metre walk from the chapel to the spring. Still, it's a very pleasant 250 metres and if you want to extend the walking, or happen to be visiting at a different time of year, there are several waymarked circuits in the vicinity, detailed in free leaflets available from the *Mairie* at Vieux Marché. The *commune* certainly has plenty of attractive countryside, its rolling

Waymarked Circuit

coppice clad hills jigsawed by skew-whiff little fields and the meanders of the River Léguer, which was once famous for its salmon and freshwater mussel pearls. The low dome of Ménez Bré, dubbed by some the spiritual hub of Brittany, is visible in the distance as we follow winding lanes flanked by newly mown hayfields to reach the hamlet of Sept Saints, a place so picturesque and well-preserved, visitors still give the handle of the old village pump a speculative crank, as if they suspect there's no running water here and that any moment now some antique crone will emerge from her cottage followed by a gaggle of gingerbread men to fetch water with a leather bucket.

The Old Village Pump

Most *pardons* take place in picturesque places and in some ways it's just as well, because these are not necessarily the most animated spectacles. Granted, if a cow makes a break for it at a bovine *pardon* or the boat at the blessing of the sea sinks resulting in an unrehearsed dunking for the assembled notables, the show can be quite diverting, but otherwise the main feature of a *pardon* is the mass and the most spectacular spectacle you're likely to get is a bunch of girls done up in traditional costumes. If you're looking for all singing, all dancing entertainment, go to the West End. The charms of a *pardon* are more understated, more sedate, and are premised more on atmosphere than animation, enchanting by evoking the past, ensnaring spectator and participant alike in a web of continuity and tradition - and then, of course, there's a good feed at the end of it all, followed by some al fresco hoofing of the amateur variety, but we'll leave that to one side for the moment.

Locals are always very proud of their *pardon* and, though their pride doesn't necessarily extend to attending the mass, you can be fairly sure there'll be a crowd gathered round the fringes of the religious ceremony, glad handing one another, clowning about, and peering over each others' shoulders to see what the priest is getting up to. And you can also rely on the priest arranging to have a crackly tannoy system set up, so that even if people stay on the fringes, they won't miss the homily. Sept Saints is no exception to this pattern and the sermon comes across loud and clear, well clearish at any rate, extolling as you would expect the advantages of tolerance and cooperation. It seems to be working, too. To one side of the chapel the shrine of the seven saints is housed in a low cellar. Inside, three local women are standing in front of the seven candles representing the seven saints. The women are nattering away, gossiping about the errant daughter of a neighbour as best I can gather, and show no sign of moving on. Meanwhile, a neatly dressed Moslem man, very couth, kempt and combed, is waiting patiently in the doorway with a camcorder.

"Are we preventing you filming?" asks one of the women.

"No," says the man, smiling broadly. "I am filming. I'm filming you."

And everyone seems very happy with the arrangement.

Elsewhere, unsupervised children have worked out their own system of concord. While everyone else is praying for peace and brotherly

love, a gang of Islamo-Christian kids are having a whale of a time clambering over the log bench in the middle of the hamlet, among them a little black girl wearing a traditional Breton frock. It's not the most practical clothing for clambering over log benches, but the girl appears to be perfectly at ease in her old fashioned outfit, and gives the boys a run for their money when a game of tag begins.

The Sacred Fountain

When the service ends, the priest makes it known that the afternoon's colloquy will concern the question of what it means to be close - with other people that is, not with your money. He then announces the procession to the seven jetted fountain for the recital of Surah 18. The fountain is at the end of a narrow grass track and there's no way everyone can get up there for the surah, so I recommend checking it out earlier. It's a pretty spot, the spring set in a fold below a field, the water bubbling over a shallow stone basin into a narrow tailored channel, and thence into a rivulet and eventually, I would guess, into the River Léguer. As it happens, there is no visible sign of the seven jets, but in the circumstances the precise number hardly matters. When you're praying for something as improbable as interfaith harmony, religious tolerance and worldwide peace, imagining a few ancillary spouts in your spring is a very modest fantasy.

The procession is lead by the priest and the imam, both wearing virtually identical hooded white robes, not so very different now that I think of it to Getafix's garb in the Asterix books. The imam's gown is slightly creamier than the priest's, but the overall cut and the shape of the long pointed hoods are remarkably similar. A quick change and nobody would notice the difference, which I guess is the whole point of the ceremony. Possibly. Though you could make an equally plausible case for the whole point of the ceremony being at the other end of the village, where the trellis tables are laid out and the volunteers on the bar tent are plugging in their barrels and the chemical loos are dotted about in strategic corners of the field.

As I suggested earlier, the pagan side will out at a *pardon* one way or another, most often with a *fest deiz* that runs into a *fest noz*, and if crowds and tannoys are part of the pattern, so too is the distant scent of roasting meat. In deference to the occasion, the traditional hog roast has been replaced by a *méchoui,* which is fair enough since the customary barbecued pork sandwiches might be taken amiss. Even so, nobody has gone so far down the road of accommodating Islamic sensibilities as to forego the fermented drinks, and there's plenty of beer and cider and wine on hand to wash down the lamb and crêpes. This is, after all, still a Breton *pardon* and Brittany is a place much given to magic potions that exact miraculous transformations. Indeed, several people seem intent on fostering interracial harmony by changing their complexions altogether through the medium of alcohol, crossing the Rubicon of race by becoming rubicund. I'll spare you the details. But let's end with a snapshot of the scene later in the evening . . .

Post pardon and we're festering again, as we did at Celtytud last year. We're *en plein air,* the Breizh Brothers are back on stage, beakers of La Mutine are lined along the bar and the *parquet* is going clappety-clap as the circles of dancers stamp their feet. The druid's here, too, still irredeemably English, but looking credibly druidical nonetheless. There is a difference, though. The difference is me.

I don't know whether it's because I've drunk too many Mutines or because I've lost my sense of direction or because somebody put some funny powders in my food, but rather than standing on the sidelines thinking "You won't catch me doing that", I find that I've been roped into the dancing. I don't 'know' the dances and my maths is no better than it was when we began bumping about Brittany, but I've been watching the druid and I've worked out that it's largely a case of muddling through, bluffing when you don't know what's going on, and generally looking vaguely benign and other-worldly to obscure the infelicities of your feet.

I don't risk any heel kicking or crossing of legs and I certainly don't take a chance on the whirling because I'm fairly sure that, however I got here, if I start whirling now, I'll be whirled right off the dance floor and there's every likelihood I'll disappear altogether. But I'm holding hands and I'm pushing out the elbows and I'm going hoppety-hop and I'm shuffling and I'm stamping. At one point, I stamp on somebody's toes, I'm not sure whose, possibly my own, but for the rest of it, I'm jiggling the elbows and putting the right foot forward and shaking it all about with the best of them. Doubtless from a distance it looks like I'm doing the Funky Chicken and very likely laying an egg, too, but never mind, I'm part of the circle and, when the time comes, I even give it a bit of the old *kof-a-kof à quatre.*

Whether one small village of indomitable Gauls can bridge the religious divide and bring harmony to a world so set upon tearing itself apart at the seams is a little doubtful, but the *pèlerinage islamo-chrétien* has achieved something equally improbable, it's got me dancing. And it occurs to me that something has happened in the course of the preceding months, that by dint of bumping about Brittany, I'm becoming Breton. I have, after all, been baptized by Breton rain at every extremity of the region; I've arrogated Mont St. Michel for Brittany and received stolen goods purloined from them-next-door-in-the-next-country; I've knocked on the gates of hell, embarked with the corsairs, been to the end of the world and back, been all at sea on the other side, and I've become cagey about revealing my private fishing holes; I've acquired a liking for *kig-ar-farz*, discovered the French cup of tea, and drunk enough cider to take up rustic toil; I've immersed myself in the *royaume de l'imaginaire*, seen little green men lurking under big stones, and learned to believe in imaginary mountains and the ubiquity of Vauban; and now I'm jigging the elbows. Perhaps this book should come with a health warning. Bump about Brittany too long and you may find you are becoming Breton yourself.

more from Charles Davis

Walk! Brittany (North)
Walk! Lake District South
Walk! Dorset
Walk! Mallorca North & Mountains
Walk! Mallorca West
Walk! La Palma
Walk! La Gomera
Walk! the Axarquia
Walk! the Alpujarras
Walk! Andorra
all published by Discovery Walking Guides

Walk On, Bright Boy (fiction)
Walking The Dog (fiction
published by The Permanent Press

Costa del Sol Walks
Costa Blanca Walks
published by Santana Books